Edwin Cone Bissell

Biblical Antiquities

A Handbook for Use in Seminaries, Sabbath Schools, Families any by all Students of the Bible

Edwin Cone Bissell

Biblical Antiquities

A Handbook for Use in Seminaries, Sabbath Schools, Families any by all Students of the Bible

ISBN/EAN: 9783743419414

Manufactured in Europe, USA, Canada, Australia, Japa

Cover: Foto ©Lupo / pixelio.de

Manufactured and distributed by brebook publishing software (www.brebook.com)

Edwin Cone Bissell

Biblical Antiquities

[GREEN FUND BOOK, No. 5.]

BIBLICAL ANTIQUITIES:

A HAND-BOOK

FOR USE IN

SEMINARIES, SABBATH-SCHOOLS, FAMILIES AND BY ALL
STUDENTS OF THE BIBLE.

BY

EDWIN CONE BISSELL, D.D.,

PROFESSOR IN HARTFORD THEOLOGICAL SEMINARY.

With Numerous Illustrations and Tables.

PHILADELPHIA:
THE AMERICAN SUNDAY-SCHOOL UNION,
1122 CHESTNUT STREET.
NEW YORK: 10 BIBLE HOUSE.
1888.

THE JOHN C. GREEN FUND BOOKS.

THIS volume has been prepared and issued under the provisions of the John C. Green Income Fund. The fund was founded in 1877, with the cordial concurrence of Mrs. Green, by Robert Lenox Kennedy, on behalf of the residuary legatees of John C. Green. Among other things, it is provided by the deeds of gift and of trust that one sixth of the net interest and income of this fund shall be set aside, and whenever the same shall amount to one thousand dollars, the Board of Officers and Managers of the American Sunday-School Union shall apply the income "for the purpose of aiding them in securing a Sunday-school literature of the highest order of merit." This may be done "either by procuring works upon a given subject germane to the objects of the society, to be written or compiled by authors of established reputation and known ability, . . . or by offering premiums for manuscripts suitable for publication by said Union, in accordance with the purposes and objects of its institution, . . . in such form and manner as the Board of Officers and Managers may determine."

The premium plan is to be followed at least once out of every three times.

It is further required that the manuscripts procured under this fund shall become the exclusive property of the American Sunday-School Union, with no charge for copyright to purchasers of the book, it being the intention of the trust to reduce the selling price of works issued under the provisions of the fund.

PREFACE.

THAT branch of biblical science known as antiquities has to do with the peoples among whom the Bible arose, especially with the Hebrews. In this work the subject is made to refer chiefly to the social, civil and religious conditions of the Hebrew people in biblical times. The antiquities of other historically-related peoples are considered only as far as they shed light on those of the Hebrews or otherwise contribute to a clearer understanding of the Bible.

The advantages of a knowledge of their antiquities to a student of the Scriptures cannot well be overrated. It serves to place him in the position of one who lived in the times when they first appeared and in the lands where they were actually written.

My aim has been to present the principal facts of biblical antiquities in the stricter sense, together with some of their moral and religious bearings, and to show their true place and significance in the plan and history of redemption. No attempt has been made to treat largely of the geography or topography, the political or natural history, of the lands of the Bible, each of which themes would require a volume.

The book has been prepared for popular use. Where Hebrew and Greek terms are used, they have been given in their simplest phonetic form. The latest accepted results of scientific study have been stated without detailing processes. Citations from authorities in general have been sparingly given; those from the Scriptures are full and explicit, and have been usually taken from the Revised Version.*

It is proper to express my sense of indebtedness to the Committee of the American Sunday-School Union, whose co-operation has greatly aided in the preparation of the work. The fitting illustrations and the attractive form which the society has given to the book will add much to its usefulness. That it may win some measure of the favor accorded to the excellent work of Dr. Nevin, which it succeeds, and be honored of God in accomplishing a similar service in his kingdom, is my most earnest hope.

EDWIN CONE BISSELL.

HARTFORD THEOLOGICAL SEMINARY,
      March, 1888.

* For a partial list of authorities, see p. viii.

CONTENTS.

[The figures after the sub-topics indicate the page.]

CHAPTER VI.

PART III.—SACRED ANTIQUITIES.

CHAPTER XI.

CHAPTER XII.

CHAPTER XIII.

CHAPTER XIV.

CHAPTER XV.

CHAPTER XVI.

LITERATURE OF BIBLICAL ANTIQUITIES.

IN addition to the Scriptures and the Apocrypha, the Targums, the writings of Philo and Josephus, the Talmud and earlier rabbinical works, Greek and Roman classical writers, the monumental remains of the East, and the accounts of travellers and explorers there, are the principal sources of our knowledge of biblical antiquities. The apocryphal and other Jewish literature which arose after the close of the Old Testament canon, though lacking the authenticity of biblical books, is not thereby unfitted to be a valid source of information on national customs. The writings of Josephus and Philo, as well as the works of rabbinical writers, are to be used with caution when not well supported.

For the antiquities of Egypt there are the standard works of Champollion (Paris, 1837), Wilkinson (London, 1878), Lane (London, 1871), Lepsius (Berlin, 1849), Brugsch (London, 1881), Ebers (Leipzig, 1881), and the several reports and publications of the Egyptian Exploration Fund; for those of Assyria and Babylon: Botta (Paris, 1849), Layard (London, 1852), Lenormant (Paris, at different times), Oppert (Paris, 1865), Schrader (Giessen, 1883), Rawlinson's works (London and New York), Smith (London, 1865), Transactions of the Society for Biblical Archæology and Records of the Past (12 vols.; London, Bagsters).

Among the numerous volumes of travel and exploration in Palestine and Syria may be mentioned Robinson (Boston, 1856), Ritter (Berlin, 1848-55), Lynch (Philadelphia, 1849), Thompson (New York, 1880), Van Lennep (New York, 1875), Palmer (New York, 1872), Conder (London, 1878), Schaff (London and New York, 1880), Bartlett (New York, 1879), Merrill (New York, 1881), Porter (New York, 1873), Baedeker (Leipzig, 1876-78), Trumbull (New York, 1884), besides the publications of the British Palestine Exploration Fund, the American Palestine Exploration Society and the Deutscher Palestina-Verein.

Of books treating directly of the antiquities of the Bible and valuable for one reason or another are worthy of notice—Jahn (Wien, 1817), Rosenmueller (Leipzig, 1823-31), De Wette (Leipzig, 1864), Ewald (Goettingen, 1866), Scholz (Bonn, 1834), Haneberg (Muenchen, 1869), Saalschuetz (Königsberg, 1855-56), Jennings (London, 1825), Keil (Frankfort, 1875), Kinzler (Stuttgart, 1884), Schegg (Freiburg, 1886), and a number of works by Edersheim.

The following monographs will be found suggestive and useful: Faber, *Von den verschiedenen Wohnungsarten* (Halle, 1873); Michaelis, *Comm. on the Laws of Moses* (London, 1814); Hartmann, *Die Hebraerin am Putztische* (Amsterdam, 1809); Saalschuetz, *Das Mosaische Recht* (Berlin, 1848); Bachr, *Symbolik des Mosaischen Cultus* (Heidelberg, 1837-39, 1874); Mielziner, *The Jewish Law of Marriage and Divorce* (Cincinnati, 1884); Kuebel, *Die Sociale und Volkswirthschaftliche Gesetzgebung des Alten Testaments* (Wiesbaden, 1870); Delitzsch, *Jewish Artisan Life* (London, Bagsters); Herzfeld, *Geschichte des Altjuedischen Handels* (Leipzig, 1863-65); Schuerer, *Geschichte des Juedischen Volkes im Zeitalter Jesu Christi* (Leipzig, 1886); Kamphausen and Fries on the Tabernacle (articles in the *Theol. Studien und Kritiken* for 1858-59); also works of Riggenbach (Basel, 1867), Brown (Edinburgh, 1872), and Paine (Boston, 1885), on the same subject; Huellmann, *Staatsverfassung der Israeliten* (Leipzig, 1834); Lowman, *Civil Government of the Hebrews* (London, 1740); Wines, *Commentaries on the Laws of the Hebrews* (Philadelphia, 1859); Loew, *Graphische Requisiten und Erzeugnisse bei den Juden*, etc. (Leipzig, 1870-71); George, *Die Aeltesten Juedischen Feste* (Berlin, 1835); Green, *The Hebrew Feasts* (New York, 1885); Kurtz, *Der Alttestamentliche Opfercultus* (Mitau, 1862); *The Lord's Day*, by Prof. A. E. Waffle (Philadelphia, 1885); *Four Essays on the Sabbath* (Edinburgh, 1886).

Among Bible dictionaries and cyclopedias may be noted those of Smith, Winer, Kitto, Fairbairn, Schenkel, McClintock and Strong, Ayre, Fausset, Schaff, Herzog and Plitt, Hamburger and Riehm. The last, in addition to valuable articles by the editor on pertinent themes, contains others by Delitzsch, Baur, Ebers, Kamphausen, Schlottmann, Schroeder, Schuerer and other eminent scholars.

For the history of the Jews there are available works of Ewald (Goettingen, 1864-68), Kurtz (Berlin, 1864), Graetz (Leipzig, from 1874), Milman (London, 1863), Stanley (London and New York, 1883), Koehler (Erlangen, 1865), Duncker (Berlin, 1880), Hengstenberg (Berlin, 1870), Wellhausen (Berlin, 1868) and others.

PART I.

DOMESTIC ANTIQUITIES.

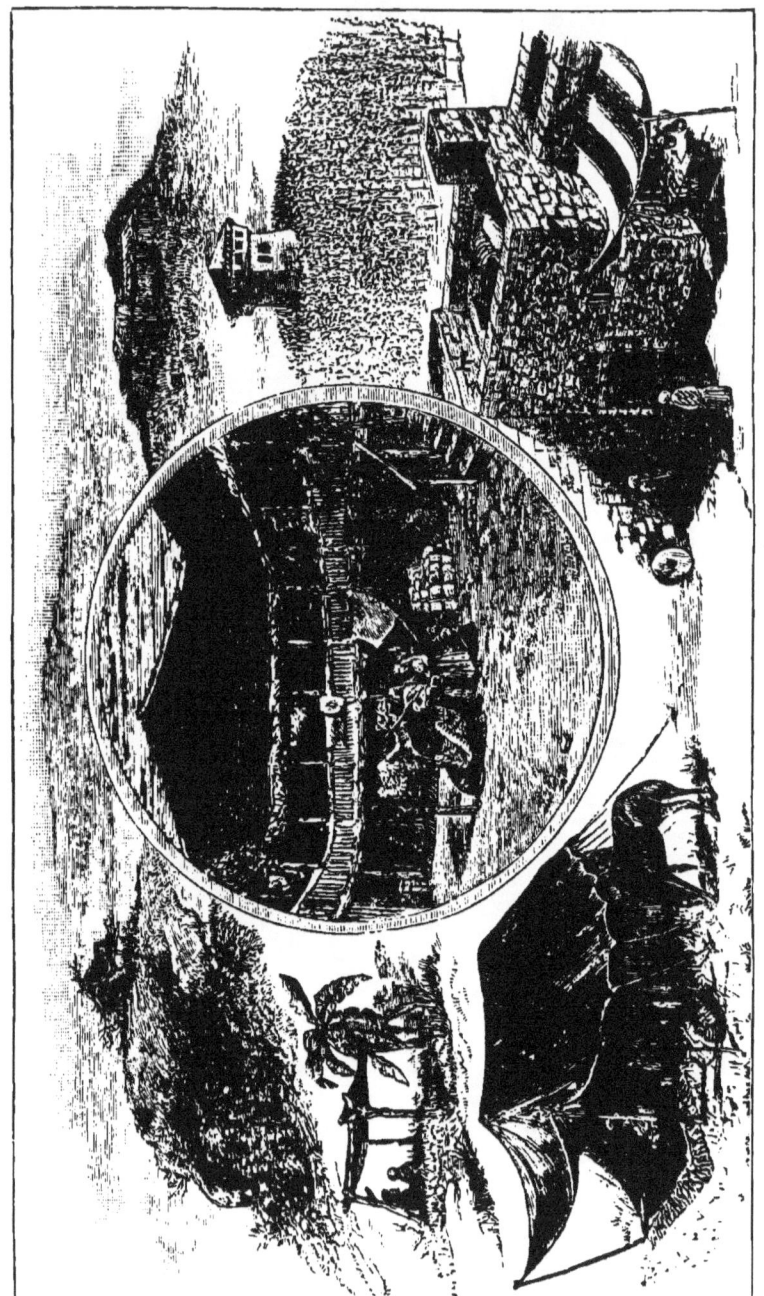

BOOTH, OR "LODGE."
CAVE, OR UNDERGROUND DWELLING.
WATCHMAN'S BOOTH.
EASTERN TENT.

CARAVANSARY, OR "KHAN."

ADOBE, OR HUT DWELLING.
TOWER IN FIELD OR VINEYARD.
HOUSE WITH "BATTLEMENTS" ON ROOF.
SHOP WITH AWNING (NEXT TO HOUSE).

CHAPTER I.

DWELLINGS AND THEIR APPOINTMENTS.

1. The Hebrew conception of the house was twofold. It referred either to the dwelling or to the family that occupied it. In the Scriptures, the principal emphasis, as might be expected, has been placed upon the family. The races peopling western Asia have always been divided into two great classes in respect to their dwellings. The one class has been nomadic, living in tents and having cattle; the other has built, and preferred to occupy, permanent habitations. This distinction ruled in the beginnings of human history as it now does throughout the Orient. Cain is said to have built a city; while Jabal was "the father of such as dwell in tents."[1] In eastern lands the nomad has always been held as, in every respect, the equal of the citizen. Abraham's wandering life did not detract from the honor with which he was regarded by representatives of the great Hittite empire.[2] On the other hand, the present Shah of Persia is a nomad by descent, and the tribe to which he belongs is one of the chief supports of his throne.

The Hebrews, in different periods of their history, belonged now to one and now to the other of these classes. The patriarchs led much the same kind of life as that of the modern Bedouin of higher rank. During the sojourn in Egypt, it is likely the Israelites occupied permanent dwellings.[3] In the wilderness, they reverted again to life in tents. The booth is nowhere mentioned in this period, but is doubtless to be included under the general designation of tent. On their occupation of Canaan, the conquerors naturally inhabited, to a considerable extent, the cities and villages of the conquered peoples, and became fixed residents of the lands, which, as families and tribes, they cultivated. The Mosaic legislation contemplates throughout an agricultural, rather than a pastoral, population. Still, in the long period of defection, lasting from the days of Joshua to the establishment of the kingdom, there was a marked tendency to return to the habits and modes of life of the early patriarchs.

2. The Booth.—In describing the various kinds of dwellings mentioned in the Bible, we begin with the booth. It was doubt-

[1] Gen. 4: 17, 20.　　　[2] Gen. 23: 5, 6.　　　[3] Ex. 12: 4, 7.

less one of the most primitive forms of human habitation. It is impossible, however, to affirm that the booth historically antedates the tent. Much less is it safe to assume that men inhabited caves at first, and that this was due to the low grade of their intelligence. It is probable that the three forms of habitation were all known to earlier peoples, and in use by them according as they found one or another more convenient.

In its primitive rudeness the booth approaches so near to the lair of the wild beast that the same original word was sometimes employed to designate it.[1] And yet, so well adapted is the structure to their mode of life that it continues to be not a little used by the nomads of the East. The ordinary booth of the Bible seems to have been constructed entirely of the leafy boughs of trees. The stoutest of them were firmly planted in the earth to form the walls, and over these the lighter ones were deftly woven together to serve as roof. Booths were of all sizes, from those capable of holding but a single person[2] to such as were used for sheltering the largest herds of cattle. Jacob, it is said, on his way from Padan-aram, erected booths at a certain place for his numerous cattle. Hence the name "Succoth"—that is, booths—which, from this circumstance, has come down to us in the sacred records.[3] Once in the history of King David, while the siege of Rabbah of the Ammonites was in progress, it is noted that the "ark and Israel and Judah" abode in booths.[4] Military campaigns being undertaken in summer, the booth, with its leafy covering, was a pleasant change from the heated atmosphere of the tent.

There are several instances in the Scriptures where the booth is made the basis of a poetic image. Much of the beauty and fitness of the trope is lost when this fact is forgotten or becomes obscured in the translation. The prophet Amos, for example, predicted that the day would come when the booth (tabernacle) of David that had fallen down would be raised up again.[5] It was a bold figure to liken the glory of David's house not only to a booth but to a booth prostrate on the earth.

3. A special kind of booth was that of the watchman in vineyards, fruit orchards and grain fields. Job says of the wicked that he "buildeth his house as the moth, and as a booth which the keeper maketh."[6] The watchman's booth was generally reared on an elevation from which the fields to be cared for could be readily seen.

[1] Job 38:40; Ps. 10:9; Jer. 25:38.   [2] Jonah 4:5.   [3] Gen. 33:17.   [4] 2 Sam. 11:11.
[5] Amos 9:11.   [6] Job 27:18.

Unless it differed from the modern style, which is unlikely, it was built of four poles stuck in the ground in the form of a square, and about four feet apart. At nearly the same distance from the ground cross-sticks were fastened to these supports, and upon them boards were laid. (See cut, p. 10.) Here was spread the simple couch of the watchman, and here, for the most part, was his home during the summer. A second covered platform was made a few feet higher up when a wider range of vision was desired. The top only was covered. The boughs of trees were generally used for the purpose, though sometimes the shelter was made more effective by means of mats. It is to a structure of this kind that the prophet Isaiah gives the name of "lodge."[1] Its insecure character is well illustrated in another passage of this prophet, where he says of the earth that under the judgments of God it shall "stagger like a drunken man" and "be moved to and fro like a hut."[2]

4. The tower mentioned in Isaiah 5 : 2, used for a like purpose as the watchman's lodge, was a somewhat similar, but a much more durable, structure, being often built of stone and of much larger size. (See illustration, p. 10.) It still bears in modern Greek the name *pyrgos*, which was used by our Lord in speaking of it in the Gospel.[3] Not infrequently it rose to the height of forty feet, and was provided at its top with roomy, well-ventilated apartments. Here the family of the owner found a much more comfortable home during the warm months than in the crowded town. The Turk uniformly applies to the structure a word which means "country house." It is doubtless one of the more elaborate buildings of this sort to which our Lord refers in Luke 14 : 28.

5. CAVE DWELLINGS.—There is no evidence that, in any period of their history, the people of Israel ever dwelt permanently in caves. They often, even down to the date of the Roman conquest, made temporary use of them, especially in times of persecution and war. The limestone hills of Palestine and Syria are exceedingly favorable to the formation of fissures and caverns of every description. In the Palestine of to-day, as at Engedi, Eleutheropolis, in the region about Hebron and Gadara and on the slopes of Carmel, such caverns not only abound but are in considerable use, particularly during the hot season. The ancient Horites, who inhabited Seir before the Edomites, seem to have been proper troglodytes, or cave-dwellers, as their name imports. Other proper names of the Bible are equally significant in this direction. Haurân[4] indicates a

---

[1] Isa. 1 : 8.   [2] Isa. 24 : 20.   [3] Matt. 21 : 33; Mark 12 : 1.   [4] Ezek. 47 : 16, 18.

land of caverns. Beth-horon[1] means "house of caverns;" and Horonaim,[2] "two caverns."

Underground places used as dwellings, or for other purposes, were by no means natural caves in all cases, but were often excavated in the solid rock at great expense of time and labor. About twenty-five years ago, Dr. Wetzstein, a distinguished German, discovered an underground city at ed-Der'aah in western Haurân. It has recently been explored under the direction of the Palestine Exploration Fund.

A passage four feet wide leads down to the gate of the city. The gate consists of a massive stone, six inches in thickness, which still swings on its ancient stone hinges. The city is made up of an indefinite number of chambers or dwellings in the solid rock, communicating with one another by means of narrow passages. Ventilation is provided for by air-shafts, many of which, in process of time, have become closed up. The weak limestone roofs are, in some instances, supported by strong pillars. The presence of troughs, mangers, and the like, shows that animals as well as men found a home here.

Lot had his dwelling in a cave after the destruction of Sodom.[3] During the wars of the Conquest, we read of five kings taking refuge at one time in the cave of Makkedah from the pursuit of Joshua's army.[4] Subsequently, in the period of the Judges, we learn that "because of Midian the children of Israel made them the dens which are in the mountains, and the caves, and the strong holds."[5] The same was true while the Philistines overran Israel, prior to their subjugation by Saul and David.[6] The hunted David found in these places his most secure retreat.[7] Elijah fled to a cave in Horeb before the fury of Jezebel.[8] In the same great persecution the faithful Obadiah hid a hundred prophets of the Lord, by fifties, in a cave.[9]

6. There are numerous allusions and poetic images to be found in the Bible, which, to say the least, are greatly obscured unless the fact is kept in mind that natural and artificial caves were much resorted to in seasons of want, danger and discouragement. In Job, for example, the depths of distress are represented as reached by those who "are wet with the showers of the mountains, and embrace the rock for want of a shelter."[10] In another place he speaks of men who are "gaunt with want and famine; they gnaw the dry

[1] Josh. 10:10. [2] Isa. 15:5. [3] Gen 19:30. [4] Josh. 10:16. [5] Judg. 6:2. [6] 1 Sam. 13:6.
[7] 1 Sam. 24:3-10. [8] 1 Kings 19:9, 13. [9] 1 Kings 18:4, 13. [10] Job 24:8.

ground, in the gloom of wasteness and desolation. . . . In the clefts of the valleys must they dwell, in holes of the earth and of the rocks."[1]

The prophets also make considerable rhetorical use of this custom. Isaiah, describing the coming of Jehovah in judgment, says that "men shall go into the caves of the rocks, and into the holes of the earth, from before the terror of the Lord, and from the glory of his majesty, when he ariseth to shake mightily the earth."[2] The same image is employed in the Revelation.[3] In the Epistle to the Hebrews the persecuted saints of old, "of whom the world was not worthy," are spoken of as going about in sheepskins and goatskins, and as "wandering in deserts and mountains and caves, and the holes of the earth."[4] The inaccessibility and security of such places is referred to in many a passage. The Psalmist prays to Jehovah, "Be thou to me a rock of habitation, whereunto I may continually resort."[5]

7. The fact that caves as well as shadowy groves were often selected for idolatrous worship is recognized by the prophet Isaiah: "Are ye not children of transgression, a seed of falsehood, ye that inflame yourselves among the oaks, under every green tree; that slay the children in the valleys, under the clefts of the rocks?"[6] It is matter of interest that some of the oldest cloisters of the East appear to have had their origin from the custom of living in caves. To some single hermit who was thus spending his life, others gradually united themselves. The cave was accordingly enlarged by the addition of separate cells to accommodate them. Little by little there arose around the old grotto or cavern, and always including it as its sacred centre, a common place of prayer, a church, and, finally, a cloister or monastery.

8. THE TENT.—According to the Bible, the custom of living in tents is of the highest antiquity. It is traced back to Jabal, who was a son of Lamech.[7] It did not, as it would seem, precede, as to matter of time or conception, the more stable dwelling. From the first there were movable as well as fixed abodes, and those who decidedly preferred the one to the other. There are peoples in the East who, as far as known, have never been engaged in anything else than strictly pastoral pursuits, or occupied any dwellings but tents. In some cases a peculiar form of tent, as distinct in style from those in common use as the modern dwelling-house is from that of two centuries ago, has been adopted by a people and held its

---

[1] Job 30 : 3, 6. [2] Isa. 2 : 19; cf. Zech. 14 : 5. [3] Rev. 6 : 15, 16. [4] Heb. 11 : 38. [5] Ps. 71 : 3; cf. Cant. 2 : 14; Isa. 33 : 16; Jer. 48 : 28; 49 : 16. [6] Isa. 57 : 5. [7] Gen. 4 : 20.

place against every innovation for a millennium. As already intimated, it would be erroneous to suppose that for a people to lead a wandering, pastoral life implies, in itself, a lower stage of civilization. This cannot have been the case when Abraham and his descendants pastured their flocks in ancient Canaan. It is as little true in the same countries to-day. For hundreds of years the only sanctuary of Israel was a simple tent-structure, and from this the magnificent temple of Solomon and those that succeeded it derived their peculiar style.

9. Cloth for tents was usually manufactured from the coarse hair of goats or camels. The name "house of hair" is given to the tent by the modern Arab. When goat's hair was used for this purpose the black or brown color was preferred.[1] If of good quality, cloth of this kind was impervious to the rain, and as a protection from the sun's rays superior to the material commonly used for tents among ourselves. Tents were also covered with skins.[2] The tents on which Paul wrought were doubtless made of Cilician hair-cloth, which was highly prized for the purpose, and were probably intended for the use of the Roman soldiers.[3] After being woven into cloth of the required width, stitched together and provided with cords and loops, the tent-cloth was spread over poles of about the height of a man and securely fastened to the ground by tent-pins.

10. The size of the tent varied according to taste and requirement. The space between the border of the tent-covering and the ground was covered, if desired, by curtains of the same material, or by mats. Tents were sometimes round in form, but more often rectangular, presenting, when spread, the appearance of the hull of a ship turned bottom upwards. The interior was divided into separate apartments, generally two or three, by means of other curtains fastened to the parallel rows of poles by which the structure was supported. One portion was appropriated to the men, another to the women, and if there was a third, it would be most likely set apart for the servants and the cattle. Separate tents for wives and children would be a mark of wealth and rank.[4] The word "alcove," coming down to us through the Spanish and the Arabic, goes back for its idea to the old tent structure, and its root is still preserved in the Hebrew word rendered "pavilion" in Num. 25 : 8, and in the margin "alcove."

11. The furniture of the tent was of the simplest description. It rarely went beyond a few mats, serving at once for chairs, couch

[1] Cant. 1 : 5.   [2] Ex. 35 : 23.   [3] Acts 18 : 3.   [4] Gen. 24 : 67; 31 : 33, 34.

and table, a hammer for driving tent-pins, a hand-mill for grinding the food, a few copper pans, and possibly a lamp. Other articles were, of course, often found in a tent, but formed no part of its proper furniture. There might be, for example, sacks of grain and other sacks used in loading camels, the camel's pack-saddle and remaining outfit,[1] distended skins containing water or curd, leathern buckets for drawing water, bowls for receiving milk, and, if there were horses, their feeding-bags and tackling. In the tent of a modern Arab, means for grinding coffee would be thought indispensable; possibly, even the stones on which the dish containing it is placed over the fire. When a fire was needed, it was built in a hole in the ground within the enclosure of the tent. The smoke was left to find its way outside as best it could.

12. When a number of tents were pitched near together they were placed in a certain determined order. If they were the tents of herdsmen or shepherds, they were generally arranged in a circle, the flocks and herds finding protection in the enclosed area. The Hebrews had special names for such collections of tents, usually rendered "encampments" or "villages" in the revised English version.[2] It was probably a small number of shepherds, or those without tents, who were keeping watch in turn over their flocks by night when the angels appeared to them with the announcement of the Saviour's birth.

13. The figurative use of the scenes of tent life is very common in the Scriptures. The most widely-employed Hebrew word for removing, journeying from place to place, referred originally to the drawing of the tent-pins.[3] Similarly the apostle Paul speaks of the bodily frame as a tabernacle or tent which may be expected to dissolve or suddenly disappear.[4] So, too, King Hezekiah, in his sickness, spoke of his life as removed and carried away from him like a shepherd's tent.[5] The prophet Isaiah, picturing the Church of his day as still inhabiting movable dwellings, addressed it in the inspiring words: "Enlarge the place of thy tent, and let them stretch forth the curtains of thy habitations; spare not: lengthen thy cords, and strengthen thy stakes."[6] The Psalmist, on the other hand, conceived of the whole earth as but the floor of a tent of which the sky was the pavilion.[7] Even the tent-pin was not overlooked. Of the servant of the Lord it is said in prophecy[8] that he shall be fastened "as a nail [tent-pin] in a sure place." With a similar metaphor the

---

[1] Gen. 31:34. [2] Gen. 25:16; Deut. 2:23; 1 Chron. 6:54; Ps. 69:25; Isa. 22:23; cf. Zech. 10:4. [3] Gen. 33:17. [4] 2 Cor. 5:1. [5] Isa. 38:12. [6] Isa. 54:2. [7] Ps. 19:4. [8] Ezra 9:8.

2

Preacher in Ecclesiastes brings his book to a close: "The words of the wise are as goads, and as nails [tent-pins] well fastened are *the words of* the masters of assemblies, *which* are given from one shepherd."[1]

14. THE HOUSE.—Of ancient Hebrew architecture the Bible has little to say. In fact, a proper architecture can scarcely be said to have arisen among the Hebrews before the time of the early kings, about B.C. 1000. When it appeared, it differed but little from that of their neighbors, the Phœnicians, Assyrians and Egyptians. The earliest mention of permanent dwellings in the Bible is the statement that Cain built a city and named it Enoch, after the name of his son.[2] Probably it consisted of a small collection of huts surrounded by a wall with a view to their defence against the "avenger of blood." The genuineness of the biblical narrative is here corroborated by the fact that the building of the first city is ascribed not to nomads but to agriculturists and those pursuing the arts of life.

15. BUILDING MATERIALS FOR HOUSES.—The materials used by the ancients for building purposes varied with the location and the object to be served. On the vast alluvial plains in the midst of which Babylon stood neither quarries of stone nor forests of trees were to be found. Accordingly, the material employed in building was necessarily bricks. These were generally dried in the sun, but sometimes, as now, burnt in kilns. Bitumen abounded in the region and was used as mortar. If we may trust the account of Herodotus, it was applied hot: "As fast as they dug the moat, the soil which they got from the cutting they made into bricks, and when a sufficient number were completed they baked the bricks in kilns. Then they set to building and began with the borders of the moat; after which they proceeded to construct the wall itself, using throughout for their cement hot bitumen, and interposing a layer of wattled reeds at every thirteenth course of the bricks."[3]

The account of the erection of the tower of Babel, found in Gen. 11 : 3–5, is also very instructive as illustrating the mode of building in that early period : "And they said one to another, Go to, let us make brick, and burn them throughly. And they had brick for stone, and slime had they for mortar." In ancient Nineveh, ordinary clay mixed with stubble was used for bricks; and from an incidental allusion in the prophecy of Nahum we infer that prepared mortar and not bitumen was employed in the structure of its walls: "Draw thee water for the siege, strengthen thy fortresses: go into

[1] Eccles. 12 : 11.   [2] Gen. 4 : 17.   [3] Herodotus 1 : 179.

the clay, and tread the mortar, make strong the brick-kiln " [lay hold of the brick-mold ?].[1]

In Egypt sun-burnt bricks were chiefly used for building. Their durable quality is attested by the fact that, in many places, they still retain their form after a period of three thousand years. If they were to be exposed to much dampness, the precaution of first burning them in a kiln was resorted to. Bricks made of the common Nile mud, in distinction from clay, were found not to be sufficiently cohesive without the addition of stubble or straw. It is to this fact that allusion is made in the pathetic passage where the oppressed Israelites complain that they must gather the needful stubble from the fields and yet deliver as usual " the tale of bricks."[2] One of the cities where the Israelites were employed was Pithom. Its ruins have recently been identified. As a matter of fact three kinds of bricks have been discovered there—some with stubble, some with straw and some without. Judging from the monuments, the process of manufacturing sun-dried bricks was much the same in ancient as in modern times. A shallow pit was used for mixing the clay or mud. Into this was thrown the necessary amount of straw or stubble. The mixing was done with the feet.[3] The prepared clay was carried in hods upon the shoulder. Possibly it is

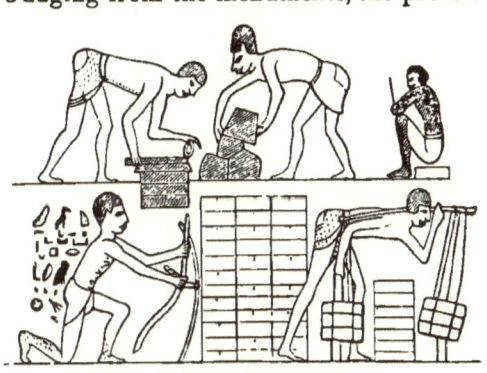

Captives making Bricks in Egypt.

to this kind of labor that the Psalmist refers in the words, "I removed his shoulder from the burden: his hands were freed from the basket."[4]

In Palestine good building-stone abounded, and at an early period noble forests of trees. Bricks, however, were probably used to a limited extent, though considered inferior to hewn stone.[5] The prophet Isaiah especially reprobated in his time the practice of constructing altars of bricks;[6] and in many passages reference is made to the instability of buildings in a manner to suggest the poor quality of the materials used.[7] In the book of Job one of the most striking

[1] Nah. 3:14.   [2] Ex. 5:18.   [3] Nah. 3:14.   [4] Ps. 81:6.   [5] 2 Sam. 12:31.   [6] Isa. 9:10; cf. Ex. 20:25.   [7] Isa. 30:13; Ezek. 13:10, 11; Amos 6:11.

images of human feebleness is found in the fact that men live in
"houses of clay, whose foundation is in the dust, which are crushed
before the moth."[1] It was no difficult matter for those so disposed
to break into houses constructed of sun-dried bricks. It is to this
circumstance that our Lord alludes in the Sermon on the Mount
when he dissuades from laying up treasures where "thieves break
[*lit.* dig] through and steal."[2] Great care too, in such cases, needed
to be taken with the foundations, he being the wise man who built
his house, not on the sand, but on the rock.[3] That there were houses
of a much finer quality built, especially in the times of the later
kings, there is ample evidence.[4]

16. STYLE OF ARCHITECTURE.—The typical form of the eastern
house is the quadrangle with an interior court around which the apartments are variously arranged. The poorer class of dwellings, which singly would not be adapted to this style of architecture, often seek to conform to it by ranging themselves in regular form around a central court. This serves for all alike, and in the winter season becomes a convenient place for the herding of cattle. Houses of the better sort, on the other hand, often consist of two or more stories, having apartments connected, like our own, by doors and stairways and opening upon

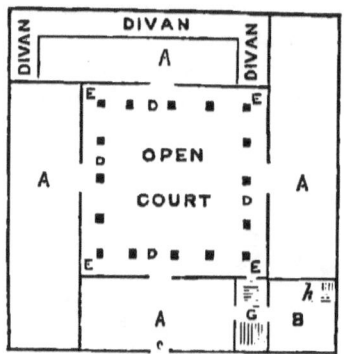

Plan of an Eastern House.

c, Entrance. A, Family-room. E, Walls, or
galleries, between the open court and the rooms.
G, Stairs to the upper stories and roof. h, Private
staircase.

roomy corridors which extend around the entire court. The stairways conducting to the upper stories either start from the porch or
from the interior court, and in some cases from both points. The roof
is reached from the upper gallery by a single staircase. (See cut, p. 10.)

17. To the exterior of his house an Oriental generally pays little
attention. It appears from without mostly as blank walls, relieved
only by the door and a high latticed window or two. Admission is
gained to the interior through a porch. This is no unimportant feature of the dwelling. Sometimes, instead of leading directly into
the main court, a smaller court intervenes connected by a door with
the larger. At other times the same result of greater privacy is
reached by curving to the right or the left the inner walls of the

[1] Job 4 : 19.   [2] Matt. 6 : 19.   [3] Matt. 7 : 24, 25.   [4] Isa. 33 : 12; Jer. 22 : 14; Ezek. 13 : 10; Hag. 1 : 4.

porch. The place is generally roomy and provided with seats where callers may temporarily await the convenience of the master of the house. Servants and retainers in considerable numbers also are often found here. We read of Uriah the Hittite that he "slept at the door of the king's house with all the servants of his lord, and went not down to his house."[1] It was in the porch that the porter kept watch over the property of his master.[2] In the porch of the high priest's house Peter denied his Lord with an oath.[3]

18. The principal interior court of an eastern dwelling answers to the yard or free plat of ground generally found around our western ones. It is made as attractive as the owner's means will allow. It is often covered with a tessellated pavement of marble or other stones. A tank or fountain of water occupies the central space, around which flowering and odoriferous shrubs are tastefully arranged. Along the sides of the court runs a colonnade, or a veranda with pillars, upon which the doors and windows of the lower apartments open. It also serves to support the piazza of the second story, if there be one. In place of doors, rooms much used are supplied with curtains or hangings of some sort. The room for the reception of guests is ordinarily found across the court and directly opposite the main entrance to it. It has a raised platform, a divan stretching around two or more sides, and is carefully, sometimes lavishly, fitted up with rugs, mats and other conveniences for day and night.

19. The rooms of eastern houses are generally square or oblong in shape. The heavy flat roof, and the thick walls needed to support it, largely determine the interior architecture. If the house consists of more than one story, the upper rooms are considered preferable, especially in the hot season. The lower ones are given up mostly to domestic uses, the storing of provisions, and to lodgings for servants. The former are often made higher and larger than the others, the second story being allowed to project over the first. They are favorite places for retirement—the roof also being easily accessible—as well for guests as for the more private social gatherings. Scriptural allusions to this portion of the dwelling are somewhat numerous. It is said, in our English version, of Eglon king of Moab, that when Ehud smote him "he was sitting by himself alone in his summer parlor."[4] The margin of the Revision, however, which is more faithful to the Hebrew, has for "summer parlor," "upper chamber of cooling." It was here that the lifeless body of Tabitha was placed previous to her burial.[5] Here the disciples first gathered

[1] 2 Sam. 11:9.   [2] Mark 13:34.   [3] Matt. 26:71, 72.   [4] Judg. 3:20.   [5] Acts 9:37.

after the ascension.[1]   Here Paul preached.   Here our Lord ate the last supper with his disciples.[2]   (See illustration, p. 10.)

20. Among the upper rooms, too, are generally found the women's apartments, unless there is a private court on the lower floor.   In any case, the most sequestered part of the dwelling is selected for the so-called "harem," and access to it is permitted only to the male head of the household, though this exclusion did not prevail among the Hebrews.   If these apartments are entered from the main court, they are carefully screened from it by means of partitions and latticed windows.   In the palace of Xerxes, as described in the book of Esther, there were separate dwellings for the women, opening on private inner courts and carefully guarded from outside intrusion, besides the palace especially devoted to the queen.[3]   In ancient as in modern times the inner walls of eastern homes were often wainscoted and inlaid with ivory.   The ceiling, too, in some cases was artistically carved and brilliantly painted.[4]

21. According to Van Lennep, the "room which the Shunammite woman induced her husband to build on the wall for the holy man of God, Elisha, was doubtless erected over the *liwan* [reception-room] of the house, as is done at the present day, and was accessible by an outer staircase leading up from the central court.   Similar was the loft where abode the prophet Elijah with the widow of Zarephath; and we can see the correctness of the expression, 'Elijah took the child, and brought him down out of the chamber into the house.'"[5] Rooms are also found in modern houses built upon and projecting over the porch.   They are provided with a window which is protected by a lattice, thus making an admirable post of observation for whatever is going on in the street.   Ancient houses were similarly constructed.[6]

It cannot be determined with certainty whether this room over the porch, or the one indicated by Van Lennep as generally built over the reception-room, answers better to the expression "upper room" as used in the Bible.   Still further, it is not clear whether this room was one particular room of several upper rooms in the same story, or was itself built on the flat roof of the house and extended a story above it.   The latter supposition harmonizes best, in the majority of passages, with the Hebrew word rendered "upper room," as also with its context.

---

[1] Acts 1 : 13.   [2] Mark 14 : 15.   [3] Esther 2 : 13, 14; 5 : 4; 7 : 1.   [4] 1 Kings 22 : 39; Jer. 22 : 14; Amos 3 : 15; Hag. 1 : 4.   [5] *Bible Lands*, p. 442.   [6] Judg. 5 : 28; 2 Sam. 6 : 16; 2 Kings 9 : 30, 32; 1 Chron. 15 : 29; Prov. 7 : 6; Dan. 6 : 10.

22. THE DOOR.—The doors of eastern houses are uniformly small and low except where, for purposes of display, the outer one is made otherwise. They seem early to have been provided with hinges turning in sockets, and with locks and keys in whose construction no little ingenuity was displayed.[1] In most modern houses the hinges are simply projecting portions of the door itself, which fit into sockets prepared for them. It is likely that the ancient hinges were generally similar; at least this is the method in which the massive stone doors and gates were hung in ancient Haurân.

Egyptian Iron Key. (*From Wilkinson.*)

And so nicely are flange and socket adjusted to one another, and so highly polished is the stone, that doors weighing many hundreds of pounds can be moved with a finger.

23. Formerly, as now, it is likely locks and keys were made both of iron and of wood according to circumstances. A wooden key now quite generally in use is described as consisting of a piece of wood about a foot in length, provided at one end with a series of pegs. It is thrust into a little opening at the side of the door and applied to the bolt. This has a corresponding series of holes into which the pegs of the key fit, displacing thereby another set of pegs by which the bolt is held in its place. The keys of the house were in the care of the steward.[2] They were carried by attaching them to the girdle with a cord. Sometimes the cord was of sufficient length to allow of their being thrown over the shoulder.[3]

24. Knockers of iron resting on a broad-headed nail, somewhat after the form of those once considerably used among ourselves, are found on the doors of the rich and on houses of public entertainment. The loose ring hanging on the door and used for the purpose of drawing it together is sometimes employed for the same purpose. The peculiar construction of eastern houses, as already described, together with the loneliness of the streets, makes admission to them at night a much more formidable process than with us. The Bible contains several allusions to this circumstance, and none more remarkable than that in the Revelation where the ascended Lord is represented as standing at the door of the human heart and seeking admission.[4]

25. It was an injunction of the Mosaic legislation that the law should be written on the posts of the doors and on the gates.[5] The

[1] Judg. 3 : 23, 25; Neh. 3 : 3; Prov. 26 : 14; Cant. 5 : 5.   [2] Matt. 16 : 19; Luke 11 : 52.   [3] Isa. 22 : 22.   [4] Rev. 3 : 20.   [5] Deut. 6 : 9.

Jews of later times understood this literally. Accordingly they inclosed a slip of parchment in a reed or cylinder on which had been written Deut. 6:4–9; 11:13–21, and attached it to the door-post of each room in the house. At present the Jews of the East often nail to the door-casing the entire Decalogue, inclosed in a tin case. This custom has been widely adopted by other peoples of the East, particularly by Mussulmans, who naturally select for this purpose passages from the Koran.

26. WINDOWS.—As already observed, the windows of eastern houses open mostly into the inner court. This seems always to have been the case, though outside windows with projecting balconies were also found.[1] The construction of a window was a matter that required little ingenuity. It was a simple opening in the wall, covered over, if desired, with thin slats of wood running crosswise so as to form a lattice. Glass was not in use for this purpose, although, as we learn from the book of Job,[2] it was not unknown to the Hebrews at an early period. It remained for a long time with them an article of luxury, being mentioned with precious stones, as though belonging to the same category in rarity and value. Two instances are recorded in the Scriptures of persons falling from windows: that of Ahaziah in the Old Testament and that of Eutychus in the New.[3] It is probable that the lattice with which the windows in these cases were provided was insecure.

27. THE ROOF.—One of the most frequented and important parts of the eastern house is the roof. It is ordinarily flat, it being more necessary to guard against heat than rain. Its structure in biblical times seems to have been much the same as now. Heavy beams are first laid upon the walls, and over these, at right angles and as thickly as possible, smaller strips or joists of wood. Next to the wood is placed a layer of heather or other strong grass. Where the luxury can be afforded, mats serve the purpose still better, the object being to prevent the remaining material of the roof from falling through into the rooms below. Over the grass some cohesive substance like clay or mud is carefully spread to the depth of several inches, and beaten or trodden down until it is sufficiently hard to be impervious to the rain. (See cut, p. 10.) In more recent times the surface of roofs is treated to a composition of oil and clay, which becomes exceedingly compact and offers a tolerably good protection against the elements.

At the best, however, a roof so constructed requires constant atten-

[1] Josh. 2:15; 2 Cor. 11:33.   [2] Job 28:17.   [3] 2 Kings 1:2; Acts 20:9.

tion. It is liable to crack under the influence of the heat, and after a rain it must be carefully rolled. Heavy stone rollers are frequently kept on the roof for this purpose. Tiles, which were first introduced for the covering of roofs by the Greeks, seem never to have been very popular with the peoples of western Asia. With all the care bestowed upon it the roof is obviously the weak part of an Oriental dwelling. That leaky roofs were by no means uncommon, even in the comparatively prosperous times of Solomon, is shown by the metaphor found in the book of Proverbs: "A continual dropping in a very rainy day and a contentious woman are alike."[1] The Psalmist speaks of the grass on the housetops "which withereth afore it groweth up;"[2] and the prophet Isaiah has a similar allusion.[3]

No part of the house in Bible lands is more generally or continually used than the roof, unless it be the court. For safety, as well as for some measure of seclusion, it is surrounded with a parapet or balustrade. (See illustration, p. 10.) In fact, special provision is made for such a protection in the code of Deuteronomy.[4] It is sometimes built of solid masonry. More often, however, the masonry extends but a little way, and is surmounted by a lattice supported on a frame and covered with vines. It is considered by Orientals a great insult for one to take pains to observe what his neighbors are doing. David on the roof of his palace was exposed to the greater danger, because he was probably able to overlook those of the neighborhood.[5] For the moment, too, he seems to have lost sight of that defence to which he so often refers.[6]

28. The roof is used for a variety of purposes requiring the heat of the sun, like the drying of fruits, grain and flax, of wool and cotton after they have been washed, and of clothing. It was among the stalks of flax which had been laid on the roof to dry that Rahab hid the spies who were sent out by Joshua.[7] It is also a favorite place for walking, for social intercourse, for occasional retirement, and even for sleeping. Peter went on the housetop at Joppa in order to pray, when he saw the vision which had such important consequences for him and for the Christian Church.[8] During the period of Israel's defection under the kings, roofs of houses were often selected as places of idolatrous worship.[9] They are now much used in the East as a post of observation on public occasions, and are still, as in Isaiah's day, resorted to in times of panic and danger.[10] Here

---

[1] Prov. 27 : 15.   [2] Ps. 129 : 6.   [3] Isa. 37 : 27: cf. 2 Kings 19 : 26.   [4] Deut. 22 : 8.   [5] 2 Sam. 11 : 2.   [6] Ps. 3 : 3.   [7] Josh. 2 : 6.   [8] Acts 10 : 9; cf. Prov. 21 : 9; 25 : 24.   [9] Jer. 19 : 13; 32 : 29; Zeph. 1 : 5.   [10] Isa. 22 : 1.

mourners attract greater attention by their lamentations;[1] and here, from the tops of buildings belonging to the government, proclamations are frequently made to the people. A similar custom in our Lord's time may have given rise to the words, " What ye hear in the ear, proclaim upon the housetops."[2] The houses in towns being generally contiguous and their roofs nearly on the same level, it was easily possible to step from one to another, and in this way to go a considerable distance without descending into the street. To this fact the Saviour appears to refer when he warns his disciples with reference to approaching calamities: "And let him that is on the housetop not go down, nor enter in, to take anything out of his house."[3]

29. There were no proper chimneys or hearths in ancient Hebrew dwellings, although it might be so inferred from the common English version of the Bible.[4] One Hebrew word which is rendered chimney means simply a lattice work through which the smoke escaped. Another so translated properly means a portable furnace or " brazier," as rendered in the Revised Version. In the most ancient times a house was dedicated after its completion.[5] What the ceremony consisted in is not known; but probably it was partly religious and partly social.

30. FURNITURE OF THE HOUSE—THE BED.—The furniture of the house, while of greater variety and more durable than that of the tent, was of the simplest description. It consisted ordinarily of little more than a bed, a table, possibly some chairs or stools, a simple lamp, mats and cushions, jars for water and culinary utensils.[6] For the bed, a mattress of some sort with or without coverings, according to the season, was considered sufficient.[7] The poor, it is likely, slept on skins, rugs, or even the bare floor. A bedstead among the Hebrews was unusual. The nearest approach to it, in general, was a raised platform on the side of the room.[8] On his flight from Absalom, King David, it would appear, was provided in his camp only with a bed, and vessels for drinking and cooking purposes.[9] That bedsteads were not unknown there is ample evidence; but they were looked upon as luxurious. The prophet Amos earnestly rebukes the spirit of those who, being at " ease in Zion," and putting afar off the evil day, " lie upon beds of ivory, and stretch themselves upon their couches, and eat the lambs out of the flock."[10] A lofty and highly-

---

[1] Isa. 15:3; Jer. 48:38.   [2] Matt. 10:27; Luke 12:3.   [3] Mark 13:15.   [4] Hos. 13:3; cf. Jer. 36:22.   [5] Deut. 20:5.   [6] 2 Kings 4:10.   [7] 1 Sam. 19:13; Luke 5:18-25.   [8] 2 Kings 1:4; Ps. 132:3.   [9] 2 Sam. 17:28.   [10] Amos 6:4.

ornamented bedstead from the tomb of Rameses III. is on exhibition, which is provided with a wooden rest for the head and steps by which the bed was reached. The bed of Olophernes, too, is described as

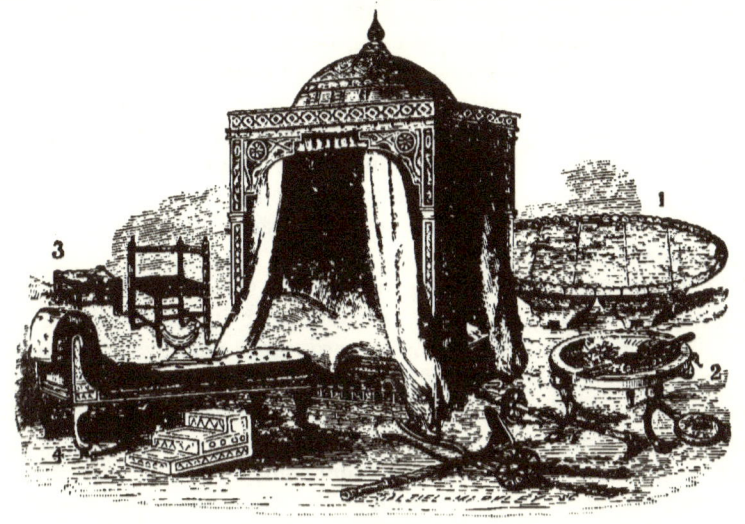

Modern Eastern Furniture.
1, A Village Table. 2, A Brazier, Tongs, etc. 3, Stool, Chair, Persian Canopy Bed. 4, Couch and Wooden Pillow.

having a canopy and even a mosquito-net.[1] In New Testament times there are several allusions to beds that could be carried.[2] They answered probably—if not consisting of a mere cushion or mattress—to our cot, which can be stretched out, and, when not in use, be easily rolled up and carried from place to place.

31. Parents and children seem to have slept, if not in the same bed as is still frequently the case in the East, at least in the same room.[3] The clothing worn during the day was not wholly removed at night. The girdle was loosed, and the outer garment was spread over the person. This, for the greater part of the year, formed the only covering of the poorer classes. Direct reference is made to this fact in a law of Deuteronomy. It is there enjoined with respect to such a garment which had been pledged for a debt that it is to be restored before the evening, " that he may sleep in his garment, and bless thee."[4] The pillow most commonly in use in the East at the present day is a goat-skin, stuffed with some soft substance like wool or cotton. The patriarch Jacob, on his way to Padan-aram, was able

<hr />

[1] Judith 10 : 21.   [2] Mark 2 : 4; John 5 : 8, 12; Acts 9 : 33, 34.   [3] Luke 11 : 7.   [4] Deut. 24 : 13; cf. Ex. 22 : 26.

to dream sweet dreams of heaven even with a stone for a pillow;[1] and our Lord, it would seem, wearied by his beneficent labors, fell asleep on the hard floor of a tossing vessel, with no other support for his head than a rower's cushion.[2] There are a number of references in the Scriptures to the custom of using the bed as a place to sit as well as to lie down.[3] In such cases it probably consisted of a raised platform or divan. The coverings of the bed, if there were any, with the mattress, we may suppose were ordinarily rolled up during the day and covered, or were placed in a closet designed for them. Such a closet or smaller apartment seems to be meant in 2 Kings 11 : 2, where the "bedchamber" of the text is better rendered in the margin "chamber for the beds."

32. CHAIRS.—Chairs were never much in use among the Hebrews. The name ("stool"), in fact, occurs but once in the English of the Old Testament; and the Hebrew word there employed is the one commonly rendered "throne."[4] No doubt there would have been a distinctive name if the custom of using chairs had prevailed to any considerable extent. It seems to have been otherwise in Egypt and Assyria, if we may judge from the monuments. Chairs, some of them of a very elaborate pattern, are there frequently seen. The seats are from eight to ten inches in height, and often composed of thongs of leather compactly interlaced. The custom has not been widely adopted in the East. To the present day the Oriental prefers to sit on the floor, the bed or the divan, with his feet drawn up under him. In places of public resort, on the other hand, especially for strangers, chairs of a rude description are not uncommon.

33. TABLES.—That the Hebrews were accustomed to the use of the table appears from the fact that it was an article of furniture in the tabernacle.[5] The monuments of Egypt, moreover, contain numerous figures of tables of various sizes and shapes. The renowned Thothmes III. numbers among the things secured in a certain campaign six chairs, manufactured from cedar-wood and ivory, with their footstools, and six large tables of the same material, inlaid with gold and precious stones. The height of the table varied according to the uses to which it was to be put. It was enjoined that the table for the shewbread should be a cubit and a half in height. The one appearing on the arch of Titus seems scarcely so high as this.[6] From the earliest times the Hebrews may, to a limited extent, have used tables for their meals, although it is more likely that the majority of the

people were satisfied with a mat or a piece of leather. At first, too, it was the custom to sit at meals instead of to recline, as in New Testament times.[1] The earliest biblical instance of the latter practice we find in the book of Amos.[2] That they sat in chairs, however, is quite unlikely. No doubt the present almost universal custom of squatting on mats before the table has always been the ordinary one.

34. The divan appears to have been comparatively a late invention, and to have been introduced into Palestine from Assyria.[3] In the modern Oriental house it often extends around three sides of the principal room. As already intimated, it is used both as a place for sitting and for sleeping.

35. THE LAMP.—The furnishing of an ancient Hebrew house seems to have been regarded as incomplete without a lamp. In the houses of the more wealthy, at least, it was customary to leave a lamp burning throughout the night. To such a custom reference is made in the book of Job, where it is said of the wicked, "The light shall be dark in his tent, and his lamp above him shall be put out."[4]

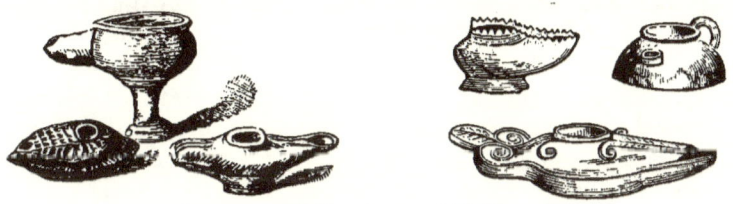

Ancient Terra-cotta and Glass Lamps of Chaldea and Assyria.
(*From Specimens in British Museum.*)

While candles are now used in the East, there is no evidence that anything corresponding to them existed in biblical times, and the word, in our version, is a mistranslation for lamp. The ordinary lamp was probably made of earthenware or of some kind of metal, and held but little oil. It was such a lamp, we may suppose, that was carried by the virgins in the parable.[5] In form it was like a small shallow saucer, with the edge projecting on one side and turned up to make a place for the wick and a little oil. Olive oil was burned. Besides the earthen lamp in which the wick floated on a surface of oil, the similar but more ornate one of metal, and that of seven branches in the tabernacle, the torch is also mentioned in the Scriptures.[6] Its material is unknown. A torch now in use by

[1] Gen. 27 : 19; 43 : 33; Judges 19 : 6; 1 Sam. 20 : 24.   [2] Amos 6 : 4; cf. Esther 1 : 6; Judith 12 : 15; Luke 7 : 37; John 13 : 23. [3] Amos 3 : 12; 6 : 4; Esther 1 : 6.   [4] Job 18 : 6; cf. 21 : 17; 29 : 3; Rev. 22 : 5.   [5] Matt. 25 : 7.   [6] Judges 7 : 16; Zech. 12 : 6; John 18 : 3.

the police of Cairo in Egypt strongly reminds one of the device employed by the soldiers of Gideon. It burns without a flame except when waved through the air. It serves the same purpose as a dark lantern. The burning end, moreover, is sometimes concealed in a small pot or jar, or otherwise covered when not in use. Metaphorical references to the lamp are not infrequent in the Bible. It is especially used as a figure of life and activity.[1] The word of God is compared to a lamp in more than one instance;[2] and the prophet Isaiah longed to see the righteousness of Zion "go forth as brightness, and her salvation as a lamp that burneth."

36. THE CARAVANSARY.—Of public buildings among the Hebrews the only one claiming special attention here, perhaps, is the caravansary or inn. It will be remembered that such a place is mentioned in the history of Joseph and in other parts of the Pentateuch, as well as in the New Testament.[3] The Hebrew word for it, literally translated, would be "lodging-place." Its most usual modern name in the East is "khan," that is, "house." A more private place where strangers are entertained is now called "menzil." A similar distinction seems to have obtained in ancient times, the more private resort being designated otherwise than the regular inn. In Jer. 41:17, for example, in the margin we read of "the lodging-place of Chimham." As a rule the inn itself was a very rude structure, providing little more than a bare shelter from the elements. This appears to have been the case with the one occupied by Joseph's brethren on their way from Egypt to Canaan. And it was also such an inn, it is likely, that Joseph and Mary, on their visit to Bethlehem, found already crowded, and were therefore compelled to lay the infant Jesus in a manger.[4]

37. The following is a description of a modern caravansary or "kahn" as given by Van Lennep:[5]—"These structures vary in size and material, and are made of mud bricks and wood, or of masonry—sometimes of hewn stone; but the form is essentially the same, consisting of a square or oblong court, with one or two stories of rooms built around it. There is a large gate in the middle of one of the sides, which is closed at night with two heavy folding-doors, adjoining which, as well as over it, are the most desirable and expensive rooms. A gallery often runs all around the court, and there is usually in the centre of the latter a fountain with a tank, or a well with troughs. Here the traveller is furnished with an empty room for a very small sum; and the innkeeper is often able to provide

---

[1] Ps. 18:28; Prov. 31:18.   [2] Ps. 119:105; Prov. 6:23.   [3] Gen. 42:27; Ex. 4:24; Luke 2:7; 10:31.   [4] Luke 2:7.   [5] *Bible Lands*, p. 803.

food for man and beast. The stables are usually situated opposite the entrance gate. They are divided into compartments or rooms, each of which has a small platform, where the muleteers or grooms sleep in order to watch over their horses or other animals." (See cut, p. 10.)

38. CITIES AND VILLAGES.—We find already in the time of the patriarchs a distinction made between cities and villages. The latter were not only smaller but were without walls, and generally dependent on some city near which they stood.[1] Such a city was their metropolis, that is, mother-city.[2] We read sometimes of "cities and their villages," and sometimes of "cities and their daughters," in both of which expressions the relation of dependence is indicated; but in the latter case possibly smaller cities in distinction from villages may be included. In Joshua 15 : 45, for example, "Ekron with her towns [Heb. "daughters"] and her villages" is spoken of. This supposition appears the more reasonable that elsewhere the same original word is applied to both walled and unwalled cities.[3] It is not possible to say what was understood to distinguish the unwalled city from the village, unless it was the larger size of the former. Cities are discriminated from villages also in the New Testament. Bethphage, Bethany and Emmaus are styled villages.[4] Bethlehem is called both a village and a city.[5]

39. It is probable that even the smaller villages were originally surrounded with some kind of defence, since one of their names means in Hebrew a hedge.[6] Another word used to designate the village seems to refer to the protection afforded by the roof or walls of the house in distinction from the walls of the city.[7] A special name, "Havvoth," was given to towns on the east of the Jordan. The word meant originally anything laid out in a circle, as an encampment, then hamlets or villages.[8] When villages grew to towns or cities, their names as villages were often retained. In Numbers 34 : 4, for example, the word Hazar-addar, which appears as the name of a city, literally means the "village of Adar." In the same way the other most common name for village is found in the word Capernaum, which signifies "village of Nahum."

Among cities a distinction is to be made between simple walled towns, where the walls served as a boundary or a slighter kind of defence, and cities regularly fortified. For the latter we find nearly the same means of protection in earlier as in later times.

---

[1] Lev. 25 : 29, 31 ; 1 Sam. 6 : 18 ; Esther 9 : 19 ; Ezek. 38 : 11.   [2] 2 Sam. 20 : 19.   [3] Deut. 3 : 5 ; Esther 9 : 19.   [4] Matt. 21 : 2 ; Luke 10 : 38 ; 24 : 28.   [5] Luke 2 : 4 ; cf. John 7 : 42.   [6] Gen. 25 : 16 ; Josh. 13 : 23.   [7] 1 Sam. 6 : 18.   [8] Num. 32 : 41.

40. It is an interesting fact that the Israelites, for the most part, inherited cities rather than built them. The land of Canaan is described as being full of cities at the time of the conquest, and it may be inferred that not a few of them were of considerable size and age. Such at least were Hazor and Jericho.[1] The two and a half tribes that settled on the east side of the Jordan seem to have laid the foundations of a few new places;[2] and we read of the rearing of a second Luz by one of the inhabitants of the old city, who had been spared by the Ephraimites.[3] The city of Samaria also was built from its foundations by Omri.[4] In most other instances where cities are referred to in the earlier records as having been "built" in Palestine, their enlargement or strengthening is probably meant.

41. THE GATES.—One of the most conspicuous and important

Gate of Damascus.

features of an eastern city was its gates. Although directly connected with the walls, they formed a peculiar structure by themselves. Their material was mostly wood or stone, or wood heavily armored with metal. The Bible speaks of gates of both brass and iron.[5] Gates were often two-leaved, and provided with heavy locks and bars.[6] In some instances there were two gates, with an open space between them. This was the case at Mahanaim, where David awaited the issue of the battle with Absalom. A sentinel kept watch on the tower over the first gate. A warder with his attendants guarded the gate below. King David himself was in the open space between the two gates.[7] This space was used for a great variety of purposes.

42. STREETS.—The Hebrew words for streets indicate three general kinds of them. There was first the ordinary one, long, narrow and winding.[8] Then there were the broad squares near the gates, in front of public buildings, or where one street crossed another.[9] And third, there was the short and contracted street or alley.[10] The narrowness of eastern streets in general is well known. They scarcely admit of two heavily-laden beasts of burden passing one another. As far as can be learned from history and from the ruins of ancient cities, they were no broader in the early times.[11] In some of the

---

[1] Num. 13:28; Deut. 1:28; 13:13; Josh. 11:13; 24:13.   [2] Num. 32:34-38.   [3] Judges 1:26.
[4] 1 Kings 16:24.   [5] Ps. 107:16; Acts 12:10.   [6] 1 Sam. 23:7; Isa. 45:1.   [7] 2 Sam. 18:24.
[8] Josh. 2:19.   [9] 2 Chron. 29:4; 32:6; Neh. 8:1, 3.   [10] Prov. 7:8; Eccles. 12:4; Cant.
3:2.   [11] Josephus, Antiq. 20, 5:3.

larger cities, however, there were doubtless streets of greater width. Absalom at least seems to have used a chariot in Jerusalem in his efforts to seduce the people from their loyalty to David.[1] The same was true of Adonijah;[2] and Jeremiah predicted that there should enter the gates of Jerusalem kings and princes "riding in chariots and on horses."[3] As a rule, no doubt, it was only near the gates and in other exceptional places that there was anything like the breadth of an avenue seen in the cities of the West.

43. Such exceptional places accordingly were all the more frequented. Here were the public gatherings of every kind. We read in the Proverbs of Wisdom uttering her voice "in the broad places; She crieth in the chief place of concourse; At the entering in of the

The Interior of the Jaffa Gate at Jerusalem. (*After Photograph by Bonfils.*)

gates."[4] Here the Pharisees paraded their good works.[5] Here, in those terrible conflicts which the Jews at various times had with their enemies, the most serious encounters always took place.[6] Here, too, was the market-place;[7] here justice was administered;[8] and here strangers entering the city were received and welcomed as guests.[9] An enemy in possession of the gates commanded the city; hence, gates are frequently used as a symbol of power. Our Lord says that the gates of Hades shall not prevail against his Church.[10] The official name of the government of the Turkish empire is the

[1] 2 Sam. 15:1.   [2] 1 Kings 1:5.   [3] Jer. 17:25.   [4] Prov. 1:20, 21.   [5] Matt. 6:5.   [6] Isa. 51:20.
[7] 2 Kings 7:1.   [8] Deut. 17:5; Ruth 4:1-3.   [9] Gen. 19:1; 23:10, 18.   [10] Matt. 16:18.

3

Sublime Porte. The last word means gate, the gate of the sultan's palace being referred to, where justice is supposed to be administered.

The streets were rarely paved in an eastern town, and almost as rarely cleaned; their mud and filth being proverbial.[1] In the streets of Pompeii the high stepping-stones used for crossing show what the ordinary condition of the streets must have been there. The only mention made of pavement in the Old Testament is in connection with buildings like the temple and others.[2] If we may trust Josephus, this king also laid "a causeway of black stone along the road that led to Jerusalem."[3] The work of cleaning and paving public streets seems to have been first seriously undertaken by the Herods, those of Jerusalem being laid with white stones by Agrippa II.[4] In view of this state of things the imagery in the book of Revelation respecting the new Jerusalem is all the more striking by contrast, its streets being represented as paved with "pure gold, as it were transparent glass."[5]

44. THE BAZAAR.—A peculiar kind of street in the Orient is the bazaar. It consists of a covered arcade with a row of narrow shops on either side. (See cut, p. 10.) It is also found to some extent in the cities of Europe. In many cases persons of a like trade congregate together in the same neighborhood. This appears to have been equally true in biblical times. We read, for example, of the prophet Jeremiah in his imprisonment that he was to receive daily "a loaf of bread out of the baker's street."[6] After the Babylonian captivity a quarter of Jerusalem seems to have been frequented particularly by goldsmiths and another by merchants.[7] There is also evidence that when one people became tributary to another, a privilege sometimes granted to the ruling powers was that they might lay out streets for the purposes of trade in the cities of their tributaries. Benhadad I. of Damascus enjoyed the privilege of such streets in Samaria; and Benhadad II. made to Ahab the same concession concerning Damascus.[8] As already intimated, the street where a certain kind of wares was sold received a corresponding name. Others were named from important points which they passed or to which they led. One street in Damascus, it will be recalled, has in the New Testament the name "Straight." It runs from east to west and is about half a mile in length. It was here that Paul received his sight after the miraculous vision of Jesus.[9]

[1] Ps. 18:42; Isa. 10:6; Micah 7:10; but cf. 1 Kings 14:10.   [2] 2 Kings 16:17; Esther 1:6; Ezek. 17:18; 42:3.   [3] Antiq. 8, 7:4.   [4] Antiq. 20, 9:7.   [5] Rev. 21:21.   [6] Jer. 37:21.   [7] Neh. 3:31.   [8] 1 Kings 20:34.   [9] Acts 9:11.

45. THE WATER SUPPLY.—For a supply of water in villages and large towns in the East dependence has always been largely placed on private wells and cisterns. While the soil of Palestine is well adapted to both, the long dry season makes cisterns the more practicable and unfailing. We read in the Bible of the private ownership of cisterns as early as the time of David, and of their use in the age of the patriarchs;[1] and the Moabite Stone informs us that the king of Moab had ordered that every resident of a certain city should provide a cistern in connection with his house. The cistern, if not hewn out of the solid rock, was generally built up with stone, a small round opening being left at the top. They were sometimes of immense capacity.[2] Water was conducted to them during the rainy season by means of troughs leading from the roofs of the houses. Various devices were used for drawing the water, the more common being that of a rope running over a wheel, to which a bucket of skin was attached, the so-called "shadoof," answering to the modern well-sweep.

Natural wells were of course of rarer occurrence and much more prized. In Numbers 21 : 17 there is recorded a song that was composed over a well and was sung by the Israelites in the wilderness at a place called "Beer," that is, "well." At an early period water was conveyed into Jerusalem by means of pipes.[3] Somewhat later Solomon's Pool, lying south of Bethlehem, was the source of water supply for the city. According to Josephus, it was the work of Pilate, the Roman governor.[4] The ruins still existing point to a much earlier date, and Jewish tradition affirms that it was the work of Solomon.[5] It is likely that Pilate only repaired what had been built long anterior to his time. The use of cisterns as places of imprisonment is marked by no less conspicuous examples than those of Joseph and the prophet Jeremiah.[6] The cistern was also a favorite subject for rhetorical figures among biblical writers. No one of them is more striking and forcible perhaps than that of the "weeping prophet," who represents the God of Israel as saying,[7] "For my people have committed two evils ; they have forsaken me the fountain of living waters, and hewed them out cisterns, broken cisterns, that can hold no water."

The population of most biblical cities was comparatively small. The tribe of Levi, made up of about twenty-two thousand males[8] in

---

[1] Gen. 37 : 22; Deut. 6 : 11; 2 Sam. 17 : 18.   [2] Jer. 41 : 9.   [3] Isa. 7 : 3; 22 : 9, 11; 2 Chron. 32 : 3, 4.   [4] *Antiq.* 18, 3 : 2.   [5] Cf. Eccles. 2 : 6; Judith 7 : 6, 7.   [6] Gen. 37 : 22; Jer. 38 : 6.   [7] Jer. 2 : 13.   [8] Num. 3 : 39; Josh. 21 : 41.

the time of Moses, was put in possession of forty-eight cities, including some of the importance of Sychem, Hebron, Heshbon and Ramoth. We find also that an army of three thousand men considered itself strong enough to capture the walled town of Ai;[1] while in the kingdom of Bashan alone there were sixty fortified cities which fell into the hands of the children of Israel.[2]

[1] Josh. 7 : 3, 4 ; 8 : 25.   [2] Deut. 3 : 4, 5.

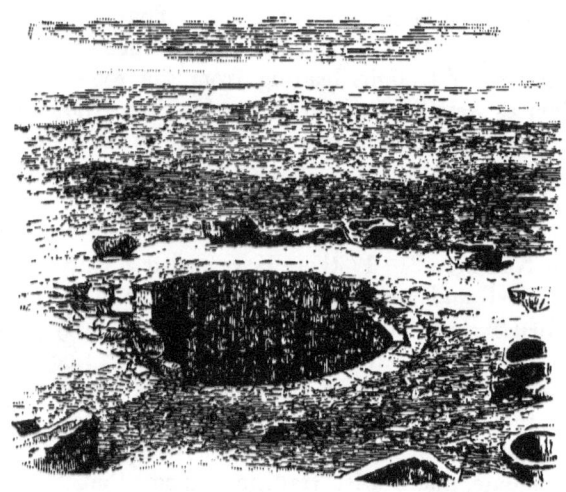

One of the Seven Wells at Beer-sheba, with Watering-troughs for Camels about it. (From *Palmer's Desert of the Exodus*.)

CHAPTER II.

THE FAMILY.

1. WE have already seen that the Hebrew conception of the house embraced that of the household. One word was employed to designate both the dwelling and its inmates.[1] Originally it meant something built up or built together. Each member of the household was an integral part of the structure. "It may be," said Sarah of her handmaid, Hagar, "that I shall be builded [that is, my family be enlarged and strengthened] by her."[2] The psalmist likewise beautifully compares a daughter to a "corner-stone" worthy to be set in the walls of a palace.[3] Another expression and one still more widely used in the Bible for the household literally signifies what is joined together;[4] in fact, the idea could scarcely be set forth more emphatically than it is by this term. Here then, imbedded in their very forms of speech, we discover how compact and indestructible an institution the family was regarded by the ancient Hebrews.

2. CHILDREN.—In harmony with this underlying idea children were looked upon as one of the greatest blessings of life, a "heritage" from the Lord and his peculiar "reward."[5] They were earnestly prayed for when not given, and their advent was marked by the heartiest congratulations of friends and neighbors.[6] No doubt the great hope of Israel that through the "Seed of the woman" the evils of the world would some day be overcome had much to do with this sentiment.

The employment of midwives at the time of birth is well-nigh universal in the East; and the process described in Exodus 1 : 16, where a chair of peculiar construction is referred to as in use in Egypt on such occasions, is still common throughout western Asia. The majority of women, especially those of the working classes, suffer but little during parturition, ordinary duties being resumed after three or four days.[7] As soon as a child is born it is washed in salted water and closely bound, or swaddled, up in a piece of cloth a few inches broad and several feet long.[8] This is wound tightly around

[1] Gen. 46:31. [2] Gen. 16:2 (margin of Revision); cf. 30:3; Deut. 25:9. [3] Ps. 144:12. [4] Ex. 6:17. [5] Ps. 113:9; 127:3–5. [6] Gen. 15:2–5; 1 Sam. 1:27; Ruth 4:11. [7] Cf. Ex. 1:19. [8] Ezek. 16:4; Luke 2:7.

the entire body. Even the arms are pinioned to the side and the whole frame held as motionless as possible, under the impression that there is danger to the child if it move about too much while the bones are soft. This practice is common also in many parts of Europe. An Oriental cradle differs but little from some in use among ourselves. "The little one lies tightly bound up in its cradle day and night, being taken up once or twice in twenty-four hours. Its mother leans over the cradle to nurse it, and hushes its cries by incessant rocking: all night long lying in her bed, spread upon the floor close by, she never lets go the cradle string."[1]

Hebrew children were uniformly nursed by their mothers.[2] A son was circumcised on the eighth day after his birth and at the same time received his name.[3] If he were a first-born son, redemption money was paid for him to the amount of five shekels. This was in memory of the fact that the first-born of Israel were passed by when those of Egypt were miraculously slain.[4] Originally, it would seem, they had been intended for service in the sanctuary. After the defection of Israel in the matter of the golden calf the tribe of Levi was set apart for this purpose, and the first-born of the other tribes became exempt by the payment of a tax.[4] On the fortieth day after the birth of a son, and the eightieth after that of a daughter, the mother presented herself at the sanctuary for ceremonial purification, bringing an offering according to her ability.[5]

Nothing could be more marked or delightful than the respect which the Bible everywhere shows for children and childhood. Tacitus, the Latin historian, thinks it worthy of mention that the Jews regarded it as a crime to kill their offspring.[6] Not only were their rights protected by statute, but the spirit of the Mosaic institutions encouraged the utmost tenderness and affection towards them. It is significant that there are no less than nine special terms in the Hebrew language used to designate different periods or characteristics of the child's life, besides the more general ones of son and daughter. What a revelation of paternal love appears in the form of the command to Abraham to offer up Isaac as a burnt-offering;[7] in the words of Jacob when he received the news of Joseph's death;[8] and in the despairing cries of David over the lost Absalom![9] No more powerful image of the love of God for his people could be found than this

---

[1] Van Lennep, *Bible Lands*, p. 570.   [2] 1 Sam. 1:23; 1 Kings 3:21.   [3] Luke 1:59.   [4] Ex. 13:12-15; 22:29; Lev. 27:6; Num. 8:17.   [5] Lev. 12:2-7; Luke 2:22-24.   [6] *Hist.* 5:5.
[7] Gen. 22:2.   [8] Gen. 37:35.   [9] 2 Sam. 19:4.

of a Hebrew father for his son. "The Lord thy God bare thee," says Moses, "as a man doth bear his son."[1]

3. But parental love might not stand in the way of correction for faults; it should rather lead to it. The work of training began with the opening life.[2] It was made not only the earliest and latest duty of both the parents, but it was to be also the special care of the state.[3] It was a fundamental principle of all education that the "fear of the Lord is the beginning of wisdom."[4] The Scriptures, not excluding the portions that treat of the ceremonial institutions of the Jewish religion, were the principal text-book at home and in the school. How well they were studied the typical example of Timothy shows us, of whom Paul could say that "from a babe" he had known "the sacred writings."[5] In his case it had been largely due to the faithfulness of a mother and grandmother. Sacred history gives us a few glimpses of these true mothers in Israel: in Samuel's mother; the pious Shunammite; the mother of King Lemuel, whose wise counsels we find in the last chapter of Proverbs; "the mother of Zebedee's children;" of John Mark; Mary the blessed, whom our Lord called mother; the "elect lady and her children," and her equally "elect sister" with her children, beloved in the truth.[6] Parents are not only admonished in the Scriptures to instruct their offspring in the precepts and ordinances of religion, but to see that they are present during religious ceremonies that they may be led to inquire concerning them and become acquainted with their import. At least as early as the time of our Lord schools had been established in connection with synagogues wherever the population would justify it. How he himself felt towards the little ones his own precious words give testimony: "Suffer the little children, and forbid them not, to come unto me: for of such is the kingdom of heaven."[7]

That Hebrew children, like those of other peoples, were accustomed to the pastimes of childhood there is no reason to doubt. The prophet Zechariah, describing the better future of Israel, says that the "city [Jerusalem] shall be full of boys and girls playing in the streets thereof."[8] Among the curiosities exhumed from the ruins of ancient cities the dolls and playthings of children form a noticeable part. Those of the ancient Egyptian youth as found laid away beside them in their tombs are constructed with a skill that would

---

[1] Deut. 1:31; cf. Ps. 103:13.   [2] Prov. 10:1; 13:24; 23:14; 29:15.   [3] Ex. 13:8; Deut. 4:9; 6:7; 11:19; 31:13.   [4] Prov. 1:7; 9:10.   [5] 2 Tim. 1:5; 3:15.   [6] 2 John 13.   [7] Matt. 19:14.   [8] Zech. 8:5.

do credit to modern times. There is a hint in the book of Job that birds were sometimes made captive and attached to strings for amusement;[1] and our Lord, in the way of illustration, intimates that the children of his day entertained themselves with the noise of trumpets and horns. In such sports they were ready to imitate either the gayety of the marriage festival or the solemnity of the funeral.[2]

4. Even during the father's life-time the first-born son was entitled to special privileges.[3] After his death he received twice as much of his property as any other child and took the place of the father as the head of the family. In the patriarchal times he seems also to have acted as the priest of the family.[4] Along with these rights naturally went the duty of providing for the mother, if living, and other dependent members of the household. The son of a concubine, if first-born, was eligible to the privileges of primogeniture, and it was exceptional when he was put off with simple presents.[5] It was understood that the father had the option, on grounds appearing sufficient to himself, to assign the rights of the first-born to a younger brother or even to make a nephew his heir.[6] On the other hand, a father was expressly forbidden to show partiality towards the son of a favorite wife and solely on that ground to deprive him of his birthright.[7]

The eldest son might sell his birthright, if so disposed, and primitive custom regarded such sale as valid though afterwards he might seek " diligently with tears" to recover it.[8] A father might direct how his property should be distributed after his death, though it interfered with ordinary customs; but we hear nothing of the will in a technical sense in the Bible, until we come to the epistle to the Galatians.[9] Daughters were generally left portionless, it being expected that they would be provided for by the eldest brother or by their husbands.[10] When there were no sons, however, they became joint heirs of their father's estate, providing they did not marry outside the family line, thereby alienating the inheritance. Even then they might claim their portion if the husband took the family name of his wife.[11] In cases where there were only daughters in the family and they unmarried, their names were entered in the registers of families as representatives of the father's house.[12]

5. MARRIAGE.—It might have been expected that marriage would be well-nigh universal among the Hebrews. Without it the life of

---

[1] Job 41 : 5.   [2] Matt. 11 : 16–18.   [3] Gen. 24 : 50; 43 : 33.   [4] Gen. 27 : 29; Deut. 21 : 17; cf. Num. 3 : 41.   [5] Gen. 21 : 10–14.   [6] Gen. 48 : 5, 6; 49 : 3, 4; 1 Chron. 5 : 1.   [7] Deut. 21 : 15–17.   [8] Gen. 25 : 33; Heb. 12 : 17.   [9] Gal. 3 : 15.   [10] Gen. 31 : 14, 15.   [11] Num. 36 : 6–9; 1 Chron. 2 : 34, 35; 23 : 22; Neh. 7 : 63.   [12] Num. 27 : 1–11.

the family and of the community as presupposed in the Mosaic institutions would be impossible. But in this relationship, as presented in the books of the Old Testament, we are carefully to distinguish between what, for the time, was ideal and what was actual; between what the Bible represents as the true relation of man and woman in marriage and that which it permitted because of the hardness of men's heart; between that which was original and divinely appointed and that to which this divine original degenerated after the fall. "In the beginning it was not so," was Christ's answer to all attempts to charge upon the Creator the later irregularities of the marriage bond. After quoting to the Pharisees the original charter of the institution of monogamy, and showing that the two persons concerned in marriage became thereby one flesh, he adds, "What therefore God hath joined together, let not man put asunder."[1] By the very expressions used the idea of polygamy is excluded.

6. But as a matter of fact, we find even in Genesis 4:19 the record of an infraction of this divine arrangement. Lamech, of the posterity of Cain, is said to have taken two wives.[2] Soon after this, as we may suppose, the practice of polygamy became somewhat common, especially among men of rank and wealth. Even some of the best of the patriarchs were not free from it. But Noah and his sons appear to have been monogamists, and there is no evidence that Moses had more than one wife at once.[3] The prophets, too, as far as we know, were all of this class. And in that ideal condition depicted in the last chapter of Proverbs, monogamy is represented as one of its most prominent and winning features. The practice of polygamy among the Hebrews, it is certain, never sank to the low level of the surrounding peoples. The Mosaic laws everywhere recognize the principle of monogamy in requiring a distinction to be made between the first or legitimate wife and those taken in addition to her. They restricted the number of wives to those most under temptation to multiply them.[4] They prohibited a second marriage in certain cases.[5] Within certain limits they definitely prescribed a man's matrimonial obligations, if he took more wives than one.[5] But down to New Testament times, though with diminishing prevalence, polygamy continued to be the custom. Then it rapidly disappeared before the clearer light and higher claims of Christianity.

7. In the patriarchal period marriage between near relatives seems not to have been uncommon. It was principally due to a de-

---

[1] Matt. 19:4-7.　[2] Cf. Num. 12.1.　[3] Deut. 17:17.　[4] Lev. 18:18.　[5] Ex. 21:10, 11.

sire to preserve, as far as possible, the family bond intact, and avoid connections with idolaters. That such a state of things could not long continue without the most disastrous effects is apparent enough. In the Mosaic laws accordingly the matter is carefully regulated, the limits being sharply defined within which marriage would be legal.[1] How important the subject was considered may be inferred from the heavy penalties attached to any infraction of the statute, and from the fact that of the curses pronounced on Mount Ebal, three related to incestuous marriages.[2]

Little need be said on the form and limits of the Levitical law respecting prohibited marriages. The wisdom of its provisions has been generally recognized among Christian nations, and tacitly, at least, by some heathen peoples. The word "incest," that is, "unchaste," which the Romans applied to the intermarriage of near relations, shows in what light they regarded it. Nothing is said of marriage to a daughter in the code of Leviticus simply because its prohibition is implied, *a fortiori*, in that of granddaughter.[3] The same seems to be true of the relation of uncle and niece, the marriage of aunt and nephew being expressly forbidden. The Jewish law did not prohibit the marriage of cousins, although in some of the United States that of first cousins has been made illegal. The same is true of step-brothers and sisters, as far as the Mosaic statutes are concerned. With obvious reference to polygamous practices, marriage with a wife's sister, during the life-time of the wife, is expressly prohibited.[4] The words "in her life-time," however, naturally lead to the inference that it was not illegal for one to marry the sister of a deceased wife; and rabbinical law has always sanctioned this view.

8. Another special exception referred to a brother's wife, where the brother had died childless. She was not permitted to marry a stranger, unless the surviving brother-in-law living near formally refused to marry her.[5] The latter form of marriage is called levirate, from the Latin word *levir*, which means brother-in-law. Such a marriage was intended, first, to prevent the extinction of the name of him who had died childless; and second, to be in harmony with the agrarian laws of Israel concerning the retention of property within the same tribe and family. The first-born son of such a union took the name of the deceased uncle instead of that of his father, and succeeded to his estate. It was at a person's option to

---

[1] Lev. 18 : 6-18 ; 20 : 11-21.   [2] Deut. 27 ; 20, 22, 23.   [3] Lev. 18 : 10.   [4] Lev. 18 : 18.
[5] Deut. 25 : 5 ; Matt. 22 : 24.

accede to or decline such a union; but in the Mosaic period his refusal was attended with a peculiar disgrace.[1] If there were no brother of the deceased husband alive, the law of the levirate was understood to be, to some extent, binding on the next of kin. In the case of Ruth's relative, we find him ready to yield to Boaz the right to the Moabitess, and doing so by means of the interesting ceremony of drawing off the shoe, as a sign of renunciation.[2] Modern Judaism does not consider the law of levirate marriage any longer binding.

9. By the law of Moses a man was forbidden to re-marry a divorced wife, provided she had married again and become a widow, or had been divorced from her second husband.[3] A rabbinical extension of this prohibition was made to cover the case of a person who desired to re-marry a woman from whom he had been divorced on the ground of a bad reputation or of barrenness, whether she had been married a second time or not. Jewish tradition, as formulated in the Talmud, also interpreted Deut. 23 : 2, where a bastard—"a person born of incest or adultery"—is excluded from the assembly of the Lord, as meaning that such a person might not intermarry with an Israelite. It applied the same rule to such as were mutilated as described in Deut. 23 : 1.

Israelites were further forbidden by statute to intermarry with any of the seven Canaanitish nations, on the ground of imperilling thereby their loyalty to Jehovah.[4] The prohibition, however, is expressly limited to these nations. We find Moses himself marrying first a Midianitish and afterwards a Cushite woman; and David, a princess of Geshur.[5] Subsequent to the exile this law of the Pentateuch was extended by the Jewish authorities so as to forbid all foreign marriages. Among others, one conspicuous case is instanced where, on refusal to break off a marriage of this kind, a grandson of the high priest was expelled from the priesthood by Nehemiah.[6] In addition to these general rules for the laity, a priest was at all periods still more circumscribed. He was forbidden to marry a harlot, a profane (polluted) person, or one who had been divorced. The high priest was limited to a "virgin of his own people."[7] Later, in the days of Ezekiel, the original law was so far modified in the direction of greater rigor that it was regarded as illegal even for an ordinary priest to marry a widow, unless she were the widow of a priest.[8]

[1] Deut. 25:7-10. [2] Ruth 4:7. [3] Deut. 24:4. [4] Ex. 34:16; Deut. 7:3,4; cf. 23:3. [5] Ex. 2:21; Num. 12:1; 2 Sam. 3:3; cf. Gen. 41:45; 1 Chron. 7:14. [6] Ezra 9:12; 10:2,3,14-41; Neh. 10:30; 13:25,29. [7] Lev. 21:7,14. [8] Ezek. 44:22.

10. Betrothal in the earliest times was mostly a matter of business, and was supposed to concern chiefly the parents and near family friends.[1] The sentiment seems always to have prevailed in the Orient, and prevails also at the present day in large portions of Europe, that love is more likely to spring up between the sexes after, than before, marriage, and that previous to marriage it is something to be deprecated rather than desired. It is probable that even in the Mosaic period there was some recognized formality of betrothal, since a distinction is clearly made between the betrothed and the married.[2] It was not until the development of rabbinical law under the second Jewish commonwealth, however, that a legal ceremonial for it was regularly established. Later practice, too, left the choice of a wife more and more to the young man. This is clear from the statement of the Talmud that annually, on the afternoon of the day of Atonement, when the maidens of Jerusalem, arrayed in white, gathered in the vineyards contiguous to the city and engaged in various festivities, the young men made their selection of partners. Betrothal at all times was regarded as more than a promise to marry: it was its initial act. It was something which could be dissolved only by death or legal divorce. Faithlessness to the vow was esteemed and punished as adultery.[3] Talmudic law held that the consent of the persons betrothed was essential to the validity of the betrothal. It might however be given in person or by deputy. The ceremony itself consisted in the simple act on the part of the bridegroom of handing to the bride, or her representative, a written engagement in the presence of two witnesses, or a piece of money, however small, accompanied with the words " Be thou consecrated [wedded] to me." Since the middle ages a ring has been substituted for the piece of coin, and is now the customary sign of betrothal.

11. In biblical times, before the betrothal actually took place it was usual to fix upon the dowry. As a rule it was given to the parents of the bride,[4] though sometimes to an elder brother.[5] The dowry was not, properly speaking, a price paid for a wife. This species of barter occurred, as a rule, only in the case of concubines. In proportion as the idea of marriage approached the ethical standard of the Scriptures themselves, as in the case of the patriarchs, the dowry was looked upon more in the light of a present made to the bride or her parents, for the purpose of sealing the engagement, or of enabling the bride to assume a worthy place in her future home.

---

[1] Gen. 21 : 21 ; 24 : 3.   [2] Deut. 20 : 7.   [3] Lev. 19 : 20 ; Deut. 22 : 23–29 ; but cf. Matt. 1 : 18, 19.
[4] Ex. 22 : 16, 17 ; 1 Sam. 18 : 25.   [5] Gen. 24 : 53 ; 34 : 12.

Had it not been so it would be difficult to understand the complaint of Rachel and Leah against their father: "For he hath sold us, and hath also quite devoured our money,"[1] that is, the price paid for us. That there are instances to the contrary is not strange; but they are to be regarded as exceptions.[2] In rabbinical law as established at least a hundred years before Christ, the dowry took the direct form of a settlement upon the wife, and was held to be as indispensable as the marriage license is among ourselves. The amount naturally depended on the circumstances of those concerned, but ordinarily ranged between thirty and fifty shekels, that is, from fifteen to twenty-five dollars.[3] It might consist of money or its equivalent.[4] Instances are on record where parents themselves bestowed presents on their daughters at the time of their betrothal.[5]

12. Marriage contracts appear to have been mostly oral and of a simple character. The earliest account of a written one is found in the book of Tobit.[6] But the oral covenant was by no means considered a mere form. It seems to have been made in the presence of witnesses, and its sacred character is several times made the subject of direct reference in the Old Testament.[7] It may have related in detail to such matters as the position and rights of the wife in the family,

A Bridal Crown.

the denial of divorce on insufficient grounds and similar topics.

13. After the betrothal a longer or shorter period, according to circumstances, was allowed to elapse before the nuptials.[8] By Talmudic law it was established at a month for widows and a full year for virgins. In the meantime no private intercourse was allowed between the betrothed. The wedding festivities were chiefly of a social character, and ordinarily lasted seven days, but might continue twice as long.[9] There is no scriptural evidence that the services of a priest were thought needful. Guests were first invited and afterwards summoned by special messenger.[10] When the wedding-day

---

[1] Gen. 31 : 15.   [2] Hos. 3 : 1, 2.   [3] Deut. 22 : 29.   [4] Gen. 29 : 18; Josh. 15 : 16.   [5] Gen. 29 : 24, 29; Tobit 10 : 11.   [6] Tobit 7 : 15.   [7] Ruth 4 : 11; Prov. 2 : 17; Ezek. 16 : 8; Mal. 2 : 14.   [8] Gen. 24 : 55, 67; Deut. 20 : 7; Judg. 14 : 8.   [9] Judg. 14 : 12, 17; Tobit 8 : 20.   [10] Luke 14 : 17.

arrived the bridegroom, richly dressed, possibly crowned with garlands or with a nuptial turban on his head, and attended by special
companions, went in procession to the house of the bride to conduct
her to his own house or that of his father.[1]   In the time of our Lord
and later the custom of having special groomsmen, "friends of the
bridegroom," seems to have been somewhat local.   It was at least
practiced in Judæa.   At the marriage in Cana of Galilee, on the
other hand, none are mentioned.   The term "children of the bride-
chamber"[2] refers to another class, that is, to guests in general.

The bride, deeply veiled, was led away amidst the blessings of her
parents and other friends.[3]   If circumstances rendered it necessary,
however, the wedding festivities were celebrated at the house of the
bride.[4]   The bridegroom, if wealthy, sometimes distributed garments
suitable for the occasion among his guests.[5]   The bridal procession
not infrequently took place at night, amidst the blaze of torches
and with the accompaniment of songs, dancing and the highest expressions of joy.[6]   Under Mosaic law, the bridegroom was exempt
for a limited period from all public duties; and such exemption
availed also for one who had become betrothed.[7]

14. The Bible sacredly guards the marriage bond by special statutes.   In harmony with prevailing custom, and during the low stage
of spiritual development in which the earlier laws arose, they assume,
for the most part, the form of protection for the husband from the
unfaithfulness of his wife, or from attempts on the part of others to
seduce her from him.   The sin of adultery was originally punished
by the death, through stoning, of both participants; nor did the Mosaic law any more than that of our Lord stop short with the outward
act; it condemned also the lustful desire.[8]   A man suspecting his wife
of unfaithfulness might subject her to a terrible ordeal which no
guilty person could well pass through without betraying her guilt.[9]
Severe as was the trial, however, it was understood to be simply a
means by which God made known what was the actual state of the
case.   In a similar manner the wife was protected by law against
the ungrounded suspicions of her husband that she had been unfaithful previous to marriage.[10]

15. DIVORCE.—The earliest fragments of sacred history and the
earliest laws furnish sufficient evidence of the radical perversion of

[1] Judg. 14: 10; Cant. 3: 11; Isa. 61: 10; 1 Macc. 9: 37–39; Matt. 9: 15; 25: 1; John 3: 29.
[2] Matt. 9; 15; John 3: 29.   [3] Ruth 4: 11; Tobit 7: 12.   [4] Gen. 29: 22; Tobit 8: 20.   [5] Matt.
22: 11.   [6] Matt. 22: 1–10; 25: 1–10.   [7] Deut. 20: 7; 24: 5.   [8] Lev. 20: 10; Deut. 22: 22;
Ezek. 16: 38, 40; Matt. 1: 18, 19; John 8: 5; cf. Ex. 20: 17.   [9] Num. 5: 11–31.   [10] Deut.
22: 13–21; 24: 1–4; cf. Ex. 21: 22.

the original relation which the Creator constituted between the sexes.[1] The Mosaic legislation attempted no more than to subject these perversions to severe restraints. The sacredness of the marital tie is assumed in it, and provision is made against its being broken and renewed at will. Divorce is presupposed as a usage of the times, and a bare legal sanction is given to it under certain fixed conditions. It is not ordered, but permitted. Our Lord, it will be remembered, corrected in this particular the false interpretation of the Pharisees, assuring them, moreover, that even so much was conceded only because of hardness of heart.[2] The important passage in Deuteronomy relating to this subject is rendered as follows: " When a man taketh a wife, and marrieth her, then it shall be, if she find no favor in his eyes, because he hath found some unseemly thing in her, that he shall write her a bill of divorcement, and give it in her hand, and send her out of his house. And when she is departed out of his house, she may go and be another man's *wife*. And if the latter husband hate her, and write her a bill of divorcement, and give it in her hand, and send her out of his house ; or if the latter husband die, which took her to be his wife ; her former husband, which sent her away, may not take her again to be his wife, after that she is defiled ; for that is abomination before the Lord."[3]

Such a bill of divorcement was in itself a decided limitation. It made needful not a little delay which might be spent in reflection. The intervention of a priest or magistrate would also be generally required, and their offices would naturally be used to procure, if possible, a reconciliation. Besides, the document provides that there shall be a real ground for the procedure, some " unseemly thing " in the woman. What this covered it is difficult to say. It could not be adultery, since that was punishable with death. The question was a matter of dispute among Jewish authorities down to the time of Christ as well as afterwards, and was differently answered by the rival schools of Hillel and Shammai. If the woman married another man subsequent to her divorce, reunion with her former husband, as we have before seen, was legally impossible, such a connection being regarded as a kind of adultery.[4] The obvious aim of the statute was to preserve the original covenant inviolate. If that were impossible or impracticable, its object was to encourage a single life with a view to a possible future reunion. It does not rise to the plane of Malachi, who says that God "hates putting away" and

---

[1] Gen. 4: 23; 16: 1, 2; Ex. 20: 17.   [2] Matt. 5: 31; 19: 7, 8; Mark 10: 4, 5.   [3] Deut. 24: 1-4.
[4] Num. 5: 20.

pathetically describes the altar of God as covered with the tears of "the wife of thy youth," "the wife of thy covenant," "thy companion," treacherously dealt with and "put away."[1] But it is in complete harmony with the remaining laws of the Pentateuch, which are largely educational in their design, and intended for a primitive stage of moral development. It is never to be forgotten what the surroundings of the Hebrew people were, and what their training hitherto had been. The divine revelation presupposes, and arranges for, advancing stages of spiritual life, and without them such a revelation would have been impossible.

16. Much stricter regulations concerning divorce are found in the New Testament. In fact, our Lord abrogates for his disciples this law of Moses and forbids divorce with the privilege of remarrying, except for one crime, that of adultery. He even declares the union of a divorced woman with another man, except in case of her divorce on this ground, an adulterous connection, both for herself and her husband. Under Mosaic laws, moreover, a woman was not allowed to separate herself from her husband for any reason. Our Lord, it would seem, puts the woman in this respect on the plane with the man. His higher standard he bases on the original divinely-constituted relationship of the sexes in marriage, affirming that they thereby became one flesh. This mysterious[2] union could only be dissolved by sexual unfaithfulness or by death.

The apostle Paul supplements, but otherwise leaves in full force, the words of our Lord. In case a difference arose between a husband and wife who were Christians, they were to become reconciled, if that were possible; but if it were not, they had no permission to remarry. If one were a Christian and the other an unbeliever, still they were called to peace and continued union. If, however, the one unbelieving actually forsook his companion, it carried with it no permission to the Christian disciple to marry another person during her husband's lifetime.[3] Paul's general estimate of the marriage bond may be inferred from the parallel which he elsewhere draws between it and the union of Christ with his Church: "Husbands, love your wives, even as Christ also loved the church, and gave himself up for it. . . . Even so ought husbands also to love their own wives as their own bodies."[4]

17. CONCUBINAGE.—In distinction from polygamy, by which is to be understood the custom of having more wives than one at the

<hr/>

[1] Mal. 2 : 14-16.   [2] Matt. 5 : 31, 32; 19 : 3-9; Mark 10 : 2-12.   [3] 1 Cor. 7 : 10-16.   [4] Eph. 5 : 25, 28; cf. Rev. 19 : 7.

same time, we have to speak also of the practice of concubinage. However many wives there might be, before the law they were on the same general plane with one another. The concubine belonged to another category. She was something less than a wife, but, on the other hand, something more than a mistress, in the modern sense. In her acknowledged position, her rights were almost as jealously guarded in the Mosaic code as those of the wife herself. Her disabilities related chiefly to the matter of divorce, the rights of her children and her own position on the death of her lord.[1] The practice of concubinage seems to have arisen at first from a desire for a numerous offspring, combined, in some cases, with the fact of the wife's barrenness. So it was with the patriarchs. The relation being here acquiesced in by the true wife, and the children of the concubine, moreover, being regarded in much the same light as those of the wife, the moral stigma naturally attaching to such a relationship largely disappeared. In no case were the children of such a connection looked upon as illegitimate.

The principal distinction in fact between the wife and the concubine was that while the former was, in some sense, on an equality of social position with her husband, the latter was a bondmaid. Not infrequently she was the servant of the wife;[2] or a captive taken in war;[3] or one purchased of her father. The taking of Canaanitish women as concubines was forbidden.[4] The case of a foreign slave, not a captive taken in war, is not provided for in the law. A Hebrew woman might become a concubine by first coming into the condition of a bondmaid; but her position and treatment are made the subject of special restrictive legislation.[5] The whole system was clearly a perversion of the natural and divinely-intended relation of the sexes. God in the wisdom of his plans, which looked forward to the end of time, allowed it temporarily to exist among the Hebrews, but under limitations unheard of among neighboring peoples. There is nowhere any attempt in the Bible to veil the terrible consequences resulting from the practice of polygamy and concubinage, even though they appear among those otherwise the godliest of men.[6]

18. In addition to those noticed elsewhere, there are three other forms of unchastity of which special cognizance is taken in the laws of the Pentateuch: the seduction of an unbetrothed maiden; ordinary harlotry; and the same indulged in under the plea of doing honor to idols. In the first instance, the maiden was left unpunished.

---

[1] Judg. 9:18.   [2] Gen. 29:24, 29.   [3] Deut. 21:10-14.   [4] Deut. 7:3.   [5] Ex. 21:7-11.
[6] Gen. 25:6; 27:1-42; 30:1-15; Judg. 19:22-30.

Her seducer, however, was obliged to marry her, unless her father objected, in which case a heavy fine was imposed. Moreover, the right of divorcing his wife was forever taken from such seducer.[1] Harlotry was forbidden in the early codes under the severest penalties. It was looked upon as a profanation of that which had been formally devoted to God. If the daughter of a priest yielded herself to it, she was burnt.[2] Harlotry in the supposed service of an idol, the sum obtained by it being appropriated to the deity, was not uncommon among eastern peoples. The abhorrent crime forbidden in Leviticus 18 : 23; 20 : 15, 16, was widely practiced in some parts of Egypt. There are several allusions to it as a practice also in the Old Testament, as well as to the gross form of licentiousness characterized as sodomy.[3]

The strongest terms of reprobation known to the Hebrew language are directed against both. The children of prostitutes were excluded from the congregation of Israel by express statute,[4] and marriage with such persons was forbidden by the Jewish authorities in the time of our Lord. That licentiousness had great sway at different periods among the covenant people, owing to their peculiar susceptibility to foreign influences, there is ample evidence. Numerous warnings in the book of Proverbs[5] show to what extent the worst vices of heathenism had taken root in Palestine. It is clear, too, from many texts that at the beginning of the Christian era, and among the best circles, the necessity for urgent admonitions on the subject had not ceased.[6]

19. SOCIAL POSITION OF THE HEBREW WOMAN.—What was the relative position of woman among the Hebrews in Old and New Testament times? Undoubtedly a false impression prevails respecting the matter. Her present position under Mohammedan influences is improperly assumed as the standard of what it has always been in the East. Women appear in the Bible as engaged to a greater extent than is common with us in out-of-door occupations. In addition to managing the affairs of the household at home, preparing the meals,[7] spinning yarn,[8] and making garments,[9] they acted as water-carriers;[10] they attended to the flocks;[11] they ground the grain for food,[12] and employed themselves in a variety of similar

---

[1] Ex. 22 : 16, 17; Deut. 22 : 28, 29.   [2] Lev. 19 : 20; 21 : 9; Deut. 23 : 17, 18; Ezek. 16 : 33–42.
[3] Gen. 19 : 4; Ex. 22 : 19; Job 36 : 14; 1 Kings 14 : 24; 2 Kings 23 : 7.   [4] Deut. 23 : 2.   [5] See chaps. 5 and 7.   [6] Acts 15 : 20, 29; Rom. 1 : 26, 27; 1 Cor. 5 : 1; 6 : 9; 2 Cor. 12 : 21; Eph. 4 : 19; 1 Tim. 1 : 10; 1 Peter 4 : 3.   [7] Gen. 18 : 6; 2 Sam. 13 : 8.   [8] Ex. 35 : 26; Prov. 31 : 19.
[9] 1 Sam. 2 : 19; Prov. 31 : 21.   [10] Gen. 24 : 15; 1 Sam. 9 : 11.   [11] Gen. 29 : 6; Ex. 2 : 16.
[12] Matt. 24 : 41.

occupations. It was impossible for them therefore to lead the care-fully-secluded life which by many they are supposed to have lived.

As distinctions in rank did not exist among the Hebrews, females moved on the same social plane, not only with one another, but with the male sex. There is every evidence that as a class they were held in the highest respect by the latter. We find them, for ex-ample, in Saul's day, celebrating with triumphal processions the vic-tories of Israelitish heroes.[1] We find, still earlier, three of them in the prophetical office,[2] one of these being also judge.[3] The full right is accorded them of making complaints to the authorities when they have been wronged and to claim justice at their hands.[4] And nothing could be more marked than the influence that, in the book of Proverbs, a wise and true woman is represented as exerting over her household, especially her sons. It is highly instructive, in fact, to note that the king Lemuel, who speaks in one of its most delight-ful chapters, is ready to acknowledge that what he there says was first taught him by a faithful mother.[5] One cannot fail, moreover, to recall the devout women who are mentioned in the gospels or their loving ministry to our Lord and his apostles. Notwithstanding the opposition that was aroused against our Lord's teaching and manner of life, not a whisper of suspicion is heard concerning these women, who humbly followed his steps from place to place that they might supply his needs; who were latest at his cross and earliest at his sepulchre.

"What the family life among the godly in Israel must have been," says Edersheim,[6] "how elevated its tone, how loving its converse, or how earnestly devoted its mothers and daughters, appears sufficiently from the gospel story, from that in the book of Acts, and from no-tices in the apostolic letters. Women, such as the Virgin-mother, or Elisabeth, or Anna, or those who enjoyed the privileges of minis-tering to the Lord, or who, after his death, tended and watched his sacred body, could not have been quite solitary in Palestine; we find their sisters in a Dorcas, a Lydia, a Phœbe, and those women of whom St. Paul speaks in Philippians 4:3, and whose lives he sketches in his epistles to Timothy and Titus.

"Wives such as Priscilla, mothers such as that of Zebedee's chil-dren, or of Mark, or like St. John's 'elect lady,' or as Lois and Eunice, must have kept the moral atmosphere pure and sweet, and

---

[1] 1 Sam. 18:6-8; cf. Ps. 68:25. [2] Ex. 15:20; 2 Kings 22:14. [3] Judg. 4:4. [4] Num. 27:1; 1 Kings 3:16-18; 2 Kings 6:26-29. [5] Title of chap. 31. [6] *Sketches of Jewish Social Life*, p. 159.

shed precious light on their homes and on society, corrupt to the core
as it was under the sway of heathenism. What and how they taught
their households, and that even under the most disadvantageous outward circumstances, we learn from the history of Timothy. And
although they were undoubtedly in that respect without many of
the opportunities which we enjoy, there was one sweet practice of
family religion, going beyond the prescribed prayers, which enabled
them to teach their children from tenderest years to intertwine the
Word of God with their daily devotion and daily life. For it was
the custom to teach a child some verse of Holy Scripture beginning
or ending with precisely the same letters as its Hebrew name, and
this birthday text or guardian-promise the child was day by day to
insert in its prayers."

20. SOCIAL LIFE IN GENERAL.—The ancient Hebrews, like
Orientals generally, were an eminently social people. Their political constitution and their religious ceremonies contributed to this
result. Many times in the popular code of Deuteronomy it is represented in one form or another, that the whole family is expected to
appear before the Lord at the sanctuary on the occasions of the so-
called pilgrimage festivals: "And thou shalt rejoice in thy feast,
thou, and thy son, and thy daughter, and thy manservant, and thy
maidservant, and the Levite, and the stranger, and the fatherless, and
the widow, that are within thy gates."[1] Other occasions for social
gatherings were the sheep-shearings, the grain and fruit. harvests,
family festivals, such as the weaning of children, wedding seasons[2]
and the ordinary arrival of guests. Not only are occasional glimpses
given us of social intercourse at the gates, in the market-places and
around the public wells, but a multitude of incidental allusions show
that the common life of the ancient Hebrew was far from being a
prosaic or an ascetic one.[3] The Bible, however, recognizes the possibility of carrying such social festivities to a criminal extreme.[4]

21. The duties of hospitality are repeatedly enjoined in the Mosaic
law, as well as recommended by the noblest examples among the earliest patriarchs.[5] Among the covenant people its moral obligation
was based on the relationship presupposed to exist between them and
God.[6] And however weak and unworthy men might be in other
respects, they seldom failed here. The conduct of Lot, for instance,
was far from being exemplary in all respects; but he was scrupu-

[1] Deut. 16:14. [2] Gen. 21:8; 1 Sam. 25:2; 2 Sam. 13:24; Luke 5:29; 15:23; John 2:2
[3] Gen. 24:11; Judg. 21:19, 21; Ps. 69:12; Matt. 11:16. [4] Amos 6:4. [5] Gen. 18:6; 19:8,
24:17; Ex. 2:20; Deut. 10:19. [6] Ps. 39:12; 1 Peter 2:11.

lously faithful to his duties as a host.[1] In the general absence of places of public entertainment the obligations of a true host required not only the provision of entertainment for man and beast as long as it might suit the convenience of visitors, but an unrequited hospitality. The offer of money in payment for services rendered would have been regarded as a direct insult. The acceptance of presents, however, from a guest is not looked upon, at least in modern times, as derogatory to the character of a worthy host. How much in harmony with the spirit of Christianity a generous hospitality is may be inferred from the many passages enjoining it in the New Testament.[2]

22. The warm, demonstrative temperament of Orientals displays itself in nothing more than in the manner in which they are accustomed to receive and welcome their guests. On the most ordinary occasions they bow low, the right hand being placed upon the left breast, and are profuse in their greetings and expressions of joy. Even on passing an acquaintance on the highway the Oriental, instead of giving the silent nod usual with us, goes through a series of movements and inquiries intended to show respect and interest, which consume no little time. It cannot have been otherwise in the earlier days, as we may judge from the command of our Lord to the seventy, "Salute no man by the way."[3] And we read of Abraham, when the three strangers presented themselves at his tent, that he "bowed himself to the earth."[4] He did the same to the sons of Heth, when he met them for the purchase of a burying-place.[5] Sometimes, in case superiors were addressed, one fell upon his knees and touched his forehead to the

Modes of Salutation in the East.

earth. It was so when Joseph's brethren greeted him as viceroy of the land of Egypt: "They came, and bowed down themselves to him with their faces to the earth."[6] Only in harmony with this general custom were some of the prostrations made before our Lord; they did not always carry with them the idea of paying him divine honors.[7] The most common form of greeting found in the Bible is, "Peace be unto thee."[8] In the book of Ruth Boaz greets his workmen with

[1] Gen. 19:1-10.   [2] Matt. 25:35; Rom. 12:13; 1 Tim. 3:2; 5:10; Heb. 13:2; 1 Peter 4:9; 3 John 5.   [3] Luke 10:4; cf. 2 Kings 4:29.   [4] Gen. 18:2.   [5] Gen. 23:7, 12.   [6] Gen. 42:6; 43:28.   [7] Matt. 17:14; Mark 10:17; but cf. Matt. 28:9.   [8] 1 Sam. 25:6; 1 Chron. 12:18; Mark 5:34; cf. John 14:27.

the words, "The Lord be with you." And they answered him,
"The Lord bless thee."[1]

23. GAMES AND OTHER DIVERSIONS.—It is unlikely that the
Hebrews indulged to any great extent in diversion for its own sake.
Such relaxation as came through social intercourse and witty repar-
tee it is evident they did not scorn.[2] The riddle seems to have been
a specially favorite intellectual pastime.[3] One of the motives that
led the queen of Sheba to take her long journey to Jerusalem was
that she might propound riddles to the wise Solomon.[4] It is not
altogether clear what the "sport" which Samson made for the Philistines consisted in.[5] It may have been nothing more than the dilem-
mas into which the giant was brought by his blindness, when he
attempted to do what was required of him. The "play" between
the soldiers of Joab and Abner, judging from its serious consequences, could have been called play only in irony. Possibly what
began as simple fencing ended in a bloody hand-to-hand conflict.[6]
The prophet Isaiah refers metaphorically to the throwing of the
ball.[7] It is known that ball-playing was practiced in Egypt at an
early day. The balls were made of leather and sometimes of dried
mud. The Egyptians were also acquainted with the simple games
of odd and even, draughts and the casting of hoops. Jerusalem is
spoken of in one passage of Scripture as a burdensome stone on
which the nations would try their strength in vain.[8] Shooting at a
mark seems to have been a pastime for royal youth and others in
the time of David.[9]

Public games, on the other hand, as trenching on the sphere of
their own religious festivals, were frowned upon by the Hebrews.
In the time of the Maccabees, the introduction of the gymnasium
and the sports connected with it into Jerusalem was regarded by
the Jews as the height of profanation.[10] The numerous New Testament references to Grecian games are incidental and for the purpose
of illustration. In Acts 19 : 31, for example, mention is made of a
theatre at Ephesus in connection with a disturbance caused by Paul's
preaching. In another passage, the apostle refers, metaphorically
it would appear, to contests with wild beasts in the same city. This
was one of the most common entertainments of those cruel times.
In other epistles there are allusions to the Isthmian and Olympic
games. The conditions of competing in them, for instance, are re-

[1] Ruth 2: 4.   [2] Prov. 26 : 19; Jer. 15 : 17.   [3] Judg. 14 : 12.   [4] 1 Kings 10 : 1; 2 Chron.
9 : 1.   [5] Judg. 16 : 25.   [6] 2 Sam. 2 : 14.   [7] Isa. 22 : 18.   [8] Zech. 12 : 3; cf. Ecclus. 6 : 21.
[9] 1 Sam. 20 : 20; Job 16 : 12.   [10] 1 Macc. 1 : 14; 2 Macc. 4 : 12-14.

ferred to in order to enhance the sense of earnestness required in the Christian life; so, too, the rigorous discipline to which contestants were previously subjected; the array of spectators before whom such trials of courage and skill took place; the high character demanded of the arbitrator, or judge; the perishableness of the garlands obtained compared with the unfading rewards of the saints.[1] Two of these contests are especially emphasized in Paul's epistles, that of boxing and the foot-race. In a single passage he refers to both.[2] In boxing the fist was not left bare, but bound around with the cestus, a piece of leather studded with nails. Every effective stroke from it made a bruise. And Paul says that he was not accustomed, in contending with his own fleshly lusts, to "beat the air" with ineffectual

Foot-race. (*Adapted from a View of the Circus Flora at Rome. Montfaucon.*)

blows. For the foot-race there was a special place set apart, called a stadium. The spectators occupied raised seats along its sides. The end from which the start was made was open. At the other end, in plain view of the contestants, was the goal, and the judge sat beside it rewards in hand. Every part of this scene is made use of in urging upon the Christian discipleship the seriousness of their calling.[3]

24. SERVANTS.—At the time the Mosaic laws were given both voluntary and involuntary servitude existed as institutions throughout the East. These laws could not ignore such a state of things. In harmony with their treatment of other existing social and political evils, their first effort was to alleviate and modify the worst features of this one. The point of view, in fact, from which slavery was regarded in Israel was entirely changed by making the institution a symbol of the nation's relationship to God himself. This is

---

[1] 1 Cor. 4:9; 9:25; Phil. 3:14; 4:1; 1 Thess. 2:19; 2 Tim. 2:5; 4:8; Heb. 10:33; Rev. 7:9.
[2] 1 Cor. 9:26.   [3] Acts 13:25; 20:24; Heb. 12:1, 2.

the motive most commonly urged for leniency and mildness toward those in servitude: "And thou shalt remember that thou wast a servant in the land of Egypt, and the Lord thy God brought thee out thence."[1] Slavery as it existed in Israel under Mosaic regulations would not have satisfied in all respects the ethical standard of Christianity, which required that the fugitive slave Onesimus be received back "no longer as a servant," but more than a servant, a "brother beloved."[2] But as it respected Hebrew servants the Mosaic laws moved even on that high plane; while with regard to others, they did not fall so very far below it. Not only was a humane treatment of servants the rule in Israel, it so far degenerated into over-indulgence and laxity, in the later time, that it called forth a rebuke on the part of at least one earnest Jewish writer.[3]

25. It is to be remembered, then, that while Israel received the institution of slavery from the patriarchal period, it began at once to limit its extent and to correct its abuses. The laws of the Pentateuch recognize two classes of servants—Hebrews and foreigners. A Hebrew might become a bondservant also in two ways. He might voluntarily assume it on account of poverty, or be forced into it for the same reason.[4] The spirit of the Mosaic laws, however, is clearly against any kind of involuntary servitude for Hebrews. This is shown by such statutes as those of Deuteronomy regarding the giving of pledges and the like.[5] In no case was it permitted to sell a Hebrew man or woman to a foreigner outside of Palestine. In Palestine the condition of servitude for such was relieved of many of the hardships attaching to it elsewhere. It was, for example, enjoined that the bondman should not be looked upon as a slave but as a "hired servant," a brother of the same race and an inheritor of the same promises. On the expiration of his term of service, he was not to be sent away empty. His master was required to load him down with gifts from the flock, the wine-press and the threshing-floor.[6]

26. A special limit of the rigors of servitude among the Hebrews was the period fixed for its duration. In case it was for debt, it would naturally cease when satisfaction had been rendered, or the year of jubilee intervened. This epoch, that is, the fiftieth year, terminated absolutely all servitude throughout the entire land. And in no instance could servitude continue for a longer time than six years, except on the election of the bondman himself. If he chose to remain indefinitely with his master, he was allowed to do so upon

<hr/>

[1] Lev. 25:42-55; Deut. 5:15; 15:15. [2] Phil. 16. [3] Ecclus. 33:24, 25, 28; cf. Prov. 19:10. [4] Lev. 25:39, 47; Matt. 18:25. [5] Deut. 24:6, 7, 17, 18. [6] Lev. 25:39, 40, 43; Deut. 15:13-15.

complying with certain formalities which served to prevent oppression and fraud.[1] If an Israelite were servant to a foreigner living in Palestine, his only hope of freedom was in being redeemed, or in the recurrence of the year of jubilee.[2] The law applied to men and women alike in service, except in the case of a daughter who had been parted with by her father on the understanding that she was to become the wife of her master. If this purpose were not carried out, she might be redeemed by the repayment of her dowry. If it were carried out, special care was taken that the rights of a wife were secured to her.[3]

27. Foreigners held in slavery among the Hebrews were in most cases captives taken in war; but some, it is likely, were procured by purchase or by arrangement with foreign immigrants who found a home in Palestine. This form of servitude, to say the least, was not encouraged by either the spirit or the letter of the Hebrew laws. At the time of the exile foreign servants made up but one-seventh of the entire population.[4] In this form of servitude, too, the contrast between Israel and neighboring peoples was most marked. By the rite of circumcision the foreign servant received a kind of adoption into the Israelitish community.[5] Like all others, he was considered entitled to the seventh day of rest.[6] He might even attain to the highest social positions. If the servant of a priest, he was allowed to eat of the holy things.[7] His life was to be held as sacred by his master as that of the freeman. Slighter injuries to his person were not indeed provided for in the laws of the Pentateuch, the self-interest of the master being concerned to guard against them. Beyond a certain limit, however, it was required that compensation should be made for personal injuries to the extent of manumission.[8]

28. We nowhere read in the Bible of slave-markets for the free selling of slaves. It contains no evidence that bondmen among the Hebrews were, as a rule, otherwise than well treated. We learn of no uprisings on their part. Cases of flight seem to have been rare.[9] The spirit of the Mosaic books on this whole matter is well illustrated in the instructions of Deuteronomy concerning fugitive slaves who took refuge in Israel: "Thou shalt not deliver unto his master a servant which is escaped from his master unto thee: he shall dwell with thee, in the midst of thee, in the place which he shall choose within one of thy gates, where it liketh him best; thou shalt not oppress him."[10] The underlying motive which was to govern in this

[1] Ex. 21 : 2, 4–6; Deut. 15 : 12; Josephus, *Antiq.*, 4, 8 : 28; 16, 1 : 1. [2] Lev. 25 : 47–55. [3] Ex. 21 : 7–11. [4] Ezra 2 : 65. [5] Ex. 12 : 44; Deut. 12 : 12, 18; 16 : 11, 14. [6] Deut. 5 : 14. [7] Lev. 22 : 11; 1 Chron. 2 : 35. [8] Ex. 21 : 20, 21, 26, 27; Lev. 19 : 20; 24 : 17–22. [9] 1 Sam. 25 : 10. [10] Deut. 23 : 15.

as in all the other relationships of life was that which our Lord sums up as the essence of the law: supreme love to God and a love to one's neighbor equalling that to one's self.[1] Job accordingly asks, "If I did despise the cause of my manservant or of my maidservant, when they contended with me: what then shall I do when God riseth up? and when he visiteth, what shall I answer him?"[2]

According to Philo, the Essenes held that involuntary servitude was subversive of the natural rights of man.[3] The moral and religious principles introduced by Christianity no doubt directly tended toward the abolishment of the institution even in that mild form of it practiced among the ancient Hebrews. That it proposed no violent overturning of existing institutions, however, is evident from the teachings of Paul.[4] The inner spiritual freedom of the Christian was the essential thing. In comparison with it freedom of the person was quite subordinate. On this broad ground the New Testament treatment of the subject may be sufficiently accounted for.

29. DEATH AND BURIAL.—The customs of the Hebrews in the matter of death and burial did not differ essentially from those of other eastern peoples. It was their practice to take formal and affectionate leave of those about to die, and to close tenderly their eyes.[5] The body was then washed and wrapped in a linen cloth, sometimes, for the sake of preserving its form, each member by itself.[6] When circumstances allowed it, sweet-smelling spices were laid among the folds of the enveloping shroud. It has been supposed by some that a part of the large amount of spices used on the occasion of our Lord's burial was intended to be burnt in his honor, such a custom being not unknown in the case of distinguished persons.[7] But it is improbable. A great deal of luxury was displayed at this period even in ordinary burials, and this fact, as well as their great love for the Saviour, would have influenced the disciples not a little in their attentions to his body.[8]

30. The practice of embalming was not general among the Hebrews.[9] Burial or entombment took place soon after death, usually on the same day. This was for the reason that the touch of a dead body and its presence in a house carried with it ceremonial defilement, and that, in consequence of the warm climate, mortification rapidly set in.[10] This usage, however, was not invariably followed.[11] The body was ordinarily borne to its final resting-place either exposed on

---

[1] Luke 10 : 27. [2] Job 31 : 13, 14. [3] Richter's ed., vi. 183. [4] 1 Cor. 7 : 20-24; Gal. 3 : 28; 5 : 1; Eph. 6 : 5; Col. 3 : 22-25. [5] Gen. 46 : 4; 50 : 1. [6] Matt. 27 : 59; John 11 : 44. [7] 2 Chron. 16 : 14. [8] Josephus, Antiq., 15, 3 : 4; 17, 8 : 3. [9] Gen. 50 : 2, 26. [10] Matt. 9 : 23; Acts 5 : 5; 8 : 2. [11] Gen. 23 : 2, 19.

a bier, or in an open casket which rested on a bier, or, rarely, on a funeral car. The order of a funeral procession in Judæa was first the women; then the hired mourners; third, the bier with bearers who were frequently changed; then the chief mourners and special friends; and finally, the general company. Women at the present day, in the Orient, are not expected to appear in a funeral procession; but this was not true at the time of our Lord.[1] Nor was it considered an impropriety for women at that time to visit the graves of dear friends to weep there. It seems to have been expected that the sisters of Lazarus would do so.[2] It is an interesting fact that rabbinical law provided for the opening of the tomb on the third day to ascertain the condition of the dead form.

31. The Israelites, contrary to the later practice of the Greeks and Romans, but in harmony with that of most other nations, notably the Egyptians, interred, and did not burn, their dead. All recorded instances to the contrary took place under exceptional circumstances, as in the case of punishment for odious crimes, or in times of pestilence and war.[3] The men of Jabesh-gilead burned the bones of Saul and his sons; but it was only to preserve them from insult. After being reduced to ashes they were carefully buried.[4] The passages Jer. 34 : 5; 2 Chron. 16 : 14; 21 : 19, simply refer to funeral pyres in honor of kings, and not to the burning of the body itself. The interment of the body was deemed essential. To leave it exposed, as did, for example, the Persians, to become the prey of birds and beasts, was regarded as the highest of indignities.[5] The law made it binding on the Israelites to bury criminals on the day of their execution. One of the most touching scenes recorded in the historical books of the Old Testament is the account of Rizpah, a concubine of Saul, who through an entire summer watched the remains of his seven sons to prevent this disgrace from coming upon them.[6]

32. It is also interesting to note that the Hebrews were accustomed to inter families together.[7] It is the more remarkable, therefore, that Joseph of Arimathæa offered what seems to have been the sepulchre of his family as a burying-place for Jesus.[8] Care should be taken, however, not to confound this custom of burying with the idea which the Israelite cherished of being at death gathered to his fathers.[9] The distinction between the grave and the under-world is made early in the book of Genesis. Abraham, for instance, was buried

---

[1] Luke 7 : 12.   [2] John 11 : 31.   [3] Lev. 20 : 14; 21 : 9; Amos 6 : 10.   [4] 1 Sam. 31 : 8-13. [5] 1 Kings 13 : 22; 14 : 11; Jer. 16 : 4; Ezek. 29 : 5; Tobit 2 : 3.   [6] 2 Sam. 21 : 10.   [7] Gen. 47 : 29, 30; Judg. 8 : 32; 16 : 31; Ruth 1 : 17.   [8] Matt. 27 : 57-59.   [9] Matt. 27 : 60; cf. 2 Chron. 24 : 16.

in the cave of Machpelah beside his wife, Sarah; while it is said of
him that he was gathered to his people.[1]

33. Eastern peoples are exceedingly demonstrative in their expressions of grief over departed friends. In all periods down to the

present day it has been customary to hire
professional mourners, generally women,[2] to
join their lamentations with those of the
family circle. The mourning begins at the
moment of death, and is kept up with little
intermission until after the funeral.[3] Grief
is expressed not alone by weeping and loud-
cries, but by beating the breast, plucking out
the hair, and scattering dust upon the head.
Male members of the household rend their
garments, put on sackcloth, pluck out the
beard, throw themselves upon the earth,
and go about shoeless and with veiled faces.

Sitting in Sackcloth.

David on the occasion of Abner's assassination refused to eat bread
until the day was over.[4]

In some cases the tears of mourners were caught in bottles and
buried with the departed as a token of affection.[5] This practice is
still kept up in Persia; the tears, however, instead of being buried
with the dead are carefully preserved as a charm. Tear-bottles are
one of the most common objects found in ancient tombs. The Israelites were forbidden in the book of Deuteronomy to cut themselves
or "make any baldness" between the eyes for the dead.[6] The law
seems to be but a repetition of one found for both priests and people
in an earlier book.[7] It is evident, however, that the heathen custom
against which it was directed did not wholly disappear, since we find
it still in vogue in Jeremiah's time.[8] Rending the garment, as a
token of grief, became at a later period largely a matter of form,
the master of ceremonies ripping down the outer robe a few inches
on the breast where there was a seam.

34. The usual period of mourning lasted seven days; but on extraordinary occasions it was extended.[9] During the period of the
second Jewish commonwealth, feasts were often given at funerals
which were occasions of great extravagance and display.[10] There is
no valid evidence that it was customary in the times covered by the

[1] Gen. 25:8.   [2] But cf. 2 Chron. 35:25; Jer. 9:19, 20.   [3] Micah 1:8; Mark 5:38, 39.
[4] Gen. 37:34; 2 Sam. 13:31; 15:30; 19:4; Job 2:12; Ps. 30:11; Amos 8:10; John 3:6.
[5] Ps. 56:8.   [6] Deut. 14:1.   [7] Lev. 19:27, 28; 21:5.   [8] Jer. 7:29; 16:6; 41:5.   [9] Gen. 50:
10; Num. 20:29; Deut. 34:8; 1 Sam. 31:13.   [10] Josephus, Wars of Jews, 2, 1:1.

canonical books of the Old Testament. Certain passages quoted in proof of it have another meaning. They simply show that food was frequently sent by friends to the house of mourning that the claims of hospitality, which were greatly enlarged on such occasions, might be properly met.[1] This seems to be the meaning of that passage in Deuteronomy also where worshippers at the altar say that, so faithfully have they discharged their obligations respecting the tithes, that no part of them has been expended even in such seasons of special need as the funerals of neighbors and friends: "I have not eaten thereof in my mourning, . . . nor given thereof for the dead."[2] The custom of making an offering for the dead appears first in an apocryphal book in the century preceding the Christian era.[3] Naturally much emphasis is laid on this passage by Roman Catholic writers in justification of their practice of praying for "souls in purgatory."

35. With rare exceptions in favor of distinguished persons, interment took place outside of the town.[4] It is unlikely that even in the case of the poorest classes the body was simply covered up in the ground, as the custom now is with us. The origin of the expression "potter's field," found in Matt. 27 : 7, may well have arisen from the fact that places from which clay had been taken for pottery were afterwards made use of as graves. There can be little doubt, although it is a matter somewhat disputed, that, as a rule, the dead among the Hebrews were laid away in vaults, that is, natural or artificial excavations in the earth or rock. These structures varied in form and arrangement according to the taste, means or needs of their owners. The rabbinical rule for a sepulchre was that it should be excavated six cubits square, or six cubits by eight. The vaults or receptacles for bodies were placed horizontally along three sides. On the remaining side was the approach to the tomb through a court, covered only on the top, and sufficiently large to accommodate the bier and its bearers.

The door might be rectangular and of solid stone, with a flange fitting into a socket for a hinge, both of the same material. Or it might be a cylindrical stone rolling in a groove to the right or the left of the opening. Or there might be a regular door of stone supported by hinges, against which a stone was rolled for further protection. It is not possible to say with certainty which of these methods was followed in the tomb of Joseph of Arimathæa.[5] The fact that

<hr/>

[1] 2 Sam. 3: 35; Jer. 16: 7; Ezek. 24: 17; Hos. 9: 4. [2] Deut. 26: 14. [3] 2 Macc. 12: 43.
[4] 1 Sam. 25: 1; Luke 7: 12; John 11: 30, 31. [5] Mark 16: 1-4; John 20: 1.

it was sealed by order of Pilate would suggest that something more at least than a simple boulder was used in closing its entrance.[1] The sealing of tombs appears to have been common throughout the East. Quite recently they have been found in Egypt, dating back to the time of the exodus, with their seals still intact upon them. Caskets

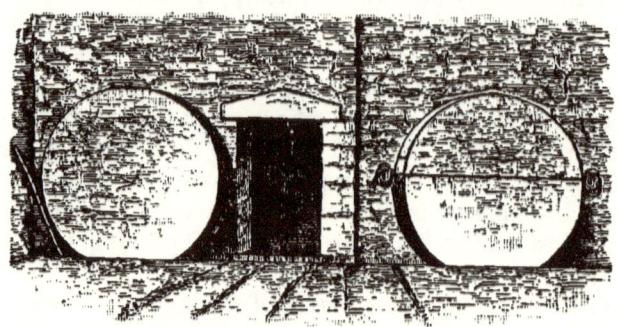

Tomb Open.   Tomb Closed and Sealed.

or sarcophagi for the dead were uncommon except in the case of distinguished or wealthy persons. They are now sometimes found in use in the Orient as drinking-troughs.

36. All graves throughout the East at the present day are marked by some sign: the humblest, by a simple uninscribed stone or a covering of tiles; those of the rich, by a pillar of hewn stone bearing an inscription. Such was doubtless the practice in the remotest periods.[2] Simon, one of the Maccabæan heroes, built a very elaborate mausoleum over the "sepulchre of his father and his brethren, and raised it aloft to the view, with hewn stone behind and before."[3] In the time of our Lord, too, it was customary to erect monuments of solid masonry for the great and those reputed to be saints. These their admirers and friends covered over with mortar, which was made more conspicuous by frequent whitening.[4] Subsequent to the exile it was looked upon as a religious duty to whiten, at the close of the rainy season, the tombs found in the neighborhood of Jerusalem, that is, before the cycle of annual festivals again began. This was to prevent persons from coming upon them unawares and contracting ceremonial defilement.[5] Natural caves and forsaken mining shafts were frequently used as places of interment, in the same way, it would seem, as the so-called "potter's field" near Jerusalem.

[1] Matt. 27:66.   [2] Gen. 35:20; 2 Sam. 18:18; 2 Kings 23:17; Ezek. 39:15.   [3] 1 Macc. 13:27-30.   [4] Matt. 23:27.   [5] Cf. Luke 11:44.

Rocky places were most sought after for such purposes; though tombs were also built in gardens and in the vicinity of groves.[1]   On the other hand, a pile of stones heaped upon a grave was sometimes a mark of special indignity.[2]

37. In the later periods, after the Jews became widely scattered among the nations, one of their strongest and most unconquerable desires was to be buried in the soil of Palestine. A beautiful rabbinical story will illustrate not only the charming family life that in all periods was common among the Israelites, but the delightful spirit with which the most trying dispensations of Providence were often received. "On a certain Sabbath Rabbi Mier was engaged in the sacred college. In his absence his two sons had died. To spare her husband some hours of grief, and not to convert the joy of the

Traditional Tomb of Absalom, near Jerusalem. (*From an original Photograph.*)

Sabbath into mourning, the mother repressed her feelings, and concealed the sad tidings. The Sabbath was past and its holy exercises ended, when she asked her husband whether it were not duty readily and cheerfully to restore to the rightful owner any property, however pleasant, which had been intrusted for safe keeping. When the astonished rabbi answered the strange inquiry in the affirmative, his weeping wife led him to the bed on which the lifeless remains of their two children were stretched, reminding him that he whose they rightfully were had only asked back what, for a time, he had intrusted to their keeping."[3]

---

[1] 2 Kings 21 : 18, 26; Isa. 22 : 16; 14 : 19; John 19 : 41.   [2] Joshua 7 : 26; 8 : 29.   [3] Edersheim, *Bible Educator*, iv., 270.

CHAPTER III.

1. THE food of the ancient Hebrews was, in general, of the simplest description, and its preparation was no less simple. Articles most commonly found on the table were bread made from wheat or barley, fish, honey, milk, and a profusion of vegetables. The use of animal food, excluding fish, was rare with the common people. In the interesting description of the land of Canaan occurring in the book of Deuteronomy, it is said to be a " land of wheat and barley, and vines and fig trees and pomegranates; a land of oil olives and honey; a land wherein thou shalt eat bread without scarceness, thou shalt not lack anything in it."[1] Grain has always grown with great luxuriance in Palestine, as it still does throughout the whole of western Asia. A single stalk of wheat not infrequently produces more than a score of stems at once, each one terminating with a full ear. Grain began to be exported by the Israelites as early as the reign of Solomon.[2]

2. PREPARATIONS OF GRAIN.—Grain, in its native state, was sometimes used as food. A marked example will be recalled in the life of, our Lord, where the disciples were censured on one occasion by the Pharisees for plucking ears for this purpose on the Sabbath.[3] More frequently the kernels were parched before they were eaten. We find "parched corn," that is, grain, referred to, along with fresh ears, as an article of food in the Mosaic period.[4] It is one of the things, too, which Boaz, in the beautiful story of Ruth the Moabitess, is represented as providing for his workmen; and which the prudent Abigail sent to David and his men while tarrying in the wilderness of Paran.[5] Then as now, it is likely, the parching was done over the fire by means of an iron pan, or in some similar way. The grain thus prepared, while still fresh and tender, was by no means an unpalatable dish. Another of the more simple preparations of grain for food was to soak or boil it slightly in water and then, after drying and crushing it, serve it up to be eaten much as is the dish called "groats" among ourselves.[6]

---

[1] Deut. 8 : 8, 9. [2] Ezek. 27 : 17. [3] Matt. 12 : 1, 2; cf. 2 Kings 4 : 42. [4] Lev. 23 : 14. [5] Ruth 2 : 14; 1 Sam. 17 : 17; 25 : 18; 2 Sam. 17 : 28. [6] Num. 15 : 20 (margin); Neh. 10 : 37; Ezek. 44 : 30.

3. Ordinarily before being converted into food the kernel was more thoroughly ground. The contrivances for reducing it to meal were of the most rudimental kind. Originally a pestle and mortar were used, and long after other methods were resorted to this was retained along with them. In fact the pestle and mortar are still regarded as an almost indispensable part of the household appointments in the Orient. The first biblical notice we have of the mortar is in Numbers 11 : 8, where the manna is said to have been pulverized by means of it. The commonness of its use in the time of the kings may be inferred from the sarcastic remark of the author of Proverbs 27 : 22, that though one "bray a fool in a mortar with a pestle among bruised corn, yet will not his foolishness depart from him."

Along with the mortar, "mills" are also spoken of as in use at an early date.[1] Doubtless the simple handmill is generally meant. It is extant in the Orient of to-day, scarcely changed, if at all, and is known to the Arabs by its old Hebrew name. It consists of a couple of cylindrical stones, from one to two feet in diameter, and about six inches thick. Each stone has a separate name. The lower one is firmly planted on the ground and provided with a convex upper surface on which the concave under surface of the other stone revolves. The upper stone or "rider" has a hole through its centre into which the grain is

Eastern Handmill.

dropped and through which also runs a shaft, or standard. By this standard the stone is held in its place. A handle attached to the rider near its outer rim enables a person sitting near to turn it around and grind the grain which is fed in with the hand that is free. If the stones be larger, two persons are required. Such service was usually assigned to women or servants.[2] It was to women thus engaged that our Saviour referred when he said that of two women grinding at the mill one should be taken and one left.[3]

It was forbidden in the Mosaic law, for humane reasons, that the whole mill, or the upper millstone, should be taken in pledge, since it was taking "the life," that is, the means of sustaining life, in

[1] Ex. 11 : 5.   [2] Job 31 : 10; Isa. 47 : 2; Lam. 5 : 13.   [3] Matt. 24 : 41.

5

pledge.[1] As it was customary to bake nearly every day, every large family would be supplied with a mill of this sort; and nothing could have been more noticeable in an Oriental town than the noise caused by their constant use. Several allusions are made to this circumstance in the Bible.[2] At a later period mills of a larger capacity, and worked by animals, came into use. It is to one of this sort that reference is made in Matthew 18 : 6, where the Revised Version renders by a "great millstone" and still more literally in the margin, "a millstone turned by an ass." The very hardest material being selected for the lower stone, the "nether millstone" became a synonym for what was extremely hard. In Job, for example, it is said of the crocodile, "His heart is as firm as a stone; yea, firm as the nether millstone."

4. Bread was made principally from wheat flour. That which was made from barley was mostly used by the very poor, or in times of special need.[3] The Bible in a number of passages clearly discriminates between the two kinds.[4] Other materials than these were sometimes used in making bread; but it was generally from necessity rather than choice. The prophet Ezekiel, for example, was instructed, in token of extreme distress, "Take thou also unto thee wheat, and barley, and beans, and lentils, and millet, and spelt, and put them in one vessel, and make thee bread thereof."[5] Millet is a species of grain of which broom corn is a variety. Its kernels are now often parched and eaten unground in the East. Spelt is also known as "German wheat," and is much used for food in Germany and Switzerland. There are two kinds of wheat flour recognized in the Old Testament, a coarser and a finer variety. They are distinguished by different names, and the latter was chiefly, though not exclusively, used in the meal offerings of the sanctuary. Both words are found together in Genesis 18 : 6, where Sarah is bidden by her husband to prepare food for their unexpected guests. The patriarch says literally, "Be quick! Three seahs of flour, fine flour! Knead and make cakes!" On the other hand, it was the coarser sort that wasted not in the barrel of the widow of Zarephath.[6]

Bread is also known in the Bible as leavened and unleavened. The latter was prescribed by law to the Hebrews for certain occasions, namely, when offered in connection with sacrifices made by fire, and for general use during the feast of the passover. There are two different words used in the original Hebrew for leaven; one of

---

[1] Deut. 24 : 6.   [2] Eccles. 12 : 4; Jer. 25 : 10; Matt. 6 : 11.   [3] 2 Kings 4 : 42; John 6 : 9, 13.
[4] 2 Kings 7 : 1; Hos. 3 : 2; Rev. 6 : 6.   [5] Ezek. 4 : 9.   [6] 1 Kings 17 : 14.

them being found in five passages only,[1] the other, in all the rest. The most common way of producing fermentation in flour or meal was to use a piece of dough which had itself been thoroughly leavened. When circumstances required it, bread and cakes were made without waiting to leaven or raise them. We find this fact mentioned occasionally as showing the haste of the meal.[2] This was notably the case on the departure of the Israelites from Egypt, and the passover loaf was its memorial.[3] Metaphorical references to leaven are somewhat prominent in the Scriptures; and it is a singular fact that it is thought of in both a good and bad sense. Our Lord, for example, refers to it in one place to represent the mysterious, penetrating influence of Christian doctrine: where he speaks of the leaven which "a woman took, and hid in three measures of meal, till it was all leavened."[4] In another passage he puts his disciples on their guard against "the leaven of the Pharisees and Sadducees."[5] This, too, was subtle and pervasive, but only for evil. It is quite a different view of the subject that is presented in the epistles of Paul. He thinks of leaven as producing decomposition, and hence as a most forcible image of the evil effects of sin.[6]

After kneading and raising the dough, the latter process sometimes requiring the entire night and being hastened by a gentle heat, it was usually divided for baking into round, flat pieces, about the width of the outstretched hand and the thickness of the finger.[7] A comparison made by our Lord suggests the resemblance of these pieces to flat stones ; and no doubt they were sometimes almost as hard as stone.[8] Three of them, when baked, seem to have been required for the meal of one person.[9] They were sometimes indented and oil poured upon them previous to baking.[10] They were then called by a different name. At other times, the dough was rolled out thin like wafers and received an outer coating of oil after it was baked.[11] At still other times, its palatability was heightened by a second kneading and the addition of some ingredient now unknown, but possibly stimulating seeds.[12] The dough was kneaded, it is likely, much as it now is in the East, by pressing it between the hands, or by passing it from one hand to the other. In Egypt, as the monuments show, it was put in baskets and trodden with the feet.

5. BAKING.—The most primitive method of baking was to place the prepared dough upon hot coals, or underneath them, with a

[1] Ex. 12:15, 19; 13:7; Lev. 2:11; Deut. 16:4. [2] Gen. 19:3; Judg. 6:19; 1 Sam. 28:24.
[3] Ex. 12:34, 39. [4] Matt. 13:33. [5] Matt. 16:6. [6] 1 Cor. 5:6-8; Gal. 5:9. [7] Hos. 7:4, 6; Luke 13:21. [8] Matt. 7:9. [9] Luke 11:5. [10] Ex. 29:2; 2 Sam. 6:19. [11] Num. 6:15, 19. [12] 2 Sam. 13:6.

slight covering of ashes. At other times, heated stones were employed, or a simple flat pan. A danger in the latter case, unless special care was exercised, was that the dough would be but partially
baked. In allusion to this circumstance, the prophet Hosea says of
Ephraim that he is "a cake not turned."[1] Ovens were also used at
an early period. They were of two kinds—the portable and the
fixed. The former is the article usually referred to in the Bible

The Arab's Portable Oven.

(It is of clay; the lower opening is for the fire of
charcoal; over it is a floor of clay; on it the dough
is placed, through the upper opening. On the top
are "loaves" of bread, leaning against the rim,
cooling.)

when the oven is mentioned. It was
little more than a large-sized clay
pot, or jar, with an opening at the bottom for the fire and sometimes in the
side for putting in the dough. A fire
of twigs or dry grass was kindled
under or within it, and when well
heated, the articles to be baked were
plastered on its sides. Nearly every
family was provided with an oven of
this kind. It was regarded, indeed,
as a mark of misfortune for several
families to be obliged to use the same
oven.[2]

The fixed oven, too, was often ex-
ceedingly rude in its construction. It might be nothing more than
a hole in the ground, with its sides plastered or built up with stones.
Possibly a flue at the bottom supplied a draft for the flame. A
fire was kindled inside of it and kept burning until it became
thoroughly heated. These methods of baking are still practiced by
the nomads of the East; but in the towns public ovens are found,
and the occupation of the baker is one of the best known. That
this was equally true in ancient times appears from many texts of
Scripture.[3] At the present day the large town bakeries in the East
are provided with brick ovens, secured by iron doors much resembling those in use among ourselves. Among the curiosities revealed
by the recent uncovering of ancient Pompeii are ovens of this sort.
In one of them were found no less than eighty perfectly-formed
loaves of bread. Figurative references to the oven or furnace are
frequent in the Bible.[4]

The Hebrews seem generally to have eaten their bread warm, and
it was not cut but broken. From this fact the expression " to break

---

[1] Hos. 7 : 8.   [2] Lev. 26 : 26.   [3] Gen. 40 : 22; 1 Sam. 8 : 13; Jer. 37 : 21; Hos. 7 : 4.   [4] Ps.
21 : 9; Lam. 5 : 10; Mal. 4 : 1.

bread" came to be synonymous with eating or taking a meal.[1]
Bread was seldom eaten alone. It was either moistened with the
sour wine of the country, as appears to have been the case in Ruth
2:14; with the gravy which was ordinarily served up with the
heavier dishes; or was eaten as an accompaniment to other food.
On two memorable occasions this general custom is illustrated in the
life of our Lord.[2]

6. MILK.—Milk and its products have always been much more
generally used as food by the peoples of the East than by ourselves.
Not only is the milk of cows made use of, but that of sheep, camels,
goats and other animals. When the New Testament speaks of milk
as suitable for babes, it is not with the purpose of disparaging its
nutritive and substantial qualities or implying that it is suitable
only for babes.[3] The Scriptures repeatedly make it, with honey, a
symbol of the highest prosperity. The son of Sirach says, "The
principal of all needful things for man's life *are* water, and fire, and
iron, and salt, and flower of wheat, and honey, and milk, blood
of the grape, and oil, and clothing."[4]

Milk was no doubt sometimes drunk fresh, but seems to have been
preferred when sour or curdled. Abraham offered his guests on one
occasion both butter and milk. By "butter" here, and elsewhere
when found in the Old Testament, it is doubtful if anything more
is meant than coagulated milk, the article now known throughout
the East as *leben*. At least it is often difficult to discriminate
between the terms employed for butter and those applied to different
varieties of cheese. One might suppose, for example, from a passage in the book of Proverbs,[5] that the churning of milk to make
butter was well known to the ancient Israelites; but the word rendered "to churn" has rather the signification "to press," and might
better refer, as it would seem, to some process of cheese-making.
Still, as there can be no doubt that the modern inhabitants of Palestine know how to make the butter known to us, and regard it as a
great luxury, the matter must not be treated too dogmatically. In
churning, the milk is put into a receptacle made of skin, which is
moved continually back and forth.

We find cheese mentioned three times in the Bible, and in two of
the instances by special terms.[6] In the other it is designated by the
same word that is given to milk, but it is called "cuttings" or

---

[1] Luke 24:35; Acts 2:42.   [2] John 13:26; 21:13.   [3] 1 Cor. 3:2; 1 Pet. 2:2; Heb.
5:12.   [4] Ecclus. 39:26; cf. Ex. 3:8; Deut. 6:3; 11:9; Joel 3:18.   [5] Prov. 30:33.   [6] 2 Sam.
17:29; Job 10:10.

"slices of milk," that is, milk in a solidified form.[1] Probably what is intended is some variety of dried curd. When pulverized, such an article is now extensively used in the East as a condiment.

7. HONEY.—The important place held in our modern culinary arrangements by sugar was supplied in ancient Palestine by honey. Not only was there recourse to it for seasoning other food, but it was itself eaten as food. It was of three kinds. There was, first, the product of the bee, and often, it would seem, of the wild bee.[2] Then there was a manufactured article known in the modern Orient under the name of *dibs*. It consists of grape juice boiled down to the consistency of a syrup. This, it is likely, was the usual honey of commerce.[3] And finally, there was a vegetable honey, so called, by which is meant a substance that exudes from certain trees, particularly abounding in the neighborhood of Mount Sinai. It has been thought by some that the honey of which Jonathan, the son of Saul, ate, and which formed a part of the simple fare of John the Baptist, was the third kind.[4] It is more likely, however, to have been that of wild bees, always extremely abundant in Palestine. A mixture of butter and honey is spoken of in the book of Isaiah.[5] Such a dish is still considered a luxury in the East. Mixing honey with the cakes of the meal offering is prohibited in the Levitical legislation.[6] Like leaven it would have the effect to produce fermentation. The ancients knew as well as ourselves the danger of eating too freely of honey.[7]

8. LOCUSTS.—Four, of the seven or more, species of locusts were allowed by the Mosaic laws to be eaten. Although there is but one instance of their use as food noted in the Bible,[8] there is no doubt that the Israelites, like

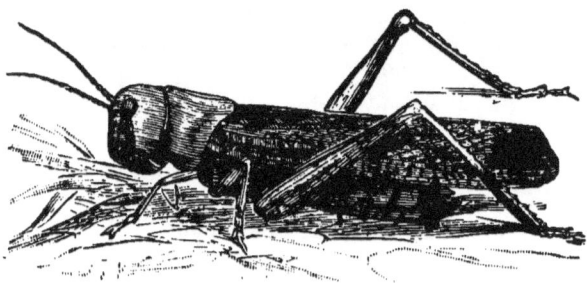

The Locust of Palestine.

other eastern peoples, considered them, when properly prepared, even a delicacy. They are to this day, to a limited extent, offered for sale in the markets of western Asia; but they are mostly bought by

---

[1] 1 Sam. 17:18.   [2] 1 Sam. 14:25; Matt. 3:4.   [3] Cf. Gen. 43:11; Ezek. 27:17.   [4] 1 Sam. 11:25, 27; Matt. 3:4.   [5] Isa. 7:15, 22.   [6] Lev. 2:11.   [7] Prov. 25:16, 27.   [8] Matt. 3:4.

the poorer classes only. Sometimes they are roasted or thoroughly dried in the sun, and eaten mixed with salt, the head, feet, wings and entrails having been previously removed. At other times they are boiled and eaten with butter and salt, or having been dried they are reduced to a powder and cakes made from them. On the restored walls of the palace of Sennacherib is a representation of the various kinds of fruits, flowers, wild game and the like, which were served up to that monarch. Among others there are seen servants bearing long sticks covered thick with dried locusts.

9. FISH.—The Sea of Galilee furnished in the olden time great quantities of fresh fish to the inhabitants of northern Palestine. There must have been no inconsiderable trade in them.[1] Jerusalem and the surrounding country, on the other hand, were probably supplied with dried and salted fish by Phœnician traders.[2]

The Eastern Cast Net.

It may be inferred that there was a regular fish market in Jerusalem, since there was a gate known as the "fish gate" on its northeast side. The Israelites had learned in Egypt highly to prize fish as food, and their laws allowed the free use of any that had fins and scales.[3] The frequent mention of fish in the Gospels as an article of diet[4] is noticeable. When fresh, a favorite way of cooking seems to have been to roast them either over embers directly or by laying them upon hot stones.[5] Besides the casting and drag nets and other similar appliances,[6] the hook and line were also used for fishing, and to some extent, it would seem, the trident and spear.[7] A peculiar method of keeping fish alive and within reach in the water after being caught

[1] Matt. 17:27; Luke 5:6.   [2] Neh. 13:16.   [3] Lev. 11:9-12; Num. 11:5.   [4] Matt. 14:17; 15:34; Luke 24:42.   [5] John 21:9.   [6] Hab. 1:15; Matt. 13:47.   [7] Job 41:1, 7; Isa. 19:8.

was by means of a ring through their gills and a cord of reeds.[1] Peter and his fellow apostles appear to have expected the best success in the night in fishing with a net.[2]

10. Game.—Mosaic regulations show that wild game was a common article of diet.[3] Hunting was, in fact, a necessity for the Israelites on entering Canaan, since otherwise it would have seriously interfered with the peaceful occupation of the land.[4] References to Nimrod "the mighty hunter before the Lord," to Ishmael as an "archer" and to Esau as a "cunning hunter," as well as numerous illustrations drawn from the chase, are significant as touching the familiarity of the Hebrews, down to a comparatively late period, with all that concerned the taking of game.[5] The sparsely-settled portions of Palestine must formerly have abounded, as to no inconsiderable extent they do still, with wolves, panthers, bears, lions, hyenas, jackals, foxes, hares, wild hogs and several varieties of the antelope. The Bible says little directly of the methods employed by the hunter, but incidental references make it clear that they were much like those set forth on the monuments of Assyria and Egypt. For the larger species of wild beasts pitfalls were constructed.[6] For other game the bow and arrow were used, as well as the snare and the net.[7] There is incidental mention in one passage of decoy birds, but there is no evidence in the Bible that trained falcons were kept, or even that dogs were taught to hunt with their masters.[8]

11. Vegetables.—Vegetables in great variety are mentioned in the Bible as articles of food. They are represented not only as products of cultivation, but as growing wild in the fields.[9] We find references, for example, to beans, lentils, cucumbers, melons, leeks, onions and garlic.[10] The bitter herbs enjoined to be eaten with the passover have not been identified with certainty.[11] According to the Mishna, endive, chiccory, wild lettuce or the nettle might be so used. Besides the species of vegetables already mentioned, there now grow luxuriantly in western Asia, and some of them it is likely in the early times, the beet, turnip, radish, carrot, cabbage, egg-plant, tomato and squash. The poorer classes were often dependent on what they found growing wild, and are spoken of in the book of Job as plucking "salt-wort" and making use of the "roots of the broom."[12] Serious consequences, it will be remembered, would have

[1] Job 41:2. [2] Luke 5:5. [3] Deut. 12:15; cf. Lev. 17:13. [4] Ex. 23:29. [5] Gen. 10:9; 21:20; 25:27; 1 Sam. 26:20; 2 Sam. 23:20; Job 10:16; 38:39; Ps. 25:15; 35:7; 142:3; Prov. 12:27; Isa. 51:20. [6] Ps. 9:15; Ezek. 19:4-9. [7] Ps. 124:7; Prov. 7:23. [8] Jer. 5:27; cf. Ecclus. 11:30; Bar. 3:17. [9] 1 Kings 21:2; 2 Kings 4:38-41. [10] Gen. 25:34; 2 Sam. 17:28; Isa. 1:8. [11] Ex. 12:8; Num. 9:11; cf. Lam. 3:15. [12] Job 30:4.

come to the sons of the prophets on a certain occasion, when one of their number "shred" wild gourds into the "pot of pottage," but for the interposition of Elisha.[1] Even now, as in our Lord's time, the dry pods of the carob tree ("husks") are food for the poor in Palestine. Among condiments mint, anise, dill and cummin are mentioned in the Bible, as well as salt, coriander seed, rue and mustard.[2] The mustard plant still grows in the neglected portions of the Jordan valley, and often reaches the height of six or more feet. To speak of anything as being as small as a grain of mustard seed seems to have been proverbial in New Testament times.[3]

12. THE VINE AND ITS PRODUCTS.—Mention is made as early as the book of Genesis of the cultivation of the vine in Palestine.[4] Its luxuriant growth in the olden time is well illustrated in the story of the spies and the one cluster of grapes which they brought from Eshcol to Joshua, carrying it "upon a staff between two."[5] The vines of Sibmah, Elealeh, Heshbon and Engedi are also especially noted in the Scriptures.[6] Formerly, as now, there was a great difference between the cultivated and wild varieties of grapes. The prophet compares Israel to a vine which brought forth wild grapes notwithstanding the pains which had been taken with it.[7] On the other hand, our Lord finds the vine and its branches the most fitting symbol of his own mystical union with his people.[8] Grapes were eaten fresh, or in the form of raisins, or dried and pressed into cakes. There is a separate word in Hebrew for the berry, the cluster and the other forms mentioned, including the seed and the wild grape. The original Hebrew word for raisin-cake survives in the modern Italian *simmuchi*. The offering of cakes of raisins was one of the idolatrous rites practiced in the time of Hosea.[9]

13. Besides water and milk, sour and other wines have always been among the most common beverages of eastern peoples, excepting Mohammedans. Boaz provided a vinegar of some kind for his workmen to moisten their bread in at their noonday meal;[10] and from Numbers 6:3 we learn that the Israelites were acquainted with a vinegar made from wine and one made from "strong drink," that is, probably, date wine, or an intoxicating drink manufactured after the manner of the Egyptians from barley. Its expensiveness would have prevented a very common use of wine among the Israelites, except by the rich. When used as a beverage, it was perhaps mixed

---

[1] 2 Kings 4:38-41.   [2] Ex. 16:31; Job 6:6; Isa. 28:25-27; Matt. 13:13; 23:23.   [3] Mark 4:31, 32.   [4] Gen. 9:20, 21.   [5] Num. 13:23.   [6] Cant. 1:14; Isa. 16:8-10; Jer. 48:32.   [7] Isa. 5:2; cf. Ps. 80:8-13.   [8] John 15:1-6.   [9] Hos. 3:1.   [10] Ruth 2:14; cf. Matt. 27:34.

with water, though we have no traces of such a custom until a late period.[1] On the other hand there were some who preferred it when made more fiery and intoxicating by the addition of stimulating spices.[2]

There are a number of terms used in the Old and New Testaments for wine. But the effort made in some quarters to show that the wine spoken of in the Bible as a blessing was unintoxicating, or even a purely vegetable product and no beverage at all, has failed for a number of sufficient reasons: the etymology of the words employed as agreed upon by the most competent lexicographers; the manner in which this supposed unintoxicating product is spoken of elsewhere in the Bible;[3] and the well-nigh universal testimony of travellers, missionaries and other residents in the East. The use of wine as a drink offering establishes the fact of its use as a beverage. It also paid its tithe like other products.[4] At the same time it is not to be overlooked that the Bible contains the most impressive warnings against the too free use of wine and strong drink;[5] forbade them in certain cases;[6] and introduced principles justifying and enforcing in some circumstances the most rigorous abstinence on the part of the Christian disciple.[7]

The Eastern Fig.

14. THE FIG.—Next to the grape, the fig holds the most prominent place among the fruits cultivated by the Israelites. Like the grape, it was eaten both fresh and in a dried state. When dried, it was sometimes pressed into the form of round cakes, and had then a special name given to it. This seems to have been the fig of commerce.[8] The fig tree appears in the very beginnings of history, and its wide distribution is indicated by the fact that, with the vine, it is made the basis of one of the most frequent figures of the sacred writers.[9] The fig was thought to have curative qualities; at least it was made in one important instance the medium of a cure by the prophet Isaiah.[10] There are two sorts of figs recognized in the Bible:

[1] Cf. Isa. 1:22.   [2] Ps. 75:8; Prov. 9:2,5; Cant. 7:2.   [3] Prov. 3:10; Isa. 62:8; Hos. 4:11; Joel 1:5; Micah 6:15.   [4] Ex. 29:40; Lev. 23:13; Num. 15:5; Deut. 18:4.   [5] Prov. 20:1; 23:29–35; Isa. 5:22; 28:1–7; 56:12.   [6] Lev. 10:9; Num. 6:3.   [7] Rom. 14:21.   [8] 1 Sam. 25:18; 30:12; 1 Chron. 12:40.   [9] Gen. 3:7; 1 Kings 4:25; Micah 4:4; Zech. 3:10.   [10] 2 Kings 20:7.

the early and the late. The latter sometimes remained on the tree
the entire winter. The fig tree which was cursed by our Lord for
being fruitless had leaves;[1] hence fruit might have been expected
from it, since the latter is usually produced before the former. In
this case, however, the leaves had *anticipated the fruit* and given
promise of that which had not been fulfilled.

15. THE APPLE AND OTHER FRUITS.—The apple tree and its fruit
are mentioned in a few passages of the Bible, and in terms showing
the relatively high position assigned them among the products of
the Holy Land.[2] Some writers think that the apple known to us is
not meant, but rather the apricot or the quince, apples being now
rare in Syria and of poor quality. Of palm trees the date palm
seems to be the only one known to Bible lands. This was widely
cultivated, and a common symbol of grace and strength with biblical writers.[3] So prolific was this tree that an entire family was sometimes sustained from the various products of a single one. The fruit
ripens in September or October. It is eaten either fresh or, the stone
being removed, is kneaded into a paste and consumed, as required,
with bread and other food. The pomegranate was another of the
natural productions of the land of Canaan. It was little more than
a shrub in size, rarely reaching a height above ten feet; but its fruit
was highly prized.[4] Representations of it were to be found on the
high priest's ephod, and carved figures of the same surmounted the
pillars of Solomon's temple.[5] It attains to the size of an orange,
but has both ends flattened like the apple, and is of a beautiful
reddish-brown color. The Israelites had learned to enjoy its taste
while in Egypt.[6] Its juice, though somewhat acid, is much esteemed
as a cooling drink; and sometimes it is manufactured into wine.

16. OIL.—Oil, it is probable, was formerly used no less commonly
in the East as food than it now is. This might be inferred from the
fact that it is one of the requirements of the meal offering.[7] It seems
not to have been consumed by itself, but only as mixed with other
food, largely taking the place of butter and lard among ourselves.
It was generally, though not exclusively, expressed from the olive
berry, which itself, doubtless, was an article of food. The Talmud
speaks of a number of other varieties of oil, including that of roses,
for medicinal purposes and perfumery, and that of nuts and the
castor bean for general use. In addition to the use of oil as food

[1] Matt. 21 : 18-22; Mark 11 : 12-14, 20-23.   [2] Cant. 2 : 3; 8 : 5; Joel 1 : 12; cf. Cant. 2 : 5; 7 :
8; Prov. 25 : 11.   [3] Ps. 92 : 12.   [4] Deut. 8 : 8.   [5] Ex. 28 : 33, 34; 1 Kings 7 : 18 (margin).
[6] Num. 20 : 5.   [7] Lev. 2 : 4, 7, 15; Num. 7 : 19.

and in the meal offerings, mention is made in the Bible of its employment for lighting, as a cosmetic, for anointing to office, and, mixed with wine, as a remedy for wounds.[1] An important trade in oil with other countries sprang up as early as the ninth century B.C.[2]

17. Nuts.—There are a few species of nuts named in the Bible. For example, among the products of Canaan which the sons of Jacob carried down to Egypt, as a present to its viceroy, were pistachio nuts and almonds.[3] The pistachio tree, which resembles the sumach, now flourishes widely in Syria and Palestine, and is known to have done so long before the Christian era. Almonds are referred to in a number of passages, notably in Ecclesiastes, where, possibly, its white blossom is made the symbol of the hoary locks of age.[4] These blossoms cover the whole tree, the green leaves not appearing until afterwards. In Canticles the walnut seems to be referred to, but it is the variety commonly known as the "English walnut."[5] According to Josephus walnut trees once grew luxuriantly around the Lake of Gennesaret.[6]

18. Eggs.—From some incidental allusions in the Scriptures it may be concluded that eggs too formed a part of the diet of the ancient Hebrews. Job, for instance, asks, "Can that which hath no savor be eaten without salt? Or is there any taste in the white of an egg?"[7] And our Lord, in illustration of the heavenly Father's willingness to hear the prayer of his children, inquires, "And of which of you that is a father shall his son ask a loaf, and he give him a stone? . . . Or if he shall ask an egg, will he give him a scorpion?"[8]

19. Animal Food in General.—It cannot be certainly inferred from Genesis 1 : 29, 30; 9 : 3 that man was at first expressly limited to a vegetable diet. The most that can be positively stated is that divine permission to eat flesh is not known to have been given until after the flood.[9] In the hot climates of the East not only would experience soon show the unwholesomeness of much animal food; but, as there was no method of preserving it for any length of time, it would also be found too expensive a custom to become a very common one. Very early, moreover, restrictions began to be placed upon the free consumption of such food, which greatly curtailed its use.

First, there was laid upon Noah, along with the permission to use as food "every moving thing that liveth," the prohibition of blood

[1] Ex. 25:6; 27:20; Lev. 8:12; 1 Sam. 10:1; 2 Sam. 14:2; Isa. 1:6; Luke 7:46; 10:34. [2] 1 Kings 5:11; 2 Chron. 2:10, 15. [3] Gen. 43:11. [4] Eccles. 12:5. [5] Cant. 6:11. [6] Wars of Jews, 3, 10:8. [7] Job 6:6. [8] Luke 11:11, 12; cf. Isa. 10:14; 59:5. [9] Gen. 4:2, 20; 7:2.

with the flesh.[1] We may suppose either that this injunction was directed against some heathenish practice of the antediluvian world already known to Noah, and likely to be followed afterwards, or that it was intended to foreshadow the still stricter Mosaic regulations on the subject.[2] Possibly both reasons may be considered as having influence, but especially the latter. The Bible is a unit, though showing a clear development, in its teaching, Genesis looking forward to Exodus and Leviticus as much as these look backward to Genesis. The strictness with which the Jews observed this regulation in the later times may be inferred from the fact that it was one of the few laid upon Gentile converts to Christianity by their Jewish brethren.[3] According to the finical rabbis the blood of fish is not covered by it, and is therefore permitted.

In natural connection with the first pre-Mosaic restriction followed another in the Mosaic laws prohibiting the use of the flesh of an animal dying a natural death, or of one found torn in the fields, or of an ox that had been stoned for unruliness. There are different phases of this law in the Pentateuch; those of Exodus and Leviticus reflecting the wilderness period, that of Deuteronomy a permanent residence in Palestine.[4] Thirdly, on account of the remarkable incident recorded in Genesis, chapter thirty-two, the Hebrews, though without special commandment, were accustomed to abstain from eating "the sinew of the hip which is upon the hollow of the thigh, unto this day." No other reference is made to this fact in the Bible, but that the rule was considered binding, and continued in force long after the beginning of the Christian era, is attested by the Talmud.

Again, certain prescribed fatty portions of the animal, such as were offered in sacrifice upon the altar, were forbidden to be eaten, namely, the fat lying about the stomach, the entrails and kidneys, that which is "by the loins, and the caul upon the liver," and the fat tail of the sheep.[5] The people of Nehemiah's time did not transgress this ordinance when they ate "the fat" on one occasion, the original word there showing that simply the more fatty portions of the flesh, and not the fat itself, are meant. Of course, too, as will be hereafter shown, animals or parts of animals designated for sacrifice or other holy uses could only be eaten under specified conditions. Still further, it was not allowed to partake of a kid which had been cooked in its mother's milk.[6] Many fanciful reasons have been con-

---

[1] Gen. 9:4. [2] Lev. 3:17; 7:26; Ps. 16:4; Ezek. 33:25; Zech. 9:7. [3] Acts 15:20, 29; 21:25. [4] Ex. 21:32, 35; 22:31; Lev. 17:15; Deut. 14:21. [5] Lev. 3:3, 9, 17; 7:3, 23. [6] Ex. 23:19; 34:26; Deut. 14:21.

jectured for such a prohibition. While it is possible that it is in some way connected with idolatrous practices, a sufficient ground for it might be the lack of feeling which would be displayed by such a course. The cultivation of kindly sentiments toward the animal creation was thought important enough to make it the subject of several precepts in the Mosaic codes.[1] Meat offered to idols was also practically forbidden in the Pentateuch, as also its use was held to be a misdemeanor by many among the early Christian discipleship.[2] With the latter the rule was so limited in the later times that it was thought to be a breach of the law to eat of such flesh before it had been presented as an offering, though known to be designed for that purpose. In all periods there were some who showed an excess of rigor in their observance of the dietary laws of Moses. Not alone such ascetics as the Essenes, but a considerable party in the Christian Church seems to have made a virtue of abstinence from meat, regarding it as a necessary means to the attainment of the highest spiritual life.[3]

Finally, there was a large class of animals which were looked upon as ceremonially unfit to be eaten. A list of them is given in Leviticus, chapter eleven, and an abstract of the same in Deuteronomy, chapter fourteen. Among quadrupeds there were excepted from this number whatever parted the hoof, that is, had the hoof divided into two parts, and that chewed, or more literally raised, the cud. An animal having one and not the other of these peculiarities was excluded, as the camel, whose hoof is only partially cloven, the hare, the coney and the swine. The hare and coney mentioned in Deuteronomy[4] as chewing the cud do this, it would seem, only in appearance. If they did so in reality, the other circumstance of their not being cloven footed would exclude them from the number of ceremonially-clean animals. It should be made no objection to the language of an inspired writer that he speaks of phenomena as they are observed rather than in scientific language. In no other way could he have been understood by the people of his time. Of fishes, as already remarked, only those having scales and fins were regarded as ceremonially clean.

Among unclean birds about twenty varieties are indicated by name. It would be too much to expect that all of these could now be identified. The list in Deuteronomy corresponds with that in Leviticus with one exception,[5] which seems to rest on a corruption in the

---

[1] Lev. 22 : 28; Deut. 22 : 6, 7; 25 : 4.   [2] Ex. 34 : 15; Num. 25 : 2; 1 Cor. 8 : 10.   [3] Dan. 1 : 8; 2 Macc. 5 : 27; Rom. 14 : 2; 1 Cor. 10 : 25.   [4] Deut. 14 : 7.   [5] The glede.

text. Again, all winged creeping things having four feet were prohibited, unless like the locust they had an additional pair of hind
legs to spring with. Among creeping things without wings classed
as unclean were the weasel, the mouse, four varieties of the lizard and
the chameleon. They were not only not allowed as food, but contact
with them caused uncleanness which required purification.

These series of laws in general, as has been remarked upon the
whole system of ritual laws, were expressly *for the Hebrews*, and
meant to be largely educational in their effects. Our Lord took a
broader view.[1] Still their underlying principle is one for all time
and for all peoples who will be his: " I am the Lord your God who
have separated you from the peoples. . . . And ye shall be holy
unto me: for I the Lord am holy."[2] While the regulations of
Moses seem to have been related partly to traditional customs and
partly to natural taste or instinct, they are not the result of them.
They had an important sanitary bearing, and a specially important
bearing on the development of the idea of the kingdom of God
among men. It is only a somewhat stronger emphasis that is laid
upon the latter aim in the New Testament.[3] It is noticeable that in
general, among both quadrupeds and birds, the law resulted in excluding as food such as themselves fed on flesh. The exceptions to
this rule, like the hare, the ass, the camel, the swine, the serpent and
other creeping things, might be readily explained on other sufficient
grounds. Part of them were serviceable animals and their prohibition
rested on an economic basis. To the others there might well have
been an instinctive aversion. The history of the serpent in Eden
could never be forgotten, nor the place of the swine in the orgies of
many heathen nations.[4]

20. COOKING ANIMAL FOOD.—It is not to be supposed that the
Hebrews as a people ever used meat as an ordinary diet. It was
found chiefly at court and on the tables of the wealthy, or it was
reserved for rare festival occasions and exhibitions of that generous
hospitality for which Orientals have always been famous.[5] In such
instances, too, animals of the bovine species and those which had been
stall fed were oftenest used.[6] The kinds of animal food most frequently
referred to in the Bible are beef, mutton and goat flesh, the young
and old of each, and various species of wild game, especially the
antelope. The animal was ordinarily killed by the master of the

[1] Matt. 15:11. [2] Lev. 20:24, 26. [3] 2 Cor. 6:17; Heb. 7:26. [4] Isa. 66:17. [5] Gen.
18:7; 27:4; Ex. 12:8; 1 Kings 4:22, 23; Neh. 5:18; Luke 15:23. [6] 1 Sam. 16:20; Prov.
15:17; Jer. 46:21; Amos 6:4; Mal. 4:2.

house and prepared for the table by the women or servants.[1] The flesh was either roasted or boiled. That boiling was the usual method in early times may be inferred from the fact that the word meaning "to boil" had even in the earliest books taken on the secondary signification of "to cook." When it meant "to boil," the words "in water" or "in milk"[2] were often added. When roasted the process seems to have corresponded to what is known among us as the barbecue, that is, the animal was roasted whole either over a slow fire of wood or in a kind of oven made by hollowing out and heating the ground for the purpose.

In preparing it for boiling, after it had been properly killed and dressed, the right shoulder was first removed. In the case of a sacrifice, this part, as a kind of first fruits, was reserved for the priest. The other joints were then successively taken out, the flesh stripped off and chopped into convenient pieces for eating, the bones crushed and the whole thrown together into a boiling caldron of water or water mixed with milk.[3] The Hebrew language has a number of expressions for pot or caldron, as well as a word for the earthen cooking range, the flesh-hook and for various sorts of dishes.[4] But it is not always possible simply from the etymology of the word to determine the form or dimensions of the article. Vegetables were commonly boiled and served up as pottage in the way found so inviting by Esau.[5] Professional cooks were only employed in extraordinary instances.[6] A single root-word was used for both cook and butcher. Rebecca seems to have understood not only how to make the flesh of kids palatable, but even to taste like venison. Men, however, did not scorn, on occasions, to attend to the cooking of food, or at least to superintend its preparation.[7]

21. CUSTOMS AT THE TABLE.—Knives, forks and spoons, as is well known, were used only in the preparation of meals, not at the table. Meat was ordinarily served in a single large dish, and was eaten with the fingers. This custom still prevails in the East. It does not, however, prevent the host, if he chooses, from offering choice bits to his guests. Thin slices of bread which could be conveniently rolled up were also made use of in conveying the food to the mouth. The broth was served in a separate dish from the meat, and was used for moistening the bread.[8] Our Lord's words will be recalled where he says of Judas, " He that dippeth his hand with me in the

---

[1] Gen. 27:9; Judg. 6:19. [2] Ex. 12:9; Deut. 17:7; 2 Chron. 35:13. [3] Ezek. 24:4, 5, 10; Micah 3:3. [4] Lev. 6:21; 11:35; Num. 11:8; 2 Kings 2:20; 21:13; Prov. 19:21; Isa. 65:4; Zech. 14:21. [5] Gen. 25:29; 2 Kings 4:38. [6] 1 Sam. 8:13; 9:22-24. [7] Gen. 27:3; Judg. 6:19; Luke 17:8. [8] Judg. 6:19.

dish, the same shall betray me."[1] This mode of eating is neither so inconvenient nor so untidy as at first it might appear.

Great attention was naturally paid to washing the hands before eating. They were not plunged into the water, as the custom is with us, but the water was poured upon them by another person. Elisha, after the translation of his predecessor, was favorably known as one who had "poured water on the hands of Elijah."[2] This practice of washing the hands before a meal, and the precise way of doing it, in the time of our Lord had come to be a matter of positive injunction on the part of the Jewish hierarchy. He refused to sanction it as a binding rule. When the Pharisees therefore complained to him that his disciples did not wash their hands in this ceremonial way before eating, he rebuked them for their hypocrisy and for making void the law of God by their traditions. It was not so much the custom that he objected to as the pretended authority of the rabbis in the matter.[3]

Orientals at a Meal.

Washing the Hands.

22. We note but a single instance in the Old Testament where a prayer is offered in connection with a meal.[4] But it seems to have been customary with the Master and his disciples, and that would be a sufficient warrant, were there no other, for what is known among ourselves as "asking the blessing" or "saying grace."[5] The later Jews laid down special regulations respecting prayer at meals, and on the basis of Deuteronomy 8 : 10 enjoined also that thanks should be

[1] Matt. 26 : 23.   [2] 2 Kings 3 : 11.   [3] Matt. 15 : 1–12; Mark 7 : 1–13.   [4] 1 Sam. 9 : 13.
[5] Matt. 15 : 36; Luke 9 : 16; John 6 : 11; Acts 27 : 35; 1 Tim. 4 : 3.

returned after the repast. How early the custom originated it is not possible to say.

23. The Hebrew language has no special terms designating meals, as the Greek and Latin have, and it is difficult to fix with certainty either their time or their number. Whatever information we have on the subject comes from purely incidental references. Still there can be little doubt that the principal meal was in the evening.[1] The foremost religious festival, the passover, at which meat was freely eaten, took place after sunset, and it is likely that this particular time was selected as best harmonizing with national customs as well as with the historical occasion of the festival. Besides the evening meal, the only other full meal customary would seem to have been taken in the morning. To Israel in the wilderness Moses said, " At even ye shall eat flesh, and in the morning ye shall be filled with bread."[2] And of the ravens that fed Elijah it is narrated that they brought him " bread and flesh in the morning, and bread and flesh in the evening."[3] Such a custom would not preclude an additional meal in exceptional cases, like that of laborers for example, who rose very early in the morning to begin their work.[4]

The writer of Ecclesiastes, in denouncing a woe upon the land where the king was a child and princes ate " in the morning," doubtless had sole reference to luxurious feasting and not at all to the customs of ordinary life.[5] From some passages in the New Testament it might be inferred that the usual time for the morning meal was about nine o'clock, that is, after the first hour of prayer.[6] Josephus states that in his day the morning meal on the Sabbath did not take place until twelve o'clock, when, as it would appear, the services of the synagogue were over.[7] Possibly at this period the Hebrews, like the Greeks and Romans, came to employ to some extent the noon and evening hours for their chief meals. But the example of Joseph in Egypt and other extraordinary cases cannot be fairly cited as establishing such a practice in the earliest times.[8]

24. It has already been remarked that the practice of reclining at table first appears in the Bible in the prophecy of Amos.[9] It afterwards became the common one. Such a custom serves to make clear several otherwise obscure passages in the New Testament. For example, it can be understood how the woman spoken of in Luke was able to wash and anoint the feet of Jesus while he was " sitting

---

[1] Gen. 19:1-3; Ex. 18:12,13; Judg. 19:4-6; Ruth 3:7; 1 Thess. 5:7.   [2] Ex. 16:12.
[3] 1 Kings 17:6.   [4] Ruth 2:14; Prov. 31:15.   [5] Eccles. 10:16.   [6] John 21:4, 12; Acts 2:15.
[7] *Life*, § 54.   [8] Gen. 43:16, 25; 1 Kings 20:16; Luke 14:12.   [9] Amos 6:4; cf. Ezek. 23:41.

at meat in the Pharisee's house," and how our Lord himself performed this service for his disciples when they were similarly situated.[1] They were reclining on their left sides, if they were following
the prevalent custom, with their heads toward the table and their
feet stretched out behind them. It will be remembered, too, that it
is said of the beloved disciple at the last supper that he, "leaning
back, as he was, on Jesus' breast," spoke to him of his betrayer.[2]
We are not to suppose, however, that this was the ordinary way in
which our Lord and his disciples took their food.

When couches were used for the purpose of reclining at meals,
the table would naturally be somewhat higher than when persons
sat down to it. Such
couches, although not
mentioned in the New
Testament except in
some manuscript au-
thorities at Mark 7 : 4,
were undoubtedly com-
mon. They were known
as the *triclinium*, that
is, couches originally
adapted for three per-
sons, although fre-
quently occupied by
more than that num-
ber.

Roman Triclinium. Mode of Eating among the Jews in
the Time of our Lord.

They were provided with cushions on which the left elbow
rested, and were arranged around a table in the form of a square or
a parallelogram. The fourth side was left open for the convenience of
those waiting on the guests. The first place on a couch was regarded
as the place of honor, and the first couch on the right was the one most
highly esteemed. In one of our Lord's parables he calls attention
to what was undoubtedly a very common fault of his time, the eager-
ness shown by guests to occupy the best places at table. The common
English version speaks of "rooms," as though separate apartments
rather than places to recline were referred to.[3] The practice of inviting guests entitled to special honor to take a higher place than they
are likely to select is still prevalent in the East. Their peculiar dietary laws, among other things, made the Hebrews exceedingly scrupulous in the matter of eating with others than those of their own nation.[4]

---

[1] Luke 7 : 36-38; John 13 : 5. [2] John 13 : 25. [3] Luke 14 : 7-11. [4] Gen. 43 : 32; Matt. 9 : 11;
John 4 : 9; 1 Cor. 5 : 11.

25. FESTIVE MEALS.—Before closing the present chapter attention should be called to festive meals, or such as were provided especially for invited guests. They were of old, and are still, an important feature of social life in the Orient. As already observed,
the occasions for such festivals among the ancient Hebrews were
very numerous. They were rated as important according to the
number and dignity of the guests,[1] the richness of the plate and
viands,[2] and the round of days consumed by the festivities.[3] To
decline an invitation to a feast for a trifling reason was considered a
great indignity.[4] The host welcomed his guests with the utmost
cordiality. Water was furnished for their feet; they were anointed
with perfumed oils; and in the houses of the rich, robes and ornamental wreaths were sometimes provided.[5]

The Hebrew language, as well as the Greek of the New Testament,
has a special word for feasts where the drinking of wine and other
liquors was made a prominent feature. In general usage, however,
these terms were applied to ordinary feasts. Parties merely for drinking and revelling are treated with marked disapprobation by both
the prophets and apostles.[6] It was customary in Egypt to remind
the guests at a feast of their mortality by exhibiting a mummy; but, as
the monuments show, this did not prevent the greatest excesses. Such
excesses, moreover, can hardly have been greater than those of the
luxurious Israelites of Samaria in the corrupt days of Jeroboam II.
The prophet Amos speaks of the women of that time as "kine of
Bashan," who while oppressing the poor and crushing the needy
cried to their lords, "Bring, and let us drink."[7] Representations on
the monuments of both Assyria and Egypt show that it was customary in those countries for men and women to feast together. This
was doubtless the rule also in ancient Israel. Women had a place
in the sacred meals, notably the passover, and cannot have been excluded from other social festivities.[8]

For every important feast it was considered necessary to have a
master of ceremonies. He answered to the well-known symposiarch
among the Greeks and Romans. Our Lord alludes to this official
when on the occasion of making the water wine he said to the servants, "Draw out now, and bear unto the ruler of the feast."[9] All
the attendants were, for the time, under his control. By his order

---

[1] 1 Sam. 9:22; 1 Kings 1:25; Mark 12:39; Luke 14:8, 16.   [2] Gen. 18:6; 43:34; 1 Sam.
9:24; Esther 1:7.   [3] Dan. 5:1; Tobit 8:19, 20.   [4] Matt. 22:3-7.   [5] Gen. 18:4; Ps. 23:5;
Prov. 21:17; Eccles. 9:7, 8; Amos 3:6; Wisdom 2:7, 8; Matt. 22:11; John 12:3.   [6] Isa.
28:7; Gal. 5:21; Eph. 5:18.   [7] Amos 4:1.   [8] Ex. 12:3; Num. 25:1, 2; Deut. 16:11, 14;
John 2:3; 12:3.   [9] John 2:8.

the tables were cleared of the different courses. He first tasted of the wine, before it was distributed to the guests. The author of Ecclesiasticus tells the master of ceremonies that he is so to demean himself as to win the approval of the assembled company.[1] The cup-bearer was a person of quite another character. His office seems to have been largely political. It will be recalled that it was this officer who was the means of freeing Joseph from prison.[2] Rab-shakeh was the cup-bearer of the famous Sennacherib, and was sent by him on a mission to Hezekiah king of Judah.[3] Nehemiah also was cup-bearer to the king of Persia.[4]

Assyrian King and Cup-bearer.
(*From the Assyrian tablets.*)

Persons who were not properly guests were often admitted to feasts as spectators. At the present day it is no uncommon thing in the East for visitors to come in when strangers are entertained, seating themselves near for the purpose of observation or to engage in conversation. This custom makes it clear how it was possible for the "woman who was a sinner" to gain admission to the Pharisee's house where Jesus had been invited.[5] Guests at banquets were frequently regaled with music and dancing. Such was the case when the prodigal returned.[6] Dancing, it is likely, was rarely engaged in by the guests. It was rather an exhibition on the part of others brought in for the purpose.[7] There is no evidence, moreover, that it was ever participated in by the two sexes together, as is customary with us. The fact that it was generally done by hired performers, and was largely a spectacular affair, may have added to the scorn of Michal when she saw David "leaping and dancing" before the ark.[8] Dancing was a favorite pastime among the women of Egypt. It is not strange that we find references to it as a religious ceremony on more than one occasion during and after the exodus.[9]

---

[1] Ecclus. 32:1, 2. [2] Gen. 41:9. [3] 2 Kings 18:17. [4] Neh. 1:2; 2:1. [5] Luke 7:38.
[6] Luke 15:25. [7] Matt. 11:17; 14:6. [8] 2 Sam. 6:16. [9] Ex. 15:20; Ps. 149:3; 150:4.

CHAPTER IV.

DRESS AND ORNAMENTS.

1. WITH the exception of the dress of the priests, which is minutely described, the Bible says but little directly concerning the clothing of the ancient Hebrews. Still, it should not be difficult for us to get a tolerably accurate representation of the matter by putting together incidental references and combining with them what we may learn from other sources. In this, as in other things, the customs of the Oriental peoples cannot have changed materially; while from Egypt, Assyria and other contemporaneous nations an ever-enlarging store of information is disclosed to us from year to year.

2. MATERIALS FOR CLOTHING.—Setting aside as exceptional the " aprons " of fig leaves which our first parents made for themselves, the primitive material used for clothing seems to have been the rough skins of animals.[1] These were not altogether cast aside at any time afterwards, as we learn from the description given us of Elijah's dress and that of John the Baptist. In fact, they continue to be worn in the East by those exposed to much hardship, down to the present day.[2] But at an early period they must have been somewhat generally abandoned for garments made from wool. We have noticed not only that the patriarchs kept sheep, but that they were accustomed to remove their fleeces; and that wool was one of the principal materials from which clothing was made, the Bible offers abundant evidence.[3] About the time of the Babylonian exile Damascus wool was highly esteemed throughout the East.[4]

From Exodus 9 : 31 we learn that flax as well as barley was cultivated in Egypt. During the captivity of the Hebrews in that land a certain family of the tribe of Judah had for its special employment the raising of flax and its manufacture into "fine linen."[5] This indicates considerable progress already in the production of cloth, since fine linen is everywhere represented in the Bible as a luxury. Even the ordinary garments of the Israelitish priesthood were made from a coarser quality of this material.[6]

---

[1] Gen. 3 : 7, 21.　　[2] 2 Kings 1 : 8; Matt. 3 : 4; Heb. 11 : 37.　　[3] Gen. 31 : 19; 38 : 12; Lev. 13 : 47; Deut. 22 : 11; Job 31 : 20; Prov. 31 : 13; Ezek. 34 : 3.　　[4] Ezek. 27 : 18.　　[5] 1 Chron. 4 : 21.　　[6] Ex. 28 : 42; cf. 1 Sam. 2 : 18; 22 : 18; 2 Sam. 6 : 14.

How early cotton was introduced as an article of clothing, it is not possible with certainty to say. Hebrew words employed seem to include both cotton and linen, the simple idea of whiteness being the one emphasized in their roots. The language has no distinctive word for cotton. It is also a singular fact that Greek and Latin authors sometimes include cotton under the more general term " linen ;" and there was much confusion among all ancient writers respecting the two products. Nor is it to be greatly wondered at, since, until recently, it has not been decided whether the material in which the Egyptian mummies are enswathed is cotton or fine linen. It is now pretty generally agreed that both were employed. In India cotton fabrics were worn as early as B.C. 800. The plant is now cultivated in Palestine and Syria, and, on account of its superior qualities as a non-conductor of heat, is much used for turbans and underclothing.

The word "silk," found three times in the common English version of the Old Testament, has been allowed by the revisers to stand only in Ezekiel 16 : 10, 13.[1] It is doubtful even here whether the product of the silk-worm or a finer quality of linen is meant. Rabbinical interpreters decide for the former. In the book of Judges mention is made of tow, that is, the coarser, broken parts of flax.[2] Sackcloth was a rough material woven from goat's hair. Both the stuff and garment had the same name. It was used not only for sacks and bags, but was very generally worn by mourners, and, sometimes, even next the skin.[3]

3. The Mosaic law forbade to Israelites the wearing of a mingled stuff, wool and linen together.[4] The reason for this prohibition was not, as Josephus alleges,[5] because such garments were worn by the priests. This was not the case. It was simply because such a practice would be out of harmony with those distinctions of nature which God had instituted. It was looked upon as a sort of sacrilege, or uncleanness ; and abstinence was enjoined upon the Israelites as a means of discipline. On the same general plane with it was another law forbidding men and women to wear the garments or appendages peculiar to the opposite sex.[6] The latter law, however, had also another urgent motive in the fact that such an interchange of garments might easily lead to immorality.[7]

4. COLORS.—The color preferred for ordinary garments by the

<hr />

[1] See Prov. 31 : 22; but cf. Amos 3 : 12. [2] Judg. 16 : 9. [3] Gen. 42 : 25; Lev. 11 : 32; Josh. 9 : 4; 1 Kings 21 : 27; Job 16 : 15; Jonah 3 : 6. [4] Lev. 19 : 19; Deut. 22 : 11. [5] *Antiq.*, 4, 8 : 11. [6] Deut. 22 5. [7] Job 24 : 15.

Hebrews was white. The art of bleaching cloth was early known.[1] White, moreover, was a symbol of joy and purity.[2] It is not likely that the Hebrews knew much of the process of coloring previous to their sojourn in Egypt. Joseph's so-called "coat of many colors" was probably nothing more than a garment with sleeves (reaching to the extremities).[3] Subsequent to the exodus we find the Israelites using colors somewhat extensively for ornamentation, as well as threads of gold, and various kinds of figures. In the book of Judges we read of "dyed garments," and in one place of "divers colors of embroidery on both sides," that is, apparently, a fabric with the same colors and figures on both the face and the back.[4]

The artificial colors named in the Bible are purple, blue, scarlet and vermilion. The first three were used in the vestments of the Levitical priests and the curtains of the tabernacle. Purple robes were worn by kings and other high officers.[5] Scarlet also was a color affected by the rich and luxurious.[6] Babylonian idols were sometimes enrobed in garments of purple and blue.[7] The Phœnicians, for the most part, seem to have provided the materials for coloring; but the Egyptians displayed the most skill in compounding and applying them. Besides the artificial colors just mentioned, the Bible recognizes as natural colors, in addition to white, black, red, yellow and green; though sometimes without a sharp discrimination in the case of the last two.[8] It is not to be supposed that the common people in Israel ordinarily indulged themselves in garments of many colors.[9] It was rather a sign of wealth and distinction. Imitating the luxurious habits of foreign nations is a frequent subject of censure on the part of the prophets.[10]

5. FORMS OF DRESS FOR MALES.—In form and general use the Oriental dress has been much the same in all ages. It consists of loose, flowing robes, which can be easily shifted and adapted to various purposes. This description especially applies to the outer garment worn by males among the Hebrews. In its simplest form it was merely a quadrangular piece of cloth, corresponding in texture to the means of the wearer. But the different Hebrew terms employed for it, attest its multiform shape, quality and use. Its most common name, for example, *simlah*, in the first instance meant merely a covering; and while ordinarily used for the wide outer

---

[1] 2 Kings 18:17; Isa. 7:3; Mal. 3:2; Mark 9:3.   [2] 2 Macc. 11:8; John 20:12; Acts 1:10; Rev. 3:4.   [3] Gen. 37:3,23; 2 Sam. 13:18; but cf. Gen. 38:28.   [4] Ex. 28:6; 36:8,35; Judg. 5:30.   [5] Judg. 8:26; Esth. 8:15; Dan. 5:7; Mark 15:17.   [6] 2 Sam. 1:24; Prov. 31:21; Jer. 4:30.   [7] Jer. 10:9.   [8] Lev. 13:30; Ps. 68:13; Isa. 37:27.   [9] 2 Sam. 1:24; Luke 16:19.   [10] Isa. 3:16; Jer. 4:30; Zeph. 1:8.

wrapper, it was used also for garments in general, and, in one case, for a soldier's cloak.[1] Another term, *beged*, etymologically meaning a covering also, and, as a rule, referring to clothing in general, sometimes meant a superior kind of outer garment.[2] A third term, *kesuth*, likewise had the ordinary sense of a covering.[3] A fourth name, *lebush*, is mostly poetical, though sometimes designating the robe of an eminent person.[4] Still another name, *mad*, distinguished the garment as long.[5] The word *gelom* was used to designate an imported wrap similar to the outer garment ordinarily worn.[6] Other designations were—*suth* (poetic, Gen. 49 : 11); *addereth* (a full, noble mantle, 2 Kings 2 : 13 and often); and *karbela* (an Aramaic term, Dan. 3 : 21).

This outer garment now, varying in size and texture, might also be worn in a variety of ways. Sometimes, like the Scotch plaid, it was thrown over the left shoulder and fastened about the body. Sometimes it was thrown over both shoulders with the ends hanging in front. Sometimes it was drawn over the head, either like the modern *poncho*, or so as wholly to envelop the face.[7] Poor people and travellers used it at night both as mattress and covering. It was on this account that the laws of the Pentateuch forbade the taking it in pawn to hold after sunset.[8]

Fringed Garment with Tassels. (*After Farrar*.)

6. It was on the four corners of this outer robe that the Hebrews wore a fringe, or, more likely, a tassel, in which was a cord of blue, intended to remind them of the precepts of the law and their obligation to obey them. How great an importance was attached to this outward symbol in the Saviour's time is well known. On the other hand, it was not the wearing it that the Saviour rebuked, as he seems to have worn one himself; but wearing it chiefly for purposes of ostentation.[9] The "purple robe" with which Jesus was

[1] Gen. 9 : 23; Isa. 9 : 5. [2] Gen. 27 : 15; 1 Kings 22 : 10; Isa. 63 : 1. [3] Ex. 22 : 27; Deut. 22 : 12. [4] 2 Sam. 20 : 8; 2 Kings 10 : 22. [5] 2 Sam. 10 : 4. [6] Ezek. 27 · 24. [7] 2 Sam. 15 : 30; 1 Kings 19 : 13; Esth. 6 : 12. [8] Ex. 22 : 26, 27; Deut. 24 : 13, 17. [9] Num. 15 : 37–41; Deut. 22 : 12; Matt. 9 : 20; 14 : 36; Luke 8 : 44.

invested at the crucifixion was a Roman garment, and probably belonged to some officer of the Roman army.[1] The "cloke" left by Paul at Troas was a kind of traveller's mantle, and not a portmanteau as conjectured by some.[2]

7. The undergarment, which was the same for both sexes, was commonly called *kethoneth* (Greek, *chitōn*). It was a sleeveless tunic or frock, of any material desired, and reached to the knees or ankles. The woman's garment was generally longer and of richer material than that of the man. The rendering coat, usually given to it in the English version, it will be seen is somewhat misleading. The tunic was fastened at the waist by a girdle. The fold made by the girdle was found convenient as a pocket, and was sometimes called a purse.[3] A person was not considered as completely dressed who wore only his undergarment, and is even spoken of in the Scriptures as naked.[4]

Another garment, called *sadin*, although sometimes confounded with the tunic, appears to have been quite a different article. It was a kind of long shawl of fine linen or wool, and used to wrap about the body during the day and as a covering at night. It is looked upon in the Scriptures as a luxury rather than a necessity.[5]

The *meïl*, on the other hand, was properly a second tunic, a sort of extra undergarment, although in our English version bearing such names as "robe," "coat" and "mantle." It differed from the common tunic in being longer and often of richer and more showy material. It was such a robe that Samuel's mother made for him while he served Eli at the tabernacle; and that Jonathan stripped off to give to David as a token of affection. It was also to this garment that our Lord referred when he said to his disciples that on their missionary journeys they were not to take "two coats" apiece.[6] Hebrews in Palestine, excepting priests on duty, were not accustomed to wear trousers; but we find them spoken of in the book of Daniel ("hosen") as forming a part of the dress of certain Hebrews in the land of Persia.[7] This interesting statement is corroborated by Herodotus, who alleges that trousers were worn by the Persians.[8]

8. WOMEN'S DRESS.—There was a general resemblance between the clothing of men and women in the East, the distinctions being far less marked than in western lands. It may be the simplest way of discriminating between their respective outer garments to note the

---

[1] Mark 15 : 17.   [2] 2 Tim. 4 : 13.   [3] Matt. 10 : 9.   [4] 1 Sam. 19 : 24; 2 Sam. 6 : 20; Job 24 : 10; Isa. 20 : 2; John 21 : 7.   [5] Judg. 14 : 12, 13; Prov. 31 : 24; Isa. 3 : 23.   [6] 1 Sam. 2 : 19; 18 : 4; Matt. 10 : 10; Luke 9 : 3.   [7] Dan. 3 : 21.   [8] Herodotus i. 71.

Hebrew terms which were applied to that of the women. While having a number of names, it served, in general, the same purpose as that of the other sex. Sometimes it was called *mitpachath*, "mantle," and again, *maatapha*, "shawl."[1] The two words being found in immediate connection in one passage, it might be inferred that a different article of dress is referred to; but the etymology shows that it could not have been very different. In both

cases a kind of long shawl seems to be meant, which could be wrapped around the shoulders or body. The *tsaïph*, rendered "veil" in the account of Rebekah and of Tamar, while doubtless used sometimes as a veil, was more properly also an outer garment of some light material.[2] The same is true of the article of dress called *radid*, "mantle," "veil," mentioned in the Canticles and in Isaiah.[3] In the context of the second passage we meet with the word *pethigil*, "stomacher," which also appears to have been a wrap of some sort, and, as the connection shows, was worn on festival occasions. Others, however, regard it as a girdle of fine linen.

Inner and Outer Garment Worn in the East.

As the garments of women were generally made more full and flowing than those of men, so, for the purpose of covering the feet, the outer one was provided with a fringe. In Isaiah the "virgin daughter of Babylon" is bidden to strip off her "train" in order to engage in menial tasks.[4] In another part of the same prophet a vision is described in which it is said of Jehovah that he sat on a throne, high and lifted up, and his "train filled the temple."[5] Here not simply the fringe is meant, but the entire lower part of the robe, as in other passages.[6]

9. It would appear that in the earliest times in the East women did not ordinarily wear veils. It was only on certain occasions when a proper modesty required it that they covered their faces.[7] This fact is sufficiently established by the monuments of Assyria and Egypt. The modern practice has been largely brought about through the influence of the Koran. Moreover, when Paul censures the Corinth-

---

[1] Ruth 3:15; Isa. 3:22.   [2] Gen. 24:65; 38:14, 19.   [3] Cant. 5:7; Isa. 3:23, 24.   [4] Isa. 47:2.   [5] Isa. 6:1.   [6] Ex. 28:33, 34; Jer. 13:22; Lam. 1:9; Nah. 3:5.   [7] Gen. 24:65; 29:23.

ian women for the disuse of veils, it should not be at once inferred that the veils referred to were used for covering the face. Often, when veiling was required, it sufficed to draw the outer garment over the head. The proper veil was doubtless sometimes worn by women in biblical times and lands, but mostly for ornament. The word rendered "muffler" in Isaiah 3 : 9 was probably a sort of veil—

Dress and Veil of a Syrian or Eastern Woman.

at least, its etymology favors the supposition—and the Talmud uses the same term for the veil commonly worn by Arab women. In another passage of Isaiah, and three in Canticles, a Hebrew word has been properly translated by the revisers "veil" instead of "locks" of hair (Common Version), and the thought has gained much in clearness by the change.[1] Moses is said to have put a veil, *masveh*, over his face after communing with Jehovah on Mount Sinai.[2] It is likely that it was his outer garment which he temporarily used for the purpose. It seems questionable whether the word translated "kerchiefs" in Ezekiel does not rather mean a veil which was worn by the false prophets. The article was evidently worn on the head, and adapted in length to the stature of the wearer. Etymologically the term might mean veil, head-dress or mantle.[3]

10. THE GIRDLE.—Where long flowing robes were customary, the girdle would be a great convenience, not to say necessity. It has always been worn by both men and women in the East, and used not only to bind the clothing about the body, but for fastening it up when greater freedom of movement was required. In the Bible, with the exception of mourning garments and the fishing-coat of Peter, the girdle is uniformly represented as bound around the tunic.[4] There are a number of different names given to the girdle in the Hebrew, but with the exception of *abnet*, the term applied to the priest's, they seem to be used in the Bible somewhat indiscriminately. Their material was ordinarily leather or some kind of cloth. They were either wound in several folds around the body or fastened with clasps. In all periods it was the fashion to ornament them,

---

[1] Cant. 4 : 1, 3 ; 6 : 7 ; Isa, 47 : 2.   [2] Ex. 34 : 33-35 ; cf. *suth*, garment in Gen. 49 : 11.   [3] Ezek. 13 : 18, 21.   [4] 2 Sam. 3 : 31 ; John 21 : 7.

more or less. Girdles of gold were not unknown, as we may infer from a few passages.[1]

As already observed, the clothing being gathered up at the breast by means of the girdle, the bosom offered a convenient place for the carrying of various articles. God is besought in the psalm to pluck his hand out of his bosom.[2] The modern Oriental carries here his handkerchief, smoking-materials, con-

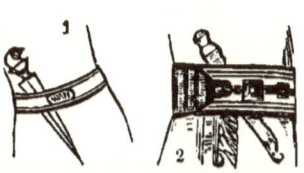

veniences for writing, and the like. So, in Ezekiel, we read of one who carried a writer's ink-horn "by his side."[3] This was a long tube containing reed pens and a receptacle for ink, all securely fastened to the girdle. Attached to the same, also, the warrior wore his

Ancient Eastern Girdles. 1. Egyptian. 2. Assyrian. (*From British Museum.*)

sword.[4] It is here that the modern Arab wears his dagger. Women wore their girdles lower down and looser than the men. Priests, on the other hand, and other dignitaries, were girded about the breast.[5] The frequent figure of girding up the loins, as referring to preparation for a journey, a race, or for battle, suggests the likelihood that the girdle was not used by the Israelites when they were engaged in their ordinary pursuits, their dress then being of a very simple character. In Luke 17 : 8 it is doubtful whether a girding up of the tunic is meant, or one like that of our Lord when he laid aside his upper garment, and "took a towel, and girded himself" (with it).[6]

11. The Turban.—From the earliest times, in the East, a simple or more complex form of the turban has been worn as a covering

for the head. In its modern style, it consists of three parts: a simple closely-fitting cap of cotton cloth; a similar, but heavier, cap of felt, generally in some bright color, and wadded; and, finally, the turban proper. This is a piece of cloth of such size and material as the wearer

Syrian Turbans.

desires or can afford. It may be of muslin, of silk, or even of cashmere. At present, where there is Moslem rule, the colors to be worn are strictly prescribed, subject races being confined to the more sombre ones. In some cases the

---

[1] 2 Kings 1 : 8; Jer. 13 : 1; Ezek. 16 : 10; Dan. 10 : 5; Matt. 3 : 4; Rev. 1 : 13; 15 : 6. [2] Ps. 74 : 11. [3] Ezek. 9 : 2. [4] Judg. 3 : 16; 2 Sam. 20 : 8; Ps. 45 : 3. [5] Rev. 1 : 13; Josephus, *Antiq.*, 3, 7 : 2. [6] John 13 : 4.

turban is of immense size, a single one being known to require as many as seventy-five yards of material. The word used in the Old Testament for the ordinary turban is *tsaniph*.[1] Its etymology shows that, like the modern article, it meant originally something wrapped about the head. Another sort, an ornamental head-dress, intended to be worn especially on festival occasions, was named *peër*.[2] The Babylonian turban, once mentioned in the Bible, was called *tibulim*;[3] and the high cap of the Israelitish priest, *migbaah*.[4] There is no direct evidence that the turban was worn by the Israelites in the Mosaic age. On its first appearance it is found among the ruling class, the wealthy or the female sex.[5] It is not improbable that ordinarily the Israelites wore nothing on their heads, unless it were a simple handkerchief as is the case with the Bedouin of the present day.[6]

12. SANDALS.—For the protection of the feet, the Hebrews, like other eastern peoples, wore sandals. In the most primitive form

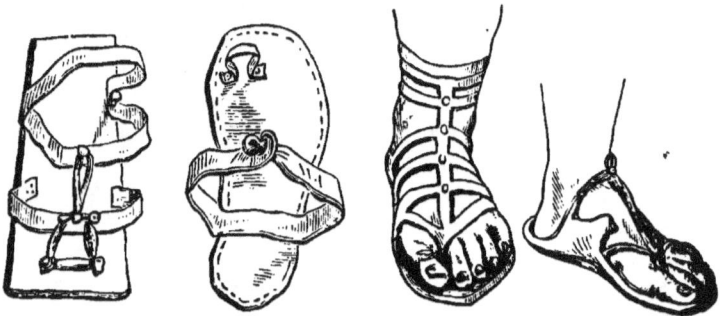

Eastern Sandals with Thongs or "Shoe-latchets."

they consisted simply of pieces of untanned hide bound to the soles of the feet by thongs. These thongs, the "shoe-latchet" of the English version, are the subject of frequent mention in the Bible.[7] In later times not only leather but felt, various kinds of cloth, and wood shod with iron, were used as material for sandals. When a piece of leather was taken it was generally cut a little larger than the foot, so that its edges being drawn up by the thongs would the better protect it. This kind of sandal, hardly worthy of the title "shoe" uniformly given it in the English Bible, is still somewhat worn by shepherds and the common people in the East, and even by the peasantry of Europe.

1 Job 29 : 14. 2 Isa. 61 : 3, 10; Ezek 24 : 17, 23. 3 Ezek. 23 : 15. 4 Ex. 29 : 9. 5 Job 29 : 14; Isa. 3 : 23. 6 John 11 : 44; 20 : 7; cf. Acts 19 : 12. 7 Gen. 14 : 23; Isa. 5 : 27; Mark 1 : 7; John 1 : 27.

The monuments of Egypt show that sandals were in use there among nearly all classes. The Egyptian sandal, however, had generally the peculiarity that it was high and pointed at the toe. In Assyria, on the other hand, an effort was made to protect more the side and heel of the foot. The ambassadors of Jehu are represented on an Assyrian monument now in the British Museum, as having sandals of this sort which reached to the ankles. It is possible that this is only a reflection of the Assyrian custom. The prophet Isaiah, in speaking of the Assyrian soldiery, in one place says that "every boot of the booted warrior" shall be fuel for the flames.[1] A single incidental reference suggests the possibility that the Israelitish soldiery had likewise a special protection for their feet.[2]

It is evident that all classes, unless it were the extremely poor like the prodigal in the Gospel,[3] wore sandals when they were out of doors. Their disuse was a token of bereavement.[4] Our Lord in sending forth his messengers forbade their taking two pairs, but did not insist upon their taking none.[5] The Israelites seem to have been provided with them on their flight from Egypt;[6] and the prophet Amos can find no more fitting illustration of the lack of appreciation for the poor in his day among their rich neighbors than the fact that they were willing to sell them even for a pair of sandals.[7] Sandals worn by women did not differ essentially from those of the men except in being often of finer material and more highly ornamented. Seal or porpoise skins were sometimes used for this class, and the thongs were beautifully embroidered. The eyes of Olofernes are said to have been "ravished" by the sandals of the designing Judith.[8] Sandals were not generally worn in the house; at least, they are not in modern times where there are carpets or mats. But the custom of leaving them at the door of private dwellings or rooms is to be carefully distinguished from that illustrated in Exodus 3 : 5, where Moses was bidden to put off his shoes because the place where he stood was holy ground. The former custom arose, it is likely, from motives of cleanliness. It is now considered the duty of servants in the East to care for the sandals of their master. We are told that when a man of wealth rides through the streets of an Oriental city, one of his throng of servants is often seen carrying his shoes. To some such service John the Baptist may have referred when he said of Christ, "whose shoes I am not worthy to

---

[1] Isa. 9 : 5, margin. [2] 1 Kings 2 : 5. [3] Luke 15 : 22. [4] 2 Sam. 15 : 30; Ezek. 24 : 17.
[5] Matt. 10 : 10; Luke 10 : 4. [6] Ex. 12 : 11. [7] Amos 8 : 6. [8] Cant. 7 : 1; Ezek. 16 : 10;
Judith 10 : 4; 16 : 9.

bear."[1]   There is no reference to gloves in the Bible; but the Talmud mentions their use by laborers for the protection of the hands. The "aprons" spoken of in Acts 19 : 12 seem to have been articles made from linen, which workmen put on after laying off the outer garment, worn much as the modern apron is worn, and for similar purposes.

13. A singular custom of the Israelites connected with that of levirate marriage is worthy of mention at this point. If the man to whom the option of such a marriage was given publicly refused to take the widow of his deceased brother under the conditions imposed

Eastern Shoes and Boots.

by the law, it was her privilege, if she chose to exercise it, to humiliate him in the manner set forth in the following passage: "Then shall his brother's wife come unto him in the presence of the elders, and loose his shoe from off his foot, and spit in his face; and she shall answer and say, So shall it be done unto the man that doth not build up his brother's house."[2]   According to Jewish authorities, the spitting was done before the face of the offender, that is, in his presence.   The drawing off of the shoe seems to have been symbolical of the surrender of the rights which the law gave to a levir, or brother-in-law.

A similar ceremony will be recalled as having taken place in connection with the marriage of Boaz and Ruth.[3]   The person legally best entitled to be a suitor for the hand of the Moabitess voluntarily drew off his sandal in token that he relinquished his right in favor of Boaz.   It seems likely that the same general meaning is to be given the passage in the Psalms where it is said, "Upon Edom will I cast my shoe."[4]   The context shows that authority is not claimed over Edom, or that Edom is expected to take the servant's place and carry the sandals of the master, but that Edom is renounced and spurned.   The Arabs of the present day often use the expression "My shoe at thee!" as an utterance of depreciation or contempt. The custom of throwing a slipper sportively after a newly-wedded pair leaving the parental roof would appear to have a like origin. The parents and family friends thereby symbolically renounce their right to the daughter or son in favor of the husband or wife.

[1] Matt. 3 : 11.   [2] Deut. 25 : 9.   [3] Ruth 4 : 7.   [4] Ps. 60 : 8; 108 : 9.

14. RHETORICAL FIGURES REFERRING TO CLOTHING.—The frequent figure of girding up the clothing as a sign of readiness for action has already been referred to.[1] A prophet named Agabus, it will be remembered, once bound his own feet and hands with Paul's girdle, saying, "Thus shall the Jews at Jerusalem bind the man that owneth this girdle."[2] So, too, "making bare the arm"—that is, rolling up the flowing sleeve—was a sign of preparation to use the arm to the best advantage in whatever service might be required of it.[3] Again, rending the garments, as we have already seen, was one of the most common outward indications of violent mental agitation, whether of fear, anger or overwhelm-

ing grief;[4] while simply shaking them was a mark of renunciation.[5] The outer robe was even sometimes stripped off and cast away in a moment of excited feeling.[6] The Hebrews, moreover, well understood the symbolism of form and colors in clothing. We read in the New Testament of those who wore "sheep's" clothing, "long" clothing, "fine" clothing, "soft" and "bright" clothing; and of others who repented "in sackcloth and ashes."[7] Homage toward a superior might be expressed by spreading one's garments in the way

Girded for Walking, with Staff.

which he would pass over.[8] To exchange garments was a sign of friendship.[9] To make a present of official robes indicated investiture with office; and taking them away, a deprivation of the same.[10] A keeper of the wardrobe is spoken of in one passage; and there is evidence that special rooms were sometimes set apart for the storing of garments.[11]

15. ORNAMENTS.—Among the ornaments worn by the Hebrews, some were common to both sexes and others were peculiar to each. It would be a mistake to suppose that male ornaments were confined in ancient times to the staff and the seal-ring. We are informed that Saul wore a bracelet on his arm even in battle; while chains for the neck and rings for the ears and fingers seem not to have been uncommon.[12] The use of the staff was by no means confined to invalids or old men. In the rough mountain-passes of Palestine it was a

---

[1] Ex. 12: 11; 2 Kings 4: 29; 9: 1; Job 38: 3; Ps. 18: 32; Isa. 5: 27; 1 Peter 1: 13.   [2] Acts 21: 11.   [3] Isa. 52: 10.   [4] Judg. 11: 35; 1 Kings 21: 27; 2 Kings 5: 7.   [5] Luke 9: 5; Acts 18: 6.   [6] 1 Sam. 19: 24; Acts 22: 23.   [7] Matt. 7: 15; 11: 8, 21; Mark 12: 38; James 2: 3.   [8] Matt. 21: 8.   [9] 1 Sam. 18: 4.   [10] Gen. 41: 42; Esth. 8: 15; Isa. 22: 21.   [11] 2 Kings 10: 22; 2 Chron. 34: 22.   [12] Gen. 35: 4; 38: 18, 25; 41: 42; Ex. 32: 2; 2 Sam. 1: 10; Ps. 73: 6.

no less grateful companion than it now is to climbers of the Swiss Alps.[1] The disciples of our Lord, notwithstanding the meagreness of their outfit, were permitted to carry a staff.[2] As a weapon of defence, moreover, it was not to be despised. The intrepid David appeared before Goliath armed only with a staff and a sling.[3] Benaiah, the son of Jehoiada, by means of his staff alone plucked the weapon out of the hands of an Egyptian and slew him with his own spear.[4] The staff seems generally to have been a long, straight stick much like the modern alpenstock. For purposes of ornament it was highly carved. Herodotus, in speaking of the ancient Babylonians, says: "Every one carries a seal, and a walking-stick carved at the top into the form of an apple, a rose, a lily, an eagle, or something similar; for it is not their habit to use a stick without an ornament."[5] Such a staff, it is likely, Judah carried with his other ornaments on the occasion mentioned in Genesis 38 : 18, 25. The prophet Hosea refers to a custom among the apostates of his day of having the image of an idol—a sort of teraphim—engraved on the top of their walking-sticks.[6] Metaphorical references to the staff are common in the Old Testament. We read, for example, of the "staff of bread." So, too, the civil and military power of a country is called its staff.[7] Much prominence is given in the Bible to the staff of Moses, of Aaron and of Elisha.

16. Finger-rings were no doubt common at all periods among the more opulent Hebrews, as the monuments and history show that they were among the Egyptians, Greeks and Romans. In the Epistle of James (2 : 2) it is the man who wears the "fine clothing" that has the "gold ring;" or more literally, according to the Greek, is "gold ringed," that is, has a profusion of rings. The use of seal-rings also prevailed in the remotest antiquity. The fact that they were known to the patriarchs is well attested. The signet of Judah was not worn on the finger, but was suspended from the neck as is made evident by the improved rendering of the revised English version.[8] The museums of Europe and this country contain numerous speci-

Assyrian Finger-rings and Bracelets.

[1] Ex. 12:11; 21:19; Zech. 8:4.   [2] Mark 6:8.   [3] 1 Sam. 17:43.   [4] 2 Sam. 23:21.
[5] Herodotus i. 195.   [6] Hosea 4:12.   [7] Lev. 26:26; Ps. 105:16; Isa. 9:4; 10:24.   [8] Gen. 38:18, 25.

mens of seal-rings, some of them dating back to days anterior to Abraham, and coming, it is claimed, from the very "Ur of the Chaldees" which was the home of his ancestors. They differ in form, but are generally cylindrical and from half an inch to three inches in length. Their material is amethyst, rock crystal, carnelian, agate, chalcedony, onyx, jasper and other like substances. Sometimes they are of composite material, black manganese being the principal ingredient. They are pierced so that they can be worn on the finger or around the neck, or conveniently rolled over the clay. In Canticles[1] there is a reference to both the former methods of wearing the signet, within the compass of a single verse. The high value put upon it is well set forth in a passage in Jeremiah: "As I live, saith the Lord, though Coniah the son of Jehoiakim . . . were the signet upon my right hand, yet would I pluck thee thence."[2] The inscription might be the owner's name with that of his father, or some title of the deity whom he served. By using a finer quality of clay, not simply papyrus and other book rolls, and letters, but also purses, doors and like things, could be sealed.[3] The custom of making an impression with the seal upon the forehead of a person is several times alluded to in the Scriptures, and is still known among the Arabians and Persians.[4] In Assyria the document to be sealed was itself often of clay, and was not hardened until after it had been inscribed and sealed. In Egypt, on the other hand, the more general custom was first to impress the seal upon a piece of clay and then affix it to the object. The use of the signet as a symbol of authority is well known.

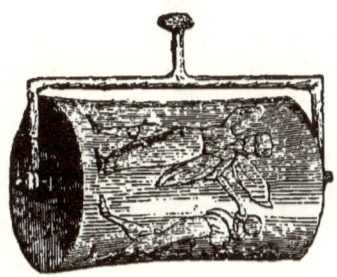

Oriental Cylindrical Metal Seal.

17. It will not be out of place to speak here of what were termed in the Old Testament "frontlets," and in the New "phylacteries." They can hardly be regarded as ornaments; but as an important part of the costume of an Israelite of the later times, they should not be overlooked. The Talmudists called them *tephillin*, a word not found in the Bible. Certain passages of the Pentateuch enjoining that the law should be a sign upon the hand and for frontlets between the eyes—symbolically referring, perhaps, to ornaments

[1] Cant. 8 : 6; cf. Ex. 35 : 22; Isa. 3 : 21.　[2] Jer. 22 : 24.　[3] 1 Kings 21 : 8; Esth. 8 : 8; Job 14 : 17; Isa. 29 : 11; Dan. 6 : 17; Matt. 27 : 66.　[4] Gal. 6 : 17; Rev. 7 : 3.

then in use—were understood literally by the Jews.[1] Accordingly, inscribing these passages upon several slips of parchment and inclosing them in a leathern case prepared for the purpose, they bound the whole on the forehead between the eyes. The same passages written on one strip of parchment and inclosed in a similar case were bound on the left arm near the elbow. The Talmud contains the most minute and finical regulations concerning the whole matter. Our Lord's strictures on this custom referred less to the custom than to its abuse.[2] The Pharisees made these awkward leathern cases as conspicuous as possible, so as to attract the more attention to themselves and their pretentious legalism. It came still later to be held that God himself wears *tephillin*, and that when he swears by his holy arm he makes specific reference to them.[3]

18. On both the Egyptian and Assyrian monuments men appear

wearing the arm-ring or bracelet; and though infrequently mentioned in the Bible, we find it used as an ornament by both sexes among the Hebrews.[4] The son of Sirach likens the instruction given to a sensible man to "a bracelet on his right arm."[5] While bone and ivory may have been made use of for bracelets, the precious metals seem to have been generally preferred. In shape, size and embellishment, as in cost, they were suited to every taste.

Royal Armlets, found at Khorsabad, Assyria.

19. The necklace, or ornamental chain for the neck, was another device employed by both sexes to heighten their personal charms. It might consist of a single band or chain, or of a series of ornaments as pearls, pieces of coral, or diamonds strung together. It is spoken of in one place as a "string of jewels."[6] The chain which Pharaoh put upon the neck of Joseph and that with which Belshazzar sought to do honor to Daniel were both of gold, and no doubt of extraordinary size and richness.[7] Even animals ridden by kings were sometimes so decorated.[8] Biblical writers knew how to distinguish between a proper and an improper use of such ornamentation. Sometimes, according to them, it only served to set forth the pride of the arrogant; but sometimes it equally illustrated the charm of inward grace and dutifulness.[9]

[1] Ex. 13 : 9, 10, 16, 17; Deut. 6 : 4–9, 13–22.   [2] Matt. 23 : 5.   [3] Cf. Deut. 33 : 2; Isa. 49 : 16; 62 : 8.
[4] Gen. 24 : 22; Num. 31 : 50; 2 Sam. 1 : 10; Ezek. 16 : 11.   [5] Ecclus. 21 : 21.   [6] Cant. 1 : 10; cf.
4 : 9.   [7] Gen. 41 : 42; Dan. 5 : 29.   [8] Judg. 8 : 26.   [9] Ps. 73 : 6; Prov. 1 : 9; cf. Ezek. 16 : 11.

20. Along with brooches, signet-rings and armlets, "all of gold," ear-rings are mentioned as in use by Hebrew women of the Mosaic period, as well as by their children of both sexes, and, it may be safely inferred, by adult males as was customary among other contemporaneous peoples.[1] One of the Hebrew words rendered ear-ring (*nezem*) sometimes means nose-ring as well; but when this is the case it is indicated by the context.[2] Pendants of various sorts were often attached to the ear-rings.[3] The size of the latter varied according to taste; but as a rule they were probably larger than those worn by the women of the western world. Layard describes some which he saw in the East, which reached to the waist and terminated in a tablet of the same material.

Eastern Women, with Nose-ring, Veils and Head-dress.

Another writer, speaking of the wife of the king of Nubia, describes her ear-rings as reaching down to her shoulders and having the appearance of wings. The rings themselves were five inches in diameter and nearly of the thickness of the little finger. The orifice pierced for them had become so enlarged that three fingers could have been passed through it above the ring. The fact that ear-rings, like other ornaments, were sometimes looked upon in the light of charms even by the Hebrews may be inferred from Genesis 35 : 4, where it is said of Jacob's household that, in response to his appeal to purify themselves, they gave him "all the strange gods which were in their hand, and the rings which were in their ears; and Jacob hid them under the oak which was by Shechem."

21. It is rare in the East at the present day to see a woman of the lower classes the cartilage of whose nose has not been pierced for the purpose of accommodating it to ornaments. The custom, to some extent, is followed by men also, cases occurring where the nose and ears are connected by a series of rings interlinked with one another. In biblical literature such a practice may be traced back to the time of Abraham. Among the gifts which the trusted Eliezer presented to Rebekah, and even placed upon her face, was a

[1] Ex. 32 : 2; 35 : 22; Num. 31 : 50; Judg. 8 : 24, 26.   [2] With Gen. 24 : 47; Prov. 11 : 22; Isa. 3 : 21; Ezek. 16 : 12; compare Gen. 35 : 4; Ex. 32 : 2; Prov. 25 : 12.   [3] Judg. 8 : 26; Isa. 3 : 19.

golden nose-ring of half a shekel's weight.[1] In modern times these
rings are often of extraordinary size. Not infrequently they reach
to the mouth and must be removed in eating, beside seriously in-
commoding the breathing at all times. It was a sharp sarcasm on
the weakness for finery often shown by persons having no intellectual or moral qualities to compel attention that inspired the proverb
"*As a* jewel of gold in a swine's snout, *so is* a fair woman which is
without discretion."[2]

22. Another occasional device of both sexes for ornamentation
was the garland, or chaplet of leaves or flowers. " Let us crown
ourselves with rosebuds before they are withered," says the Epicurean
author of the apocryphal book of Wisdom, "and let there be no
meadow untrod by our luxury."[3] The custom probably originated
with the simple fillet employed to keep the hair in place. In contrast with the fading substances used for such purposes the prophet
Isaiah declares that Jehovah of hosts shall be " for a crown of glory,
and for a diadem of beauty, unto the residue of his people."[4] In
similar language the apostle Paul calls attention to the wreaths of
pine and laurel given to the victors in the Grecian games: "Now
they *do it* to receive a corruptible crown ; but we an incorruptible."[5]

Although glass was not unknown, the mirrors mentioned in
the Bible were doubtless made of metal. This was certainly true,
judging from the use to which they were put, of those spoken of in
Exodus 38 : 8. It is likely that the Hebrews obtained their first
mirrors from Egypt, where, even before the exodus, the art of making them had attained a high degree of perfection. The monuments
show that in form they closely resembled the hand-mirrors of the
present day, and were seldom much larger. They were made principally of copper, or of copper mixed with tin, although silver and
other more costly metals were also employed for the purpose, especially in the later times. They were kept bright by polishing.[6]
Whether little mirrors were ever substituted by the Hebrew women,
as by those of some other peoples, for ornamental purposes in place
of precious stones cannot be determined with certainty. Two New
Testament writers refer to the mirror by way of illustration.[7]

23. Of ornaments usually worn or carried by women alone the following claim attention here: cauls, anklets and ankle-chains, scent-
bottles, and decorated purses or "satchels." They are all mentioned

---

[1] Gen. 24 : 22, 47; cf. Ezek. 16 : 12.   [2] Prov. 11 : 22.   [3] Wisd. 2 : 8; cf. Ecclus. 1 : 11; 3 Macc.
7 : 16.   [4] Isa. 28 : 5; cf. Prov. 1 : 9; 4 : 9.   [5] 1 Cor. 9 : 25; cf. 2 Tim. 2 : 5; James 1 : 12; 1 Pet.
5 : 4; Rev. 12 : 1.   [6] Wisd. 7 : 26; Ecclus. 12 : 11.   [7] 1 Cor. 13 : 12; James 1 : 24.

in a single passage of Isaiah.[1] The caul, nowhere else referred to in the Bible, seems to have been a band or fillet, which was worn across the forehead for the purpose of attaching to it the net in which the flowing hair was retained. The anklet was a more or less embellished band of gold, silver or other metal fastened around the ankle.

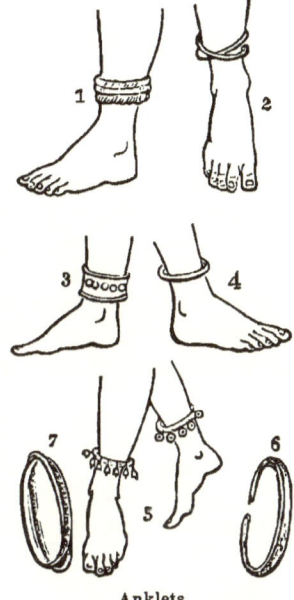

Anklets.

1, 2, 3, 4. Egyptian Anklets. 5. Modern, worn by dancing-girls. 6, 7. Assyrian, of iron and bronze. (*From Nineveh. Now in British Museum.*)

The sound the anklets made as one walked and struck them together seems to have been one of their chief attractions. They are still worn in Egypt and in the rural districts of western Asia. Livingstone found the custom prevailing also in Africa, where rings of iron are used. To these, little bits of metal are attached in order that, like the women of ancient Israel, they may "make a tinkling with their feet."

Attached to the anklets also, besides pendants of various kinds, including, it is likely, little bells, there were in the ancient times so-called "ankle-chains," which connected the feet together. They were intended to compel those who wore them to take short, mincing steps, which seem to have characterized the fashionable gait of that period. The prophet has only censure for those "daughters of Zion" who are haughty, and "walk with stretched forth necks and wanton eyes, walking and mincing as they go."[2]

24. PERFUMERY.—The "perfume boxes" mentioned in Isaiah were little caskets or vases filled with perfume and carried, it is to be presumed, in the girdle. Perfumes manufactured from native and imported spices were very much used by the Hebrews, and various methods of applying them are noted. In Canticles 1 : 13, for example, there is an allusion to a kind of scent-bag worn on the person. In another passage of the same book the use of incense for a similar purpose is referred to.[3]

25. When ornamental purses are spoken of in the Scriptures, it is probable that the ordinary purse, embroidered in bright colors or decorated with jewels, is meant. Besides the girdle, which was often made use of for this purpose, the Hebrews employed, especially on

---

[1] Isa. 3 : 18.   [2] Isa. 3 : 16.   [3] Cant. 3 : 6; cf. Prov. 7 : 17; 27 : 9; Isa. 57 : 9.

journeys, a little bag in which to carry their money and the weights needed to determine its value.[1]

26. THE HAIR.—The hair was always highly esteemed by the Hebrews as an ornament of the person, whether in youth or in old age.[2] It is a singular fact that while it was customary in Egypt for males to shave the head and to wear wigs, and for the Assyrians to let the hair grow long, the Hebrews adopted neither of these methods, but regularly trimmed the hair both of the head and beard to prevent too great luxuriance. This custom may have been brought about, in the first instance, by the very common practice among heathen nations of offering locks of hair in sacrifice to their gods. The Mosaic laws, it is true, prescribe no one way of wearing the hair, except that both priests and people are prohibited from interfering with its orderly growth, whether on the head or the face. They might not cut it off in certain spots only, as a sign of mourning, and in imitation of the heathen nations about them.[3]

But in the book of Ezekiel the priests are bidden to "poll," that is, trim, their hair, in distinction from shaving it off or letting it

Egyptian Mode of Wearing the Hair. (*From a painting in British Museum.*)

grow long in the form of locks;[4] and there is every reason to suppose that the laity followed the same practice without being specially enjoined to do so. Extremely long hair was the acknowledged badge of the Nazarite.[5] The case of Absalom was clearly an exception to ordinary rules for adults;[6] and Josephus mentions it as a singular habit of the body-guard of Solomon that they wore long hair.[7] The same conclusion is reached when we consider that to let the hair grow and remain uncared for was regarded as a symbol of distress and sorrow, and was also particularly enjoined on the leper.[8] Still, it is probable that the Hebrews wore their hair somewhat longer than is common with us, and may have taken some means of confining it close to the head. This would seem to follow from some incidental expressions of the Bible, such as letting the "hair go loose" and "uncovering the ear," that is, to hear.[9] Luxuriant black hair was specially prized, and none the less if it was curly.

[1] Gen. 42:35; Deut. 25:13; Micah 6:11; Luke 10:4; 12:33.   [2] 2 Sam. 14:26; 2 Kings 2: 23; Prov. 16:31.   [3] Lev. 19:27; 21:5; Deut. 14:1; but cf. Job 1:20; Jer. 7:29; 16:6; 41:5. [4] Ezek. 44:20.   [5] Num. 6:5; 1 Sam. 1:11.   [6] 2 Sam. 14:25.   [7] Josephus, *Antiq.* 8, 7:3. [8] Lev. 13:45; 21:10.   [9] Lev. 10:6; 1 Sam. 20:2 (margin), 12; cf. Ezek. 24:17.

There is no evidence that the Israelites ever sought to disguise the signs of age appearing in gray hair. Josephus, however, alleges that Herod did this, and we know that it was common with the Greeks and Romans.[1] With the Hebrews, on the contrary, the hoary head was looked upon as a mark of dignity and honor. This is not only directly stated, but is incidentally confirmed by the fact that God himself is represented in vision with snowy-white hair.[2] The occupation of the barber was well known at all periods.[3] A woman named Mariam, acting in this capacity, is mentioned in the Talmud. The Bible gives us little information concerning modes of dressing the hair. That of women, which was worn long, seems often to have been braided. New Testament writers, in making reference to this fact, did so, it is likely, less with the view of censuring the practice than of cautioning Christian women against giving too much attention to the "outward adorning of plaiting the hair, and of wearing jewels of gold, or of putting on apparel."[4] Egyptian women used combs and other similar devices for keeping the hair in place. It is most probable that the same appliances were early adopted in Palestine. According to Josephus, in Solomon's time gold-dust was sometimes sprinkled on the hair in order to increase the brilliancy of its effects.[5] The custom of anointing it, especially on festival occasions, dates back to the earliest periods.[6] Head-tires, too, are several times spoken of in the Scriptures, but without any definite description of them.[7]

27. PIGMENTS.—The practice of applying pigments to the eyelids and eyebrows in order to enhance the apparent brilliancy of the eyes was common throughout the East in Bible times. The prophet Jeremiah, addressing Israel, says, " Though thou clothest thyself with scarlet, though thou deckest thee with ornaments of gold, though thou enlargest (roundest) thine eyes with paint, in vain dost thou make thyself fair; *thy* lovers despise thee, they seek thy life."[8] The material used for this purpose was often kept in a horn, a fact which seems to have given rise to the name of Job's third daughter, *Keren-happuch*, which means, literally, "the pigment-horn."[9] Besides *puch*, the paint was also called *kachal*, and is so named to this day among the Arabs. It is a preparation of antimony, and, singularly enough, it is from this word that the term "alcohol" comes; the fineness of the powder suggesting the idea of highly-rectified

[1] Josephus, *Antiq.* 16, 8 : 1; cf. Matt. 5 : 36.   [2] Lev. 19 : 32; Prov. 16 : 31; Dan. 7 : 9; Rev. 1 : 14.   [3] Num. 6 : 5; Ps. 52 : 2; Isa. 7 : 20; Ezek. 5 : 1.   [4] 1 Tim. 2 : 9; 1 Pet. 3 : 2.   [5] Josephus, *Antiq.* 8, 7 : 3.   [6] Ruth 3 : 3; 2 Sam. 14 : 2; Ps. 23 : 5; Matt. 6 : 17; Luke 7 : 46.   [7] 2 Kings 9 : 30; Isa. 3 : 20; 61 : 3, 10.   [8] Jer. 4 : 30; cf. Prov. 6 : 25; Isa. 3 : 24.   [9] Job 42 : 14.

spirits. This pigment is applied to the eyelids by modern Egyptian women by means of a small, blunt piece of wood or ivory, which is moistened, dipped in the mixture and then drawn carefully along the edges of the eye. Boxes containing the substance have been brought to light in considerable numbers from Egyptian tombs.

Egyptian Woman, with Eyes and Skin Tattooed.

28. That Hebrew women tattooed their skin or painted the soles of their feet, the palms of their hands, or their nails, as is now customary with the women of western Asia, does not appear to be supported by valid evidence from the Scriptures.[1] That all classes made great use of the bath is clear from the Mosaic laws of purification— which are based on this custom—as well as from certain uniform rites of hospitality.[2] The practice of anointing the skin was also widespread in the East at all times. That the Hebrews highly regarded it might be inferred from the fact that the holy anointing oil used in consecrating the priests was prohibited to the laity for ordinary purposes.[3] We read in the poetic language of Canticles of one whose "hands dropped with myrrh" and her "fingers with liquid myrrh;"[4] and it is said in the Psalms, of the royal bride, "All thy garments smell of myrrh, and aloes, and cassia."[5]

[1] See Lev. 19:28; 21:5; Deut. 14:1.   [2] Gen. 18:4; 24:32; Ruth 3:3.   [3] Ex. 30:22-33.
[4] Cant. 5:5.   [5] Ps. 45:8.

CHAPTER V.

1. The earliest occupations of men, according to the Scriptures, were tilling the ground and rearing cattle and sheep. Down to the present day forms of labor directly connected with these two have always engaged the attention of large portions of our race. Pastoral life in the East, in which the calling of the herdsman as well as that of the shepherd is here included, is doubtless at the present time very much what it was in the times of Abraham and David. We read of the former that the Lord gave him " flocks and herds, silver and gold, and menservants and maidservants, and camels and asses."¹ When the family of Jacob went down into Egypt they asked permission of Pharaoh to settle in the rich pasture-lands of Goshen. " Thy servants," they said to him, " have been keepers of cattle from our youth even until now, both we, and our fathers."² It was with their herds that they made their exodus from Egypt.³ Two and a half tribes finally settled east of the Jordan, for the reason that this region was especially suited to grazing.⁴

Some conception of the extent to which this business was carried on may be gained from the ever-recurring metaphors of the Old and New Testaments based upon it, from the immense number of cattle that were yearly required for sacrifice, and from the fact that sheep and cattle are so often mentioned among the blessings of a prosperous people. Numerous laws of the Pentateuch were shaped with express reference to the fact that property consisted largely in cattle. In fact, the same Hebrew word signified property in general and property in flocks and herds.

2. REARING OF SHEEP.—Formerly, as now, sheep were the most numerous and important of domestic animals in the East.⁵ Just previous to their crossing the Jordan the Hebrews took away from the Midianites, along with other booty, not less than six hundred and seventy-five thousand head.⁶ Nabal, the rich Carmelite, had a flock of three thousand sheep and one thousand goats.⁷ At the dedication of the temple Solomon is said to have offered in sacrifice

---

¹ Gen. 24:35.　² Gen. 46:34; 47:3.　³ Ex. 12:32.　⁴ Num. 32:1.　⁵ Deut. 8:13; 28:4; Jer. 31:27; Zech. 2:4.　⁶ Num. 31:32.　⁷ 1 Sam. 25:2.

twenty-two thousand oxen and a hundred and twenty thousand sheep.[1] In later times the king of Moab paid to King Ahab an annual tribute of a hundred thousand rams with their wool, and as many more lambs;[2] and on the monuments of Assyria it is recorded that Sennacherib in a war with Merodach-Baladan captured on one occasion eight hundred thousand sheep and goats.

The sheep most common in Syria and Palestine is what is known as the broad-tailed species. A variety of the sort generally found among western peoples is also seen, but far less frequently. The former have been reared in the East from time immemorial. They are mentioned by classical writers, and are doubtless referred to in several passages of the Pentateuch in connection with sacrifices.[3] The tail of this sheep is little else than a mass of fat, which is described as of delicate quality, being superior to tallow, though not equal to butter. It is made great use of in the preparation of a large number of Oriental dishes. Ordinarily the entire tail weighs about twenty pounds, though sometimes considerably more.

The color of sheep was usually white, and only exceptionally black or speckled.[4] They bear in the East twice yearly, the later lambs being regarded as the stronger. We find many illustrations in the Scriptures based on the natural qualities or habits of this animal. Its uncomplaining patience, for example, is noticed; its tractability; its strong attachment to the shepherd, especially that of a pet lamb; its innocence; the peculiarity that leads the whole flock to follow the leader; its helplessness when left without a shepherd; and the miserable plight of a wandering and lost sheep.[5]

It is customary now in the East, as it was in Bible times, to give names to individual sheep, to which they respond. Our Lord, speaking of himself as the true shepherd, declares, " the sheep hear his voice: and he calleth his own sheep by name, and leadeth them out."[6] And it is said of him in prophecy that " he shall feed his flock like a shepherd, he shall gather the lambs in his arms, and carry them in his bosom, *and* shall gently lead those that give suck."[7]

Of the various uses to which sheep were put, emphasis is laid in the Bible chiefly on their employment as offerings and for food and clothing. For the first object lambs of the first year were the most common; although sheep under three years old, and especially rams,

---

[1] 1 Kings 8 : 63.   [2] 2 Kings 3 : 4 (margin).   [3] Ex. 29 : 22; Lev. 7 : 3; 8 : 25; 9 : 19.   [4] Gen. 30 : 32; Cant. 4 : 2; Dan. 7 : 9.   [5] Num. 27 : 17; 2 Sam. 12 : 3; 24 : 17; 1 Kings 22 : 17; Isa. 53 : 7; Ezek. 34 : 5; Dan. 8 : 3; Matt. 9 : 36; Luke 15 : 4; 1 Pet. 2 : 25.   [6] John 10 : 3.   [7] Isa. 40 : 11.

were also selected.[1] In this connection some titles of our Lord as the great sacrifice will be recalled, he being styled "the Lamb of God" and "the Lamb slain from the foundation of the world."[2] The rich milk of sheep was a favorite article of diet.[3] Formerly too, it is likely, as at the present day, the trappings of horses, camels and asses, the saddle-bag and the water-bottle, were mostly made from the skins of sheep. Their horns were possibly used as vases for oil and other purposes.[4] Rams are not infrequently met with in the East having a number of horns, sometimes as many as eight. The representation in Daniel 7 : 7, accordingly, of a beast having ten horns, and in Revelation 5 : 6 of a lamb with seven horns, is by no means extraordinary. That the sheep-shearing was made a festival occasion has already been observed.[5] For a few days subsequent to their shearing the sheep were driven regularly into the water for cleansing, and possibly to harden them to the changes of the atmosphere.[6]

3. THE SHEPHERD.—The life of an eastern shepherd is by no means so easy or so uneventful as might be supposed. When Jacob reproached his father-in-law for unfair dealing with him, he said of his own service, "Thus I was; in the day the drought consumed me, and the frost by night; and my sleep fled from mine eyes."[7] David, also, makes record of some of his experiences at the time he kept his father's flocks. "When there came a lion, or a bear," he says, as though it was no uncommon occurrence, "and took a lamb out of the flock, I went out after him, and smote him, and delivered it out of his mouth."[8] Nor was the danger from wild beasts the only one to which the flock was exposed. It is highly suggestive, for example, of the state of society in the time of Saul that the outlawed David and his men should demand some recognition from the rich Nabal, because they had not interfered with his property, as others in like circumstances most probably would have done.[9] Faithfulness and success in such a calling could only be expected from one who had a personal concern in the well-being of the flock. "The good shepherd layeth down his life for the sheep. He that is a hireling and not a shepherd, whose own the sheep are not, beholdeth the wolf coming, and leaveth the sheep, and fleeth."[10] It is the custom now in the East for the owner of a flock, if he cannot care for it himself, to employ some one who will assume a pecuniary interest in

---

[1] Ex. 29 : 38; Lev. 9 : 3; 12 : 6; 22 : 27; Num. 28 : 9.   [2] John 1 : 29, 36; Rev. 13 : 8; 22 : 1, 3.   [3] Deut. 32 : 14; Isa. 7 : 21, 22.   [4] Josh. 6 : 4; 1 Sam. 16 : 1.   [5] Gen. 38 : 12; 1 Sam. 25 : 4; 2 Sam. 13 : 23.   [6] Cant. 4 : 2.   [7] Gen. 31 : 40.   [8] 1 Sam. 17 : 34, 35; cf. Amos 3 : 12.   [9] 1 Sam. 25 : 7.   [10] John 10 : 11, 12.

it, requiring from him only a certain yearly income. It was such a bargain that Laban made with Jacob.[1]

For sustenance the shepherd ordinarily depends on his flock and on what he can obtain from the country where he may happen to be.[2] Members of his family, however, occasionally visit him with provisions, as Joseph visited his brethren in Dothan.[3] The modern shepherd always carries a knife in his belt, and not infrequently a pistol. These weapons are in addition to a heavy cudgel, which seldom fails in a sheep-master's outfit. The so-called " crook " is a staff of a different kind, bent at one end into a semi-circle form for convenience in controlling the flock.[4] David, in his shepherd-life, carried a "scrip," that is, a kind of bag or wallet, and found use also for a sling.[5] Both these articles are still found among eastern shepherds. The former is commonly made of an entire skin of a sheep or lamb—the wool having been removed—and is carried by straps passing over the shoulders. Shepherds, moreover, ancient and modern, have been accustomed to while away lonely hours with the music of some simple instrument like the flute or flageolet.[6] This fact has given rise to the name " pastoral," which is applied to a certain kind of poetical composition, and to " pastorale," a peculiar style of music.

The ordinary duties of the shepherd consisted in leading out the flock to pasture, actually going before them, as is noted in the gospel; watching them while feeding, generally, it would seem, with the help of a dog; supplying them with water; restoring the straying ones, and bringing them all safely back to the fold at night.[7] To find out whether any were missing he made them pass under a rod as they entered the fold, indicating the presence of each one by an inclination of the hand. It is to this custom that reference is made in the prophecy of Ezekiel, where Jehovah tenderly says of Israel, "I will cause you to pass under the rod, and I will bring you into the bond of the covenant; and I will purge out from among you the rebels, and them that transgress against me."[8]

4. THE FOLD, ETC.—The fold varied in construction according to circumstances. Sometimes it was a simple inclosure, surrounded, for its better protection, by a wall of stone, which was itself surmounted by thorn bushes. At other times, probably, it was only a palisade of sticks interlaced with such bushes. The whole arrangement was naturally one of extreme simplicity, since the flock remained but a

[1] Gen. 31:39.   [2] Amos 7:14; cf. Luke 15:16.   [3] Gen. 37:13.   [4] Ps. 23:4; Micah 7:14; Zech. 11:7.   [5] 1 Sam. 17:40; cf. Matt. 10:10.   [6] Gen. 4:21; 1 Sam. 16:18; Job 21:12. [7] Gen. 29:7; Job 30:1; Ps. 23:2; Luke 15:4; John 10:4.   [8] Ezek. 20:37; cf. Lev. 27:32; Jer. 33:13.

little while in any one place. Before the door—now generally consisting of a few sticks laid across the entrance—watched the shepherd and his dog. Where there were several shepherds they took turns in watching.[1] Towers for observation and defence were also used by sheep-masters in the ancient times. Traces of the custom still survive in certain proper names occurring in the Old Testament, as the "tower of Eder," that is, tower of the flock. Places of this sort were built by the kings Uzziah and Jothan.[2]

Eastern Sheepfold.

5. The metaphorical use of the shepherd's calling is very common in the Bible. Princes, prophets and distinguished teachers are styled shepherds,[3] and, in some instances, Jehovah himself. He is described, for example, in one place as leading his people "like a flock, by the hand of Moses and Aaron."[4] It was a specially favorite image with our Lord. As already observed, he named himself the "good Shepherd;"[5] and after the resurrection, in his solemn charge to the restored Peter, he recurs to the same thought, bidding him feed his lambs, tend and feed his sheep.[6] So, too, it is said concerning the people of God in heaven, that "the Lamb which is in the midst of the throne shall be their shepherd, and shall guide them unto fountains of waters of life."[7]

6. GOATS.—The Bible everywhere makes a clear distinction between sheep and goats. The latter as well as the former were numerously reared in the East in ancient times. There are seven different words in the Hebrew Scriptures used to designate the goat. The he-goat and wild goat are especially distinguished in this respect, each name putting emphasis upon some peculiarity of the animal. Goats are generally pastured in different flocks, and have a separate fold, from the sheep; accordingly, their formal division from one another, when they become mixed, is no uncommon affair.[8] It is the young of goats that are most frequently mentioned in the biblical books as furnishing food for special entertainments.[9] A kid cooked with milk seems to have been looked upon as a special delicacy, since

[1] Luke 2 : 8 (margin).   [2] Gen. 35 : 21 ; 2 Chron. 26 : 10 ; 27 : 4 ; Micah 4 : 8.   [3] Eccles. 12 : 11 ; Isa. 44 : 28 ; Zech. 11 : 5.   [4] Ps. 77 : 20.   [5] John 10 : 11.   [6] John 21 : 15, 17.   [7] Rev. 7 : 17.   [8] Matt. 25 : 32.   [9] Gen. 27 : 9, 16 ; 38 : 17 ; Judg. 15 : 1 ; 1 Sam. 16 : 20 ; Luke 15 : 29.

the Mosaic laws contain three distinct prohibitions against the use of the milk of the dam for this purpose.[1]   The milk of the goat was more commonly used for food than that of any other animal; and its black hair was manufactured into a variety of articles, notably tent-cloth and the coarser kinds of garments.[2]

7. CATTLE.—Among domestic animals mentioned in the Scriptures, neat cattle were held in scarcely less esteem than sheep and goats. They have always been the chief assistants of man in the pursuits of agriculture.   It is significant as showing the high value that was put upon them everywhere that divine honors were paid in Egypt to Apis, their representative, and that it was with the greatest difficulty that the Israelites could be kept from imitating their more cultivated neighbors in this respect.[3]   Figures of the ox are found on the most ancient monuments, and it was probably among the earliest animals domesticated. Its image was also stamped on the most ancient coins. Before the invention of money, cattle were made the medium of exchange in commercial transactions.   In some parts of the world this is still the case, the daughter of a south African father being valued by him, for purposes of marriage, at so many head of cattle.

8. A principal Hebrew term for the ox and cow is one based on their ordinary employment, which was the breaking up of the soil preparatory to tillage.   There is a peculiar law in Deuteronomy forbidding the yoking together of these animals with the ass for such a purpose.[4]   It is in strict harmony, however, with other laws of the Pentateuch.[5]   The inequality of strength and contrariety of temper would not only stand in the way of the best work, but would entail an unnecessary hardship upon the animals themselves.   In addition to breaking up the land, cows and oxen were employed, as already intimated, to tread out the grain, to draw together in carts and wagons, carry burdens on their backs, and serve in a variety of other capacities.   Cows also supplied milk and butter, and, to a limited extent, their flesh, as well as that of oxen, was consumed as food.[6] As a rule, cattle are smaller in the East than with us; but there is reason to suppose that this was not so uniformly the case in early times, especially since sufficient causes exist for their deterioration.[7]

9. There is a species of buffalo now extensively employed in the East for the same purposes as the ox.   It is a more powerful, but a far less tractable, animal; and while resembling the American buf-

---

[1] Ex. 23: 19; 34: 26; Deut. 14: 21.   [2] Ex. 26: 7; 35: 26; 1 Sam. 19: 13, 16; Cant. 1: 5.   [3] Ex. 32: 8; 1 Kings 12: 28, 29.   [4] Deut. 22: 10.   [5] Ex. 23: 12; Deut. 22: 1, 4; 25: 4.   [6] Num. 7: 3; Deut. 32: 14; 1 Sam. 6: 7; 2 Sam. 6: 6; 1 Kings 1: 9; 4: 23; Isa. 7: 22; Hos. 10: 11; 1 Cor. 9: 9; 1 Tim. 5: 18.   [7] 1 Kings 4: 23; Ps. 22: 12; Prov. 14: 4; Ezek. 39: 18.

falo in general appearance, its habits are peculiarly its own. It is exceedingly fond, for example, of swampy places, and will lie contentedly for hours in the water and mud. The animal was introduced into western Asia from India considerably after the Christian era, and the only reason for mentioning it here is to distinguish it from the wild ox of the Bible, improperly represented as a "unicorn" in the Authorized Version. The wild ox was of a very different temperament from the modern buffalo of the East. "Will the wild-ox be content to serve thee? Or will he abide by thy crib? Canst thou bind the wild-ox with his band in the furrow? Or will he harrow the valleys after thee?"[1]

10. THE HORSE.—Other domestic animals of the Bible which should have brief notice are the horse, the camel, the mule and the ass. The dog receives little attention, being a despised animal and less thoroughly domesticated than with us.[2] Still, as we have seen, it was made useful by the shepherd, and in the later times, as we learn from the case of Tobias, was sometimes looked upon as a companion.[3] Hens are not mentioned at all in the Old Testament, although it can scarcely be doubted that, at all periods, they were common with the Hebrews, as we know they were with their neighbors the Egyptians.[4] Moreover, from a single passage only are we able to infer directly that bees were domesticated in Palestine, notwithstanding it was a land "flowing with milk and honey."[5] The most of the honey was probably wild.

11. The centre from which horses seem to have been distributed throughout the East was the table-lands of central Asia. They still run wild there in great numbers. Among the possessions which Abraham brought back from Egypt horses are not named, and it is likely that they were not known there at that time.[6] The first indication of them on the monuments appears during the eighteenth dynasty, that is, about the time of Jacob's pilgrimage thither. Until the period of David they were never used in war by the Israelites. Afterwards the custom became common, Solomon importing them for himself and neighboring kings from Egypt.[7] A couple of centuries later we have evidence of their employment, to a limited extent, in agriculture.[8] No class among the Hebrews seems to have taken kindly to horseback riding for its own sake. The food of horses, besides grass, was cut straw, barley, and probably meal made

[1] Job 39 : 9, 10; cf. Num. 23 : 22; 24 : 8; Ps. 22 : 21; Isa. 34 : 7.   [2] Ex. 22 : 31; Deut. 23 : 18; 1 Kings 14 : 11; 16 : 4; 21 : 19; 2 Kings 9 : 36.   [3] Tobit 5 : 16; 11 : 4; cf. Matt. 15 : 27.   [4] Job 6 : 6; Matt. 23 : 37; 26 : 34, Mark 14 : 30.   [5] Isa. 7 : 18.   [6] Gen. 12 : 16.   [7] 1 Kings 10 : 29.   [8] Isa. 28 : 23.

from beans and the stones of dates.[1] They were not shod, nor generally provided with saddles when ridden.

We find references in the Bible to the whip, bridle and bit, and
to some peculiar trappings worn by chariot horses.[2] In Assyria it
was customary for women in the earliest times to ride astride the
animal, as they now do in the Orient as well as in some other parts
of the world. But this practice seems not to have been universal,
since Etruscan vases dating back to a period before the foundation
of Rome represent them as riding in the manner common with us.
The metaphorical use of the peculiarities of the horse in the Bible
is relatively limited.[3] In heathen religions, especially the Persian,
horses of a white color were dedicated to the sun.[4] This fact may
have been of influence, as some suppose, in the representation which
we find in the Revelation where Christ is made to ride on a horse
of this color, as are also the "armies which are in heaven" that
follow him.[5] But it is more likely that the circumstance which lies
at the basis of both these facts is that white is a natural symbol of
light and purity. That the prophet Zechariah uses symbolically the
colors of the horses of which he speaks is extremely doubtful.[6]

12. THE CAMEL.—The variety of camel found in Palestine and
Syria now, as well as in the times of the Bible, is that having one
hump on its back—the dromedary or Arabian camel, so called in
distinction from the Bactrian, which has two humps and belongs to
another region of the earth. Though the camel is sometimes found
in a wild state in the interior of Asia, it is chiefly known in history
as the servant of man. It is docile, can be easily led by a halter
and be made to lie down to receive its burden; but of all the
domesticated animals it perhaps submits the least graciously of any
to the services imposed upon it. On an emergency and for short
stages it will carry a load of a thousand pounds or more, and without hardship will make a continuous journey of thirty miles a day.
Although the camel is mentioned as among the possessions of the
relatively-opulent patriarchs,[7] with this exception we do not find it
in any considerable numbers elsewhere among the Hebrews previous to the exile save in the case of David;[8] and for his camels
David provided an Ishmaelite keeper. The Hebrews, in fact, in
their mountainous country had comparatively little use for such
an animal as the camel, especially as long as they devoted them-

[1] 1 Kings 4:28. [2] 2 Kings 19:28; Ps. 32:9; Prov. 26:3; Isa. 30:28; Zech. 10:3; 14:20;
James 3:3. [3] Isa. 63:13; Amos 6:12; Wisd. 19:9. [4] 2 Kings 23:11. [5] Rev. 6:2, 4,
5, 8; 10:11, 14. [6] Zech. 1:8; 6:2, 3. [7] Gen. 12:16; 24:10; 30:43; 31:17, 34; 32:7; Job
1:3; 42:12. [8] 1 Chron. 27:30.

selves chiefly to the pursuits of agriculture. We accordingly find it mentioned throughout the Old Testament mostly in connection with neighboring peoples, particularly those given to trade.[1]

13. The camel was used both for riding and as a pack animal. That it was ever har-nessed into a chariot is improbable. The only passage of the English Bible favor-ing such a supposition has been properly changed by the revis-ers, so that we read, instead of "chariot of camels," "troop of camels."[2] Camel's milk is considered in the East very nutri-tious; although there is no positive evidence that the Israelites were accustomed to drink it.[3] Its flesh was

Eastern Bactrian Camel.

forbidden to them.[4] The skin was used in the manufacture of sandals, water-bottles and other similar articles. Of its hair, which regularly falls out in the spring, a rough kind of cloth was manufactured, suit-able for the covering of tents and the cheapest clothing.[5] The pro-cess of making a finer material from it, however, was not unknown to the ancients. The saddle used on the camel for riding was much the same as that employed for loading it. It generally consisted of a wooden frame, under and within which cushions were placed. The frame was sometimes covered over in the form of a palanquin. It is not unusual to see now, as in ancient times, a chain with various pendants suspended from the neck of the camel when in service.[6]

The animal known as *becer*, and mentioned in two passages of the Bible, seems to have been only a younger, and hence a stronger and fleeter, kind of camel.[7] Respecting the *kirkaroth* of Isaiah 66 : 20, rendered in the Revised Version "swift beasts" (marg.,

---

[1] Gen. 37 : 25; 1 Sam. 15 : 3; 27 : 9; 30 : 17; 1 Kings 10 : 2; 2 Kings 8 : 9; Isa. 60 : 6; Jer. 49 : 29, 32. [2] Isa. 21 : 7. [3] Gen. 32 : 15. [4] Lev. 11 : 4. [5] Matt. 3 : 4. [6] Judg. 8 : 26. [7] Isa. 60 : 6; Jer. 2 : 23.

dromedaries), there is a difference of opinion, some preferring the rendering "paniers" or "baskets," that is, such as were borne on the backs of camels. But modern usage among the Bedouins of the desert rather justifies the other rendering, the root of the word referring to the swinging gait of the animal when in rapid motion. The expressions used by our Lord respecting the camel were probably proverbial for anything conceived to be naturally impossible.[1]

14. THE MULE.—The mule is not mentioned in the Bible previous to the time of the kings. One of the more radical changes made in the recent revision of the Old Testament is that found in Genesis 36 : 24, where the word "mules" has been altered to "hot springs." A law of Leviticus prohibited the rearing of animals which were the product of the union of two diverse species, and there is no evidence that the Israelites ever transgressed it.[2] After the establishment of the kingdom, however, mules, like horses, were somewhat numerous. David had a special one on which he was accustomed to ride.[3] Absalom was endeavoring to escape on one of these animals when he lost his life.[4] It is stated that mules were among the things rendered in yearly tribute to Solomon by the neighboring peoples.[5] They were used as pack animals, but far less generally than for riding.[6] On their return from the Babylonian captivity the Israelites brought back two hundred and forty-five mules, as against seven hundred and thirty-six horses and six thousand seven hundred and twenty asses.[7] At the present time in the East this animal has a higher pecuniary value than the horse, and largely outnumbers it, as well as the ass, in the uses of commerce. This fact might be inferred from the word "muleteer," which is applied to the man who has charge of the animals of all sorts making up a caravan.

15. THE ASS.—One of the best-known and most useful animals of the Bible was the ass. It was very early domesticated, although at all periods, even down to the present, it has existed in a wild state. The monuments of Assyria represent the hunting of this animal as one of the favorite sports of royalty. In speed and endurance no horse could approach it. Its flesh, though forbidden to the Hebrews, was much prized as food.[8] The straits to which the inhabitants of Samaria were once reduced during a siege may be inferred from the fact that an ass's head sold for eighty shekels.[9]

---

[1] Matt. 19 : 24 ; 23 : 24.   [2] Lev. 19 : 19.   [3] 1 Kings 1 : 33, 38, 44.   [4] 2 Sam. 18 : 9.   [5] 1 Kings 10 : 25 ; 2 Chron. 9 : 24.   [6] 2 Kings 5 : 17.   [7] Ezra 2 : 66 ; Neh. 7 : 68.   [8] Lev. 11 : 1-8 ; Deut. 14 : 3-8.   [9] 2 Kings 6 : 25.

Throughout the history of the covenant people the ass, among their domestic animals, always largely outnumbered the horse and the mule. It is mentioned several times in the history of the patriarchs, and the remarkable journey of the prophet Balaam on the back of one occurred before the Israelites settled in Palestine.[1] In the book of Job, driving away the ass of the fatherless is noted as an act of excessive oppression, proving both their great number and their relatively small value at that period.[2] David's asses were so numerous that he had a special keeper for them;[3] and in the time of our Lord the ox and ass were the most familiar and the most widely-inclusive description of a man's possessions in domestic animals.[4]

Eastern Wild Ass. (*After J. G. Wood.*)

The ass of eastern countries has generally a brighter color and more graceful figure than that of the Occident. Previous to the tenth century B.C. it was the animal most used by the Hebrews for riding and as a pack animal. At about that time the mule came largely into use for the former purpose, especially on the part of the rich. From the time of Solomon the horse was the animal chiefly ridden, particularly in battle, and the ass came to be looked upon, in distinction from it, as the animal for periods and scenes of peace. This serves to account for the language of the prophet concerning the Messiah: "Rejoice greatly, O daughter of Zion; shout, O daughter of Jerusalem: behold, thy king cometh unto thee: he is just, and having salvation; lowly, and riding upon an ass, even upon a colt the foal of an ass."[5] The female, on account of its softer step, was especially prized for riding, as well as for its nutritious

[1] Gen. 12:16; 30:43; Num. 22. [2] Job 24:3; cf. 1 Sam. 12:3. [3] 1 Chron. 27:30. [4] Luke 13:15; 14:5. [5] Zech. 9:9; John 12:15.

milk. Women as well as men were accustomed to ride the ass. A driver was sometimes found necessary on such occasions. A journey made by Moses in this way, his wife and sons being mounted on the animal while he walked at its side, seems to be the only historical foundation for the design of the familiar picture of the flight of Joseph and Mary into Egypt with the child Jesus.[1]

16. The saddle, several times spoken of in connection with the ass, was probably no more than a simple covering of skin or cloth, for convenience in riding or for the protection of the animal.[2] The ass was also used as a draught animal to some extent. In the earliest times it was attached to the plough; in those of the New Testament it was made to work in the larger mills for grinding grain.[3] The docility and usefulness of the ass appear to have protected it in former times from the opprobrium so widely attaching to it in our own day. The name "Hamor," that is, ass, was that of a titled family of Shechem previous to Jacob's going thither.[4] And Homer seeks to do honor to Ajax by comparing him with the animal which is now so much the object of ridicule.[5]

17. AGRICULTURE IN GENERAL.—As already noted, the Bible represents agriculture as one of the earliest pursuits of man.[6] The patriarchs, however, seem to have engaged in it only occasionally; that is, when circumstances required it. It is said, for example, of Isaac that during the prevalence of a famine in Palestine he cultivated land in the vicinity of Gerar, which produced a hundredfold.[7] Joseph's dream of the sheaves suggests an acquaintance on the part of his family likewise with the business of sowing and reaping.[8] During the sojourn in Egypt the Hebrews doubtless became practically familiar with the highly-developed processes of agriculture there known. Moses makes an interesting allusion in Deuteronomy to a method of gardening which his own countrymen carried on there.[9] On settling in Canaan the major part of the people must have become agriculturists. The laws of the Pentateuch certainly recognize land as the principal possession of the Hebrews, and its cultivation as their chief business.

According to these laws every family was to have its own piece of ground. It could not be alienated, except for limited periods. Such family estates were carefully surveyed; and it was regarded as one of the most flagrant of crimes to remove a neighbor's landmark.[10]

[1] Ex. 4:20; Matt. 2:13-15.   [2] Gen. 22:3; Num. 22:21; 1 Kings 13:13; 2 Kings 4:24.   [3] Deut. 22:10; Isa. 30:24; 32:20; Matt. 18:6 (margin); Luke 17:2.   [4] Gen. 33:19; cf. 49:14.   [5] Il. 11:557.   [6] Gen. 3:17; 4:2; 5:29; 9:20.   [7] Gen. 26:12.   [8] Gen. 37:7.   [9] Deut. 11:10.   [10] Deut. 19:14; 27:17; Job 24:2; Prov. 22:28; 23:10; Hos. 5:10.

Estates were divided into so many yokes ("acres"), that is, portions such as a yoke of oxen could plough in a single day.[1] The value put upon land was according to its yield in grain.[2] Labor in the fields was not thought beneath the dignity of any, although day-laborers as a class, and the calling of the overseer, were not unknown.[3] Some of the kings gave particular encouragement to agriculture.[4] Irrigation was practiced in Palestine, though not carried to the same extent as in Egypt. The chief dependence for moisture was on the dew and the drenching rains of the rainy season. There are not less than eight synonyms for rain in the Hebrew language. The climate of Palestine has undoubtedly changed somewhat in more modern times, and many of the earlier methods of cultivating the soil, like terracing the hills, have been abandoned. It is accordingly unsafe to draw too confident conclusions concerning its lack of fertility from what it now produces. The ground was fertilized by the ashes of burnt straw and stubble, the chaff left after threshing and the direct application of dung.[5]

18. THE SABBATIC YEAR.—A special circumstance that contributed to heighten the natural fertility of the soil was the custom enjoined on the Israelites of letting it lie fallow every seventh year. Not only was the seventh day and the seventh month to be observed, but also the seventh or so-called "sabbatic" year. This law is found in three different books of the Pentateuch.[6] Undoubtedly its different forms were meant to be mutually supplementary. That of Exodus is incomplete, and would be scarcely intelligible without that of Leviticus. To say, however, with some, that the law in Exodus fails to recognize any one period of rest for land and people at once, is to overlook the context. The law of the Sabbath as obligatory on all is made the norm of the new regulation. And while rest on the seventh year is not positively enjoined, it is clearly meant to be inferred from the command to sow the fields six years. The form in Deuteronomy, on the other hand, bears to that of Leviticus the relation of a by-law, providing for a special case arising from carrying out the statute.

The law as a whole then required that on each seventh year the land should enjoy a sabbath. It was not to be tilled. What grew spontaneously was to be not alone for the owner, but, on equal terms, for the poor, for strangers and for cattle; that is, the rights of the

[1] 1 Sam. 14:14.   [2] Lev. 27:16.   [3] Lev. 19:13; Ruth 2:5; 1 Sam. 11:5; 1 Kings 19:19; Matt. 20:1; 1 Cor. 3:9.   [4] 1 Chron. 27:26; 2 Chron. 26:10.   [5] Ex. 15:7; 2 Kings 9:37; Ps. 83:10; Isa. 5:24; Jer. 8:2; 9:22; 16:4.   [6] Ex. 23:10-12; Lev. 25:1-7; Deut. 15:1-11.

owner were for the time kept in abeyance. Such a law has been pronounced quite impracticable by some critics. But aside from the economic advantage of a rest of this kind for the land, there was nothing to hinder the owner from laying aside from previous crops a sufficiency to maintain him and his family during the "sabbatic" year. The code indeed makes express provision for his doing so.[1]

To what extent this law was observed in post-Mosaic times it is not possible with certainty to say. That it was pretty generally neglected for a long period is extremely probable. This might be inferred from a passage in the book of Chronicles, where the exile in Babylon is represented as a punishment for the failure to observe it.[2] A reference to the form of the law in Deuteronomy, and possibly more, occurs in Nehemiah 10 : 31 ; and the fact that it was

Egyptian Wheat.

customary to reckon years in cycles of seven is established by Daniel 9 : 24. After the close of the canon of the Old Testament, we learn from the first book of Maccabees that the sabbatic year was kept ;[3] and according to Josephus, Julius Cæsar took account of it in levying tribute on the Jews.[4] A strong incidental support to the genuineness of the law as a product of the Mosaic period is found in the Deuteronomic statute of the tithe for the third year. It seems to presuppose the institution of the sabbatic year. If it did not, there would be needful a twofold system of indicating the periodic recurrence of the year of release and that of the tithe.[5] On the supposition, however, of the existence of this institution, the two nicely harmonize in the cycle of seven years, the special tithe falling on the third and sixth, while there was none on the seventh, year.[6]

19. GRAINS OF PALESTINE.—The grains which have been the most widely cultivated at all times in Palestine are wheat and barley. In connection with these spelt and millet, or the so-called "German wheat," are noticed in a few passages.[7] Indian corn, rye and oats are not spoken of in the Hebrew Bible. Fitches and cummin, the

[1] Lev. 25 : 20–22.   [2] 2 Chron. 36 : 20, 21.   [3] 1 Macc. 6 : 20, 49, 53.   [4] Josephus, Antiq. 14, 10 : 6.
[5] Deut. 14 : 28, 29.   [6] Deut. 15 : 1–11.   [7] Ex. 9 : 32 ; Isa. 28 : 25 ; Ezek. 4 : 9.

former being simply a variety of the latter, are mentioned together in Isaiah, and the process described by which the grain was separated from its husk.[1] Of plants that produced pods the most common in the early times were beans and lentils. The products of the land which Jacob sent down to Egypt as a present to its viceroy are not, it is likely, a fair representation of their variety. They were necessarily limited by the dearth which had prevailed as well as by the requirements of such a journey.[2]

20. THE SEASONS.—The dependence of the husbandman on the natural order of the seasons and the productive forces of nature ordained by God is well set forth by the prophet Isaiah.[3] The "early rain" usually began to fall in the latter part of Tishri (September–October), or soon after the close of the fruit-harvest. The "latter rain" was due just before the beginning of the barley-harvest, in Nisan (March–April). The six months intervening between Tishri and Nisan were mostly devoted to the cultivation of the soil; those from Nisan to Tishri to the gathering of the crops. The expressions "early rain" and "latter rain," although so frequent in the Scriptures, should not be understood as necessarily meaning that there were only two periods when rain fell. There is reason to suppose, on the contrary, that formerly, as now, there was often little distinction between them, the rainy season being, for the most part, unbroken, except that, perhaps, a larger amount of rain fell near its beginning and near its end.

21. THE PLOUGH.—From what we learn of the plough of the ancient Hebrews we judge that it had the general form of the modern plough, but was of rude construction. The share was of iron and could be removed for sharpening.[4] The frame was of wood and furnished with a handle by means of which the plough was guided.[5] Judging from the modern Syrian plough, there were also a pole and cross-bar for attaching the animals that drew it. It has been supposed from the alleged circumstance that different names are given it in the Hebrew that, even at an early period, there was more than one style of plough in use. But it is uncertain whether by the Hebrew word so rendered in a few closely-related passages the plough

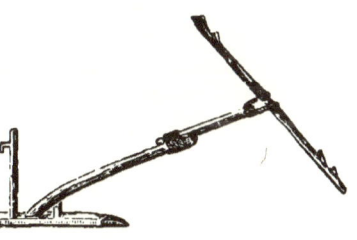

Arab Plough.

is meant or some other agricultural tool.[1]   The most probable conclusion is that, the frame of the plough remaining much the same,
there were different styles of the share to which different names were
applied; or that the alternative word referred to a knife which was
attached to the plough in front of the share.   The plough was
ordinarily drawn by two oxen, cows or asses; never, among the

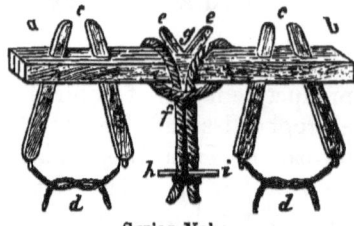

Syrian Yoke.

a, b, timber of the yoke; *c, d*, the bows; *e, e*, pegs
between which, at *g*, the end of the shaft comes, the
shaft itself having been run through the rope between
f and the cross-piece of wood *h i.*

Hebrews, by one of the last-named
animals and one of the former.[2]
They were connected with the plough
by means of a yoke.   The Egyptian
monuments represent this as fastened to the head of the animal near
the horns; but it is not the common
method in modern Syria.   The outfit of the ploughman included a
goad.   It consisted of a long heavy
stick made sharp at one end or

armed with an iron point.   How formidable a weapon it could be in
a strong hand we learn from the incident of Shamgar, recorded in
the book of the Judges, who slew six hundred Philistines with one
of them.[3]

22. PREPARATION OF THE SOIL.—Unbroken land, having first
been cleared of stones and bushes, was ploughed more than once.[4]
According to Isaiah 37 : 30, it was not until the third year after the
withdrawal of the Assyrians from Palestine that the Israelites were
able to sow and reap.   It would appear that sometimes the sowing
preceded the ploughing, and
that the latter might begin
before the opening of the
rainy season; but ordinarily
the sowing immediately succeeded the early rain.[5]   Where
the ground was moist the
seed was sometimes covered
by means of the trampling of
cattle.[6] The use of the harrow

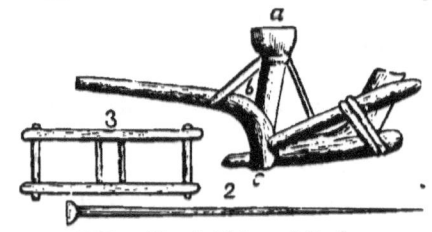

Eastern Plough, Yoke and Goad.

a, Bowl for the seed; *b, c*, pipe for dropping seed, as a drill.
2, Goad. *3*, Square yoke.

—which was probably a strong board armed in some way for the purpose, or a cluster of thorn bushes—is established by several passages.[7]

[1] Isa. 2:4; Joel 3:10; Micah 4:3.   [2] Deut. 22:10; 1 Sam. 11:7; 1 Kings 19:19; Job 1:
14; Amos 6:12.   [3] Judg. 3:31; see Eccles. 12:11; Acts 9:5 (Authorized Version).   [4] Isa.
5:2; 32:20; Jer. 4:3; Hos. 10:12.   [5] Matt. 13:4.   [6] Isa. 32:20.   [7] Job 39:10; Isa. 28:
24; Hos. 10:11.

From the Egyptian monuments we learn that it was the custom there for a person to follow the ploughman and knock the clods and furrows to pieces by means of a heavy wooden instrument. The seed was generally sown broadcast with the hand. A more careful sowing in drills was practiced by those seeking a larger crop.[1] There was a regular order observed in the sowing, beginning with the more hardy products and ending with barley and wheat.

23. Owing to a prohibition of the Pentateuch against sowing the same field with two kinds of seeds under the penalty of the confiscation of the products to the sanctuary, the Hebrews were scrupulous to mark exactly the borders of their fields.[2] The rabbins of a later day invented the most painful regulations for avoiding the juxtaposition of different kinds of products in the field. On their approaching ripeness the field fruits were carefully watched, although it was the privilege of any chance comer to help himself to what he required to supply immediate needs.[3]

The beginning of the harvest was signalized by bringing a sheaf of new grain—Josephus informs us that it was barley[4]—into the sanctuary and waving it before the Lord.[5] The Scriptures intimate that this ceremony took place on the day following the passover Sabbath—that is, the sixteenth of Nisan. It was intended as an acknowledgment that the bounty of the earth was dependent on the divine favor. Seven weeks from this date, at the feast of pentecost, a similar ceremony took place, two loaves of bread, made of the new flour, being waved before the Lord as the passover sheaf had been.[6] Between these two periods the grain harvest continued, the time required being lengthened by the fact that the threshing of the grain was considered a part of its harvesting.

24. HARVESTING.—Grain in Palestine was generally cut with the sickle, as was also the case in Egypt.[7] Pulling it up by the roots was a rarer practice, the preference being to leave much of the stalk still standing. The prophet Isaiah, describing the judgments which should fall on Israel, says: "And it shall be as when the harvestman gathereth the standing corn, and his arm reapeth the ears; yea, it shall be as when one gleaneth ears in the valley of Rephaim."[8] After gathering as much as could be conveniently carried, the reaper left the grain in little piles behind him on the field. This was afterwards gathered up and bound into sheaves and the sheaves stacked

---

[1] Isa. 28 : 25.   [2] Lev. 19 : 19; Deut. 22 : 9.   [3] Deut. 23 : 25; Matt. 12 : 1.   [4] Josephus, *Antiq.* 3, 10 : 5; Ruth 2 : 23; 2 Sam. 21 : 9.   [5] Lev. 23 : 5, 6, 10-12.   [6] Lev. 23 : 15, 17; Num. 28 : 26.   [7] Deut. 16 : 9; Jer. 50 : 16; Joel 3 : 13.   [8] Isa. 17 : 5; cf. Ps. 129 : 7.

together.[1] In a number of passages of Scripture we are introduced
to the busy scenes of the harvest-field, and even shown how the har-
vesters working under a burning eastern sky were accustomed to
refresh themselves. The joy of harvest is proverbial in the Bible;
and the benign features of the Mosaic laws are conspicuous in the
reiterated injunction that at such times the needy were not to be forgotten.[2] Vineyards and olive-yards were included in the benevolent
intent of the statute. Fields and fruit-orchards were not to be
gleaned by their owners, or the corners of the former even reaped.
This was to be the portion of the poor and the stranger, who also
were thus to know the harvest joy. It will be recalled how liberally
this ancient law was interpreted by her generous kinsman in favor
of Ruth the Moabitess.[3] And it was no unmeaning compliment that
Gideon paid to one of the tribes of Israel when he said, " Is not the
gleaning of the grapes of Ephraim better than the vintage of Abi-
ezer ?"[4]

25. THRESHING.—The threshing of the straw, following close upon
the harvest, was carried on in the same field or in one adjacent, and

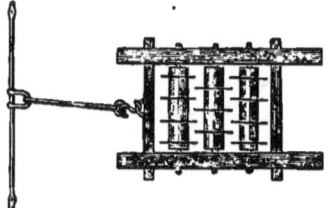

Eastern Threshing Instrument
(upper view).

Eastern Threshing Instrument
(side view).

generally under the open sky. This was possible on account of the
dry climate of Palestine at this season of the year.[5] An elevated
spot was selected, that the wind might carry away the dust and lighter
chaff. Sometimes, at least, the grain was borne to the threshing-
floor in carts.[6] The place itself was simply a spot of ground made
hard by beating or treading it. In area it was from fifty to a hundred feet in diameter. Often the same floor served the purpose for
a long time, until, like that of Atad and that of Araunah, it became
well known.[7] The heavier grain was sometimes beaten out with
sticks, and in the case of fitches and cummin this was the ordinary
process.[8] The method early adopted in threshing was to drive cat-

[1] Gen. 37:7; Jer. 9:22.   [2] Lev. 19:10; 23:22; Deut. 24:19-22; Ps. 4:7; 126:5; Isa. 9:3.
[3] Ruth 2:9, 15, 16.   [4] Judg. 8:2.   [5] 1 Sam. 12:16, 17.   [6] Amos 2:13.   [7] Gen. 50:10;
2 Sam. 24:16.   [8] Isa. 28:27.

tle over the straw, several being yoked together abreast. This was also customary in Egypt.[1] Later a threshing-sledge was made use of. It consisted of a frame with two or three revolving cylinders fitted into it. Each cylinder was armed with iron projections in the form of wheels, so arranged with respect to each other that the whole space under the machine would be covered. It was drawn by oxen or horses, and an elevated seat for the driver was placed in front of it.[2] A threshing-machine of a still ruder sort was sometimes found. Two or three planks, bent upward in front, were fastened side by side in a form corresponding to the modern stone-sledge. In the under side of the planks holes were bored and filled with sharp sticks and stones, by means of which the grain was forced out and the straw cut in pieces.[3] It was inevitable that in such processes the grain would be more or less injured. Threshing-machines seem also to have been sometimes used in those cruel days for the purpose of torturing enemies.[4]

26. WINNOWING.—The process of winnowing followed immediately upon that of threshing. It was one that required both strength and skill. The instruments used for winnowing and spoken of in the Bible as the "shovel" and the "fan" are not clearly distinguished from one another.[5] It seems likely, however, that the former was a kind of pitchfork with several tines, by means of which the straw was flung into the air;

Eastern Winnowing-fans.

the latter, a wooden shovel with a long handle. The winnowing was commonly done in the evening, when there was likely to be sufficient wind.[6] The wind might be too strong, so as to carry away the grain as well as the chaff.[7] Following the winnowing came the sifting, by which the grain was still further separated from dust and dirt.[8] It

[1] Hosea 10:11; Micah 4:12.   [2] Prov. 20:26; Isa. 28:27.   [3] 2 Sam. 24:22; 1 Chron. 21: 23; Isa. 41:15.   [4] 2 Kings 13:7; Isa. 25:10; Amos 1:3.   [5] Isa. 30:24.   [6] Ruth 3:2. [7] Jer. 4:11; 51:1, 2.   [8] Amos 9:9; Matt. 3:12.

was customary for some one to sleep near the grain at night, during the period of harvest, to protect it from marauders until it was safely stored in the granaries.[1] Both in ancient and modern times excavations in the earth, including dry cisterns, have been favorite places for the storage of grain. The chaff and straw remaining after threshing and winnowing, as already remarked, were burnt for the enrichment of the soil.[2]

27. GRAPES.—The gathering of the later fruits closed the harvests of the year. By far the most important of them were the grape and the olive. A vineyard in the East is generally surrounded with a ditch a few feet wide, the earth from which is thrown up on its inner side. Into this pile of earth posts are driven, and the entire space surrounded with a close fence of branches and twigs, or, if these are wanting, with walls of stone or dried mud. This is to protect the fruit from foxes, jackals and other marauding animals.[3] The tower of the vineyard has already been described. The soil is spaded over rather than ploughed, and for this purpose companies of workmen are hired from the nearest market-place.[4] Trellises are not commonly used for vines; accordingly they are kept closely pruned.[5] Grapes which are to be converted into raisins are cured by a very simple process. The clusters are dipped in a strong lye and then allowed to dry in the sun. They are afterwards picked from their stems and packed away in bags, or, perhaps quite as frequently, they are left on the stem. Raisins form an important article of diet with eastern peoples.[6]

28. If wine or syrup is to be made, the grapes are carried directly from the vineyard to the wine-press, either that of the owner of the vineyard or of the professional wine-maker. The wine-press is an elevated tank of brick or wood, with a hole on one side near the bottom, from which the juice escapes into the vat. The tank being filled with grapes, men mount to its top by a ladder and, holding on to cords fastened to the roof or ceiling, tread out the grapes with their naked feet.[7] The monuments showing that this form of wine-press was common in ancient Egypt, it is fair to suppose that it was the one in general use among the Hebrews. The gathering of the vintage, in which all ages and classes engaged, was a time of great joyousness.[8] Moslems, to whom wine is forbidden, when they do not dry their grapes for raisins, or eat them while fresh, boil down their

[1] Ruth 3:7.   [2] Ps. 1:4; 35:5; Matt. 3:12.   [3] Ps. 80:8-13; Cant. 2:15; Isa. 5:4-6; Matt. 21:33.   [4] Matt. 20:1-5.   [5] Ezek. 15:2-4; John 15:2-6.   [6] 1 Sam. 25:18; 30:12; 2 Sam. 16:1; 1 Chron. 12:40.   [7] Isa. 63:2, 3.   [8] Isa. 16:10.

juice to the consistency of a syrup, known as *dibs*, or, mixing it with fine flour, make sun-dried cakes of it. When wine is made, the grape juice is poured into jars and allowed to ferment, or enclosed in bottles of skins. Such bottles are made from the whole skins of animals, generally the goat. After the animal is killed and its feet and head removed, in order to preserve the skin as complete as possible the rest of the body is drawn out entire; hence the unique form of these bottles, which is well known. Care is taken to put wine that is to be fermented into new skins, or such as are able to withstand the pressure required of them.[1] Vineyards are frequently rented to persons who pay their rent in kind, the amount being generally one-half the yield.[2]

Egyptian Wine-press (*Wilkinson*).

29. THE OLIVE. — The olive grows wild in western Asia; but when cultivated it is grafted. From Romans 11 : 17–24 it is not to be inferred that the wild olive is generally grafted upon the cultivated stock, the apostle himself showing that this was reversing the natural process. Olive trees are planted as close together as they can conveniently stand, and the soil about them is kept loose. The olive is a long-lived tree, and sometimes an orchard of olives passes from one hand to another while the land remains with the same owner, or *vice versa*. It is noticeable that when Abram bought the field of Ephron, "the cave which was therein, and all the trees that were in the field, that were in all the border thereof round about, were made sure" to him.[3] The olive reaches about the height of the apple tree, and when in its prime is a beautiful specimen of vegetation.[4] Its blossoms are white and easily scattered by the wind.[5] The fruit is well known in our markets. It is gathered not earlier than November. The finer portion is reserved for pickling; oil is made from the rest.

30. The olive-press is generally constructed of a platform of masonry, on which a large circular stone, hollowed out in the form of a pan, is placed. The olives to be ground are put in this recep-

¹ Matt. 9 : 17.   ² Matt. 21 : 33, 34, 41.   ³ Gen. 23 : 17.   ⁴ Ps. 128 : 3 ; Jer. 11 : 16 ; Hos. 14 : 6.
⁵ Job 15 : 33.

tacle. They are crushed by means of another stone of the shape and
size of a large grindstone, set upright and moved about by means of
a pole extending through its centre. The oil flows out through a
hole in the side of the vat. The pulp, inclosed in bags or baskets,

is afterwards subjected to still further
pressure by the feet or otherwise, until
all the oil has been removed. There
is every reason to suppose that the
ancient process was similar to the
modern.[1] The oil is kept either in
earthen jars or in bottles of skin.

31. The cultivation of the apple,
fig, pomegranate, mulberry and various species of nuts has already been
referred to, and needs not to be more
particularly described. The lotus is

Syrian Olive-mill.

twice mentioned in the Bible.[2] Orig-
inally the grape and the olive alone paid the tithe, and came under
the law of the first fruits.[3] The Mosaic laws, however, contain an
injunction concerning all trees bearing fruit which deserves notice.
Such fruit was regarded as unclean for three years after the tree
began to bear. That of the fourth year was consecrated to Jehovah;
and not until the fifth year could it be freely used by the owner as his
own.[4] In the code of Deuteronomy the Israelites are prohibited from
felling fruit-bearing trees in the case of the siege of a hostile city.[5]

32. GARDENING.—Gardening also, using the word in its ordinary
sense, was a form of agriculture well known to the Hebrews.[6] But
in many cases the term "garden," when used in the Scriptures, refers
not to a place where vegetables were raised for the support of life,
but to one planted with flowers, shrubs and ornamental as well as
fruit-bearing trees, intended to minister especially to the enjoyment
of life. They were not often found in connection with private houses,
unless they were those of the rich and persons in high station.[7] Such
gardens in the Occident are called "parks." The "garden of Eden,"
in which our first parents were put, seems to have been principally
a garden of this kind; and doubtless the memorable spot known
as the "garden of Gethsemane" was originally such, although now
marked only by a few gnarled, straggling olive trees. These places

[1] Deut. 32:13; 33:24; Job 29:6; Ezek. 32:14.   [2] Job 40:21,22.   [3] Lev. 27:30; Deut.
14:23; Neh. 13:5, 12.   [4] Lev. 19:23-25; cf. Ex. 22:30; Deut. 20:6.   [5] Deut. 20:19.   [6] Deut.
11:10; 1 Kings 21:2; Isa. 1:8; Jer. 29:5; Amos 4:9; 9:14; Epist. of Jer. v. 70; Luke 13:19.
[7] 2 Kings 25:4; Eccles. 2:5; Neh. 3:15; Esther 1:5; Susan. v. 4.

were well fitted for quiet meditation and prayer, and for the burial of those beloved.[1] Previous to the exile they were the favorite resort of idolaters too, who sought their shade and retirement for the celebration of forbidden rites.[2]

33. METAPHORS FROM AGRICULTURAL LIFE.—An extraordinary number and variety of illustrations from agricultural life, taken, in fact, from almost every phase of it, are found in biblical writers. Among those of the Old Testament none, perhaps, is more comprehensive or fitting than that of the prophet Isaiah, where he seeks to impress the fact that as surely as the ploughman is not content simply to plough, so Jehovah will not be satisfied with the beginnings of spiritual husbandry in connection with Israel.[3] Our Lord himself found no more fruitful field than this for parable and simile with which to enliven and carry home divine truths to the hearts of men. Among many other metaphors he introduced that of ploughing; of sowing; of the growing grain; of the tares among the wheat; of the fruitful and the barren tree; of the mustard seed; of the plant of his Father's planting; of the laborers in the vineyard, under a burning sun; of unfaithful tenants and stewards; and, most suggestive and moving of all in its application, of the vine and its branches.

[1] 2 Kings 21:18; Matt. 26:36; John 19:41.   [2] 2 Kings 16:4; Isa. 1:29; 65:3; 66:17.
[3] Isa. 28:23-29.

An Egyptian Threshing-floor. (*After Wilkinson.*)

CHAPTER VI.

OF the seven so-called sciences of the ancients, grammar, logic, rhetoric, geometry, arithmetic, astronomy and music, the last three are the only ones to which the Hebrews at all devoted themselves. Theology has been in all ages the sum and crown of sciences to them: the knowledge of God and a service comprising whatever he has prescribed as duty toward him and toward men. Every other science, as far as it was not simply a means of livelihood, was merged in this or made subsidiary to it.

1. THE HEAVENLY BODIES.—Astronomy cannot be said to have attained among the Hebrews the position of a science. Along with mathematics it was chiefly studied as a necessary means for the adjustment of the calendar. There was not only a very imperfect knowledge of facts touching the sidereal heavens, but there is little evidence of any effort to systematize and arrange them. The stars were known as the "host of heaven."[1] The sun and moon seem always to have been distinguished from one another and from the remaining heavenly bodies; but no distinction is made in the Old Testament between planets and fixed stars, nor is there, apparently, any recognition of comets. Silence, however, is not here to be taken as a sure sign of ignorance. The unique purpose of the Bible is never to be forgotten. Since the Hebrew calendar was so largely based on the phases of the moon, it had a peculiar prominence in their thought. The appearance of the new moon was always hailed with the blast of trumpets and with special sacrifices.[2]

Certain single stars and constellations are mentioned in the Old Testament. Venus is called the "morning star" in Isaiah 14 : 12. The Pleiades are referred to in a few passages;[3] so too Orion, under the poetic image of a giant chained to the skies; as well as Arctùrus, or the Great Bear, and the Serpent.[4] It will be recalled that in the New Testament the "sign" of the ship on which Paul sailed from Melita to Rome was Castor and Pollux (Gr., *Dioscuri*), rendered in the Revised Version the "Twin Brothers."[5] In the prophecy of

---

[1] Isa. 40 : 26; Jer. 33 : 22.   [2] Num. 10 : 10; 28 : 11-15; 29 : 1; 1 Chron. 23 : 31; 2 Chron. 2 : 4; 8 : 13; Ezek. 46 : 6.   [3] Job 9 : 9; 38 : 31; Amos 5 : 8.   [4] Job 26 : 13.   [5] Acts 28 : 11.

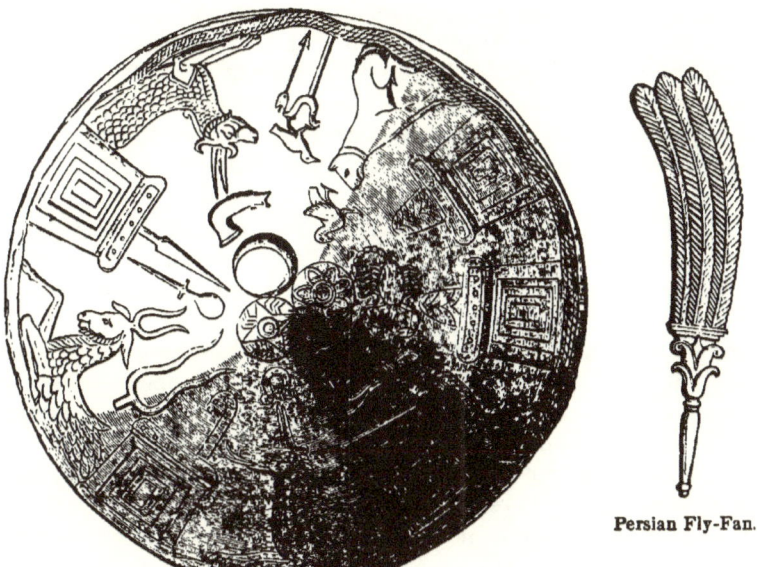

Persian Fly-Fan.

Babylonian Zodiac (?) or "arrangement of Constellations." (*From Babylonian Black Stone, twelfth century B.C., in British Museum.*)

Gate and Gateway engraved on a Babylonian Cylinder.

Egyptian Siphons, B.C. 1450.

Fig 1 pours the liquid into vases c from the cup b. Fig. 2 draws it off by siphons a into vessel d.

Chaldæan Clay Tablet bearing notice of the Deluge.

Amos it is noted that divine worship was paid in the northern kingdom to Saturn under its old Shemitic name of Chiun.[1] The word "mazzaroth," in Job 38 : 32, has been translated in the margin of the Revised Version "the signs of the Zodiac," as also a similar word in 2 Kings 23 : 5. Both expressions seem to refer to supposed stations in the progress of the sun and moon through the skies.

The Bible everywhere recognizes the fixed course and determined order of the heavenly bodies.[2] Their vast number is often used as an illustration.[3] Their majesty and glory is not overlooked, or even the different degrees of it when they are compared together.[4] They are always looked upon as a part of the one universe of God, being named, numbered, controlled and called into service as well as originally made by him.[5] Repeated warnings appear in the Old Testament against the practice of astrology, which, as a kind of magic, was wide-spread among neighboring peoples.[6]

2. STRUCTURE OF THE EARTH, ETC.—Concerning the structure of the earth and its relations to the remaining heavenly bodies too much knowledge must not be expected of the ancient Hebrews. That, however, they are not to be put on a simple equality with the other nations of antiquity the first chapter of Genesis and many other scriptural evidences of the superiority of their information amply show. There is special danger of interpreting the highly-poetical language used by Old Testament writers, when the creation is referred to, in a way to do great injustice to their real sentiments.[7] God is described in Isaiah as sitting on the "circle of the earth;" and the author of Job represents that the earth was created subsequent to the other planets and was suspended "upon nothing."[8] In surprising harmony, however, with the facts of science, we read in Genesis 1 : 6 of the heavens as an expanse ("firmament"); in Genesis 2 : 6 of a mist that went up "from the earth and watered the whole face of the ground." The Hebrew word for mist itself indicates something that goes and returns. In like manner there are some remarkable statements in the book of Ecclesiastes concerning the course of the winds, which imply, to say the least, a more than ordinary keenness of observation.[9]

3. RECKONING AND NUMBERS.—It would appear that men began first to reckon by means of the five fingers. The number five in Hebrew is derived from a root signifying to draw the fingers together.

---

[1] Amos 5 : 26.   [2] Judg. 5 : 20; Job 38 : 33; Jer. 31 : 35; 33 : 25.   [3] Gen. 15 : 5; 22 : 17; 26 : 4.
[4] Job 25 : 5; Dan. 12 : 3; 1 Cor. 15 : 41.   [5] Gen. 1 : 16; Job 9 : 7; Ps. 8 : 3; 147 : 4; Isa. 40 : 26.
[6] Gen. 41 : 8, 24; Isa. 47 : 13; Jer. 10 : 2; Dan. 1 : 20.   [7] Job 9 : 6; 38 : 4; Ps. 75 : 3.   [8] Job 38 : 7; Isa. 40 : 22.   [9] Eccles. 1 : 6; cf. Gen. 2 : 6.

Provision is made in the language by special words only for the units, ten, one hundred, one thousand and ten thousand. All the other numbers are indicated by the plurals or duals of these. The use of five as a multiple was naturally very common. It is probably due to the simplicity of this decimal system on the one hand, and on the other to the preference of the Hebrews for round numbers, that we find so little use made of fractions where otherwise they might have been expected. That it is intended to give simply round numbers is shown by the fact that not infrequently other numbers, the next higher or the next lower, are mentioned as being possibly more nearly correct.

The Hebrew alphabet was also used as signs of numbers. When this method of reckoning started it is not possible to say. In the absence of proof to the contrary it may be held that it began with the use of the perfected alphabet itself. The verses of the alphabetical psalms are so numbered. The first documentary evidence of the custom outside of the Bible is found on Maccabæan coins. It was adopted by the Greeks after the time of the Ptolemies. That they took it from the Hebrews through the Phœnicians has been argued but not proved. From the Moabite Stone it might be inferred that besides these methods of reckoning, numbers were also indicated by words written in full. And it is not impossible that a system of distinct numerical signs also early existed, as was the case in Phœnicia, Egypt and Babylon. Some of the variations of numbers in parallel passages of the Bible, it is likely, arose from different ways of reckoning and the changes necessary in passing from one system to another.[1]

4. There are certain numbers used in the Bible in a representative capacity, apparently without any intention of giving precise figures. Seven and its multiples, for example, is a number of completeness, and on this account is especially used of sacred things.[2] The same is true, though to a less extent, of ten; so "two and three," like our "two or three," often indicates an indefinitely small number; while "three and four," "six and seven," "seven and eight," denote a number indefinitely large.[3] For an unlimited period of past time the Hebrews had a formula signifying "yesterday and the day before."[4] A symbolical or typical sense was also given to numbers. The numbers three and four, for instance, were invested with a mystical sig-

[1] With 1 Kings 4:26 cf. 2 Chron. 9:25, and with 2 Kings 24:8 cf. 2 Chron. 36:9.   [2] Judg. 9:56; 2 Kings 10:1; Jer. 25:11; 29:10; Matt. 18:22.   [3] Ex. 20:5; Job 5.19; Amos 1:3; Micah 5:5.   [4] Deut. 19:4; 1 Sam. 4:7; 2 Sam. 3:17.

nificance, as well as their sum and their multiple. The same is true of five, ten, forty and seventy. The whole subject, however, especially in its prophetical aspect, is surrounded with grave difficulties. No one theory respecting it meets with general approval. For its fuller discussion the reader is referred to the Bible dictionaries.

5. DIVISIONS OF DAY AND NIGHT.—The method of reckoning the time of day by the lengthening of the shadows and of the night by the position of the constellations is doubtless the most ancient. The word hour, for which the Hebrew has no specific term, is quite commonly used in a vague sense in the Scriptures.[1] The dial of Ahaz, which he seems to have procured from Assyria, was apparently a series of steps on which the shadow of a pillar or obelisk fell.[2] The number of its divisions and the length of time they indicated it is not possible to determine. It is certain that in Babylon, as early as the eighth century before Christ, the day was divided into periods of twelve hours each. The same was true, and at a much earlier period, of Egypt.

The Egyptians divided both the day and the night into twelve parts; and, according to the highest authority, the word used for one of these divisions dates back to the fifth dynasty. Hence it would be hazardous to infer that the Hebrews, previous to the exile, were unacquainted with such a twelvefold division of time. When an hour is spoken of in the New Testament, it should be borne in mind that simply one of these twelve divisions is meant, reckoning from sunrise to sunset or *vice versa*. They varied in length according to the season of the year. The length of the day in Palestine ranged between one of fourteen hours and twelve minutes and one of nine hours and forty-eight minutes. Accordingly, when the third or any other hour is mentioned, the exact astronomical time, the time of sunrise being given, can only be determined by computation. The sixth hour of the day would always be at noon, but the third hour fell half way between sunrise and the time that the sun reached the zenith.

6. The division of the night into watches of four hours each dates at least from the time of the judges.[3] In Lamentations mention is made of "the beginning of the watches;" and elsewhere, of the "morning," or third, watch.[4] The ancient Greeks, also, divided the night into three watches; but the Romans had four, each of three hours. After the Roman occupation of Palestine their divisions of time were to some extent adopted by the Jews in ordinary life;[5] but

---

[1] Dan. 3:6; Matt. 8:13; Luke 12:39.   [2] 2 Kings 20:9-11; Isa. 38:8.   [3] Judg. 7:19.
[4] Lam. 2:19; cf. Ex. 14:24; 1 Sam. 11:11.   [5] Mark 6:48; 13:35; Luke 12:38; Acts 12:4.

in the temple service the old method was adhered to. In Talmudic usage a watch is always equivalent to one third of the night. What instruments, other than dials, the Hebrews may have had for marking the lapse of time it is not now possible to say. It is probable that, like their contemporaries, they made use of gnomons and the so-called clepsydra, among other devices. The clepsydra, or water-clock, was an Alexandrian invention of the second century before Christ, and of tolerable accuracy.

7. Like some other ancient peoples, the Hebrews were accustomed to begin the day with the evening. It was notably not the custom of the Babylonians or of the Romans, from the latter of whom our method of reckoning it from morning to morning is derived.[1] It is an interesting fact that in the first chapter of Genesis, where a day of labor—that is, a day proper in distinction from the night—is spoken of, it is made to begin with the morning. We find also indications that in ordinary life the day was sometimes understood to continue until its work was over and the rest of the night began. The days of the week, excepting the Sabbath and in later times Friday, the "day of preparation" for it, had no special designation, but were simply numbered from one to seven. The three principal parts of the day were known as morning, midday and evening. A variety of names was given to them, as "dawn," "sunrise," "sunset," "the light of the day," "the heat of the day," "the cool (lit., the wind) of the day."[2] In the ceremonial law the date for the celebration of the passover is fixed on the fourteenth of Nisan, "between the evenings," that is, at twilight. Later usage, however, extended the time from about three o'clock to sundown.

8. Allowing for difference of time in different seasons of the year, the three hours of prayer observed by the Jews were the third hour, or about nine o'clock; the sixth hour, or noon; and the ninth hour, or three o'clock in the afternoon.[3] The word day is often used metaphorically in the Bible. A man's day, for example, might be either his birthday or the day of his death.[4] The "day of the Lord" in the mouth of the prophets meant a time when Jehovah would come in judgment or in some new development of his providence.[5] To a distinction between so-called "lucky" and "unlucky" days, so common in both the ancient and modern Orient, the Scriptures give no encouragement.[6]

9. THE WEEK.—The institution of the week of seven days we

[1] Ex. 12:18; Lev. 23:32; Dan. 8:14.   [2] Gen. 3:8; 24:63.   [3] Matt. 27:45; Mark 15:25; Luke 23:44.   [4] 1 Sam. 26:10; Job 3:1; 18:20.   [5] Mal. 3:2.   [6] Isa. 47:13.

find recognized as an established fact in the oldest books of the
Bible. It appears to be taken account of in the narrative of the
flood, and of Laban's arrangements with Jacob.[1] In the legislation
of Moses it is made a specially prominent feature in settling the
calendar of the feasts.[2] The question when it arose is much discussed. The account in Genesis 2 : 2, 3 strongly supports the
hypothesis that, like the family, it was an original institution of
the race and began with the beginning of human history. It is
certain that as yet there has been no period discovered when the
week was unknown to the Shemitic peoples, to whom the Hebrews
belonged. When Abraham went out from Ur of the Chaldees, he
no doubt carried with him a knowledge of this fundamental division
of time; and whatever their practice may have been, the Hebrews
as a race can never have been wholly without acquaintance with it.[3]

10. THE MONTH.—The length of the Hebrew month was determined, in general, by the course of the moon. The names for month
and moon have the same root. Previous to the exile the months
were for the most part simply numbered; and the same was true,
to a considerable extent, after the exile. Of post-exilian writers,
the books of Ezra, Esther and Zechariah give both the name and
numerical order of the month; Nehemiah, the name only; Daniel
and Haggai, the number only. During the former period names
are given in the Bible to only four of the months—Abib, Ziv, Bul
and Ethanim.[4] Of the last three the number in the series is also
indicated.

11. It is now generally agreed that the names applied to the
months after the exile are of Assyrian or Babylonian origin. In
fact all of them have been found together on a tablet unearthed at
Nineveh. Their etymological significance has not been satisfactorily
settled in every case. These names and their order are as follows :—
Nisan,[5] Iyar, Sivan,[6] Tammuz, Ab, Elul,[7] Tishri, Marcheshvan, Chislev,[8] Tebeth,[9] Shebat,[10] Adar,[11] and an intercalary month, Veadar.
Of these names five do not occur in the Bible; but they are to be
found in the Talmud and other Jewish literature. The later Nisan
corresponds to the earlier Abib; Iyar to Ziv; Tishri to Ethanim;
and Marcheshvan to Bul. As the ordinary Hebrew month was
lunar, while our own is solar, it is not possible to identify them precisely; but Nisan (Abib) corresponds very nearly to April, Iyar

---

[1] Gen. 7 : 4; 8 : 10; 29 : 27; cf. 17 : 12.   [2] Lev. 23 : 15.   [3] Ex. 16 : 23.   [4] Ex. 13 : 4; 1 Kings
6 : 1, 38; 8 : 2.   [5] Neh. 2 : 1.   [6] Esth. 8 : 9.   [7] Neh. 6 : 15.   [8] Neh. 1 : 1.   [9] Esth. 2 : 16.
[10] Zech. 1 : 7.   [11] Esth. 3 : 7.

(Ziv) to May, and so on through the series. After the establishment of the Syro-Macedonian empire the names of the months were for a third time changed in Hebrew literature. Josephus uses the Macedonian calendar only. Instances of the same usage are found in the Old Testament apocryphal books.[1]

12. The question whether the earlier Hebrews were acquainted with the solar as well as the lunar month must be answered, it would appear, in the affirmative. Their names for the months, as found in the oldest books of the Bible, seem to require such an hypothesis. They are significant only as referring to certain definite seasons of the year. Abib, for example, was the month of "the ears of corn;" Ziv, the month of "blossoms." Such designations would scarcely have been employed if the lunar month only had been known. In that case Abib and Ziv could only occasionally have been the months of "the ears of corn" and of "blossoms," respectively. It is well known, too, that in Egypt the solar year was in use long before the exodus. It had twelve months of thirty days each, together with five other intercalated days. The Bible itself indirectly furnishes other facts confirmatory of the theory. In its statement concerning the time the flood continued, the month is reckoned as a period of thirty days, five of them being equal to a hundred and fifty days.[2] In the same account the flood is described as lasting from the seventeenth day of the second month to the twenty-seventh of the same month in the following year, that is, during one lunar year, plus eleven days, which would be equal to the solar year.[3]

13. The Mosaic legislation for the feasts was based on the lunar month; and this system subsequently prevailed. The passover took place at the full of the moon in Nisan. The beginning of the month, that is, the appearance of the new moon, was carefully noted by observers appointed for the purpose, and officially announced. Owing to obscuration uncertainty might arise concerning the exact time of the moon's appearance; but it was not difficult to secure a sufficient degree of accuracy in a number of ways.[4] The days of the month were reckoned at twenty-nine and thirty alternately. This would give a year of three hundred and fifty-four days. The actual lunar year was longer by eight hours, forty-eight minutes and thirty-eight seconds. To correct this discrepancy, and adjust the calendar to the course of the sun, it was customary about every third year to add a thirteenth month, called, as above, "Veadar," that is, another Adar,

---

[1] 2 Macc. 11 : 30, 33, 38.   [2] Gen. 7 : 11, 24; cf. 8 : 4; Num. 20 : 29; Deut. 34 : 8.   [3] Gen. 7 : 11; 8 : 14.   [4] 1 Sam. 20 : 5, 24, 27.

that being the name of the twelfth month. In a period of nineteen years it required the intercalation of seven such months in order to bring the Jewish calendar into harmony with our own. We find nothing concerning this intercalary month in the Bible.

14. THE YEAR.—The Mosaic law enjoined that the year should begin with the month Abib (Nisan).[1] Throughout the Old Testament, in writings which arose both before and after the exile, this mode of reckoning is followed. But it is evident that, at least from the period of the exodus, there was also another way of beginning the year. In Exodus 23 : 16, for example, the feast of tabernacles, which began on the fifteenth of Tishri, is spoken of as taking place at "the end of the year."[2] But Tishri was only the seventh month of the calendar. It seems quite likely therefore that a distinction was ordinarily made between what was known as the ecclesiastical, and the agricultural and civil, year. For an agricultural people in Palestine a natural time to begin the year would be in the fall, when the harvests were over and the seed-time began. Josephus directly states that Moses appointed Nisan as the first month of the festivals, and that it began the year as to "all the solemnities they observed to the honor of God, although he preserved the original order of the months as to selling and buying and other ordinary affairs."[3] It is certain that both the sabbatic and jubilee years began with the seventh month.[4] The custom of celebrating the first of Tishri as New Year's day was not introduced until after the exile.

15. The first period adopted by the Hebrews from which to number their years was the exodus.[5] After the establishment of the kingdom, years were often numbered from the accession of certain kings to the throne.[6] Subsequent to the Babylonian captivity the Seleucidian era was adopted, which began B.C. 312. With the re-establishment of the commonwealth under Judas Maccabæus, that event was taken as an epoch or era, but was soon after abandoned for the Seleucidian, which continued in use until near the twelfth century A.D. At that time the Jews began to reckon from the "creation of the world." This practice is still followed. Accordingly, to arrive at the number of the Jewish year we have to add to the year of our era the number 3761. The Hebrews distinguished but two seasons in the year, summer and winter; but the various harvests were used to indicate special periods. We read frequently, for

---

[1] Ex. 12 : 2; cf. 9 : 31.   [2] Ex. 23 : 16; cf. 34 : 22; Isa. 29 : 1; 32 : 10; 37 : 30.   [3] Josephus, *Antiq.* 1, 3 : 3.   [4] Lev. 25 : 9, 10.   [5] 1 Kings 6 : 1.   [6] 2 Kings 11 : 4; 12 : 1; 15 : 1.

example, of the time of barley harvest, wheat harvest, or the harvest of grapes and the time of seed-sowing.[1]

16. MUSIC IN GENERAL.—To music, both vocal and instrumental, a high position is assigned in the Bible. In his noted eulogy of famous men the son of Sirach classes those who "found out musical harmonies, and set forth poetic compositions in writing" with such as "bore rule in their kingdoms, and men renowned for *their* power; who gave counsel in their discernment, and uttered prophecies."[2] Then, as now, men were capable of abusing their musical gifts, as did some in

Stringed Instruments, Cymbals and Kettle-drum.   Trumpets, Pipes or Double Flute, Cornet and Sistrum.

luxurious Samaria, who fell under the rebuke of Amos, singing "idle songs to the sound of the viol;"[3] still, the study and practice of music was regarded as worthy of the noblest minds. Music was the pastime of the lonely shepherd.[4] It formed a principal attraction of the social gatherings of youth at the city gates.[5] It was the indispensable accompaniment of every festival occásion, whether family or national.[6] Above all, it was an exceedingly important feature of the worship of the temple at every period.

Previous to the time of David, the music of the Hebrews seems to have been of the simplest character. It was probably such that the people could easily join in it without instruction. Such was the song of Miriam and the women of Israel at the crossing of the Red Sea, and the wild melody which appears to have accompanied the worship of the golden calf.[7] The silver trumpets provided for the tabernacle and the horns used at Jericho, as we shall see, were not musical instruments, but intended for the purpose of giving signals.[8]

[1] Gen. 30 : 14; Lev. 26 : 5; Ruth 1 : 22; 2 Sam. 21 : 9; Amos 7 : 1.   [2] Ecclus. 44 : 2–4.   [3] Amos 6 : 5.   [4] 1 Sam. 16 : 18.   [5] Lam. 5 : 14.   [6] Gen. 31 : 27; Judg. 11 : 34; 1 Sam. 18 : 6; 1 Kings 1 : 40; Ps. 4 : 7; Luke 15 : 25.   [7] Ex. 15 : 20, 21; 32 : 17, 18.   [8] Num. 10 : 1–10; Josh. 6 : 5.

The first direct efforts among the Israelites to cultivate music appear in connection with the schools of the prophets, founded by Samuel.[1] It is, however, very likely that at a considerably earlier period some attention had been given to it by the Levites as a part of their duties at the sanctuary.

17. MUSIC OF THE TEMPLE.—Under David's direction not less than four thousand musicians, or more than a tenth of the whole tribe of Levi, praised the Lord with "instruments" in the service of the temple.[2] Each great division of the tribe, Kohathites, Gershonites and Merarites, had a representative family among this number. They were those of Heman, Asaph and Ethan or Jeduthun. A select body of two hundred and eighty-eight trained musicians led this chorus of voices, one person being placed as leader over a section consisting of twelve singers.[3] This smaller body of skilled players formed the orchestra of the temple.[4] They generally used stringed instruments, like the psaltery and the harp, the leaders of the smaller sections only being provided with cymbals, probably for the purpose of marking time.[5] Men and women were associated together in the choir.[6] It is a fact worth noting that there is no positive injunction to be found in the legislation of the Pentateuch respecting the use of music in the sanctuary. David doubtless had a divine warrant, through the prophets Nathan and Gad, for the changes introduced by him.[7] The way was prepared for the innovation by the cultivation of music in the schools of the prophets. The fact that no detailed account of the changes made by David in the temple service is found in parallel passages in the books of Kings in no wise affects the authenticity of the narrative in Chronicles. The books of Kings corroborate the latter as far as they go. They speak of men and women singers whom David employed at his court; of his instructing the people on one occasion to sing a funeral ode which he had composed; and of his making use of a service of song on the occasion of his bringing the ark to Mount Zion.[8] In what they say of Solomon, too, that he had harps and psalteries of sandal wood prepared for the singers, they presuppose that there existed at that time a musical class composed of musicians and singers who were employed in the temple. The context clearly shows that the reference cannot be to any supposed court band.[9]

The orchestra originally had its place to the east of the altar of

¹ 1 Sam. 10:5; 19:20.   ² 1 Chron. 15:17; 23:5, 6; 25:1-6.   ³ 1 Chron. 25:6, 7.   ⁴ Ps. 68:25.   ⁵ 1 Chron. 15:19; 16:5.   ⁶ 1 Chron. 25:5, 6; Ezra 2:65.   ⁷ 2 Chron. 29:25.   ⁸ 2 Sam. 1:17; 6:5, 14; 19:35.   ⁹ 1 Kings 10:12.

burnt offerings, but in the temple of Herod, on the steps that led from the court of the people to that of the priests.[1] Although there is frequent mention of the use of trumpets by the priests, it seems never to have been intended as, strictly speaking, a part of the music of the temple.[2] This was true at least in the time of our Lord. The priests stood on the west side of the altar, that is, somewhat removed from the orchestra. They also, contrary to the Levitical perform-ers, faced toward the people and away from the sanctuary. Their instruments, as already remarked, were simply for blowing blasts or signals, to mark, for example, the transition from one part of the service to another. On ordinary days there were seven occasions for their doing so, three blasts being given in each case. On the Sabbath there were additional ones blown,—three just before the beginning of the day, three when it began, and still others in con-nection with its additional services.

Among the later kings, Hezekiah and Josiah are specially men-tioned as having given unusual attention to the musical services of the sanctuary.[3] They were not altogether neglected even during the depressed condition of the people subsequent to the captivity.[4] It is certain that the service of song formed a prominent feature of Jewish worship in the time of our Lord. Each day, in connection with the morning and the evening sacrifice, a psalm was sung, the following serving for the several days of the week : 24, 48, 82, 94, 81, 93, 92. It was required that not less than twelve voices should join in it, the number of instruments being unlimited. The psalm was divided into three sections, at the close of each one of which the priests blew three blasts with their trumpets and the people bowed in worship. There is still preserved as a part of the heading of Psalm 92 the words " A Psalm, a Song for the sabbath day." There were also certain psalms that were used on the feast days. Psalm 30 has the super-scription, " A Song at the Dedication of the House."

18. Little can be said of the kinds of music practiced by the Hebrews, or of its development as an art. It would appear that the music of the temple was at no time mere cantillation, such as is common in modern synagogues. Much less was it an adaptation of the music of the people. It was a cultivated music, in which antiphony had a prominent place. Solo- joined with chorus-singing seems also to have been a common form in public service, both among the Jews and early Christians.[5] The singing was in unison, and not

[1] 2 Chron. 5 : 12.   [2] 2 Kings 11 : 14; 2 Chron. 7 : 6; 29 : 26.   [3] 2 Chron. 29 : 25 ; 35 : 15.
[4] Neh. 11 : 17, 22; 12 : 28.   [5] Neh. 12 : 31 ; Ps. 24 : 7-10 ; Rev. 4 : 8, 10 ; 19 : 1.

with the several parts in harmony. The only variation was probably in the use of different octaves. Support for the theory that the singing was in unison is found in the Bible in 2 Chronicles 5 : 13. Some of the musical expressions occurring at the beginning of psalms have the same bearing.[1] Others of them indicate the style of instrument that was to accompany the singing. Quite a number of the psalms are provided with these and other musical directions.[2] That they are very old is clear from the circumstance that they were no longer fully understood when the oldest translation of the Bible was made. Some of the headings, it would appear, are the names or the first words of airs to which it was desired that the singing of the psalm should be conformed. About one third of all the psalms have retained as a part of their superscription the words "To the chief musician;" the work being thus committed to him for liturgical use in the temple. It was for him to see that it was sufficiently practiced and properly executed. There is no evidence that musical notes were in use in Bible times, or later before the seventeenth century. The whole matter is largely one of tradition.

19. MUSICAL INSTRUMENTS—THE TIMBREL.—The musical instruments of the Hebrews, like those of other nations of antiquity, were of three kinds: stringed and wind instruments and such as were beaten or shaken to produce sound. Of the last-named the "tabret" or "timbrel" (Heb., *toph*) was one of the most common. It was used chiefly by women. We find it mentioned in the opening chapters of the Bible, and often throughout the earlier history of Israel.[3] It is frequently spoken of in connection with the "harp" (Heb., *kinnor*) as furnishing music on occasions of family and public festivities.[4] It closely resembled the modern tambourine in form, and was beaten with the fingers of the right hand while held in the left. If the Egyptian style as it now appears on the monuments furnished the model, it might have been either round or four-sided. To make it resonant the tanned skin of some animal was tightly drawn over a shallow frame of wood or metal; and generally, to the edges of the frame thin pieces of metal were attached, whose jingle, when the instrument was beaten, was thought to improve its otherwise dull sound. The timbrel was much used for marking time in orchestral music, as also in circular dances and public processions.[5] It appears to have had no place in the religious services of the tabernacle or temple.

---

[1] Ps. 6, 12, 46; cf. 1 Chron. 15 : 20, 21.   [2] Ps. 9, 22, 45, 56, 57, 58, 59, 60, 69, 75, 80.   [3] Gen. 4 · 21 ; 31 : 27 ; Ex. 15 : 20 ; Judg. 11 : 34 ; Jer. 31 : 4 ; Ps. 149 : 3 ; 150 : 4.   [4] Job 21 : 12 ; Isa. 24 : 8 ; 30 : 32.   [5] Ps. 68 : 25.

20. CASTANETS AND CYMBALS.—Besides the timbrel there are but two other instruments belonging to its class which are mentioned in the Bible—castanets and cymbals. The former appear only in a single passage, and the revisers here give as an alternative rendering "sistra," instruments of quite a different character.[1] The modern castanet of the Orient consists of a small concave plate of brass, with a handle for holding it, and is principally used by professional dancers. The Hebrew word for cymbal—*tsiltsel*—indicates the kind of sound produced by it. The cymbal was of two sorts. One of them was made up of four small plates of metal, two of which were held in each hand. They were smitten together to produce sound. The other one, called in our version "the high-sounding cymbal,"[2] more resembled the modern instrument of this name. It consisted simply of two large plates of metal, one for each hand. It was probably this form that was used by leaders in the temple music for marking time. It is uncertain whether triangles were in use among the Hebrews. The word is found as an alternative rendering in 1 Samuel 18 : 6. What is probably referred to is an instrument having three strings, or a sistrum with three bars.

21. STRINGED INSTRUMENTS IN GENERAL.— Stringed instruments were always played in ancient times either with the fingers or with the plectrum, and not, like the modern violin, with a bow. The strings were made from the covering of the intestines of different animals. Various kinds of wood were utilized in their manufacture, the most common being the fir or cypress. It is said of Solomon that he made them from the "almug" tree, by which, possibly, sandal wood is meant.[3] The stringed instruments principally in use among the Hebrews were the harp (Heb., *kinnor*) and the psaltery (Heb., *nebel*). They are very frequently mentioned together in the Bible. The former has received a variety of names in the Septuagint version of the Old Testament, being confounded, in some cases, even with the psaltery. This has given rise to not a little confusion. The Revised Version has consistently translated everywhere the Hebrew word *kinnor* by "harp" and *nebel* everywhere by "psaltery," except in Isaiah 22 : 24 ("flagon") and in Amos 5 : 23 ; 6 : 5 ("viol"). There is considerable difference of opinion among scholars concerning the nature of the instruments. It is very probable that each of them had more than one form ; and it would appear to be safer to depend on the representations of the ancient monuments in determining their character than on those of

[1] 2 Sam. 6 : 5.   [2] Ps. 150 : 5.   [3] 1 Kings 10 : 12.

late writers like Josephus, who might easily be too much influenced in their judgments by the customs of their own times.[1]

22. THE HARP.—What we know of the harp of the Bible answers fairly well to the lyre, or harp, of the Egyptian monuments. The latter in general appearance resembles the modern harp, and is provided with a varying number of strings. In its smaller form it could easily have been carried about in processions. The same instrument was also well known to the Assyrians. When in use, it was held before them, as the pictorial representations show, with the left arm, and the lower end allowed to rest on the hip. The Egyptian lyre, moreover, would seem to have come originally from western Asia. The earliest figures of it on the monuments of Egypt are in connection with the immigration of Shemitic families during the twelfth dynasty. At this period it consisted only of a board nearly square, in the upper half of which a hole was cut, and across it a number of strings, apparently seven or eight, were stretched. The same instrument, considerably improved in form, reappears on the monuments of succeeding dynasties. The probability that this is the instrument known among the Hebrews as the *kinnor* is strengthened by the fact that one closely corresponding to it is found on coins belonging to the Maccabæan period.

23. THE PSALTERY.—The etymology of the Hebrew word rendered "psaltery" would suggest an instrument having considerable body. It was for this reason, perhaps, that the revisers did not think it best to change the rendering of the common version in Amos 5 : 23; 6 : 5, where it is given as "viol." In Isaiah 22 : 24 the context shows that "flagon," that is, skin-bottle, properly stands as its representative. Over a resonance chamber, doubtless resembling such a skin-bottle, the strings passed. They were fewer than those of the harp, since ten were regarded as an uncommonly large number for it.[2] If right conclusions have been reached respecting the harp, the psaltery, it is likely, resembled what is now known in the East as the tamboora, or guitar, an instrument which also figures largely on both the Egyptian and Assyrian monuments. In its present shape it is thus described by Van Lennep:[3] "In its most complete and perfect form, this instrument is three feet and nine inches long, has ten strings of fine wire, and forty-seven stops. It is played with a plectrum, and is often inlaid with mother-of-pearl and valuable woods. It is oftener, however, of smaller size and less costly materials. . . . It is represented, in these plainer forms, on many of the

[1] Josephus, *Antiq.* 7, 12 : 3.   [2] Ps. 33 : 2.   [3] *Bible Lands*, p. 612.

monuments of ancient Egypt, for it seems to have been a great favorite with her people, though it has wholly disappeared from among their posterity." The revisers have left the rendering "psaltery" in our English Bible for the Aramaic word *pesanterin*, in which others find the "dulcimer," while giving the latter rendering (marg., "bagpipe") to *sumponeyah*, by which others suppose the bagpipe is meant.[1]

24. THE SACKBUT.—A peculiar instrument, rendered "sackbut" in our version, is mentioned in the book of Daniel.[1] The translation, however, seems to be somewhat wide of the mark; since the instrument known in modern times as the sackbut is a wind instrument, "a bass trumpet with a slide like the modern trombone" (Fr., *saquebute*, and Span., *sacabuche*). The Hebrew *sabbekha*, on the other hand, was doubtless a stringed instrument, the Greek *sambyx* (Lat., *sambuca*). In form it appears to have been intermediate between the guitar and harp. It is found represented on the Egyptian monuments, and was well known throughout the East in the later biblical times. It had but a few short strings, and its tones were sharp and piercing. The resounding-board was in shape like the keel of a ship, the three or four strings being stretched from stem to stern.

25. WIND INSTRUMENTS—THE FLUTE.—A favorite wind instrument of the ancients was the flute, or flageolet. It was found in a great variety of forms, two even being sometimes bound together with one mouth-piece. In its simplest form it was a reed, or some variety of wood in the shape of a reed, eighteen inches or more in length, bored throughout evenly and pierced with holes in the sides for notes. Provision was made at first, it would seem, for only two or three notes; but gradually the number was increased until now the so-called *nay* of the East is arranged for six. The *nay* is played by blowing across the sharp edge of the upper end, and great skill is required to produce anything like a musical tone. There seem, however, always to have been pipes of the same general class which were played by blowing into a hole at the side. This instrument is mentioned among others in the Bible as used on festival occasions, both private and public, as also on those of mourning.[2] Among the later Israelites it was considered indispensable, even for the poorest man, to have not less than two performers on flutes present at the funeral of a wife.

---

[1] Dan. 3:5, 7, 10, 15. [2] 1 Sam. 10:5; 1 Kings 1:40; Isa. 30:29; Matt. 9:23; 11:17; Rev. 18:22.

10

26. The "Pipe."—Another wind instrument, mentioned a few times in the Bible, is the *ugab* (" organ ;" Revised Version, "pipe "). It apparently consisted of a number of pipes of different sizes, open only at one end, and so constructed as to admit of being blown into at the other, either successively or simultaneously. There was a very ancient instrument of this kind known to the Greeks as the *syrinx* (Lat., *fistula*). It is not strange that the original word was rendered by the earlier English translators, following the Vulgate, "organ ;"[1] the principal difference between it and what for a long time has been known as the organ being that the pipes of the former answer better to the ordinary flute, while those of the latter correspond to the *flute à bec*, that is, a flute with a beak, a mouth-piece at its extremity directing the column of air against a sharp perforated edge. The *ugab* is named among the earliest musical instruments invented by men, and is more likely to have been developed into an organ than to have been developed from one at so early a period.[2] It is directly suggested by the double flute, which must have been well known to the Hebrews, though we have no con-clusive evidence from the Bible that they were accustomed to use it.

27. The Trumpet.—The trumpets spoken of in the Bible, known under three names, appear to have been of only two kinds (*keren-shophar, chatsotsera*). The word *keren* occurs in two passages only, being translated in the former " horn," and in the latter " cornet."[3] Most authorities render the word *yobel*, found in connection with *keren* in the book of Joshua, by "jubilee" (so "jubilee horn," not "ram's horn," with the Revised Version). Undoubtedly this instrument originally consisted of the horn of some animal, like the ram, chamois or ox, the tip of which had been perforated ; or, if made of metal, having the same general form. Its most common name was *shophar*, and it was blown either in blasts or with a prolonged note. Only on rare occasions was it used as an accompaniment to other musical instruments, particularly when a specially startling effect was de-sired.[4] It was made use of to proclaim war, for signalling an attack, and for ordering a retreat or disbandment.[5] It was blown by watch-men to give an alarm,[6] and as a token of joy at the coronation of kings.[7] Its use on religious occasions was mostly confined to usher-ing in the festival of the new moon in the seventh month and the year of jubilee.[8]

---

[1] Gen. 4 : 21 ; Job 21 : 12 ; 30 : 31 ; Ps. 150 : 4.   [2] Gen. 4 : 21.   [3] Josh. 6 : 5 ; Dan. 3 : 5, 7, 10, 15.
[4] 2 Sam. 6 : 15 ; 1 Chron. 15 : 28 ; Ps. 47 : 5 ; 98 : 6 ; 150 : 3 ; Dan. 3 : 5, 7, 10, 15.   [5] Judg. 3 : 27 ;
7 : 16 ; 2 Sam. 2 · 28 ; 20 : 1, 22 ; Job 39 : 24.   [6] Hos. 8 : 1 ; Amos 3 : 6.   [7] 2 Sam. 15 : 10 ; 2
Kings 9 : 13.   [8] Lev. 23 : 24 ; 25 : 9 ; Num. 29 : 1 ; Ps. 81 : 3.

28. The trumpet proper, on the other hand (*chatsotsera*), was almost exclusively a priestly instrument. There were at first but two of them, and by express divine command they were made of silver.[1] Though like the horn sometimes used for giving signals for the people to assemble both in peace and war, these silver instruments were commonly appropriated to religious services.[2] In the temple of Solomon their number was increased from two to one hundred and twenty.[3] The form it had in later times is seen on Jewish coins, and is definitely described by Josephus.[4] It appears to have been a little more than two feet in length (Josephus says that it was "a little less than a cubit long"), was narrow and straight, and at the bottom had a bell-like protuberance much like the hautboy of the modern Orient.

29. THE ART OF WRITING.—That the Israelites at the time of the exodus understood the art of alphabetical writing is no longer subject of dispute. That the art was practiced by the patriarchs of an earlier period the Bible furnishes little positive evidence. It does allude incidentally to the fact that Judah had a seal-ring; and from other sources we know that seal-rings provided with written characters would not have been an anachronism at that time.[5] The Bible certainly contains the oldest literature yet discovered, written in this, the most perfect outward form of literature. Although Moses is the first one spoken of in the Bible as a writer, the art is not represented as anything new.[6] In addition to the priests, a class of persons whose special business it was to write would seem to have existed in his day.[7] The Hebrew word *shoterim* does not in itself necessarily mean "writer;" still the connection in which it is used in the Pentateuch shows that a knowledge of the art of writing on the part of this class is generally presupposed.

In Deuteronomy the injunction to write an abstract of the law on the posts of the doors of course implies the ability to write.[8] In the book of Joshua we find that a copy of the law of Moses was written on stones prepared for the purpose; also, that a description of the land of Canaan was drawn up in order to facilitate its division by lot.[9] And in Judges it is related of a young man who is incidentally captured that he is able to write down a long list of names comprising the eldership and the princes of Succoth.[10] It is difficult, moreover, to see how such extended pieces of poetic composition as

---

[1] Num. 10:1–10.   [2] Num. 31:6; 2 Kings 11:14; 12:13; 2 Chron. 13:12, 14.   [3] 2 Chron. 5:12.   [4] Josephus, *Antiq.* 3, 12:6.   [5] Gen. 38:18.   [6] Ex. 17:14; 24:4; Num. 33:2.   [7] Ex. 5:6; Num. 5:23; 11:16.   [8] Deut. 6:9; 11:20.   [9] Josh. 18:6, 8, 9; cf. 10:13.   [10] Judg. 8:14.

we find in Numbers and in Judges could well have been preserved
unless they had been in a written form.[1] After the time of David
the practice of writing in all its forms, as letters, despatches, business contracts, legal documents, and the like, was common with
every class of the people.[2]

30. It is now pretty generally agreed that Tacitus was right in
ascribing the discovery of alphabetical writing to Egypt. Allowing
then the long sojourn of Israel in Egypt, there is no difficulty in
understanding how the art came to be developed to such a degree
among them in Moses' day ; or the otherwise most surprising literary
products presented to us in the Pentateuch and the book of Joshua.
From the time of Isaiah, it would appear that besides the customary
written character there was another representing a more running
hand, and possibly letters of a smaller size.[3] Others find in the
prophet's "pen of a man" an indication that already the larger
Aramaic character had been introduced, and that he was bidden to
use the old, rather than the new, style.[4] But this is questionable ;
although the Aramaic was doubtless understood by some persons in
Israel at this date. This Aramaic character, which is the one now
solely in use in our Hebrew Bible, supplanted the original Hebrew
alphabet after the Babylonian exile. The latter, however, still
exists, in its general features, in the Samaritan alphabet, the inscription of the Moabite Stone, belonging to the ninth century B.C., and
on extant coins of the Maccabæan period.

31. LANGUAGES OF THE BIBLE.—The entire Old Testament was
originally written in the Hebrew language, excepting Daniel 2 : 4–
7 : 28 ; Ezra 4 : 8–6 : 18 ; 7 : 12–26 ; Jeremiah 10 : 11, which were
written in the closely-allied Aramaic. The expression "Hebrew
language" is not found in the Old Testament. It is there called the
"language of Canaan," a strong incidental proof of the origin of
the language itself.[5] Most scholars are in fact agreed that some
dialect of the Hebrew was spoken in Canaan at the time of Abraham's migration thither. This theory is corroborated by the circumstance that the Phœnician language, still preserved in numerous
inscriptions, is strikingly analogous to the Hebrew in vocabulary
and in many characteristic formations of nouns and verbs. The
language which Abraham had previously spoken was also, like the
Hebrew, Shemitic ; but it was probably that which is now being so
marvellously brought to light in connection with the Babylonian

---

[1] Num. 21 : 27–30 ; Judg. 5.   [2] 1 Kings 21 : 8, 11 ; 2 Kings 10 : 1 ; 2 Chron. 30 : 1 ; Job 31 : 35 ;
Jer. 32 : 10.   [3] Isa. 8 : 1.   [4] Isa. 36 : 11 ; cf. Ezra 4 : 7.   [5] Isa. 19 : 18.

Timbrel. (*After specimen in Kensington Museum, London.*)

Egyptian Harp.

Moabite Stone, with Inscription of King Mesha. About B.C. 900.

שקל ישראל שב
ירושלים הקדושה

Ancient and Modern Hebrew Writing.
Lines 1 and 3 read: *Shekel Israel* (and date); 2 and 4 read: *Jerusalem, the Holy.*

Writing on Cameo of Nebuchadnezzar. About 575 B.C.

Writing on a Phœnician Seal. About 1200 B.C.

Portion of a Turkish Letter.

and Assyrian monuments of the East. That the original dialect of Canaan was largely developed and adapted to its higher use in connection with the immigration and peculiar history of the Israelitish people is more than probable.

32. One has remarked that the Hebrew language indeed appears as fully developed in the time of Moses as though it had been for a long period the language of books :—" But why should this gifted man, who to this end had been instructed in all the wisdom of Egypt, not have been possessed of the means to take an original path in the province of language, and have served as a model for future centuries, without having himself worked from extant models? What model or predecessor in his work had Luther? Did not Ulfilas give to the wild Goths along with the alphabet a translation of the Scriptures? Particularly instructive is it that the beginnings of the art of writing among the Korashites were shortly before the rise of Mohammed; and yet the Koran was fully composed in writing." [1]

33. MATERIALS FOR WRITING.—Not only did the Israelites learn from Egypt the art of writing, but also borrowed thence, as it would

Pens and Writing-materials.

seem, nearly all the requisites for its practice. There are two expressions in the Bible for pen, both of which carry etymologically the idea of a graving-instrument.[2] One of them is even characterized sometimes as a " pen of iron." [3] This is due to the fact that the same style of utensil was used for writing and for engraving on wood or metal. For ordinary writing the reed-pen was undoubtedly the most common.[4] Both the pen and the little store of ink were carried by professional writers in the girdle.[5] A knife was also found convenient for keeping the reed-pen in order and for cutting the material on which the writing was done.[6] The ink was ordinarily black. We are not informed how it was prepared in the earliest times.

34. It is probable that the first writing-material was papyrus-paper. The plant grows luxuriantly in Egypt, and somewhat abundantly also, at the present day, in some parts of Palestine.[7]

[1] Kinzler, Bib. Altertümer, p. 415.   [2] Ex. 32 : 4 ; Isa. 8 : 1.   [3] Job 19 : 24 ; Jer. 17 : 1.   [4] Ps. 45 : 1 ; Jer. 8 : 8 ; 3 John 13.   [5] Ezek. 9 : 2, 11.   [6] Jer. 36 : 18, 23.   [7] Ex. 2 : 3 ; Job 8 : 11 ; Isa. 18 : 2 ; 35 : 7.

Insignificant fragments of papyrus-paper, inscribed with Phœnician characters, have been found, but none with the ancient Hebrew. The first actual mention of this material in the Bible is in 2 John 12; but there is no good reason, save lack of sufficient occasion, why it should not have been noticed in the Old Testament.

It is still matter of discussion whether the Hebrews wrote on the prepared skins of animals. Most authorities hold that they did; but there are very good ones who regard it as at least doubtful. There is no direct evidence that the Egyptians used this material. It can only be said with certainty, at present, that there are some passages of Scripture where leather as a material for books seems to be most naturally implied.[1] It is urged by some that in the passage from Jeremiah, it is unlikely that the king would have thrown any considerable amount of leather on an open fire in his own apartments. But considering his angry mood and what he actually did, it is hard to say without positive knowledge what he would or would not do.

Parchment, which is claimed to have been a discovery of the time of the Ptolemies, is spoken of in the Bible only in the New Testament.[2] As is well known, the early form of books was that of the roll. The papyrus or parchment having been cut into long strips and written over on one side was nicely fastened together, and then rolled up as maps are often rolled at the present day. Doubtless engraving on wood, stone and the metals was well understood by the Hebrews. The only recorded instance in the canonical books of continuous writing on stone, excepting the Decalogue, is in Joshua 8 : 32.[3]

35. HEBREW POETRY.—Of the three kinds of poetry cultivated by the ancients,—lyric, epic and dramatic,—the Hebrews gave little attention to any but the first. But to these three another species of poetic composition, for which the Hebrews had a special liking, should be added—the gnomic. Gnomic poetry was in its bloom shortly after the time of David. Another common name for it is didactic poetry. It is a kind of philosophy of human life, presented in its results rather than in its processes, and in a poetic form. The books of Proverbs and Ecclesiastes are marked examples of this kind of composition, as are also the books of Ecclesiasticus and Wisdom among the Apocrypha of the Old Testament. The nearest approach to anything like dramatic poetry in the Bible is in the Canticles and the book of Job; but neither represents much more than a simple dialogue in which a number of persons participate.

36. Scholars, unfortunately, have not yet, arrived at fixed or

[1] Num. 5 : 23; Jer. 36 : 23.   [2] 2 Tim. 4 : 13.   [3] See Deut. 27 : 4, 8; Job 19 : 24; 1 Macc. 8 : 22.

generally satisfactory conclusions respecting the peculiar style and form of Hebrew poetry. It is pretty well established, however, that rhyme and metre, both common in sister dialects, were unknown to it. What have been represented as examples of rhyme are examples rather of simple assonance; and the most recent attempts to reduce Hebrew poetry to a metrical system have only succeeded in making something else of it than Hebrew, the results attained being dependent on the rejection of the present rules of Hebrew accentuation. Taking Hebrew poetry as we find it, it may be said that the matter is broken up into lines and strophes, the latter being composed of several of the former. A still more striking feature of it is what is known as parallelism. Attention was first called to this characteristic by Lowth in 1787. The subject was further developed by Herder and others. Parallelism consists in recalling in some way, in a second or third member, one or both, the thought expressed in the first, before passing on to a new one. Lowth recognized three species of parallelism—synonymous, antithetic and synthetic. To these others have been added, as the syntactic and the introverted. All these forms, more or less interchanged and modified, may be found in a single poem.

37. In addition to this peculiar structure of Hebrew poetry, it was no doubt intended to be highly rhythmical. In not a few instances the rhythmical movement may still be easily recognized, even in the English version. Whether it will ever be possible to discover the actual literary principles underlying the poetry of the Bible is questionable. Such a result would seem to demand an acquaintance with the original pronunciation of Hebrew words. And here it is significant that the later Hebrew scholars who have affixed the accents to the original text have accentuated as poetry only the books of Job, Proverbs and the Psalms. It also requires the supposition that the Hebrews *had* an elaborated system of poetic composition, with fixed principles to which they more or less rigidly conformed—a matter which still lies wholly in the realm of hypothesis. Besides the device of assonance, already noticed, and of alliteration, Hebrew poets also understood the use of the acrostic arrangement. Quite a number of psalms in our collection are acrostic, besides Proverbs 31 : 16–31 and all of the Lamentations of Jeremiah except the last.[1] Poets also adopted a peculiar literary style, making special use of archaic words and forms, particularly those having fullness of tone and sonorousness.

[1] Ps. 9, 10, 25, 34, 37, 111, 112, 119, 145.

Ancient Egyptian Bellows.

Roll or Book of the Law, rolled up.

Modern Egyptian Potter.

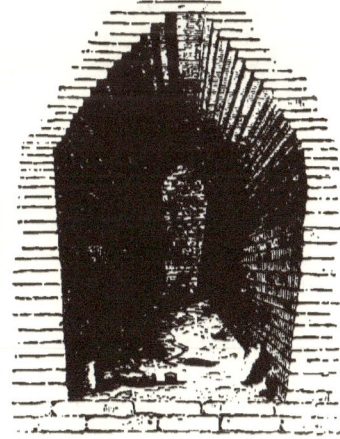

Ancient Brick Vault, at Mugheir.

Arched Drain, S. E. Palace, Nimrud. (*Layard*.)

38. THE MEDICAL ART.—Efforts to heal the sick naturally reach back to the remotest antiquity. The fact that the Israelites looked upon disease and death as a direct infliction from God did not hinder them from doing what they could to stay their ravages. That master of the gnomic wisdom of his time, the son of Sirach, puts the matter correctly when he says, " Honor, with reference to thy needs, a physician with the honor due unto him, . . . for the Lord hath created him."[1] The frequent symbolical use in the earliest books of the Bible of the processes of physical healing shows how important it had already come to be regarded.[2] An instance of the superstitious use of plant-life as a medicament is found in the history of Rachel and Leah.[3] Midwifery also was recognized as a special occupation in patriarchal times.[4] The names of two patriotic and God-fearing women of this class are found in connection with the history of Israel in Egypt.[5] An ordinance of the Mosaic law enjoined that a person wounded in a brawl should be surgically treated at the expense of him who gave the wound.[6] Circumcision itself was really an operation in surgery, rough as, in some instances, the instruments were.[7]

So early a knowledge of this subject on the part of Israel need not surprise us if we remember that already before the exodus physicians formed a distinct profession in Egypt. Outside of the Bible there is ample documentary evidence not only that physicians abounded there, but physicians of almost every sort, not excepting oculists and dentists. The word chemistry is derived from *chemi* (Gr., *chēmeia*), which is an old name for the land of Egypt. When King Asa, afflicted with a disease of the feet, is blamed for seeking not "unto the Lord, but unto the physicians," evidently no disparagement of the profession of medicine is intended.[8] He is blamed simply for *depending on* physicians rather than on God. He did not look to God for his blessing on the means used. King Hezekiah was medically treated by direct command of a prophet of the Lord.[9]

It is needless to say that, compared with its modern development, the medical art never got beyond the period of infancy in Bible times. The work of the earlier physicians was mostly surgical,— that is, it consisted in applying remedies to outward injuries. The treatment of wounds is referred to in a number of passages.[10] After the exile the practice of medicine became more general ; and it is a pathetic record that we have in the Gospel of a woman with a bloody

---

[1] Ecclus. 38 : 1, 2.   [2] Job 13 : 4; Jer. 17 : 14.   [3] Gen. 30 : 14.   [4] Gen. 35 : 17; 38 : 28.   [5] Ex. 1 : 15.   [6] Ex. 21 : 19.   [7] Ex. 4 : 25.   [8] 2 Chron. 16 : 12.   [9] 2 Kings 20 : 7; Isa. 38 : 21.
[10] 2 Kings 8 : 29; Isa. 1 : 6; Jer. 8 : 11; 51 : 8; Ezek. 30 : 21; Luke 10 : 34.

flux, who had "suffered many things of many physicians, and had spent all that she had."[1] Quacks were not unknown even in the earliest times; but the profession as such always stood in high honor.[2] It is worthy of note that the writer of one of the gospels and of the Acts was a "beloved physician."[3] In the times of our Lord the services of the profession were much required at the temple, the duties of the priests and others there exposing them to certain peculiar physical ailments.

39. The Mechanic Arts.—As preparing it for an independent national life in Canaan, Egypt was in many respects an admirable school for Israel. If it had been of the same race or the same religion, there might have been too great an assimilation, possibly even an absorption of the weaker in the stronger. As it was, Israel was able to learn what it most needed to know, while retaining its national peculiarities and above all its historic faith. Not alone agriculture, but the mechanic arts, had reached in Egypt at this time a high degree of development. The Israelites on settling in Canaan not only did not attain to its standard in this particular, but fell far below it. Their wanderings in the wilderness, and the wars of the conquest that followed, were no doubt a wise providential discipline, but they were a great hindrance to progress in the mechanic and useful arts. Besides, their apostasy from God, which soon followed, and their consequent tribal jealousies and conflicts, left them in no condition for such progress in the arts of civilized life.

It is a sorry picture which the historian draws of the times preceding the activity of Samuel: "Now there was no smith found throughout all the land of Israel: . . . but all the Israelites went down to the Philistines, to sharpen every man his share, and his coulter, and his axe, and his mattock; yet they had a file for the mattocks, and for the coulters, and for the forks, and for the axes; and to set the goads."[4] With the harmony and prosperity that came with David's reign, especially with the building of Solomon's temple and the introduction of skilled labor and its products from without the bounds of Israel, the mechanic arts began at length to flourish. Still, the Israelites were never much devoted to them in the early times. Agriculture and the rearing of cattle were their favorite pursuits. Subsequent to the exile, however, the force of circumstances compelled them to engage so generally in the other occupations of civilized life that the rabbis held it to be one of the signs of a neglected education if a person had not learned in youth some useful trade.

[1] Mark 5:26; Luke 8:43.   [2] Job 13:4.   [3] Col. 4:14.   [4] 1 Sam. 13:19-21.

40. Of the artisan classes, those working in wood and metals were always, perhaps, the most numerous in Israel. Among the former were carpenters, cabinet-makers, wood-carvers, manufacturers of wagons, of baskets, of various household utensils including the distaff and the loom, and of the tools used in agriculture, such as ploughs, yokes, threshing-machines, goads and winnowing-shovels.[1] The tools incidentally mentioned in the Bible as in use among workers in wood are the hammer, saw, different kinds of axes, the

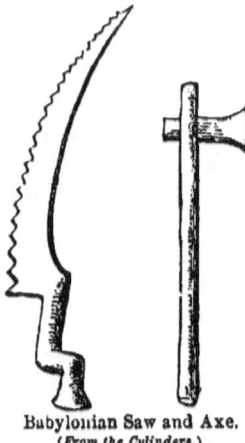

Babylonian Saw and Axe.
(From the Cylinders.)

measuring-line, the draughting-pencil, the compasses and the plane.[2] Like the Egyptians, their neighbors and predecessors in civilization, the Hebrews doubtless understood also the use of the awl, drill, mallet, chisel and many other similar instruments.

41. METALS.—The principal metals of modern times were well known to them. Even the antediluvians are represented as skilled in metallurgy, Tubal-cain (that is, "Tubal the smith") being "the forger of every cutting instrument of brass and iron."[3] After the flood the patriarch Abraham is represented as rich not only in cattle, but in gold and silver.[4] Tin and lead also are both mentioned in the Pentateuch.[5] The Hebrew word rendered "steel" in a number of passages in the common version has been translated "brass" by the revisers.[6] Brass is properly an alloy of copper and zinc; while bronze is an alloy of the same material with tin, a small proportion of zinc being sometimes added. That the process of hardening copper by such additions was understood by the ancients is undoubted. The distinction between bronze and iron weapons, as indicated by their color, is plainly shown on the monuments of Egypt. But it is not always possible to say with certainty whether the material called "brass" in the revised English version resembled most what is now known as brass, or bronze, or copper,—the same uncertainty attaching to the original Hebrew word as to the Latin aes and the Greek chalkos. That it was quite a different article from steel is clear. The Hebrew word chasmal, rendered "amber" in Ezekiel 1:4, 27; 8:2, seems also to have been a com-

[1] Ex. 35:33; 37:1, 10, 15, 25; Deut. 20:2, 4; Judg. 6:19; 1 Sam. 6:14; 2 Sam. 24:22; 1 Kings 19:21; Jer. 28:13.   [2] Deut. 19:5; Ps. 74:5, 6; Isa. 10:15; 44:13.   [3] Gen. 4:22.   [4] Gen. 13:2.   [5] Ex. 15:10; Num. 31:22.   [6] 2 Sam. 22:35; Job 20:24; Ps. 18:34; Jer. 15:12.

posite brilliant metal of a quality similar to brass.[1] Whether the "iron from the north" spoken of in Jeremiah 15:12 was not a hardened iron answering somewhat to modern steel is still a question.[2]

Gold and silver were not native in Palestine.[3] The same is true of tin and lead; but iron and copper were both mined there.[4] An interesting and instructive passage in the book of Job shows that the methods used in mining were much the same then as now.[5] There are still to be found mines on the Sinaitic peninsula which, as it is supposed, were worked by the Egyptians before the days of Moses. The remains of smelting-furnaces, hammers of porphyry, reservoirs for water, and even the piers and wharves on the adjacent coast whence the ore was shipped, are still visible. There is abundant evidence that the process of separating metals from their alloys was to some degree early understood.[6] In two passages of Scripture, mineral soda, or natron, is mentioned in a way to indicate a knowledge of its chemical qualities.[7]

42. WORKERS IN METALS.—Those employed with metals who are specially referred to in the Bible are gold and silversmiths and workers in brass and iron.[8] Some of the tools of which they made use were the anvil, the bellows, the smelting-furnace and "finingpot," the hammer and tongs.[9] Among the various products of their labor which are referred to are settings for precious stones and numerous other articles used for ornamentation, gilding, axes, sickles, knives, swords, spear-heads, fetters, chains, bolts, nails, hooks, penstocks, pans for cooking purposes, ploughshares, and the wheels of threshing-instruments.[10] It would appear that in the earlier periods copper or bronze was oftener used in the manufacture of these articles than iron. The weapons of Goliath, for example, as also those of Samson, were of the former material;[11] and it is worthy of attention, as bearing on some questions of the higher criticism, that relatively a much larger amount of copper was used in building and furnishing the tabernacle than the temple. This might have been expected if the account of the tabernacle be genuine and authentic; but it is out of harmony with the theory that the tabernacle is a product of the imagination—simply a purposed reflection of the temple backward into a mythical period.

[1] Cf. Rev. 1:15; 2:18.　[2] Cf. Nah. 2:3.　[3] 1 Kings 9:11; 10:22; 22:48.　[4] Deut. 8:9.
[5] Job 28:1-11.　[6] 1 Chron. 29:4; Ps. 12:6; Prov. 8:19; 10:20.　[7] Prov. 25:20; Jer. 2:22.
[8] Judg. 17:4; 1 Kings 7:15; 2 Chron. 24:12; Isa. 41:7; Mal. 3:2; Acts 19:24; 2 Tim. 4:14.
[9] Ex. 39:3; Prov. 17:3; Isa. 6:6; Jer. 6:29; Ezek. 22:18.　[10] Num. 35:16; 1 Sam. 13:20;
17:7; 2 Sam. 12:31; Job 19:24; Ps. 105:18; 107:16; Isa. 45:2; Jer. 17:1; Ezek. 4:3;
Amos 1:3; Acts 12:10.　[11] Judg. 16:21; 1 Sam. 17:5.

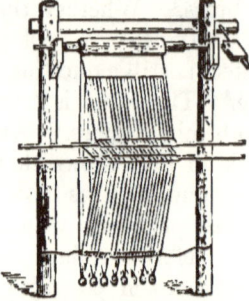

Ancient Roman Loom.

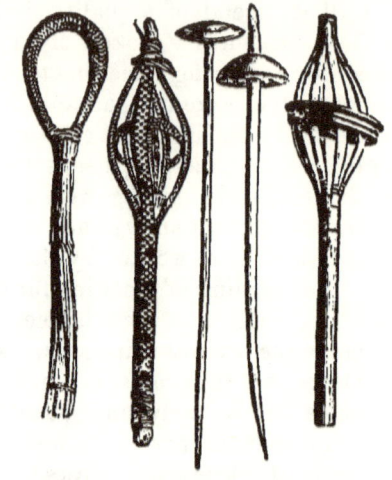

Ancient Spindles. (*From Specimens in British and Berlin Museums.*)

Loop to place over the thread; basket-work spindle; wood spindle; spindle with head of gypsum; spindle of split cane.

Assyrian Brick inscribed with Shalmaneser's Name and Title.

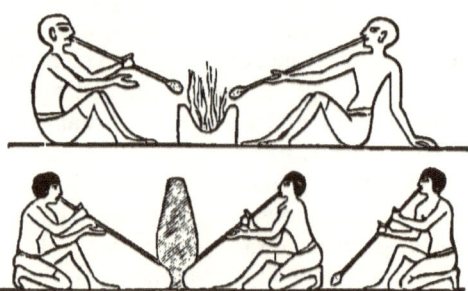

Egyptian Glass-blowers. (*After Wilkinson.*)

Glass Bottle inscribed with the Name of Thothmes III.
(*After Wilkinson.*)

Ancient Egyptian Glass Bottles. (*After Wilkinson.*)

43. OTHER ARTISANS.—Mention is made in the Bible also of stone-masons—who are at the same time plasterers—of brick and tile-makers, engravers, apothecaries, perfumers, bakers, tanners, fullers, spinners, weavers and potters.[1] The business of the fuller included that of fulling, that is, thickening, shrinking the cloth, as well as cleansing it.[2] He had no machine for the purpose, but as the Hebrew word for his name indicates ("the treader") he made a vigorous use of his hands and feet. Weaving was mostly done by women.[3] Looms of a very primitive type are still seen in the East, to some extent, although machines superior to them were introduced in Egypt two centuries before the exodus. When Job says, "My days are swifter than a weaver's shuttle," he cannot refer to the old method of supplying the filling for the web by the fingers, or by a rod armed with hooks.[4] The potter's trade is often alluded to, especially by the prophets. The Israelites had doubtless been acquainted with it in Egypt. The clay was first trodden with the feet. It was then shaped by the potter by the use of wheels, which were sometimes turned with the foot. The process of glazing was also early understood.[5] After being smoothed and glazed the vessel was hardened in a furnace. In Jeremiah 48 : 12 there is a peculiar class of laborers referred to. They were those who tilted casks or other vessels for the sake of emptying them of their contents.

44. While there seems to have been nothing in antiquity precisely corresponding to the modern association of the trades into guilds or orders, for mutual protection and advantage, there is evident a tendency to local association. Certain parts of a city, sometimes whole streets, received their names from the character of the business carried on there.[6] Some of the trades, as, for example, that of the tanner and the fuller, were looked upon with less public favor than others, and could be pursued only in the suburbs. A well-known proverb of the Talmud voiced this popular sentiment: "The world cannot exist either without the perfumer or the tanner. Happy is the perfumer, and woe to him whose calling is that of a tanner." Josephus mentions a valley in the neighborhood of Jerusalem called the "valley of the cheesemongers."[7]

45. The honor put upon skilled labor, and in fact upon manual labor of all sorts, in the Bible, is specially noteworthy. Of Oholiab

---

[1] Ex. 5:8; 31:5; 35:33; 2 Kings 18:17; 1 Chron. 4:23; Prov. 31:13, 19, 22; Isa. 7:3, 20; 29:16; 36:2; 41:25; Jer. 2:22; 17:1; Ezek. 5:1; 18:11; Hos. 7:4,6; Nah. 3:14; Mal. 3:2; Acts 10:6.   [2] Cf. Matt. 9:16; Mark 2:21.   [3] 1 Sam. 2:19; Prov. 31:22, 24.   [4] Job 7:6.
[5] Prov. 26:23; Ecclus. 38:29, 30.   [6] 1 Kings 20:34; 2 Kings 18:17; 1 Chron. 4:14; Jer. 37:21.
[7] Josephus, *Wars of the Jews*, 5, 4:1.

Dressing and Working in Flax. (*After Wilkinson.*)

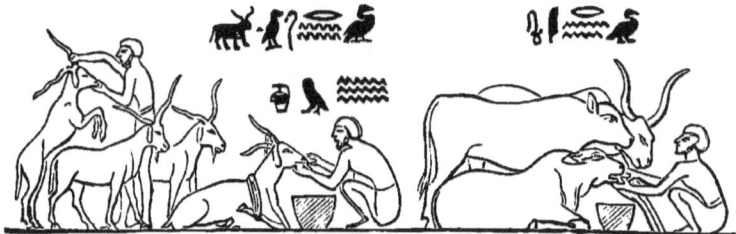

Egyptians Treating sick Animals. (*After Wilkinson.*)

The Nilometer.

For measuring the height of the river Nile.

Egyptian Furnace. (*After Wilkinson.*)

Brazier for burning Charcoal.

and Bezaleel, for example, it is represented that they were divinely endowed with "wisdom of heart" to do what they did.[1] Physical toil was never regarded among the Hebrews, as it was among the Greeks and Romans, as in any sense degrading. Saul and David in early life were both day-laborers. Elisha was taken from the plough to become the follower and successor of Elijah.[2] The prophet Amos was "a herdman and a dresser of sycomore trees."[3] It is meant for high praise of a faithful wife and mother when it is said that "she riseth also while it is yet night, and giveth meat to her household."[4]

Even such philosophers as Aristotle and Plato taught that manual labor was unworthy of a free man, and that the state should never give the right of citizenship to an artisan. How unlike is this to the spirit that rules in the book of Proverbs: "Seest thou a man diligent (skillful) in his business? he shall stand before kings."[5] The same principles prevailed among the Jews of our Lord's time and still later. A certain Phineas is spoken of who was busy with his work as a mason when word was brought to him that he had been chosen to the high priesthood. It was in strict harmony with the sentiments of his countrymen and the customs of his time, therefore, for Paul, scholar and orator though he was, to engage, as opportunity offered or circumstances required, in the trade of making tent-cloth, which in his youth he had learned. But a still higher honor is it to handicraft that the Redeemer of the world was not only the son of a carpenter, but, as we have reason to believe, himself worked at that trade in the humble shop at Nazareth.

[1] Ex. 36 : 1.   [2] 1 Kings 19 : 19.   [3] Amos 7 : 14.   [4] Prov. 31 : 15.   [5] Prov. 22 : 29.

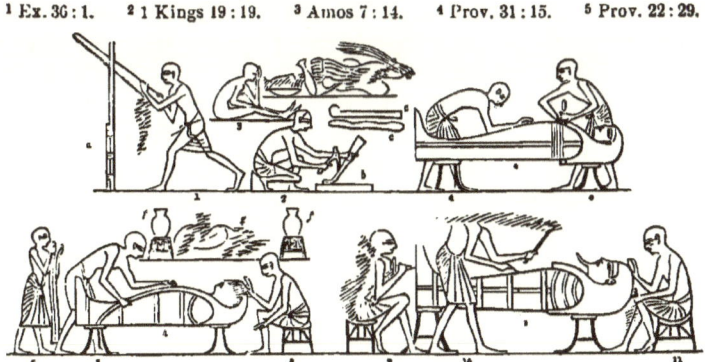

Embalming, Making the Cases and Bandaging Mummies.

Fig. 1, sawing wood; a. timber fastened to a stand. 2, cutting the leg of a chair, on a stand, b, indicating the trade of a carpenter. 3, a man fallen asleep. c, c. wood ready for cutting. d, onions and other provisions, which occur again at g, with vases. f. f. 4, 5 and 7, binding mummies. 6, bringing the bandages. 9, using the drill. 8, 10 and 11, painting and polishing the cases. e, h, i, mummy-cases.

CHAPTER VII.

TRADE AND COMMERCE.

1. THE Hebrew words used for trader show that, among the Israelites, he was originally a travelling salesman.[1] These words, however, do not exclude the idea of a place where trade was carried on.[2] The principal one of them is still current among the German Jews of Europe in the form *schacher*, that is, traffic. Trade in some form undoubtedly goes back to the beginnings of human history. Life in cities was only possible as the necessaries were supplied from the surrounding country. There is evidence that even in the patriarchal period there was not only a limited domestic trade carried on, but that it had assumed an international character. Gold and silver were known both in the form of ornaments and of money, and were freely circulated.[3] "Abraham weighed to Ephron the silver, which he had named in the audience of the children of Heth, four hundred shekels of silver, current *money* with the merchant."[4] Somewhat later we read of a caravan made up of Ishmaelite and Midianite merchants going down into Egypt with such articles as spicery, balm and myrrh. It appeared also that they were not averse to trading in slaves. To them Joseph was sold by his hard-hearted brethren.[5] Still later, in a period of scarcity, we learn of the importation of grain into Canaan from Egypt and of its being paid for with silver pieces which were weighed.[6]

2. PALESTINE UNSUITED TO COMMERCE.—Geographically, Palestine would seem to have offered the most natural highway to connect the renowned and opulent nations bordering on the Euphrates with those inhabiting Egypt and Arabia. As a matter of fact, however, owing to its peculiar situation and its physical features, there was little opportunity for the Israelites to become, like their Phœnician neighbors, a great commercial people. It lacked sea-coast. The course and nature of its principal river were unfavorable. It was traversed by high mountain chains; and to the east and south lay an almost impassable desert. Undoubtedly this state of things was

---

[1] Gen. 23:16; 37:28; 1 Kings 10:28; Prov. 31:14; Ezek. 27:12, 15.   [2] Isa. 23:18; cf. "Racal" (= trafficking), 1 Sam. 30:29.   [3] Gen. 13:2; 20:16; 24:22, 53.   [4] Gen. 23:16. [5] Gen. 37:25; 39:1.   [6] Gen. 42:1, 2.

providentially intended. It was morally necessary that while holding a central position relative to the great nations of the earth, the holy land should also, for a time—that is, until salvation had been duly prepared for the race—be in a degree secluded from them. Opportunity was thus given for maturing undisturbed the germ whose fruit was to be offered to all mankind.

The needed seclusion was provided for not alone in their land but also in the institutions of the chosen people. The Mosaic laws are based largely on the supposition that the Israelites are, and will remain, agriculturists. In so far, too, these laws have the peculiar stamp of the Mosaic period when grazing and agriculture were their almost exclusive occupations. And while, in letter, the law recognizes the legitimacy of trade and offers rules for its regulation, its spirit indisputably favors the cultivation of the soil and the utmost restriction of foreign intercourse.[1] The prophetical books face in the same direction. Isaiah calls on the "house of Jacob" to come and walk in the light of the Lord. "For," he says, addressing Jehovah, "thou hast forsaken thy people the house of Jacob, because they be filled *with customs* from the east, . . . and they strike hands with the children of strangers."[2]

3. TRADE OF ISRAEL UNDER THE KINGS.—Previous to the time of David the trade of the Israelites was mostly confined to the exchange of the products of their own country among themselves. Caravans were only occasionally made up for adjacent lands, especially Phœnicia, Syria and Egypt. Even this limited foreign trade was carried on mostly by foreign merchants. The extension of the bounds of the kingdom by David's conquests and the great increase in its wealth furnished both the occasion and the means for an enlarged commerce with other nations. In the time of Solomon it reached its highest stage. His ships, built and manned mostly by Phœnicians, sailed to the remotest lands then known, and brought back their products to enrich his capital. There were exported grain, balsam, nuts, spices, ship-timber, skins, wool and flax. There were brought back in exchange for them and for money, among other things, the various metals, in a crude state and in the form of ornaments and useful vessels, the rarer woods and spices, precious stones, ivory, peacocks and apes.[3]

Nor was this commerce carried on simply from Phœnician ports. Every three years the conjoined fleets of Hiram and Solomon sailed

---

[1] Lev. 19:35; 25:36, 37; Deut. 17:16, 17; 25:13-16; 28:12.   [2] Isa. 2:6, 7; Nah. 3:4.
[3] Gen. 37:25; 43:11; 1 Kings 5:11; 2 Chron. 8:17, 18; 9:10; 27:5; Ezek. 27:6, 17.

from Eloth and Ezion-geber, harbors on the Red Sea which had
been secured through the power of David. These fleets visited for
purposes of trade the principal countries bordering on the Indian
Ocean and the Persian Gulf.[1] During the reign of Solomon, too,
horses began to be imported on a large scale from Egypt, although
in direct contravention of a Mosaic statute.[2] His marriage with an
Egyptian princess opened the way not only for this innovation, but
for many another breach of national custom and law. A reference
to the "king's merchants" gives color to the theory that there was
a sort of royal trading-company formed at this time with special
reference to trade with foreign countries;[3] and from one passage it
would appear that some kind of a tax was laid on this foreign trade
for the benefit of the public revenue.[4] The natural effects of such
free intercourse with foreigners were not slow in coming. Crowds
of Gentiles flocked to Jerusalem not only with their wares, but with
their heathenish tastes and customs. The frequent references in the
book of Proverbs to the "strange women" are very suggestive as it
respects the state of morals that then existed. In one place it is dis-
tinctly stated that it is the wife of a foreign merchant who, as a
harlot, lies in wait "at every corner."[5]

The division of the kingdom, with the internal strife and external
oppression and robbery brought about by it, naturally put an end to
any considerable foreign trade among the Israelites, as well as to the
former wide-spread prosperity of the people. Still the prophetical
books bear witness to the fact that notwithstanding expensive wars
and heavy tributes paid to heathen princes there remained no inconsiderable amount of luxury among certain classes.[6] It is said of
Jehoshaphat that he made "ships of Tarshish to go to Ophir for
gold: but they went not; for the ships were broken at Ezion-geber."[7]
Phœnicia was still supplied with such natural products as wheat,
oil and honey in exchange for skilled labor and its fruits. Even
the impoverished exiles from Babylon found means for paying it in
provisions or money for the timber needed to build the second temple,
and for the fish with which it provided their scanty market.[8] But
the trade that was carried on was relatively unimportant, and passed
principally through the hands of others than Israelites.

Phœnician traders, especially, traversed the country as peddlers and
also erected markets for their wares in the principal towns. It was

1 1 Kings 9 : 26.   2 Deut. 17 : 16.   3 1 Kings 10 : 28, 29; 2 Chron. 1 : 16.   4 1 Kings 10 : 15,
6 Prov. 7 : 8-20.   6 Isa. 3 : 18-25; Ezek. 26 : 2; Hos. 12 : 7; Amos 2 : 6; 8 : 5; Mic. 6 : 10.
7 1 Kings 22 : 48.   8 1 Kings 5 : 11; Ezra 3 : 7; Neh. 13 : 16.

to them that the "virtuous woman" of the Proverbs is represented as selling her "fine linen" and "girdles."[1] The feasts in Jerusalem offered to them a rich harvest. The very name "merchant" became finally synonymous with Canaanite.[2] In Nehemiah's time these traders were so numerous and so defiant of Hebrew customs that he was obliged to resort to harsh measures against them.[3] At a still later period, after the Israelites became dispersed among other peoples, especially in Egypt, they themselves became to no inconsiderable extent the middle-men of commerce. Yet it was productive of little change among the inhabitants of Palestine. In the brief space of national independence under the Maccabees some efforts were made to restore Israel's commercial prosperity, but without lasting results.[4] The attempts of Herod in the same direction contributed principally to the prosperity of Greek and Roman traders.[5] In fact, the Israelites were always disinclined to come into any closer contact with foreigners than was absolutely necessary. The apostle Peter sets forth in the Acts what was their habitual practice: "Ye yourselves know how that it is an unlawful thing for a man that is a Jew to join himself or come unto one of another nation."[6] And Josephus writes to the same effect in his work against Apion: "We neither inhabit a maritime country, nor do we delight in merchandise, nor in such a mixture with other men as arises from it."[7]

4. TRADE AFTER THE TIME OF CHRIST.—Subsequent to the time of our Lord, the circumstances of the people having greatly changed, "their views as to commerce also underwent a slow process of modification, the main object now being to restrict such occupations, and especially to regulate them in accordance with religion. Inspectorships of weights and measures are of comparatively late date in our own country. The rabbis in this, as in many other matters, were long before us. They appointed regular inspectors whose duty it was to go from market to market, and more than that, fix the current market prices. The prices for produce were ultimately determined by each community. Few merchants would submit to interference with what is called the law of supply and demand. But the talmudical laws against buying up grain and withdrawing it from sale, especially at a time of scarcity, are exceedingly strict. Similarly, it was prohibited artificially to raise prices, especially of produce. . . . Cheating was declared to involve heavier punishment than a breach of some of the other moral commandments. For the

[1] Prov. 31:24. [2] Prov. 31:24 (margin of Revised Version). [3] Neh. 10:31; 13:16-22.
[4] 1 Macc. 14:5. [5] Josephus, *Antiq.* 15, 9:6. [6] Acts 10:28. [7] Josephus, *c. Apion* 1:12.

latter, it was argued, might be set right by repentance. But he who
cheated took in not merely one or several persons, but every one;
and how could that ever be set right !"[1]

5. ROADS IN PALESTINE.—Roads in the East at the present day,
even those most travelled, are extremely poor. Excepting the period
of Greek and Roman occupation, there have been but few roads
artificially made in Palestine at any time. Traces of those of the
Romans are still to be seen, especially on the east of the Jordan.
The Old Testament contains no reference to bridges, although the
idea is not foreign to the Hebrew language, being contained in the
proper name Geshur.[2] There is but one passage that speaks of a
conveyance for passengers across a stream.[3] The usual method of
crossing the Jordan, the principal stream of Palestine, was by ford-
ing. This was not difficult during most seasons of the year. The
Hebrew language contains a number of terms for roads, including,
with that for the simple foot-path, others suggesting no little care in
their construction. Such roads must have existed in the very earliest
times, being absolutely necessary for the passage of armies and caravans, as well as for that commercial intercourse of which we have
knowledge. One of these expressions, *mesillah*, found in several
passages, represents an elevated road answering to the modern "highway."[4] It is used as an illustration by the prophet Isaiah in his
notable prediction concerning John the Baptist.[5] In the construction of such roads deep places were filled up, hills levelled and rough
places made smooth, so that journeying on them should be as unimpeded as possible.

That the idea of road-building was not foreign even to the Mosaic
period is shown by the instructions given in the Pentateuch respecting the roads leading to the cities of refuge.[6] And when the Israelites seek permission of the Edomites to cross their land they promise that they will not pass through field or through vineyard, but
will go along the "king's *high* way."[7] A road built by the government seems to be meant, and toll was sometimes demanded from those
making use of it.[8] The same conclusion is reached respecting the
early existence of tolerable roads if we consider the numerous biblical passages referring to the use of chariots of war and other vehicles.[9] It is not to be supposed, however, that wheeled carriages
for ordinary travelling were in use in Palestine before the times of

[1] See Edersheim, *Sketches of Jewish Social Life*, p. 206.   [2] 2 Sam. 3 : 3.   [3] 2 Sam. 19 : 18.
[4] Num. 20 : 19; Judg. 20 : 31; 1 Sam. 6 : 12; 2 Sam. 20 : 12.   [5] Isa. 40 : 3.   [6] Deut. 19 : 3.
[7] Num. 20 : 17, 19.   [8] Ezra 4 : 13, 20; 7 : 24.   [9] Gen. 45 : 19; 50 : 9; Judg. 4 : 13.

David. There are infrequent allusions to them at a later period.[1] It is likely that commercial reasons, if no other, would have led Solomon to make the means of communication throughout his kingdom as abundant and easy as possible. If we may trust Josephus here, this king had the roads leading to Jerusalem paved with black stone, probably the basalt found near the Sea of Tiberias.[2] Not far from this time there are certain traces of the erection of khans for the convenience of travellers in otherwise uninhabited wastes.[3]

Somewhat later there were four great public roads made use of by the military powers and by the traffic of the world which passed along the four sides of the holy land. In the south was one extending from Gaza, by way of Petra and Duma, to the Persian Gulf. On the west was the great thoroughfare along the coast of the Mediterranean connecting Egypt with Phœnicia and Syria. On the north lay the route from the Phœnician ports of Tyre and Sidon, running across Lebanon to Damascus, Palmyra and on to the Euphrates. Along the east border stretched the road from Damascus to the Ælanitic Gulf and the peninsula of Arabia, skirting in its course the western part of the great Syrian desert.

In the time of our Lord there were six main arteries of commerce and general intercourse traversing the country within, "the chief objective points being Cæsarea the military, and Jerusalem the religious, capital. First, there was the southern road, which led from Jerusalem, by Bethlehem, to Hebron and thence westward to Gaza and eastward into Arabia."[4] Second, there was the main road just described, running along the sea shore from Egypt to Tyre, with which Jerusalem was connected by a branch diverging at Lydda. Paul, it is likely, escorted by Roman soldiers, travelled by this route to Cæsarea, a little more than seventy miles from Jerusalem.[5] A third road led from Jerusalem to Joppa by way of Beth-horon and Lydda. A fourth great highway of Palestine at this date was one leading from Galilee to Jerusalem through Samaria.[6] At Sichem it intersected another running from Cæsarea to Damascus. It was on the former of these roads, it will be remembered, that our Lord was when, while resting by Jacob's well at Sichem, he had the notable conversation with the woman of Samaria.[7] A fifth road, extending north from Jerusalem, was by the way of Bethany to Jericho, thence across the Jordan into Peræa,

[1] 1 Kings 12:18; Acts 8:28.   [2] Josephus, *Antiq.* 8, 7:4.   [3] Jer. 41:17 (margin).   [4] Edersheim, *Sketches of Jewish Social Life*, p. 42.   [5] Acts 23:31, 32.   [6] John 4:4, 45; cf. Luke 9:53.   [7] John 4:6.

and thence again across the Jordan at Decapolis into Galilee.[1] It was the road ordinarily travelled by Jews who wished to avoid Samaria. The last principal line of internal communication in Palestine at this period was one which passed directly through Galilee, and was the main thoroughfare between the east and the west. Its eastern terminus was Damascus. In Galilee it passed through such familiar places as Capernaum, Tiberias, Nain, Nazareth, and terminated at Ptolemais on the sea coast.

6. TRAVELLING.—The Bible speaks of journeys of all sorts and for almost every purpose. Travelling by sea is the most seldom mentioned.[2] The long journey which Abraham took with his family from Ur of the Chaldees to Haran and from Haran to Canaan is among the earliest recorded facts of history.[3] The hardships and perils to which one was exposed in travelling even in the more civilized times of the apostle Paul are fully set forth by him in one of his epistles.[4] Thrice he had suffered shipwreck; a day and a night he had been in the deep; he had been in perils of rivers, in perils of robbers, in labor and travail, in watchings often, in hunger and thirst, in fastings often, in cold and nakedness. Losing one's way and getting out of provisions was by no means the most serious peril to which a traveller was exposed. Unless protected by a numerous guard, he was pretty generally at the mercy of roving freebooters. Even the large company of exiles returning from Babylon were not without their fears lest they might be assailed and overpowered by bands of robbers.[5]

Journeys by land were commonly made on foot.[6] If an animal was used for riding, it was generally the ass. After the period of the kings, horses were ridden in war, but not on ordinary journeys.[7] The camel was sometimes so used, but mostly served as a beast of burden.[8] The yearly pilgrimages of the people to the feasts at Jerusalem were, as it would seem, universally made on foot, large numbers banding together both for the sake of protection and with a view to social intercourse.[9]

7. WAGONS.—As already intimated, wagons for purposes of travel—that is, for the carriage of persons—were very little used by the Israelites, although known to them and not uncommon in Egypt in the time of the patriarchs.[10] In the tenth century B.C., King Rehoboam is described on one occasion as fleeing in a char-

---

[1] Matt. 20:17, 29; Luke 10:30; 19:1, 28.   [2] 1 Kings 10:11, 22; Ps. 107:23; Jonah 1:3.   [3] Gen. 11:31; 12:4, 5.   [4] 2 Cor. 11:25.   [5] Ezra 8:22, 31; cf. Neh. 2:6, 9.   [6] Gen. 29:1 (margin); Isa. 52:7; John 4:6.   [7] 1 Sam. 25:42; 2 Sam. 17:23; 1 Kings 2:40; 2 Chron. 23:15.   [8] Gen. 24:61.   [9] Mark 10:32, 46; Luke 2:42, 44.   [10] Gen. 45:19, 27.

iot.[1] Ahaziah also used the same means of flight from the wrath of Jehu ;[2] but in both cases it is doubtless a light war-chariot that is meant. Between it and the vehicle intended for the transportation of goods or persons the Hebrew language makes a clear distinction. A considerable variety of the latter seems to have been known to antiquity. They were mostly two-wheeled, and the wheels, which were generally made solid, revolved around an axletree. On this axletree the body of the wagon or cart was directly placed. Vehicles of this sort and of very rude construction are still found in western Asia. The state of the roads has always been such in Palestine as to make it appear unlikely that wagons were often used for anything else than the transportation of goods.[3] They were drawn by cattle, and might be either covered or open.[4] If more than two animals were used, they were attached, whatever their number, side by side. The " cart rope" of which the prophet Isaiah speaks was perhaps that by which the extra cattle were connected with the vehicle.[5] Both the Assyrian and Egyptian monuments have representations of two-wheeled wagons, with seats for those riding and with spoked wheels. It was probably in a chariot of Egyptian manufacture that the Ethiopian eunuch was riding, on his way from Jerusalem to Gaza, when Philip joined him.[6] As far as we are informed, the first attempt to lift the body of the vehicle from the axletree and make the comfort of travellers a matter of concern was at the beginning of the fifteenth century A.D. A queen of France is spoken of who rode into Paris, in the year 1405, in a carriage whose seat was suspended on leathern straps.

8. THE PALANQUIN.—Something answering to the modern palanquin of China and India appears to have been in use in the earliest times. In its first occurrence it was borne not on men's shoulders, but on the back or (with something to balance it) the side of the camel or other animal.[7] It consisted of a covered frame firmly attached to the saddle and fitted up with cushions and other conveniences. " Litter" was another name for it. The Hebrew uses three words to which much the same significance was attached. In answer to the question " Who is this that cometh up out of the wilderness like pillars of smoke, perfumed with myrrh and frankincense, with all powders of the merchant?" the answer is, " Behold, it is the litter of Solomon ; threescore mighty men are about it, of the mighty men of Israel." The revisers give us " palanquin" as

[1] 1 Kings 12 : 18. [2] 2 Kings 9 : 2". [3] 1 Sam. 6 : 7, 8 ; Amos 2 : 13. [4] Num. 7 : 3. [5] Isa. 5 : 18. [6] Acts 8 : 28. [7] Gen. 31 : 34.

the rendering of another word in the context; but doubtless a similar vehicle is meant.[1] In Isaiah, likewise, the exiled Israelites are spoken of as returning " upon horses, and in chariots, and in litters, and upon mules, and upon swift beasts."[2]

The modern litter of the East, which cannot greatly differ from the ancient one, is thus described by Van Lennep: " Persons of wealth and rank, when journeying, often ride, either themselves or their families, in a litter or *taktravan*, probably referred to in Isaiah 66 : 20, and which corresponds to the palankeen of India, the traveller reclining on a mattress and cushions. . . . This vehicle is similar to an oblong box or the body of a carriage, with a latticed door on each side, and usually covered with crimson cloth. It is set and firmly fastened on the middle of two long parallel poles or shafts, whose extremities are attached to the pack-saddles of the front and hind mule."[3] Notwithstanding their nearness to the coast and the fact that for a time the tribes of Dan and Naphtali were in possession of strips of territory along the Mediterranean, the ancient Israelites, as we have already seen, had little to do with a seafaring life.[4] The voyages actually undertaken by them were made not from the coasts of Palestine, but from harbors in the Red Sea. Even these exceptional enterprises were not entered upon independently, but in connection with Phœnician ship-builders and mariners. It will be recalled, too, that the timber with which King Hiram of Tyre supplied Solomon for the temple at Jerusalem was transported to Joppa, its nearest seaport, by him, the land-carriage only being attended to by the servants of Solomon.[5]

9. JOURNEYING BY WATER.—It is a noteworthy circumstance that no mention is made in the Old Testament of the use of boats on the Sea of Galilee. It is quite otherwise in the New Testament. During the ministry of our Lord this province enjoyed a commercial and political activity unknown before. It was the scene of the most of his public life, and the first three gospels are made up largely of events that occurred there. The majority of the apostles were Galilæans, either by birth or residence. A number of them were fishermen.[6] Jesus on several occasions makes use of their boats, as well as those of others, in traversing the lake which formed, with the Jordan, the eastern boundary of the province. Josephus informs us that he himself once, in a feint that he made against the Romans,

---

[1] Cant. 3 : 6, 7, 9.   [2] Isa. 66 : 20.   [3] *Bible Lands*, p. 226.   [4] Gen. 49 : 13; Deut. 33 : 19; Josh. 19 : 28; Judg. 5 : 17.   [5] 2 Chron. 2 : 16; 20 : 36.   [6] Matt. 4 : 21; Luke 5 : 2, 3; John 6 : 23; 21 : 3.

Egyptian Bags of Money. (*After Wilkinson*.)

Vessels for Measuring Liquids and Grains.

Ancient Drinking-cups.

Egyptian Scales for weighing Rings of Gold.

Camel or Dromedary saddled for Travelling.

An Eastern Water-seller, with Skin Bottle filled with Water.

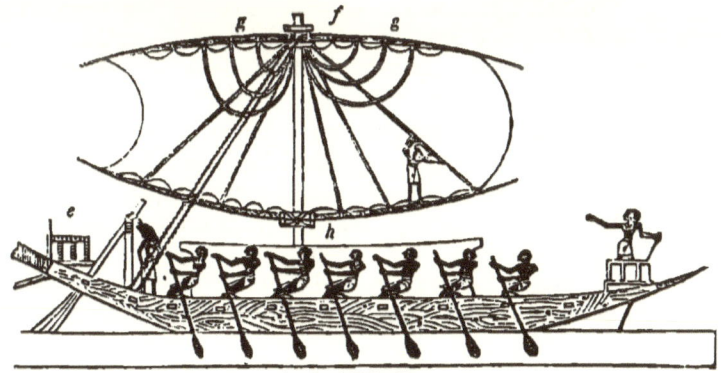

Ancient Nile Boat.
e, Forecastle. *f*, Hole for ropes to haul in sail. *g, g*, Yard. *h*, Mast.

was able to gather together on this lake no less than two hundred and thirty boats carrying four men each.[1] The usual size of the craft may be inferred from this fact. It is not to be wondered at, therefore, that a boat carrying the Master and his disciples should be in danger of sinking in a storm.[2] A passage in Deuteronomy has been unjustly thought to imply that journeying by sea was specially distasteful to the Israelites.[3] The graphic description of an ocean tempest found in the Psalms is probably the result of experience.[4] In other passages, too, a practical acquaintance with life at sea is presupposed.[5] Allusions to war-vessels are far less frequent than to merchantmen.[6] Even among the various kinds of the latter a distinction is recognized. "There," says the prophet Isaiah, "the Lord will be with us in majesty, a place of broad rivers and streams; wherein shall go no galley with oars, neither shall gallant ship pass thereby."[7]

10. The Ancient Merchant-vessel.—A somewhat detailed description of the ancient merchant-vessel is incidentally given in the prophecy of Ezekiel.[8] The city of Tyre is compared with such a vessel, and, as might be expected, with one of the richest and most highly ornamented. Her planks are said to be from trees of Senir (Hermon). Her mast is a cedar from Lebanon. The oaks of Bashan furnish the oars. Her benches (or decks) are of ivory inlaid in boxwood from the isles of Kittim (Cyprus and other islands of the Mediterranean). For a sail only the embroidered linen of Egypt will satisfy, and for awnings only blue and purple from the isles of Elishah (the Grecian Archipelago). The rowers come from Zidon and Arvad (an island near Tyre). The pilots are of the "wise men" of Tyre itself. As calkers (or ship-carpenters) the elders of Gebal (a place near Tyre) and the "wise men thereof" are taken along. Merchants are also found aboard who trade in the goods with which the craft is laden, and soldiers to defend them as well as to keep order in the numerous company. Other scraps of information on this subject are furnished here and there in the Old Testament. In the prophecy of Jonah, for example, we find the modern name of "salts" given (in Hebrew) to sailors, together with another referring to their skill in handling the ropes.[9] Here, too, we learn that passengers were received on board merchant-vessels to be carried, for a stipulated sum, from place to place, accommoda-

---

[1] Josephus, *Wars of Jews*, 2, 21 : 8.　[2] Mark 4 : 37.　[3] Deut. 28 : 68.　[4] Ps. 107 : 23–30.
[5] Ps. 48 : 7; Ezek. 27 : 26.　[6] Num. 24 : 24; Dan. 11 : 30; 1 Macc. 1 : 17; 11 : 1; 15 : 4; 2 Macc.
11 : 1.　[7] Isa. 33 : 21.　[8] Ezek. 27 : 5–9, 27.　[9] Jonah 1 : 5, 6.

tions being provided for them below the deck. Already the method of lightening a vessel in danger of swamping, by casting overboard its lading, is understood, as well as the means for spreading the sail and making firm the mast.[1] The reference in Proverbs to lying down on "the top of a mast" seems to imply a knowledge of the cross-trees, or main royal yard.[2]

11. NAVIGATION IN NEW TESTAMENT TIMES.—When we pass from the Old Testament to the New the additional information obtained concerning early methods of navigation is something remarkable both in quality and amount. From a simple narrative of one of Paul's journeys recorded in the Acts more is learned of the structure and management of ancient vessels than can be gleaned from the whole body of contemporaneous profane literature.[3] This eventful journey of the apostle was made in three different ships. The first was an Adramyttian coasting-vessel. The second, in which he was wrecked, was an Alexandrian corn-ship. The third, which succeeded in landing him safely at Puteoli, the port from which he reached Rome, was also an Alexandrian corn-ship. The second of these vessels was of a size sufficient to carry, in addition to its cargo, two hundred and seventy-six passengers. These passengers were afterwards transferred to the third vessel, which already had a crew and cargo of its own, and apparently without overloading it.[4] Accordingly, it may be safely inferred that trading-vessels at the beginning of the Christian era were not much smaller than those of the present day.

The interesting narrative of Luke also furnishes us with an item respecting the appearance of the hull of vessels at that day. That in which Paul was wrecked seems to have had an eye painted on each side of the bow, a custom which is still followed on the Mediterranean; at least, when it is said that the vessel could not "face the wind," the Greek is "eye," or "look at, the wind." The vessel in which the apostle re-shipped is said to have had for its sign "The Twin Brothers," that is, Castor and Pollux. Images of these fabulous heroes were doubtless either painted or engraved on the prow. A hint is given, too, concerning the steering apparatus. From a passage in James it has been supposed that some ancient vessels were provided with but a single rudder, although this is not directly stated.[5] That on which Paul was shipwrecked at Malta had at least two, and the process of lashing and unlashing them when an anchor

---

[1] Isa. 33 : 23. [2] Prov. 23 : 34. [3] Acts 27, 28. [4] Cf. Josephus, *Life*, chap. iii. [5] James 3 : 4.

was thrown out is described. The rudder at this period seems to have been only a larger kind of oar working through a hole or row-lock on the quarter of the vessel.

The anchors, if we may trust representations of them preserved on ancient coins, were scarcely inferior in workmanship to our own and much resembled them in form. They were carried at the stern. The ship's boat is twice mentioned in the account in the Acts. It seems at first to have been towed behind; but was hoisted on board when the storm came on and wholly cut loose when the sailors sought to escape by it. The "undergirders" referred to were chains or ropes used to bind around the vessel to prevent its planks from starting. The rig of ancient ships consisted ordinarily of one mast provided with a single square sail fastened to a yard. If more sails were used they were set on the same general principle. In the Acts a foresail is expressly mentioned, and its use, to bring the ship around in order to beach her, is noteworthy.[1] Vessels so rigged made good progress before the wind, but were not well fitted to sail against it.[2] Using the lead on approaching the shore was already common, and being so was naturally much more common than in modern times, owing to the absence of compass, charts and other helps.[3] The practice of anchoring at night, when sailing was dangerous, was often resorted to for the same reasons.[4]

12. MONEY.—Previous to the Babylonian captivity coined money did not circulate among the Israelites. The history of uncoined money dates back to the earliest times. In a business transaction which Abraham some time after his arrival in Palestine had with Ephron the Hittite, we read that he "weighed to Ephron the silver, which he had named in the audience of the children of Heth, four hundred shekels of silver, current *money* with the merchant."[5] This seems to mean that the amount of money paid over was equivalent in weight and quality to fifty of the shekel-pieces then current in trade. Numerous other instances of the weighing of money occur in the Old Testament; and where it is said to be counted, it is in cases where it probably consisted of a considerable number of pieces.[6] When a definite sum had to be determined or was transferred from hand to hand, the scales were invariably resorted to, as in the con-text of one of the passages last cited. In Isaiah 46 : 6 a distinction is thought by some to be made between gold and silver as it respects coinage, certain persons being mentioned who lavished "gold out of

---

[1] Acts 27 : 40.   [2] Acts 27 : 3–5; 6 : 8; 28 : 12, 13.   [3] Acts 27 : 28.   [4] Acts 20 : 13, 16; 21 : 1.
[5] Gen. 23 : 16; cf. 17 : 13.   [6] 2 Kings 12 : 10; Jer. 32 : 9; Zech. 11 : 12.

a bag," while they " weighed silver in the balance." It is possible that pieces of gold of a fixed valuation and weight are meant; but it is quite as likely that it is merely accidental that the gold as well as the silver is not spoken of as weighed. That the money of the ancient Israelites was generally weighed to determine its value is incidentally confirmed by the word shekel, which being the most common form of money has also the root-meaning to weigh. Nor is the argument weakened by the circumstance that there were half and quarter shekel-pieces. On the other hand, the Hebrew word for talent, *kikkar*, meaning a ring, suggests the probability that it was the largest pieces of money only that were found in the shape of rings. (See illustration, p. 171.)

There is definite monumental evidence that gold and silver, sometimes in the form of rings which were apparently of much the same size and quality, circulated in Egypt considerably anterior to the exodus. During the prevalence of the famine described in Genesis 41 : 53-57, Joseph at first sold grain to the people for money. This Egyptian money is frequently represented, on the monuments, lying on scales, and though looking much alike it would appear that the pieces were of different quality, or were not actually all of the same weight. There is certainly no evidence that such money circulated by authority of the government and with its stamp upon it. Undoubtedly the precious metals were used as money in other forms than that of the ring. We read in Joshua, for example, of a " wedge" (literally, " tongue") of gold, whose weight is fifty shekels.[1] The first biblical reference to gold as a medium of exchange is where David purchases of Ornan (elsewhere "Araunah") the Jebusite his threshing-floor in order to erect an altar there. The practice of weighing money still obtains among half-civilized peoples. It is said that in the island of Madagascar the Spanish dollar is often cut into fragments by dealers and weighed in small scales which they carry with them. Even among civilized nations large pecuniary transactions are not infrequently effected by means of gold and silver transferred in bulk.

13. VALUE OF HEBREW MONEY BY WEIGHT.—After a careful examination of conflicting theories respecting Hebrew money, that supported by R. S. Poole of the British Museum (art. " Money" in Smith's *Bible Dictionary*), and adopted by Madden in his *History of Jewish Coinage* (London, 1864), seems to us to have the most to commend it. Previous to the Babylonian exile four denominations

[1] Josh. 7 : 21.

Denarius, Roman Penny of Tiberius.

[On one side is a portrait of Tiberius, with the inscription "Ti. Cæsar Divi. Aug. F. Augustus" (Tiberius Cæsar Augustus, son of the divine Augustus). On the other side is a female figure and the inscription "Pontif. Maxim." (Pontifex Maximus).]

Jewish Shekel, ascribed to Simon Maccabæus.

[One side has the Hebrew legend "Shekel Israel," a cup or chalice, and above it the date of the year when the coin was struck. On the reverse side is the legend "Jerusalem the Holy," and a triple lily or hyacinth.]

The Tetradrachma, or Stater, the Equivalent of the Jewish Shekel.

[The one figured above bears the name of Lysimachus, but the type and profile are those of Alexander the Great. It is from a specimen in the British Museum.]

Coin of Augustus, in Berlin.

The Roman Denarius "Penny." Common form of Roman "Pence."

Golden Daric.

Coins to Commemorate the Capture of Judæa.

[On the left-hand coin is seen the emperor Titus; Judæa is weeping at the foot of a palm tree. On the right hand, a Jewish captive with hands tied behind his back looks upon a Jewess seated at the foot of a palm tree.]

Coin of Claudius. (*British Museum.*)

Assarion (farthing). Actual size. (*From specimen in British Museum.*)

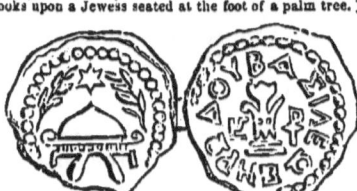

Coin of Herod the Great.

Coin of Herod Agrippa I.

COINS OF THE BIBLE.

of money were in use: the *talent*, the *maneh* (Gr., *mina*) or pound, the *shekel* with its divisions (*bekah*, $\frac{1}{2}$; *gerah*, $\frac{1}{20}$), and the *kesitah*. Nearly all of these terms are the same with the Babylonian. Much light has been shed on the whole subject by recent discoveries in the East, especially from a collection of stamped weights that has been gathered in the British Museum.

In the Hebrew money-system there was a gold and a silver talent, the one containing one hundred manehs, or ten thousand shekels, the other fifty manehs and three thousand shekels. There was also a copper talent of fifteen hundred copper shekels, each one of which was four times as heavy as the shekel of gold. The gold shekel contained about one hundred and thirty-two grains troy of the metal; the silver, two hundred and twenty; the copper, two hundred and sixty-four. There are good reasons for supposing that the Hebrew system, if not the original of the others, most nearly approaches the original, the Egyptian alone, possibly, being excepted. An effort has been made to show from Ezekiel 45 : 12 that the maneh of gold was not composed of one hundred shekels, but of sixty. It is extremely doubtful whether the passage, if it is genuine, can be so applied. Meantime two important manuscripts, the Vatican and the Alexandrine, have fifty instead of the fifteen in the common text, making the whole number of shekels ninety-five, thus bringing it nearly into harmony with other passages. It is not possible to say with certainty what value was assigned the coin called kesitah, mentioned in a few places.[1] From the connection in which it is used, it has been estimated to be worth four shekels. Jacob gave a hundred kesitahs to Hamor for the "parcel of ground where he had spread his tent;" and each of Job's acquaintances gave him one of them, besides a ring of gold. The expression "shekel of the sanctuary," found in Exodus 30 : 24, probably means simply a full shekel. With it is to be compared that used of the shekels paid by Abraham to the children of Heth (one "current with the merchant"[2]) and the so-called "king's weight" mentioned in 2 Samuel 14 : 26.

14. COINED MONEY.—Soon after the exile coined money began to circulate in Palestine. A Persian gold coin called a *daric* (worth about five dollars) is several times mentioned in the books of Ezra and Nehemiah.[3] It is by no means certain that this was the first piece of coined money known to the Jews. All that can be said is

---

[1] Gen. 33 : 19; cf. 23 : 15; Josh. 24 : 32; Job 42 : 11.   [2] Gen. 23 : 16.   [3] Ezra 2 : 69; 8 : 27; Neh. 7 : 70–72.

that it was the first to gain much currency among them.   Upon the overthrow of the Persian monarchy, Greek coins of the denomination of talents and drachmas began to be used by them.[1]   The right to coin money was first granted to Simon, one of the Maccabæan heroes, B.C. 143, and specimens of the coins then minted are still extant.[2]   The Jewish coinage, however, did not wholly supplant the Greek.   The Greek coin of smallest value was the *lepton*.   The word means a fish's scale.   The widow's mite was a piece of this kind.[3]   It required, according to the context in Mark, two to make a farthing, that is, the Roman coin called *quadrans*.   There is another word rendered farthing in the English version (*assarion*) which was four times as valuable as the quadrans.[4]

Besides the quadrans and the assarion, another Roman coin in circulation in the time of our Lord was the *denarius*, a silver piece worth about sixteen cents.[5]   Of coins common to the Greeks and Romans there were the *drachma* and the *stater*.   The former was valued at about one fourth of a shekel; hence the *didrachma* or double drachma, noted in one place[6] as tribute money, was equivalent to one half a shekel, about twenty-five cents—the exact sum required by law for that purpose.   The stater was equal in value to the shekel.[7]   (See illustrations, p. 176.)

15. RELATIVE WORTH OF MONEY.—The worth of money in biblical times as represented in what it would purchase, though different at different periods, was scarcely ever so high as is generally supposed.   In the Mosaic era a ram was considered to be worth about two shekels of silver.[8]   David paid but fifty shekels— but compare 1 Chronicles 21 : 25—for the threshing-floor of Araunah, including two yoke of oxen with which the latter was ploughing.[9] An Egyptian horse imported into Palestine in the time of Solomon cost one hundred and fifty shekels and a chariot six hundred.[10] Omri bought the mountain on which Samaria afterwards stood for two talents of silver—that is, six thousand shekels.[11]   In the times of Isaiah a vineyard sold for as many shekels as it had vines.[12]   The ordinary price of a slave was thirty shekels, although Joseph's brethren sold him for twenty.[13]   In the period of the judges the wages of a man by the year, including board and one suit of clothing, was but ten shekels of silver.[14]   Tobit at a much later date is represented as giving a drachma—about twelve and a half cents—a day to the

---

[1] 1 Macc. 11 : 28; 2 Macc. 4 : 19.   [2] 1 Macc. 15 : 6.   [3] Mark 12 : 42; Luke 12 : 6.   [4] Matt. 10 : 29.   [5] Matt. 22 : 19.   [6] Matt. 17 : 24.   [7] Matt. 17 : 27; cf. Ex. 30 : 13.   [8] Lev. 5 : 15 (shekels = 2 shekels).   [9] 2 Sam. 24 : 24.   [10] 1 Kings 10 : 29.   [11] 1 Kings 16 : 24.   [12] Isa. 7 : 23.   [13] Gen. 37 : 28; Ex. 21 : 32; Zech. 11 : 12; Matt. 26 : 15.   [14] Judg. 17 : 10.

servant who accompanied his son on his journey.[1] The wages for a day's work in our Lord's time was a denarius, which was about the same amount, and was actually a higher sum than was paid to field-hands in Greece at that time.[2]

It is an interesting circumstance that while the Master is represented as saying to the twelve whom he was sending forth, " Get you no gold, nor silver, nor brass in your purses," in the parallel passage in Mark he is said to instruct them to take no " money," the word rendered money being in the original " brass" or " copper." That is to say, Mark, in his succinct way, sums up the fuller account, and uses for money the word for that kind of money with which the disciples doubtless were the most familiar, namely, the smaller copper coins. Luke, on the other hand, who might have been more influenced by considerations of style, uses the word "silver" (*argurion*) for money.[3]

16. Such changes as we have noticed in the currency of the Hebrews, their laws remaining the same, necessitated the frequent exchange of one coin for another. A law of Exodus, for example, required that whenever the Israelites were numbered, each male among them over twenty years of age should pay into the treasury of the sanctuary one half a shekel, or ten gerahs.[4] In later times, after the Hebrew shekel had ceased to circulate so commonly, it was still required that this tax should be paid in Hebrew money. Hence the occupation of the money-changer sprang up. At the great feasts of New Testament times, when such multitudes from various parts of the world gathered at Jerusalem, there must have been no inconsiderable trade of this kind carried on. Incidental references show that it was one recognized as quite legitimate.[5] According to the Talmud the ordinary charge made for supplying the necessary half-shekel for other money was a "collybus," whose value was about three cents. This would be at the rate of twelve per cent. for the transaction of the business. It is by no means certain that a much larger premium than this was not sometimes exacted for the service. While therefore the ground for our Lord's driving the traders out of the temple and overthrowing the tables of the money-changers was not the unfairness of their dealings ; still, the epithet he applied to the whole class shows that their business was carried on with little reference to just methods.[6]

17. MEANS FOR WEIGHING.—The means for weighing metals and

---

[1] Tob. 5 : 14.　　[2] Matt. 20 : 2.　　[3] Matt. 10 : 9; Mark 6 : 8; Luke 9 : 3.　　[4] Ex. 30 : 13.
[5] Matt. 25 : 27.　　[6] Matt. 21 : 12.

other articles in ancient times were not very dissimilar from those now used. Ordinary stones seem originally to have served as weights among the Hebrews. That is the literal meaning of the word rendered weight in a number of passages.[1] When they were small they were often carried with the metal itself in the purse attached to the belt. This is still the custom in Persia. Great emphasis is laid in the Mosaic legislation on the importance of having correct weights and measures. It is enjoined, for example, in Deuteronomy,[2] "Thou shalt not have in thy bag divers weights, a great and a small. Thou shalt not have in thine house divers measures, a great and a small. A perfect and just weight shalt thou have; a perfect and just measure shalt thou have: that thy days may be long upon the land which the Lord thy God giveth thee." The temptation naturally was to use the old and depreciated weights for one purpose and the full weights for another, as it might seem best to serve one's interest. We are not informed how the accuracy of weights was to be secured. It may be, as there was a "shekel of the sanctuary," that the weights and measures used as standards were kept there. The fact that certain Levites were appointed by David to the service of overseeing the matter "of measure and size" supports such a conclusion.[3]

There were two kinds of instruments for weighing in use among the Hebrews. The more common one consisted of a simple beam resting at its central point on a standard, while from its two ends were suspended scales or basins in which the weights and the substance to be weighed were respectively placed.[4] Balances of this sort were used for weighing both money and other articles.[5] The possibility of falsifying them is several times alluded to in the Scriptures.[6] In later times, it is likely, the Egyptian device of a sliding ring on one of the arms contributed to more accurate results. The instrument known as *peles* was a balance of a somewhat different kind, answering better to the modern steelyard.[7] The beam was poised, as in the former case, on its middle point, but one of its arms was furnished with a graduated scale. The weight of an object was determined by finding out at what point an adjustable ring would bring the beam to a horizontal position. The monuments of Egypt and Assyria show that great skill was early displayed in the manufacture of various kinds of scales and in devices for securing their accuracy.

[1] Lev. 19:36; 2 Sam. 14:26; Prov. 11:1; Mic. 6:11; Zech. 5:8. [2] Deut. 25:13-15. [3] 1 Chron. 23:29. [4] Job 6:2; 31:6; Ps. 62:9; Prov. 11:1; 16:11; 20:23. [5] Jer. 32:10; Ecclus. 28:25. [6] Hos. 12:7; Amos 8:5; Mic. 6:11. [7] Prov. 16:11; Isa. 40:12; cf. Isa. 46:6.

18. MEASURES OF LENGTH.—Measures of length in the Bible are derived from some common standard, and for the most part from members of the human body.   The hand and forearm were especially employed for this purpose.   We have, for example, the finger's breadth; the handbreadth; the span, by which is meant the distance between the end of the thumb and little finger of the hand when it is extended; the cubit, as most suppose the distance from the extremity of the middle finger to the elbow; and the fathom, from six to six and a half feet.[1]   In addition to these more common measures there was the reed used for building purposes, whose length was six cubits.[2]   The cubit was the ordinary unit of measure, but, as might be inferred from its origin, needed itself to be defined.[3]   It is certain that more than one kind of cubit is referred to in the Bible; the question is mooted whether there are not three.[4]   The subject is surrounded with much difficulty; but it would appear from a comparison of several passages of Scripture with what can be learned from other, especially Egyptian, sources, that the ordinary cubit of the Bible is somewhat shorter than is commonly supposed.

19. The three principal measures of distance in the Old Testament were the pace, "some way," and the day's journey.[5]   Of these the first corresponded nearly to our yard, though the Roman pace was four feet and ten inches.   The second has not yet been determined.   By inference it is judged to be equivalent to the distance from Bethlehem to Rachel's burying-place.   If we may trust tradition this was about one mile and a half.   A day's journey is differently estimated by different nations.   Among the Jews it was thirty miles when the travelling was unimpeded, and ten if it was in connection with a large company or train.   In the apocryphal books of the Old Testament and in the New Testament there occur three other measures of distance: the Sabbath day's journey, the furlong and the mile.   The rabbinical limit fixed for the first was two thousand paces, that is, a little more than an English mile.   The furlong, or stadion, a measure borrowed from the foot-races of the Greeks, was a little more than six hundred and six feet of English measure.[6]   The mile of the New Testament was a Roman measure of a thousand paces, or about four thousand eight hundred and fifty-four English feet.[7]   The only recognition of square measure in the Bible is in the acre.   As the Hebrew shows, it was a piece of ground which a yoke

---

[1] Gen. 6:15; 1 Sam. 17:4; 1 Kings 7:26; Jer. 52:21.   [2] Ezek. 40:5-8; 41:5; 42:16-19.
[3] Cf. Lev. 19:35.   [4] Deut. 3:11; 2 Chron. 3:3; Ezek. 41:8.   [5] Gen. 30:36; 35:16; 2 Sam.
6:13.   [6] See Luke 24:13.   [7] Matt. 5:41.

of cattle could plough over in a day.[1] In English this word had the indefinite sense of an open field until the time of Edward the Third.

20. MEASURES FOR LIQUIDS.—The Hebrew measures for liquids were the bath, the hin and the log. We are largely dependent here, as in the case of dry measure, on Josephus and the rabbins for a knowledge of their relative capacity. In dry measure the homer represented the largest amount; the same term, however, designated a measure for liquids. In the latter case it was equal to ten baths. In dry measure it represented ten ephahs, or thirty seahs, or one hundred omers, or one hundred and eighty kabs.[2] The omer was also called issaron, that is, tenth of an ephah. A measure called lethech is mentioned once in the Old Testament. It was equal to one half an omer.[3] The seah was also sometimes known as shalish, third, that is, the third of an ephah.[4] The kab is named but once in the Bible.[5]

21. Certain other measures are noted in the New Testament exclusively. These are the firkin (metretes, John 2 : 6), which the context shows was for liquids, and contained a little more than eight gallons; the measure (chœnix, Rev. 6 : 6), for dry articles, holding about a quart; the pot (xestes, Mark 7 : 4), a word probably applied to any small vessel, though in Greek meaning the sixth and representing a wooden receptacle holding about a pint and a half; and the bushel (modius, Mark 4 : 21; cf. Matt. 5 : 15), which, in like manner, was used for any small vessel. As a Roman measure it contained not far from eight quarts.

TABLES OF COINS, WEIGHTS, MEASURES AND DISTANCES MENTIONED IN THE BIBLE.

1. SILVER MONEY (shekel = $0.73).

1 gerah								$	.0365
10	"	=	1 bekah						.365
20	"	=	2	"	=	1 shekel			.73
1,200	"	=	120	"	=	60	"	= 1 maneh	43.80
60,000	"	= 6,000	"	= 3,000	"	= 50	"	= 1 talent	2,190.00

2. GOLD MONEY (ounce troy = $19.476).

1 shekel					5.35
100	"	= 1 maneh			535.00
10,000	"	= 100	"	= 1 talent	53,500.00

----

[1] 1 Sam. 14 : 14. [2] Gen. 18 : 6; Ex. 16 : 36; 1 Kings 7 : 26, 38; 2 Kings 6 : 25. [3] Hos. 3 : 2 (margin). [4] Ps. 80 : 5; Isa. 40 : 12. [5] 2 Kings 6 : 25.

3. Roman Money.

1 lepton (mite)..					$	.0012
2	"	"	= 1 quadrans (farthing)...			.0024
8	"	"	= 4	"	" = 1 assurion	.0096

4. Greek and Roman Money.

1 denarius (penny) = 1 drachma..				.183
2	"	(½ shekel) = didrachma...		.366
4	"	= 2 didrachma = tetradrachma (shekel).....................		.732

5. Silver Weights (gerah = 11 grains, or about $\frac{1}{40}$ of an ounce avoird.).

1 gerah..							11 grains.
10	"	=	1 bekah...				110 "
20	"	=	2	"	=	1 shekel............................	220 "
1,200	"	= 120	"	=	60	" 1 manch.................................	13,200 "
60,000	"	= 6,000	"	= 3,000	"	= 50	" = 1 talent (= about 6 lbs. avoirdupois)........... 660,000 "

6. Gold Weights (shekel = 132 grains).

1 shekel..				132 grains.
100	"	=	1 maneh..	13,200 "
10,000	"	= 100	" = 1 talent (= nearly 12 lbs. avoirdupois).............. 1,320,000	"

7. Measure of Capacity (dry).

1 4-5 kab =	1 omer.							
6	"	=	3½	"	=	1 seah.		
18	"	=	10	"	=	3	" = 1 ephah.	
180	"	=	100	"	=	30	" = 10	" = 1 homer (cor.) = 86,696 gall. or 10¾ bushel.[1]

8. Measure of Capacity (liquid).

12 log = 1 hin.
72   "   = 6   "   = 1 bath (ephah) = 8.6696 gall.[1]

9. Measure of Length.

1 finger (width)..								.7938 inch.
4	"	= 1 palm..						3.1752 "
12	"	= 3	" = 1 span.......................................					9.5257 "
24	"	= 6	"	= 2	" = 1 cubit............................			19.0515 "
144	"	= 36	"	= 12	"	= 6	" = 1 reed (about 9 ft. 6 inches)..........	114.3090 "

10. Measure of Length (foreign).

1 Roman foot..									11.64 inches.
5	"	feet =	1 Roman pace...					4 feet	10.248 "
6¼	"	" =	6 Greek feet =	1 Greek fathom..................				6 "	0.81 "
625	"	" = 600	"	" = 100	"	" = 1 furlong...		606 "	9.00 "
5,000	"	" = 4,800	"	" = 800	"	" = 8	" = 1 Roman mile.		
							.9193 mile = 4,854 feet.		

[1] So Josephus (*Antiq.* 3, 8 : 3). According to the rabbins 4.4286 gallons, or 5½ bushels.

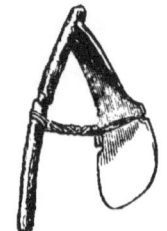

Mattock or Egyptian Hoe.
(See page 123.) (*After Wilkinson.*)

Egyptian Basket. (*After Wilkinson.*)

The Egyptian Shadoof.   (See Deut. 11 : 10, 11.)

Assyrian Basins. (See p. 80.) (*British Museum.*)

Egyptian Household Chest or Box.

Eastern Stone Water-jars. (See p. 80.)

Mode of Wearing Nose-jewel, Plaiting the Hair and Covering the Head by Eastern Women. (See p. 101.)

PART II.

CIVIL ANTIQUITIES.

185

Head-dress of Assyrian King and Queen.
(*From Nineveh Marbles.*)

Tomb of the Judges, near Jerusalem. (See
page 61.) (*From Photograph by Good.*)

Beards of Assyrian and other Nations.
(*After Rosellini and Layard.*)

Profile of Rameses II., the Pharaoh of the
Oppression. (*After Lepsius.*)

Throne or Chair of State. (*From the Assyrian
Monuments at Khorsabad.*)

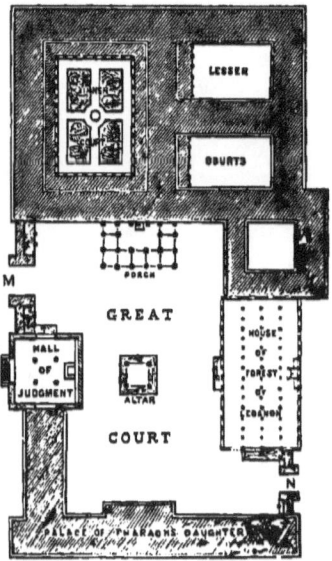

Supposed Ground-plan of Solomon's
Palace.

186

CHAPTER VIII.

The spirit and teaching of the Bible throughout are in harmony with the declaration of Paul that the powers that be are "ordained of God."[1] Rudimentally, at least, it furnishes at the outset of human history the foundation of a civil polity. As soon as the family began to exist, there existed in the world a divine institution which more than any other lies at the basis of the state—is the vital unit of its composite structures and the chief visible foundation of its strength and authority. The beginning of human government and the germ of all right human government is family government. The theory of a so-called natural society at the start, where all were exactly equal and all free and independent of one another, has no foundation in fact.[2]

1. THE FAMILY THE NORM.—It would perhaps be possible to trace, in the antediluvian period, the dominance of family influence in whatever government then existed.[3] It certainly asserts itself conspicuously in what ·is technically known as "sacred history." Of Abraham Jehovah says that he has "known him, to the end that he may command his children and his household after him, that they may keep the way of the Lord, to do justice and judgment."[4] So from family government, which was the original form, sprang patriarchal government. The patriarch was the father of his race. This fact carried with it, to the Oriental mind, primarily the idea of rulership—a rulership which, in an inferior degree, was transmitted to the first-born son of each succeeding family. The authority of the patriarch was not merely civil; it was absolute and universal. Under God, and as responsible only to him, his will was law to his descendants.[5] As families multiplied, the bond that united them was still their relation to a common ancestor. After they grew to numerous and powerful tribes and the influence of consanguinity was less felt, the necessity arose for new provisions by means of which a natural tendency to disintegration might be checked.

---

[1] Rom. 13:1. [2] Gen. 1:26–28. [3] Gen. 4:16, 17, 23, 24; 5:1; 7:1. [4] Gen. 18:19; cf. Amos 3:2. [5] Gen. 22:9.

2. On going into Egypt, the tribes of Israel seem to have kept up, in its principal features, the patriarchal form of government. Together they formed what was known as the family or house of Israel. This whole was genealogically subdivided into tribes, families, households or fathers' houses, and individuals, the last including the persons of a family, the husband and wife with their children. This division of the nation is perhaps most clearly set forth in a passage in the book of Joshua where the discovery of Achan's transgression is described. First among the tribes, Judah was taken; of this tribe, the family of the Zerahites was taken; of this family, the household of Zabdi; and of this household, Achan was taken.[1] The father of each household, and so too the head of each family, was supreme within his circle. The tribe obeyed its prince, who originally was the first-born son of its founder. Down to the time of the captivity the number of tribes remained the same.[2] The Levites, however, having no inheritance with their brethren, there would have been but eleven tribes to possess Canaan had not Jacob, just before his death, adopted the two sons of Joseph as his own in their father's place.[3] The names of Ephraim and Manasseh, accordingly, survive as heads of tribes. The number and designation of families and households, on the other hand, was constantly undergoing change. While yet in the wilderness, two enumerations of the people of Israel, according to their families, were made.[4] From the second of them it appears that of the fifty-seven families found, the most, as might be expected, are named from sons of the tribal prince; but others from grandsons and even great-grandsons. The same change in title may safely be assumed to have taken place also in households or fathers' houses, although direct evidence for it may not be found. Just what principle ruled in the selection of the head of a family or a household, the son of a founder failing, it is not possible to say. There is even reason to suppose that no one principle governed at all times. In fact, the whole subject is involved in not a little confusion. In 1 Samuel 10: 21, for example, we read that Saul was of the family of Matri, of the tribe of Benjamin; but on turning to the book of Numbers, where the families of Benjamin are enumerated, we do not find one of this name among them.[5]

3. Another source of confusion is the fact that the Hebrew word for family is used in the Scriptures in several different senses. Besides being the designation of the main subdivision of the tribe, it is

---

[1] Josh. 7: 14, 16-18.   [2] Gen. 49: 28; Ex. 24: 4; Acts 26: 7.   [3] Gen. 48: 5, 6.   [4] Num. 1 and 26.   [5] Num. 26: 38-41.

used also as an equivalent for nation, and even for the tribe itself.[1] The same is true of the Hebrew word for household, or father's house. It is used not alone as a title for the second largest division of the tribe, but more definitely for the principal father's house, which might be the title also of the whole tribe.[2] While Israel remained in Egypt it is not to be supposed that the authority of tribal chiefs or princes was much superior to that of heads of families or even those of households. Jacob himself had set the example of depreciating this dignity, in refusing on the ground of crime, to Reuben his first-born, the double portion to which otherwise he would have been entitled.[3] It was given to the two sons of Joseph. Of these sons, moreover, he assigned to the younger a higher position than to the elder. It seems probable that in the necessary lack of unity among the people at this time, heads of families gradually attained to a position of influence scarcely second to the highest; at least we find the same title—that of " prince"—given to them in the Pentateuch.[4]

4. THE ELDERSHIP.—Already before the beginning of the Mosaic era there had arisen a class of persons called elders, who exercised the very highest authority among the people. It is before them that Moses and Aaron appear to deliver the message from God respecting the deliverance from Egypt.[5] It is through them that Moses afterwards issues instructions that are intended for the whole people.[6] At first, undoubtedly, the word elder signified simply " aged;" then, an office mostly filled by the aged.[7] At what time it came to designate almost solely an office it is not possible to say. The eldership in Israel is not to be regarded as a ruling class distinct from the heads of tribes and families. It was one with them, or at least to a large extent included them. The title "elders" was given to them when tribal and genealogical distinctions were less in view and the people as a whole were thought of.

5. BEGINNINGS OF REPRESENTATIVE GOVERNMENT.—During the sojourn in the wilderness, calls for the administration of justice between man and man grew to such an extent that Moses, on whom it fell, found himself inadequate to the task. On the suggestion, therefore, of his father-in-law he appointed seventy elders to be " rulers of thousands, rulers of hundreds, rulers of fifties, and rulers of tens."[8] The business assigned them was to "judge the people at all seasons;" and only in case a matter was too difficult for them, to

---

1 Gen. 12:3; Josh. 7:17.   2 Num. 1:4; 17:2; Josh. 22:14.   3 Gen. 35:22.   4 Num. 3:24, 30, 35.   5 Ex. 3:16, 18.   6 Ex. 4:29.   7 Josh. 24:31; 1 Kings 12:6.   8 Ex. 18:13-22.

appeal to Moses. It is clear that in appointing these men Moses took them from the eldership already existing—that is, made his choice dependent on the existing organization of the tribes. The term "thousands" is itself afterwards applied to the families of Israel.[1] So, too, the persons indicated by "hundreds" and "tens" are not simply individuals taken indiscriminately from the tribes, but from those smaller sections into which the people, from the first, had been divided. Each one of them was composed of a variable number of persons. It seems probable that Moses, without interfering with the functions of the eldership in other respects, on finding that body too unwieldy for this special matter of civil processes, adopted the present expedient to meet the difficulty. After his death it does not appear to have been perpetuated. In fact, while Israel was still in the wilderness he instituted another method for the administration of justice, intended for the period after the conquest. It was by means of local courts, which were allowed to carry the more difficult cases up to a supreme court to be found at the capital or the central place of worship.[2]

Most of the public business was transacted by the eldership. They represented the people so fully that, in some passages, elders and people are used as interchangeable terms.[3] After the settlement in Canaan, it was from this body, as previously in the case of the seventy elders, that all new officials were selected. They not only continued to act as national representatives when occasion called for it, but also as local rulers and magistrates.[4] The body survived, at least in name, the hard experiences of the exile, and we continue to hear of it in the time of the Maccabees, and even at the beginning of the Christian era.[5] At this last period they did not, as might be supposed, exclusively make up the sanhedrin, but were a distinct class by themselves, though one among others from which the sanhedrin was formed.[6] After the occupation of Canaan, it was only on rare occasions and where matters of great importance required it that the whole congregation was ever convened. When it was desired to summon the eldership for any public business, the signal was a number of blasts on a single trumpet. Two trumpets were used when the congregation was to assemble.[7]

6. THE SHOTERIM OR "OFFICERS."—A class of persons generally styled in the English version "officers" begins to appear in the

---

[1] Num. 1:16; 10:4; 1 Sam. 10:19.   [2] Deut. 16:18-20; 17:8-13.   [3] Josh. 24:1; cf. vs. 2, 19, 21.   [4] Ruth 4:9, 11; 2 Sam. 19:11.   [5] 1 Macc. 12:6; 2 Macc. 1:10.   [6] Matt. 16:21; 21:23; Luke 22:66; Acts 22:5.   [7] Num. 10:4.

earliest history of Israel.[1] From the etymology of the word and other considerations, it is safe to infer that their first business was to act as scribes or registrars. It is likely that, at first, the care of the genealogical tables was committed to them. Afterwards a number of other corresponding services were required. During the enslavement of Israel in Egypt, the Egyptians employed them as subordinate to native task-masters in the capacity of overseers of their own people. Their duty was to secure from their countrymen a certain specified amount of work, at the risk of being themselves beaten if it were not done.[2] These same persons, at least persons similarly named, we find somewhat later acting in the capacity of officers of the highest authority in military affairs; and subsequently still, as adjutants to Joshua.[3] In connection with the judiciary, too, after the conquest they are assigned important positions, second only to the judges themselves.[4] And after the rise of the kingdom, though now become numerous, they are still found in stations of power and influence.[5] At the beginning they formed a part of the eldership.[6] The Scriptures do not inform us how the office arose or how its incumbents were chosen.

7. GOVERNMENT IN THE PERIOD OF THE JUDGES.—The period which followed the Egyptian thralldom in the history of Israel was peculiar; accordingly, peculiar methods of government were adopted. For example, the position and influence of Moses, Joshua, and the other military leaders who succeeded them in the time of the judges, were extraordinary. They form no essential part of that system of government which we find outlined in the earlier books of the Bible. They were especially raised up to introduce the theocracy. To the theocracy, as a system of civil government, their offices were not essential; they were not provided for in it. They were even independent of one another. Joshua followed Moses, but was in no proper sense his successor. His function was quite a different one. Like the staging used in the construction of a building, to be taken down when the building is completed, so these offices passed away with the individual men who, in the providence of God, were called on to fill them.

8. Moses speaks of a "prophet" who would come after him and who would be like him; but only as a religious instructor and guide.[7] It is certain that in this utterance he makes no reference to the civil polity of Israel. He has in view, as it would seem, that long line

[1] Ex. 5:6. [2] Ex. 5:6, 14–16. [3] Deut. 20:5, 8, 9; Josh. 1:10; 3:2. [4] Deut. 16:18.
[5] 1 Chron. 23:4; 26:29; 2 Chron. 19:11. [6] Num. 11:16. [7] Deut. 18:15–21.

of Israelitish prophets which, beginning with Samuel, culminated in him who proclaimed himself "the way, and the truth, and the life."[1] Joshua's work, though less important and far-reaching than that of Moses, was no less unique. His special training as well as the call of God set him apart as the military leader of Israel in the conquest of Palestine.[2] When that work was done he retired to Timnath-serah, a place that had been allotted him among his own tribe, without a thought of permanently holding his high office, much less of transmitting it to his posterity.[3] There is scarcely anything more extraordinary in the extraordinary history of Israel than the biblical account of the lives of these two great men in connection with the enfranchisement of their people and the establishment of the Hebrew commonwealth in a newly-conquered country.

The period of the judges was hardly less abnormal than that of Moses and Joshua had been. The land was, at first, pretty thoroughly subdued. The people had inherited a code of laws more than sufficient for present necessities. But tribal difficulties were continually arising which needed to be adjusted; and Israel was very imperfectly prepared morally to enter upon the high state of self-government which the theocracy both permitted and imposed. Above all, there arose among them, on a large scale, defections and apostasy. A generation came up "which knew not the Lord, nor yet the work which he had wrought for Israel."[4] Hence, as a specific provision for the occasion, there was providentially raised up a series of judges. They were not rulers in any proper sense of the term. They were not regarded as having any organic connection with the government. Their authority was limited not only to the time that called it forth, but it was also much limited in extent. Rarely did the tribes act in concert.[5] The elders still had the widest and most permanent influence in civil affairs.[6]

9. POSITION OF THE LEVITES.—The Levites, in harmony with the peculiar prerogative given them in the Mosaic laws, were scattered among the several tribes.[7] Some religious rites enjoined by the law continued to be observed.[8] The national sanctuary was maintained, and for the most part at Shiloh.[9] Here Phinehas, grandson of Aaron, officiated as priest,[10] and here the annual festivals enjoined in the code seem to have been, to some extent, celebrated.[11] There is evidence too, as in the case of the idolater Micah

<hr/>

[1] John 14:6.   [2] Num. 27:18-23.   [3] Josh. 19:50; cf. 24:1-32.   [4] Judg. 2:10.   [5] Judg. 1:3, 17, 22-25; 5:14-18; 6:35; 8:1-3, 22, 23; 20:10.   [6] Judg. 21:16.   [7] Judg. 17:5-13; 19:1, 2.   [8] Judg. 14:3; 15:18.   [9] Judg. 18:31; 19:18.   [10] Judg. 20:28.   [11] Judg. 21:19.

and the ephod of Gideon, that there remained in the hearts of the people a consciousness that the evil courses they were pursuing were a defection from the right way.[1] The names of fifteen so-called judges, who exercised power in Israel between the death of Joshua and the establishment of the kingdom, are given in the Bible. They are Othniel, Ehud, Shamgar, Deborah and Barak, Gideon, Abimelech, Tola, Jair, Jephthah, Ibzan, Elon, Abdon, Samson, Eli, and Samuel. In the case of most of them, however, the office of judge was greatly subordinated to that of military leader, especially at the beginning of their career. But this was not true of Samuel nor Eli. Nothing is said of feats of arms performed by them, or by Tola, Ibzan, Elon and Abdon.

10. LAWS OF THE EARLIEST PERIOD.—Our account of the government of Israel in this its first period would be incomplete without some reference to the laws which originated in it. It is to be confessed that it is not easy to discriminate between the Mosaic code in its civil and ecclesiastical aspects. All the laws of the Pentateuch have a direct ethical and spiritual bearing. It could not be otherwise when Jehovah is recognized as the one supreme Ruler. Some, however, relate more directly to sacred places, seasons, persons and service; these will be treated specially by themselves. Besides them there are other laws of a more general character. One series of them, for example, relates to idolatry.[2] In a theocracy, idolatry was equivalent to high treason, and the severest penalties were accordingly visited upon it. Again, there are the more temporary regulations concerning the treatment of Canaanitish and other heathen cities.[3] Then follow laws relating to mourning customs and food;[4] to Hebrew and to foreign servants;[5] to the establishment of a judiciary;[6] to the number of witnesses required in capital cases;[7] a law limiting the custom of blood-revenge by the appointment of cities of refuge;[8] one prohibiting magic arts;[9] forbidding the removal of landmarks;[10] punishing unchastity;[11] and one against bearing false witness.[12]

11. We have, too, a description of the process to be pursued in the case of a murderer where the murderer is unknown;[13] a regulation

<hr />

[1] Judg. 8:24-27; 17:5-13.   [2] *Deut. 4:15, 19; 7:5, 25, 26; 12:2-4, 29-31; 17:2-5; 18:10; 20:18.   [3] Deut. 13:12-18; 20:10-20.   [4] Deut. 14:1-20.   [5] Deut. 15:12-18; 16:19, 20; 21:10-14; 24:14, 15.   [6] Deut. 16:18-20; 17:8-13.   [7] Deut. 17:6, 7; cf. 19:15, 16.   [8] Deut. 19:1-13.   [9] Deut. 18:9-14.   [10] Deut. 19:14.   [11] Deut. 22:13-21; 23:1.   [12] Deut. 19:15-21.   [13] Deut. 21:1-9.

<hr />

* It has seemed best to limit the citations to the forms of the law found in Deuteronomy. For the parallel passages a reference Bible may be consulted.

defining how a disobedient son is to be treated;[1] one showing what course is to be adopted on the occasion of a public execution with impaling;[2] one concerning the property of a brother Israelite;[3] concerning kindness to animals;[4] the protection of life;[5] regulating the dress;[6] relating to the classes of persons to be denied citizenship with Israel;[7] fugitive slaves;[8] prostitution;[9] usury;[10] divorce;[11] man-stealing;[12] sanitary regulations in the case of leprosy;[13] gleaning;[14] levirate marriage;[15] the degree and method of punishment by flogging;[16] the penalty for gross immodesty;[17] the rights of inheritance;[18] and the provision for just weights and measures.[19]

It is marvellous to what extent these regulations cover the ground of civic and social duties from the point of view of the Mosaic period, or indeed of any period. Add to them the laws already spoken of as being of a more religious character and it is not surprising that, on any theory of natural development, critics are wholly unable to find a place for them in the period of the exodus. Without the assumption of a special divine interposition and training such as has been seen in the history of no other people, we can just as little account for Israel as for its legislation. It was a people and nation organized on a divine plan. It was made up not of a mass of heterogeneous individuals held together by stress of circumstances or force of custom. It existed rather as a well-developed organism, itself divisible into other organisms, the principal and most potent one of all being the compact organism of the family as God constituted it at the beginning.

12. PRACTICABILITY OF THE MOSAIC LAWS.—Fault has been found with the political constitution of Israel as formulated in the Pentateuch as impracticable. Undoubtedly it was in no small degree impracticable for such a people as Israel then was. But was not this one of its principal objects and benefits: to show the distance between the real and the ideal, stimulate to the highest endeavor, and, especially, demonstrate the hand of God? With at least equal justice the moral precepts of Jesus Christ may be said to have been impracticable for the generation in which he lived. Divine foresight is particularly shown in the Mosaic laws not only in the unique and noble ideal that is set before Israel in them, but in the provisions which they themselves contain for such exigencies as might

<hr>

[1] Deut. 21 : 18-21. [2] Deut. 21 : 22, 23. [3] Deut. 22 : 1-4. [4] Deut. 22 : 6, 7. [5] Deut. 22 : 8. [6] Deut. 22 : 5, 9-12. [7] Deut. 23 : 2-9. [8] Deut. 23 : 15, 16. [9] Deut. 23 : 17, 18. [10] Deut. 23 : 19, 20. [11] Deut. 24 : 1-4. [12] Deut. 24 : 7. [13] Deut. 24 : 8, 9. [14] Deut. 24 : 19-22. [15] Deut. 25 : 5-10. [16] Deut. 25 : 1-3. [17] Deut. 25 : 11, 12. [18] Deut. 21 : 15-17. [19] Deut. 25 : 13-16.

arise from any imperfect execution of them. If Israel, for example, had been morally prepared to adopt and act on that early declaration that they were to be a " kingdom of priests, and a holy nation,"[1] it would have been quite unnecessary to establish a distinct class of priests, and impose on the people the burdensome ceremonial ritual. So, too, if they had been prepared to execute in full the civil laws given them through Moses, they would never have needed to change their form of government and take upon themselves the additional burdens of the kingdom. It was from this point of view, in fact, that Samuel condemned the project of a kingdom when it was introduced, as Gideon had done before him.[2] It was essentially a retrogression from the standard which had been set for Israel. The prophet therefore only yielded, under protest, to the popular clamor. Still the fact that the Israelitish people would thus conduct itself had been foreseen, and this precise exigency provided for in the original scheme of Moses.

13. THE KINGDOM.—Already in Genesis there are intimations that a kingdom would ultimately arise among the Hebrews.[3] In the code of Deuteronomy there is a distinct section relating to such a change in the civil polity.[4] It looks forward to the times of the peaceful occupation of Canaan. The period would then come when there would be a popular demand for a king. Consent is to be yielded to it on certain conditions. Definite directions are given for the choice of the sovereign, the title he shall bear, the government of his household, his income, his relative position among his brethren, the succession and other matters, in a way to set this future king of Israel quite apart from contemporary kings. They make it imperative, in short, that if there is to be a king over the chosen people, he is to reign under the peculiar conditions imposed by existing laws, and that the government shall still be recognized as, in the end, theocratic.

14. The objection made by a certain class of critics to this law that it is of later origin than the times of Moses, was in fact concocted after the establishment of the kingdom, is conclusively refuted by its contents. No such law defining the succession as one to be confined to Israelites and prohibiting the leading of the people back to Egypt would have been thought of after the establishment of the succession in the line of David and at such a remove from the experience of the Egyptian bondage. What the contents of the book

---

[1] Ex. 19:6.   [2] 1 Sam. 8:10–19; cf. Judg. 8:22, 23.   [3] Gen. 17:16; 49:10.   [4] Deut. 17:14-20.

were which Samuel is said to have written and to have laid up before the Lord respecting the "manner of the kingdom" it is not possible to say. It may have been simply a reproduction of this Deuteronomic law.

15. That on the change of government it was understood that Jehovah was not to exercise any less authority is plain from the constitution of the new kingdom. The king was to be one whom Jehovah should choose. He was to be anointed by his prophets. He was to feed his people in being a prince over them. Above all, he was himself to be subordinate to the laws of his country and to govern in harmony with them.[1] The selection of the first king from the least important family of the least important tribe was, perhaps, meant to show that the real sovereign of Israel was still Jehovah. It has been thought by some that the king among the Hebrews was not always anointed, the fact of anointing being recorded only in the case of a few of them. It is quite as likely that the anointing was regarded as so much a matter of course that it was recorded only in those instances where the succession was in some way exceptional.[2]

Royal Crowns. (*After Wilkinson, Layard, and Rawlinson.*)

1. Crown of Upper Egypt. 2. Crown of Upper and Lower Egypt United. 3. Assyrian Crown, from Nineveh Marbles. 4. Laurel Crown. 5. Crown of Herod the Great. 6. Crown of Aretas, King of Arabia.

16. INSTALLATION OF THE KING. —Other ceremonies besides the anointing which accompanied the inauguration of a king we find recorded in the historical books.[3] Surrounded by soldiers he was conducted to a public square or the court of the temple, and there the ceremonial of anointing took place, the high priest performing the rite. The crown was then placed on his head and a copy of the law, either that of the king or the code of Deuteronomy, or possibly the whole Pentateuch, was put in his hands. When Joash was crowned it is said that the high priest "brought out the king's son, and put the crown upon him, and *gave him* the testimony."[4] The crown was probably little more than a fillet of gold, possibly studded with precious stones. It was a part of the royal costume, and

---

[1] Deut. 17: 14–20; 1 Sam. 10: 1, 24.   [2] 2 Sam. 19: 10; 1 Kings 1: 39; 2 Kings 11: 12; 23: 30.
[3] 2 Kings 11: 4–18.   [4] 2 Kings 11: 12.

sometimes worn in battle.[1] After the anointing, crowning, the presentation of a copy of the law and the exchange of mutual covenants,
there followed, in some cases, the kiss of homage, the acclamations
of the people, and the formal seating of the king on his throne.[2]

17. THE LAW OF SUCCESSION.—The law of succession as found
in Deuteronomy[3] refers only to the one circumstance that the king
must be an Israelite. What practice was followed is not altogether
clear. It would seem that the king ordinarily named his successor
during his own lifetime. This we know to have been true in the case
of David and some others.[4] Where no such preference had been
expressed it is likely that the law of primogeniture would be allowed
some weight.[5] During the minority of a king his mother, in some
instances, held the regency.[6] The chief functions of the king were
to act as commander-in-chief of the army and perform the duties of
a supreme magistrate. In the latter capacity he might give decisions in cases which were brought before him on appeal from lower
courts, as well as in such as came to him directly.[7] He seems to
have had no special jurisdiction over the national judiciary or to
have been held responsible for it. It was not left to his option to
execute the laws or to leave them unexecuted.[8] Still less was he regarded as competent to repeal laws which had been previously made.
In instances where this was attempted by apostate rulers their conduct was visited with the severest reprobation by the prophets.[9]
The subject is the more important since, according to some modern
theories, the laws of the Pentateuch were brought into their present
form, after the period of the earlier kings, by some persons unknown.

18. ROYAL PREROGATIVE.—The king might, on special occasions, proclaim a fast.[10] He was expected to execute rigorously the
laws against idolatrous worship;[11] but with the ordinary duties of
the priesthood he had nothing to do.[12] It was his privilege sometimes, however, to nominate the high priest, provided he kept within
the line of Aaronic descent.[13] What was done by David in the matter of arranging the public services of the sanctuary was something
for which the Mosaic laws had made no express provision. It
evinced no disposition on his part to usurp authority which did not
belong to him.[14] The kings of Israel, in addition to the restraints
of the laws, were continually under those imposed upon them by

---

[1] 2 Sam. 1 : 10.   [2] 1 Sam. 10 : 1, 25 ; 2 Sam. 5 : 3 ; 1 Kings 1 : 35, 38 ; 2 Kings 9 : 13 ; 11 : 19 ;
1 Chron. 11 : 3 ; Ps. 2 : 12.   [3] Deut. 17 : 15.   [4] 1 Kings 1 : 30 ; 2 : 22 ; 2 Chron. 11 : 21, 22.
[5] 2 Chron. 21 : 3.   [6] 1 Kings 2 : 19 ; 2 Kings 11 : 1, 3 ; 24 : 12, 15.   [7] 2 Sam. 15 : 2 ; 1 Kings 3 : 17.
[8] Deut. 17 : 19 ; 1 Kings 21 : 4.   [9] 1 Kings 12 : 33.   [10] 1 Kings 21 : 12.   [11] 2 Kings 18 : 4.
[12] 2 Chron. 26 : 18, 19.   [13] 2 Sam. 8 : 17 ; 1 Kings 2 : 27, 35.   [14] 1 Chron. 15 : 16, 17.

the order of the prophets. They ventured on no important business without consulting them, or, in the earlier periods of the monarchy, the Urim and Thummim. How dominant the influence of the pro-

phetical order was in shaping the course of the government may be seen in the relations which Samuel held to Saul, Nathan to David and Elijah to Ahab.[1] It can only be explained on the theory that the Mosaic laws, however inoperative they may have been among the masses of the people, were still "the power behind the throne."

19. INCOME AND EMOLUMENTS.— The income of the king naturally varied greatly at different periods. It consisted in part of presents made to him by citizens and strangers. These so-called "presents" were often, in fact, tribute which was required to be paid with more or less of regularity. King David was the owner of a considerable amount of real estate under cultivation on the Mediterranean coast. He had also large herds of cattle, camels, asses and sheep scattered in various parts of the kingdom. This property seems to have been principally acquired in war and accorded to him as his portion of the spoils.[2]

Assyrian King on his Throne holding a Sceptre. (*From Monuments at Kouyunjik.*)

From 1 Samuel 8 : 10–18, where the prophet relates the "manner of the kingdom," he tells the people that their king will exact from them service of many kinds, and demand a tenth of their flocks. How far a ruler would go in this direction might depend quite as much on his caprice as on his actual needs. When a tribute was imposed on Israel by Pul of Assyria, Menahem, the king, assessed the rich men of his realm to the amount of fifty shekels apiece in order to raise it.[3] Jehoiakim of Judah is said to have exacted money in a similar way to pay tribute demanded by Pharaoh of Egypt.[4] It would not appear that these exactions

[1] See also 1 Kings 12 : 21–24 ; Isa. 37 : 21–36.   [2] 2 Sam. 8 : 2, 7, 8, 10 ; 1 Kings 4 : 21 ; 2 Chron. 27 : 5.   [3] 2 Kings 15 : 19, 20.   [4] 2 Kings 23 : 35.

were ever made by Israelitish kings except in extraordinary circumstances.

20. EXPENSES.—In the time of Solomon a tax was paid to the government by merchants of other countries who traded in the land.[1] At the same time his vassal the king of Moab brought him the enormous yearly tribute of the wool of two hundred thousand sheep.[2] Solomon also, as we have seen, had trading-vessels, and it is not unlikely that he derived a considerable income from his commercial enterprises.[3] He certainly needed a large revenue to support the state which he kept up. We are told that the daily provision for his table was "thirty measures of fine flour, and threescore measures of meal; ten fat oxen, and twenty oxen out of the pastures, and an hundred sheep, beside harts, and gazelles, and roebucks, and fatted fowl."[4] If we consider, in addition, the levies he made on the laboring classes to carry out his immense building enterprises, it will appear as a necessary result that the rate of taxation was high. During his own reign, and while the wealth he had received from his father lasted, this was not so seriously felt. Under his successor it was sufficiently serious to be made the occasion of a revolt on the part of the ten tribes, and ultimately led to the division of the kingdom.[5]

21. HOUSEHOLD.—The royal household seems always to have been large. One of the most important officials whom the king kept near him was the historiographer, or chronicler. He is the first source of most of the information we have concerning the events of Jewish history. He committed to writing not only the royal edicts, but all other matters of a public nature thought worthy of remembrance. It was his business, too, to keep the king informed of what was transpiring in his kingdom. The position of chronicler was looked upon as one of the highest honor and responsibility.[6] A somewhat similar official, but of a lower grade, was the scribe, or secretary. Elihoreph and Ahijah are named as scribes during the reign of Solomon.[7] In connection with the military establishment there were two other officers who had a place near the king: the general commanding, often known as "captain of the host," and the chief of the body-guard.[8] The latter was an official common to most Oriental courts.[9] He was of the highest rank. Commissions of the most delicate and dangerous character were intrusted to the

[1] 1 Kings 10:14, 15. [2] 2 Kings 3:4. [3] 1 Kings 9:28. [4] 1 Kings 4:22, 23. [5] 1 Kings 12:4. [6] 2 Sam. 8:16; 20:24; 1 Kings 4:3; 2 Kings 18:18, 37; Isa. 36:3, 22. [7] 1 Kings 4:3. [8] 1 Sam. 14:50; 2 Sam. 8:16; 20:23; 1 Kings 2:32; 4:4. [9] Gen. 37:36; 2 Kings 11:4; 25:8.

body of men whom he controlled. The person of the king was in their charge, and they executed without intervention his public and secret orders.[1]

King David's body-guard, for some reason not clearly understood, was known by the name of the "Cherethites and the Pelethites."[2] Some, considering the words etymologically, have supposed them to mean the "executioners and couriers." Others, and the majority, have maintained that they were foreign mercenaries, like Ittai the Hittite and the six hundred whom he commanded.[3] The latter hypothesis is favored by the circumstance that not only have the original Hebrew words the usual gentilic ending, but the former one is mentioned a number of times in such a connection with the Philistines as to make their identity nearly certain.[4] The word Pelethite might even be a corruption of Philistine. Besides, these people appear in Israelitish history just at the time when David succeeded in bringing the Philistines into subjection.[5]

Another officer of the royal household was the one who, like Adoniram of Solomon's time, attended to the business of raising levies for the public service.[6] Again, there was the king's counsellor, like Ahithophel whose counsel to Absalom David sent Hushai the Archite to defeat; and the "king's friend," a more private and intimate adviser and companion.[7] There was also an officer answering to "keepers of the wardrobe."[8] In two passages of the Revised Version a person is mentioned under the name of "priest," the original word being the same as that ordinarily so rendered. In the margin of the same version, however, the translation "chief minister" is substituted.[9] This is probably correct. It would scarcely be expected, from what we know of David, that he would allow one of his own sons to usurp an office which belonged exclusively to descendants of Aaron. Moreover, in a parallel account of David's officials we read, in place of "David's sons were priests," "the sons of David were chief about the king."[10] Also in 1 Kings 4:5, where a list of the officials of Solomon is given, one by the name of Zabud is mentioned who "was priest, the king's friend." The root-meaning of the word rendered "priest" is to stand, and so to minister. In these exceptional instances, therefore, it goes back to the prim-

---

[1] 1 Kings 2:25, 34, 46.   [2] 2 Sam. 8:18; 20:23; 1 Chron. 18:17.   [3] 2 Sam. 15:18–22.
[4] 1 Sam. 30:14; Ezek. 25:16; Zeph. 2:5.   [5] 2 Sam. 8:1.   [6] 2 Sam. 20:24; 1 Kings 4:6.
[7] 2 Sam. 15:32–34; 1 Kings 4:5; 1 Chron. 27:33; Isa. 3:3; 19:11.   [8] 1 Kings 4:6, 7; 2
Kings 10:2; 22:14; 1 Chron. 27:25–31.   [9] 2 Sam. 8:18; 20:26.   [10] 1 Chron. 18:15–17.

itive sense instead of taking the specific one of serving as a priest or
minister of God.

22. FALL OF THE KINGDOMS OF ISRAEL AND JUDAH.—The
kingdom of the twelve tribes, as is well known, ended with Solomon.
After his death ten of the tribes set up an independent government
whose principal capital was Samaria. It lasted about two hundred
and fifty years, when Samaria was taken and a large body of Israelites were carried away as captives to Assyria.[1] The kingdom made
up of the tribes of Judah and Benjamin, whose rallying-point was
the house of David and its capital Jerusalem, holding on with more
tenacity to the principles of the theocracy, maintained its existence
for a longer period. But, finally, it too yielded to other influences,
and so was obliged to succumb to the world-power. Its end came in
the first quarter of the sixth century before Christ.[2] The captivity
lasted until the accession of Cyrus to the throne of Babylon, B.C.
536. By him and his successors the Jews were allowed to return to
Palestine. The first company, numbering about fifty thousand, were
led back by Zerubbabel, who was appointed tirshatha, or governor,
by the Persian monarch. Associated with him were the high priest,
Joshua, and ten of the principal elders. Twenty-eight years afterwards, during the reign of Artaxerxes I., a second company of exiles, dismissed with the good wishes and generous gifts of their Persian rulers, returned under the leadership of Ezra. Fourteen years
later still, B.C. 444, came Nehemiah.

23. GOVERNMENT SUBSEQUENT TO THE EXILE.—The people who
returned in these successive companies belonged, for the most part,
to the tribes that had been most recently carried into captivity; that
is, Judah and Benjamin, which were the tribes, too, that had longest
kept up their devotion to the institutions of their fathers. No ob-
stacle seems to have been thrown in the way of those desirous to
return. The great mass of exiles showed a singular indisposition to
do so. Some, as we know, remained from choice in the more productive land of their conquerors, though purposing to adhere scrupulously to the customs of their compatriots in the father-land. There
were, however, many more, including the majority of the ten tribes,
who never lost their propensity to idolatry, and so finally sunk out
of sight as Jews in the heathenism that surrounded them. Representatives of the ten tribes were found among those who returned
with Zerubbabel and Ezra ; but there is no evidence that as tribes
they continued to exist after that time. While it was matter of

[1] 2 Kings 17 : 6.   [2] 2 Kings 25 : 8, 12.

frequent prediction with the prophets that the kingdoms of Judah
and Israel should be again united in the restored house of David,

Assyrian Palace Restored. (*After Fergusson.*)

these prophecies seem never to have contemplated a complete restoration. It was uniformly of a remnant that the prediction was made.[1]

[1] Isa. 6:13; 10:22; Micah 2:12; 5:3; Zeph. 2:9; Hag. 1:12, 11; Zech. 8:6, 12.

24. During the Persian period, B.C. 536–333, the province of which Judæa formed a part was under an officer called a satrap. Smaller districts, like Judæa itself, were ruled by governors (tirshathas). Such a governor was Zerubbabel (whose Persian name was Sheshbazzar), and later, Ezra and Nehemiah. Ample power was accorded to these Jewish officers by the Persian monarchs; but regular tribute was required. The exact amount of it is not stated. If Palestine was treated like other provinces, and the statements of Herodotus are to be trusted, it was no inconsiderable sum, the ground tax alone amounting to about twenty talents of silver.[1] Besides this there would be taxes for the support of troops and the households of officials, including the Jewish governors themselves unless they declined it.[2] The so-called "Great Synagogue," which existed in this period, was in no sense a political body, and the functions of the high priest were essentially religious. The people no longer attempted to keep up their former tribal organizations or to occupy their original tribal districts. Even the distinction between Judah and Benjamin largely disappeared, especially in Jerusalem where the chief representatives of both tribes had their home. Only the priests and Levites maintained their genealogical lists relatively uncorrupted.

25. During the brief reign of Alexander, the Jews were treated with marked favor. The story of Josephus concerning this ruler's visit to Jerusalem cannot be accepted as authentic.[3] Undoubtedly, however, many Jews voluntarily entered the ranks of his army on his victorious march into Egypt. Among his successors, the attempt of Antiochus Epiphanes forcibly to Hellenize the Jewish people led to an extended revolt and a bitter conflict, which lasted for forty years. Largely through the valor and wisdom of the Maccabæan heroes, Judas, Jonathan and Simon, the yoke of Syria was at last broken and the Jewish commonwealth once more restored. From the year in which this event occurred, B.C. 143, the Jews subsequently dated, as well on coins as on private and public contracts, their national independence. It is an attractive picture which the historian gives of the close of Simon's reign. He "made peace in the land, and Israel rejoiced with great joy. And every man sat under his fig tree, and there was none to make them afraid. And no one was left in the land to fight against them."[4] Great were the admiration and gratitude felt for Simon by his countrymen. A brazen tablet inscribed with a record of his deeds and those of his

[1] Herodotus, iii. 91.   [2] Neh. 3:15, 18.   [3] Josephus, Antiq. 11, 8:5.   [4] 1 Macc. 14:11,12.

family was raised to his honor within the precincts of the temple, and the office of prince and high priest was made hereditary in his family until there should arise a "trustworthy prophet."[1]

26. THE MACCABEES.—The independent government founded by the Maccabæan family lasted about one hundred years, or until the year B.C. 63, when Jerusalem was captured and destroyed by Pompey. He made Hyrcanus II., of the Maccabæan line, prince and high priest, on condition that he make no attempt at revolution and that the nation should be tributary to Rome. A Roman governor was stationed in Syria, and had a general oversight of affairs in Palestine. In the year B.C. 57, on account of an insurrection led by Aristobulus, the proconsul Gabinius degraded Hyrcanus from his political position, and restricted his authority to the temple. In the year B.C. 54 another proconsul, Crassus, robbed the temple of ten thousand talents in treasures. In the year 40, Antigonus, having the Hebrew name Mattathias, succeeded Hyrcanus, with the title of king and high priest, but with the same limited authority as his predecessor. Three years later, by order of the triumvir Antonius, and on the petition of Herod the Great who succeeded him, he was beheaded.

27. THE HERODS.—Herod was an Edomite, and with him the line of succession in the Maccabæan family came to an end. He reigned until the year B.C. 4. His authority extended over the whole of Palestine, including the provinces of Judæa, Galilee, Peræa, and what is generally known as Decapolis. It was just before his death that our Saviour was born, and several events of the New Testament history, notably the slaughter of the children in Bethlehem, occurred during his reign.[2] After Herod's death his kingdom was divided into four parts, called tetrarchies. Tetrarchy was the name given to a government in which four had part. One of these divisions, including Judæa, Samaria and Idumæa, was presided over by Archelaus as tetrarch. Antipas, known in the New Testament as "Herod the tetrarch," was assigned to Galilee and Peræa. The large district east of the Sea of Galilee, embracing Gaulonitis, Ituræa, Auranitis, Batanæa and Trachonitis, fell to Philip II. The fourth tetrarchy, governed by Lysanias, consisted of a very moderate territory lying between Mount Hermon and Damascus, called Abilene. This district did not originally belong to the kingdom of Herod the Great. Archelaus and Antipas were both sons of this Herod by a Samaritan woman. Philip II. was his son by Cleopatra. Of the

1 1 Macc. 14: 41.   2 Matt. 2: 1-16.

Lysanias who is mentioned by Luke as tetrarch of Abilene little is known. He is not to be confounded with the Lysanius of whom Josephus speaks in connection with the reign of Antony and Cleopatra sixty years before.[1]

28. On the removal of Archelaus, in A.D. 6, the important provinces of Judæa, Samaria and Idumæa came directly under the rule of the imperial government at Rome. A legate of the emperor was sent out to administer their affairs. When our Saviour was crucified this legate or governor was Pontius Pilate. He was the sixth in the line that had followed Archelaus. In A.D. 41, Herod Agrippa I., a grandson of Herod the Great, having previously held the tetrarchies of Philip and Lysanias, received from Caligula, along with the title of king, the government of all Palestine, including the tetrarchy of Abilene. He is the person of whom we read in the Acts under the name of "Herod the king."[2] It was he who slew the apostle James, imprisoned Peter, and died in such agony at Cæsarea not long after. Herod Agrippa II., a son of the former, being only seventeen years old when his father died did not at once succeed him. But in A.D. 52 he was given the tetrarchies of Philip and Lysanias, also with the title of king. He was the Agrippa before whom Paul appeared.[3] At this time the province of Judæa had been enlarged to include Samaria, Galilee and Peræa, and was governed by a Roman procurator whose headquarters were at Cæsarea. With the destruction of Jerusalem by the Roman forces under Titus, A.D. 70, the entire country became politically subordinate to Syria and was ruled as a part of that province.

29. ROMAN CITIZENSHIP.—A few words on the matter of Roman citizenship may be of service in understanding a number of incidents in the life of the apostle Paul. This franchise was his by birthright. How his father, who was a resident of Tarsus in Cilicia, had obtained it, it is not possible to learn. Among the special advantages possessed by a citizen of Rome were exemption from punishment before trial, from stripes and physical torture under any circumstances, and the power of appeal to Cæsar. The privilege might be obtained by purchase, by noted military services or by manumission. More than once the great apostle to the Gentiles availed himself of this high political prerogative.[4] According to the tradition which puts the martyrdom of Peter and Paul on the same day, the latter was slain with the sword.

---

[1] Luke 3:1.   [2] Acts 12:1.   [3] Acts 25:26.   [4] Acts 16:35-39; 22:23, 30; 25:11; 26:32; 28:19.

30. Throughout the whole of western Asia, during and long after the time of Alexander, a process of Greek colonization was going rapidly on. Greek cities sprang up in and around Palestine to a remarkable extent. About forty of them of considerable importance are mentioned by historians. In their government these cities took for their model those of their own land. A council, often made up of several hundred persons, was constituted, to which all matters of common interest were by general consent referred. The whole of Palestine, however, was not Græcized. The strictly Jewish sections of it may be broadly characterized as made up of Judæa and parts of Galilee. In these districts Jews were at least in the majority, and formed largely the ruling class.

31. CIVIL REGULATIONS IN THE TIME OF CHRIST.—As far as the Jewish civil regulations had depended on the constitution and relations of the various tribes and families, they necessarily ceased when the tribal connections and genealogies of families fell into confusion. But the important governing body, known already in the time of Moses and throughout the Persian and earlier Greek periods as the "elders of the city," was most happily adapted to the era of the new civilization.[1] In addition to this body it is natural to suppose that in the larger cities a sort of local court would also be provided. The existence of such a court is, in fact, confirmed by Josephus.[2] It consisted of not less than seven persons, who took cognizance of all civil and ecclesiastical questions requiring judicial decisions. As in the neighboring Greek communities, the villages in Jewish districts were politically subordinate to the adjacent city and the smaller cities to the larger ones. For convenience of administration, mostly perhaps for the purpose of raising the taxes easily, Judæa, during the Roman period, was divided into eleven toparchies, with Jerusalem as the middle point.

32. The local Jewish court just referred to was originally composed exclusively of Levites. Later it consisted of a body of scribes who by special knowledge and experience were fitted for the responsible position. Hearings and trials took place in the synagogues, and were held ordinarily on market-days in order the better to accommodate those living at a distance. Punishment, on conviction, was not infrequently administered on the spot.[3] Such cases alone as involved points about which the judges of the local court were not clear were referred to Jerusalem. In the larger places the

---

[1] Deut. 19 : 12 ; Ezra 10 : 14 ; Judith 6 : 16, 21.   [2] Josephus, *Antiq.* 4, 8 : 14.   [3] Matt. 10 : 17 ; 2 Cor. 11 : 24.

number of judges seems to have been greater, the Mishna stating that a city which had at least a hundred and twenty men was entitled to a sanhedrin of twenty-three persons. In Jerusalem there were several such smaller courts, though they were naturally limited and overshadowed in their activity by the Great Sanhedrin.

33. THE GREAT SANHEDRIN.—The origin of the latter body is uncertain. The name is of Greek derivation, and its first appearance as the title of a Jewish court is after the beginning of the Roman dominion. It is highly probable that Sanhedrin is but another name for the Senate of which we read occasionally in works of the Maccabæan period and shortly after it.[1] In the New Testament it is often mentioned, and continued to exist until after the destruction of Jerusalem. It was composed of seventy-one members, of whom one third formed a quorum sufficient for the transaction of business. Members were inducted into office by the laying on of hands. An interesting feature of the meetings was the attendance of a considerable number of young men, who thus became acquainted with the details of its rules and methods. Its ordinary meetings, like those of the smaller judicial bodies, were held on the second and fifth week-days. Probably they might, on emergency, be held daily, with the exception of the Sabbath and special holidays. The body was made up of priests, elders and scribes. The high priest presided at the sittings.

Among the priests were included any who had served as high priest, as well as members of leading families that had furnished incumbents of this office. The elders were generally distinguished laymen, but might be priests. The scribes were depended on for the interpretation of all abstruse points of law. Both Pharisees and Sadducees had seats in the body. In the later times the former seem to have had the numerical majority, or at least to have had the greater influence. As distinguished from the lower courts the Great Sanhedrin was the administrative and judicial body for all matters except such as the Roman government claimed jurisdiction over. The decision of the Sanhedrin at Jerusalem was binding on Jews outside of Palestine, as far as it related to religious matters. For the rest, its authority was confined to the eleven toparchies of Judæa. The ordinary place of meeting was in one of the buildings connected with the temple. Irregular, and especially night, sessions might be held elsewhere, the gate of the temple-mountain being closed and under strict watch during the night. This probably accounts for the

[1] Judith 4 : 8 ; 1 Macc. 12 : 6.

fact that our Saviour's trial took place at the palace of the high priest.[1]

34. TRIBUTE TO FOREIGN POWERS.—Reference has been made to the tribute imposed on the Jews by their foreign oppressors. After their return from Babylon, with the exception of the brief reign of the Maccabæan family they were never exempt from foreign taxation. During the most of the Persian period the burden was comparatively light.[2] Under the immediate successors of Alexander, also, although the taxes were farmed out to the highest bidder, and room was thus given for the greatest injustice, the total tribute demanded amounted only to about thirty thousand dollars a year. This does not include, of course, that which the Jews contributed for the maintenance of their own religious institutions, or the large sums expended for military purposes and the support of a foreign court among them. During the reign of the Seleucidæ the taxes consisted of a duty on salt, a third of the income of the grainfields, one half the product of all fruit trees, a poll-tax, custom duty, and a kind of tribute called crown-money. When Jonathan, the Maccabee, procured from Demetrius freedom from taxation, he was obliged to pay three hundred talents for the exemption.[3]

How burdensome these foreign impositions were in the time of the Herods may be inferred from the fact that the yearly revenue of Archelaus, whose tetrarchy included Judæa and Samaria, is estimated at two hundred and forty thousand pounds sterling. That of Herod the Great, who had a larger extent of territory, was not less than six hundred and eighty thousand pounds, and that of Agrippa II. was five hundred thousand. "The Romans had a peculiar way of levying these taxes—not directly, but indirectly—which kept the treasury quite safe, whatever harm it might inflict on the tax-payer, while at the same time it threw upon him the whole cost of the collection. Senators and magistrates were prohibited from engaging in business or trade; but the highest order, the equestrian, was largely composed of great capitalists. These Roman knights formed joint-stock companies, which bought at public auction the revenues of a province at a fixed price, generally for five years. The board had its chairman, or *magister*, and its offices at Rome. These were the real Publicani, or publicans, who often underlet certain of the taxes. The Publicani, or those who held from them, employed either slaves or some of the lower classes in

[1] Matt. 26:3, 57. See also Prof. Bissell's work on the *Apocrypha* (New York, 1880), pp. 30, 31.
[2] Ezra 4:13, 20; 7:24. [3] 1 Macc. 11:28; 13:15.

the country as tax-gatherers—the publicans of the New Testament. . . . Of course, the joint-stock company of Publicani at Rome expected its handsome dividends; so did the tax-gatherers in the provinces, and those to whom they on occasions sublet the imposts. All wanted to make money of the poor people; and the cost of the collection had of course to be added to the taxation."[1]

[1] Edersheim, *Sketches of Jewish Social Life*, pp. 55, 56.

The Cross in Monogram.
(*Used by the early Christians.*)

Prisoner, bound or chained between two Guards.
(*From an old Roman sketch.*)

Augustus Cæsar, Roman Emperor in the time of Christ. (*Copy of a marble statue lately found near Rome.*)

14

CHAPTER IX.

1. By Hebrew usage, as recorded in the Bible, it was made a part of a ruler's duty to pronounce judicial decisions in all matters brought before him. The titles ruler and judge are, in fact, often used synonymously. The supreme Ruler and Judge was Jehovah. All others were his vicegerents. "Ye shall not respect persons in judgment," was the command of Moses; "ye shall hear the small and the great alike; ye shall not be afraid of the face of man; for the judgment is God's."[1] Taking a case before a judge is spoken of as inquiring of God, or going before God.[2] To stand before the one was regarded as equivalent to standing before the other. "If an unrighteous witness rise up against any man to testify against him of wrong doing; then both the men, between whom the controversy is, shall stand before the Lord, before the priests and the judges which shall be in those days."[3]

2. EARLIER LEGAL PROCESSES.—The simplicity of legal processes in the earlier times has been already referred to. As family relations became more and more involved and the unity of the people was more emphasized, heads of families ceased to exercise, to the same extent, the ancient right of sitting in judgment in civil matters. To Moses, as God's vicegerent and the recognized medium of communication with him, this right was transferred. But already loaded down as he was with a multitude of other cares and duties, Moses found his strength inadequate for such a task. On the advice of Jethro, therefore, a body of men, seventy in number, was constituted a court for the consideration of all the less important matters. Putting together the several accounts of the subject found in the Pentateuch, we learn that the body was composed of seventy "elders," that is, of men who already represented the nation in an official capacity.[4] They were named by the people and inducted into office by Moses.

3. This organization, while having for its first object the consideration of matters requiring judicial decisions, was clearly intended to

---

[1] Deut. 1:17. [2] Ex. 18:15; 21:6; 22:8. [3] Deut. 19:16, 17. [4] Ex. 18:13-27; Num. 11:16, 17; Deut. 1:13-18.

serve the further purpose of being a kind of official military board. This alone can account for the fact that it was made up of men who are spoken of as heads over tens, fifties, hundreds and thousands, respectively.[1] There can have been no such graded series of courts. Each judge or officer was independent in his own sphere. The only appeal possible was to Moses himself; and in every such appeal it was not the people, but the judge, who carried the case to the higher court. If, for any reason, he felt himself incompetent, as for instance from lack of information concerning facts, or because the case involved matters of supreme importance, or because it was something new concerning which the law did not definitely speak, he applied directly to the lawgiver. Some cases regarded as of more immediate public concern continued to be tried by the old method, that is, by a full assembly of the elders of the people.[2]

4. SUBSEQUENT CHANGES.—This primitive arrangement for the administration of justice came to an end along with the peculiar circumstances that called it forth. It was adapted only to the earlier periods of the national history. As early as the book of Deuteronomy, provision is made for the time when the people shall become settled in the land of Canaan:[3] " Judges and officers [assistants] shalt thou make thee in all thy gates, which the Lord thy God giveth thee, according to thy tribes: and they shall judge the people with righteous judgment. . . . If there arise a matter too hard for thee in judgment, between blood and blood, between plea and plea, and between stroke and stroke, being matters of controversy within thy gates: then shalt thou arise [i. e., the judge] and get thee up unto the place which the Lord thy God shall choose; and thou shalt come unto the priests the Levites, and unto the judge that shall be in those days: and thou shalt inquire; and they shall show thee the sentence of judgment: and thou shalt do according to the tenor of the sentence. . . . And the man that doeth presumptuously, in not hearkening unto the priest that standeth to minister there before the Lord thy God, or unto the judge, even that man shall die; and thou shalt put away the evil from Israel."

5. It is clear that in this provision we have simply an adaptation to altered circumstances of those previously made.[4] Like the council of seventy, these judges are to be selected from the elders of the people " according to their tribes." They are assigned to positions of different importance " in all thy gates," that is, in cities small

[1] Ex. 18 : 25.　[2] Num. 35 : 24; Josh. 20 : 6.　[3] Deut. 16 : 18-20; 17 : 8-13.　[4] Ex. 18 : 13-26; Num. 11 : 16, 24-29.

aud great. They have the privilege of appeal in difficult cases to the priest or judge, or to both together, who might at any time be at the head of affairs. This corresponds exactly to the earlier ordinance, where appeal could be taken to Moses and Aaron as the civil and ecclesiastical heads of the nation. As matter of history, moreover, we find a tribunal similar to this in existence not long after the time of Moses. In the ceremony of rehearsing the law on Mount Ebal there are present elders, officers and judges in distinction from the rest of the people.[1] It is to this body, apparently, that Boaz makes application in his efforts to befriend Naomi and Ruth.[2]

6. The times of the judges being to a considerable extent abnormal, we find the people, not only in other respects but especially in the administration of justice, reverting to primitive usages. The ruler, or temporary military leader, by virtue of his office is recognized as judge; and since in times of peace this was his principal function, the title of judge is accorded to him. Jephthah, for example, is said to have "judged Israel six years;" and after him Ibzan of Bethlehem "judged Israel."[3] In Eli the office of judge is once more joined to that of high priest; while after Samuel the Mosaic ordinance comes to its full right. In harmony with it David appointed a large number of judges and officers, the same terms being used for them as in the Deuteronomic law.[4]

7. In the Time of Jehoshaphat.—The next change which, as far as we are informed, took place in the judiciary, occurred during the reign of Jehoshaphat. It is said of him that he "set judges in the land throughout all the fenced cities of Judah, city by city, and said to the judges, Consider what ye do: for ye judge not for man, but for the Lord. . . . Moreover in Jerusalem did Jehoshaphat set of the Levites and the priests, and of the heads of the fathers' *houses* of Israel, for the judgment of the Lord and for controversies."[5] If this were our only information concerning the matter we might suppose that, with one exception, the king meant to act in precise conformity with the Deuteronomic law. But in the context we observe a further departure from the original form in the tribunal constituted by Jehoshaphat. "And, behold," he says, "Amariah the chief priest is over you in all matters of the Lord; and Zebadiah the son of Ishmael, the ruler of the house of Judah, in all the king's matters: also the Levites shall be officers before you."[6] This court of Jehoshaphat, then, differed from that provided for in Deuter-

---

[1] Josh. 8:33; cf. 24:1.   [2] Ruth 4:1-9.   [3] Judg. 12:7, 8.   [4] 1 Chron. 23:4; cf. 26:29.
[5] 2 Chron. 19:5-8.   [6] 2 Chron. 19:11.

onomy in three respects. It was composed of priests and Levites instead of Levitical priests alone. It had a civil and ecclesiastical head acting at one and the same time, instead of independently. The civil head is represented by a family chief of Judah, an officer unknown to the earlier legislation, and is supported by the chief of the fathers of Israel.[1]

8. It is the more important to note the essential distinction between these two forms of judicial procedure, since an effort has been made to confound them. Critics who give a later date to many of the laws hitherto ascribed to Moses hold that in the present case the law of Jehoshaphat's time antedates that of Deuteronomy. But if the facts be as we have stated them, this cannot be successfully maintained. The tribunal of Jehoshaphat did not, any more than previous ones, exclude the authority of the eldership in matters properly belonging to its jurisdiction. When Ahab sought unjustly to possess himself of the vineyard of Naboth, it is said that "the men of his city, even the elders and the nobles who dwelt in his city, did as Jezebel had sent unto them."[2] From this passage and others, it may be inferred that in alleged capital offences the judgment of the eldership was particularly sought. The prophet Jeremiah, complained of by the priests and false prophets of his day as worthy of death, is cited to answer for his life before the representatives of the whole people, and before them he pleads his case.[3]

9. DURING AND AFTER THE EXILE.—In the apocryphal book of Susanna it is assumed that during the Babylonian exile the people of Israel executed justice among themselves according to their own usages.[4] It is certain that this privilege was accorded to them by their Persian rulers, and to some degree by their successors the Ptolemies.[5] Josephus, who quotes Strabo, informs us that to such Jews as had found a home in Egypt special places were assigned besides those allotted them in Alexandria. "There is also an ethnarch allowed them," he says, "who governs the nation; and distributes justice to them, and takes care of their contracts and of the laws to them belonging, as if he were the ruler of a free republic."[6] In Palestine itself local courts continued to exist down to the time of the Romans; and the right of attending to all ordinary civil processes was freely granted to the Jews. Several allusions are made to these courts in the New Testament.[7] Exactly how they were con-

---

[1] Deut. 17 : 12.   [2] Deut. 19 : 12; 21 : 19; 25 : 7; 1 Kings 21 : 11.   [3] Jer. 26 : 11, 12.   [4] Susan. vs. 5, 41.   [5] Ezra 7 : 25; 10 : 14.   [6] Josephus, *Antiq.* 14, 7 : 2; 14, 10 : 17.   [7] Matt. 5 : 22; 10 : 17; Mark 13 : 9; Luke 12 : 14, 53.

stituted it is not possible to say. In the so-called city of Bethulia of the book of Judith three men are represented as its rulers. In the same connection, however, a council of elders is mentioned, and it is likely that these men are only among the higher officials of this body.

10. IN THE TIME OF CHRIST.—According to the Talmud, the local provincial courts were composed of twenty-three members. Any place containing a hundred and twenty men—other authorities say two hundred and thirty—might have such a court. But it is more probable that the size of the bodies also corresponded to that of the places in which they were situated. In the larger cities the sittings were more frequent than in the smaller ones. Places favored with a rabbinical college, like Jabneh where the famous Gamaliel once presided, would be likely to entrust to it very largely the administration of justice. Under the Roman government these courts, while regarded as competent to try any, even capital, cases, were limited in the execution of sentences. Beyond forty stripes they were not allowed to inflict any bodily punishment. The Great Sanhedrin at Jerusalem, which was the highest governing body among the Jews as well as their supreme court, has already been described, in its main features, in the preceding chapter.

11. PRINCIPLES GOVERNING COURTS OF LAW.—The processes by which justice was administered among the Hebrews were largely dependent on ancient usage. The Mosaic law of course, where it spoke, was the highest rule; but in many cases it was silent. Even as it respected the principles on which decisions were to be reached, it was far from being a complete guide in civil affairs. The judge, accordingly, was often left to that spirit of fairness and wisdom with which, from the nature of his office, it was expected he would be endowed. It was because so much depended on the impartiality of the magistrate that this quality was so strongly insisted on in the law. It is said, for example, "Thou shalt not wrest the judgment of thy poor in his cause. . . . And thou shalt take no gift: for a gift blindeth them that have sight, and perverteth the words of the righteous."[1] The law abounds in appeals and exhortations of this sort.[2]

A careful examination into all the details of a case was rigorously enjoined.[3] In capital crimes, it was not permitted to condemn a person to death on the testimony of a single witness. Two or three were needful; three, it is likely, when circumstances did not make the

[1] Ex. 23:6-8.　[2] Lev. 19:15; Deut. 1:16, 17; 16:19.　[3] Deut. 13:14; 17:4; 19:18.

matter clear without them. By comparing the two passages just cited, it will be found that the one in Deuteronomy shows an advance on that in Numbers.[1] It is likely that his experience in the wilderness had led the lawgiver to see the importance of modifying the original regulation, especially of making it more definite. Jewish practice was uniformly based on the Deuteronomic form.[2] It has been thought that the apocryphal book of Susanna was written for the purpose of illustrating the necessity of more than two witnesses in certain cases. Special emphasis was laid on the character of witnesses. Besides the ninth commandment, we find numerous other laws relating to the subject.[3] If after "diligent inquisition" it was found that a witness had testified falsely, it was required that it should be "done unto him as he had thought to do unto his brother." The rabbis held that a false witness was only to be put to death when the person against whom he had testified had not been already executed. This can hardly have been the meaning of the original statute.

12. PLACE OF TRIAL, ETC.—The place of trial, in ancient times, was ordinarily near the principal gate of the city.[4] Moses heard causes at the door of the tent of meeting, and Deborah, under a palm tree.[5] In Jerusalem hearings took place in front of the temple. The trial was public, and as a rule was conducted orally. In the case of kings, to whom, especially in the earlier times, was accorded the right of pronouncing decisions in important causes, the court of the palace was the place of assembly, or some special room

Oriental Court in Session.

within it devoted to the purpose.[6] Parties at variance appeared in person and pleaded for themselves before the judge.[7] There is no evidence that advocates were appointed on the part of the government either to make complaint or to defend one who had been incriminated. But the cause of the widow, orphan, stranger, and the helpless generally, was laid especially upon the heart by the Mosaic laws, and it was demanded that nothing favorable to them should be overlooked.[8] A person in confinement for a capital offence was brought into court,

[1] Num. 35 : 30; Deut. 17 : 6; 19 : 15.   [2] John 8 : 17; Acts 7 : 58; Heb. 10 : 28.   [3] Ex. 23 : 1; Lev. 19 : 12; Deut. 19 : 15–21.   [4] Deut. 21 : 19; 22 : 15; Job 5 : 4; Ps. 127 : 5; Prov. 8 : 3; 22 : 22. [5] Num. 16 : 19; Judg. 4 : 5.   [6] 1 Kings 7 : 7.   [7] Deut. 1 : 16; 21 : 20; 25 : 1.   [8] Isa. 1 : 17; 29 : 21; Amos 5 : 10.

and others under indictment who did not appear when wanted were made to do so. The complainant took his station at the right of the prisoner.[1] According to Josephus the latter wore a peculiar garb, and appeared with dishevelled hair in the way of appeal to the sympathies of his judges.[2]

13. It was necessary to sustain an accusation by facts. Circumstantial evidence was sometimes considered as an aid to a judge in reaching an equitable decision where nothing else was available.[3] In the case of a disobedient son, severe as was the punishment, the simple complaint of parents was considered as sufficient evidence of guilt, provided both parents were concerned in lodging and supporting it.[4] It has been justly inferred from Leviticus 5 : 1 that witnesses were put under a certain form of oath. The passage reads, "And if any one sin, in that he heareth the voice of adjuration, he being a witness, whether he hath seen or known, if he do not utter *it*, then he shall bear his iniquity." This appears to refer only to a person who has been summoned as a proper witness, and is actually in circumstances to know something about the case. He was adjured to speak of whatever he knew concerning it.[5] If he failed to do it, being so adjured, he must bear his iniquity, that is, be held guilty.[6] If he afterwards repented of his silence, he had to make full restitution to any one whom he had injured by it and also present a guilt-offering in the temple.[7]

14. NO USE OF TORTURE.—Applying torture to witnesses was never a practice of the Hebrews; but was introduced, along with many other atrocities, by Herod the Great and his successors.[8] Calling in the aid of prophetical insight in judicial matters was also unknown in Israel. In instances where crime was charged and legally competent witnesses were not forthcoming, the solemn oath of the accused to that effect was accepted as proof of innocence. This oath was called the "oath of the Lord," that is, the divine name was introduced into it.[9] In somewhat later periods of Israelitish history the following form of imprecation is often met with: "The Lord do so unto me," etc. The use of an oath was generally attended by some such formality as raising the hand, placing the hand on the head or under the thigh of another, dividing a victim and passing between the pieces, or appearing before the altar.[10] Our Lord refers to some peculiar forms of oath, but they were

---

[1] Ps. 109 : 6; Zech. 3 : 1, 3. [2] Josephus, *Antiq.* 14, 9 : 4. [3] 1 Kings 3 : 26. [4] Deut. 21 : 18-20; cf. Ex. 21 : 17; Lev. 20 : 9; Prov. 19 : 18; 30 : 17. [5] See 2 Chron. 18 : 15; Matt. 26 : 63. [6] Prov. 29 : 24. [7] Lev. 6 : 5, 6. [8] Josephus, *Wars of the Jews*, 1, 30 : 2-4. [9] Ex. 22 : 11. [10] Gen. 11 : 22; 15 : 10-17; 24 : 2; 47 : 29; Ex. 6 : 8; 1 Kings 8 : 31; Jer. 34 : 18.

simply refinements of a later day and of no force in judicial matters.[1]

15. CASTING LOTS.—Casting lots in order to obtain a decision in doubtful cases was practiced, to a limited extent, in the early history of Israel.[2] It was considered in no sense an appeal to chance, but to the supreme Judge. A proverb current in Solomon's time ran, "The lot is cast into the lap, but the whole disposing thereof is of the Lord."[3] With a single exception, this was the only use of extraordinary means for determining the guilt or innocence of an accused person. A woman suspected by her husband of adultery was subjected to a peculiar trial. The proceedings, which are fully detailed in Numbers 5 : 11–31, are probably based on some pre-Mosaic custom. Many a modern victim of marital jealousy would gladly submit to an ordeal as trying as this to receive a vindication as conclusive. A law found in Deuteronomy covers a somewhat similar case, but is not to be regarded as a later modification of that in Numbers, as some critics maintain.[4] On the contrary, without superseding that of Numbers in the special case it had before it, the former emphasizes, in the heavy penalties imposed on the husband if he prove a false accuser, a principle of equity there unrecognized which should be always understood to rule in like circumstances.

16. DECISIONS BOTH ORAL AND WRITTEN.—In the more ancient times the decision of the judge was announced orally; at a later period it would seem to have been written.[5] The penalty determined on was exacted immediately, and, if the offence was not a capital one, before the eyes of the judge himself.[6] The death penalty was ordinarily inflicted by the whole community; and since the responsibility largely rested on the witnesses, the natural solemnity of the execution was enhanced by the part assigned them. The usual method of putting to death being by stoning, their hands were to be first against the condemned man to put him to death, "and afterwards the hand of all the people."[7] The case of Stephen's martyrdom will be recalled, when the witnesses "laid down their garments [the more easily to cast the stones] at the feet of a young man named Saul."[8] In the instance of manslaughter the guilty person was delivered into the hands of the goël, or avenger of blood, for execution. Kings, as we have seen, assumed the right to put to death at once those whom they considered amenable to it without waiting for

the forms of law. The perversion of justice on their part, as well as the corruption of judges, is one of the most common subjects of complaint by the prophets.[1] Matters concerning the sale and exchange of property, the renunciation, or the establishment, of rights and the like, were not brought by the Hebrews into courts of justice. As will hereafter appear, they were settled either by mutual agreement or by reference to an assembly of elders.

17. METHODS OF THE SANHEDRIN.—The method of procedure in trials before the Sanhedrin is especially interesting in view of the trial of our Lord by it. Members sat in a half circle. Two secretaries stood before them, one on the right hand, the other on the left, to record all opinions expressed. The prisoner was expected to appear in humble mien and, as already stated, in garments befitting his position. Where the case was one of life and death, it was understood that the first argument should be in the prisoner's favor. No one could speak against him who had already spoken for him; but the reverse was possible. The prisoner was allowed to testify in his own behalf. Students of the law who were present were permitted to take part, if they had cogent reasons to adduce in favor of the culprit. The debate being over, the vote was taken and recorded along with the reasons for it. A majority of one was sufficient to acquit; a majority of two necessary to condemn. If no decision was reached, additional judges were selected from students of the law who were present. The sentence once passed the execution was immediate. The hasty and notably irregular trial of Jesus on the night preceding his crucifixion is the more remarkable in view of the ordinary fairness and even mildness of this judicial body.

18. PENALTIES.—Two things served to modify, to a considerable extent, Hebrew legislation as it respects the penalties affixed to crimes: first, the fact that the national government was a theocracy; and second, the institutions and customs which had been inherited from the past. To the former circumstance it is due that the punishment of certain offences is so much severer than might otherwise have been expected; to the latter, the peculiar form which some penalties assume. The general principle on which punishment was inflicted is stated with great frequency in the book of Deuteronomy: to "put away the evil" from the midst of Israel; or, as otherwise given, that "Israel shall hear, and fear, and do no more any such wickedness."[2] The quality and form of punishments were, as far

---

[1] Isa. 1:23; Amos 5:12; Micah 3:11; Mal. 3:5.   [2] Deut. 13:5, 11; 17:7, 12, 13; 19:13, 19, 20; 21:8, 21; 22:21, 22, 24; 24:7.

as possible, fixed in harmony with the principle that satisfaction was to be rendered for the wrong done. Guilt and its requital were in some sense to correspond. What the evil man had done, or purposed to do, to another, was to be visited in punishment on his own head.

This is the ethical basis of the so-called *lex talionis*, which required an eye for an eye, a tooth for a tooth.[1] It was never designed, if we may judge from Hebrew history, to be carried out literally, except, perhaps, in the case of murder and a few other instances of willful injury, where retaliation in kind would have a salutary influence in checking violence and passion. It seems intended rather to be a norm or guiding principle for the authorities, in harmony with which just penalties might be visited upon offenders. The human law was content to restore the disturbed equipoise of the social order. Exact justice was left to God. And our Lord in his utterances, on one occasion, over this matter is not to be understood as taking an exception to such a principle as used to govern the civil authorities in the ancient times.[2] He had expressly stated just before that he had not come " to destroy the law and the prophets."[3] He excepted to it only as a rule by which the individual Christian was to be controlled in his conduct toward his fellow man. In this sphere he was to consider himself bound by the higher law of brotherly love.

19. If certain forms of punishment found in the penal code of the Hebrews appear still, at first sight, disproportionate, the state of public sentiment at that period is to be considered in connection with the fact above stated, that one of the principal objects of punishment with them was that it might serve as a deterrent. The Hebrew laws are at least free from those extremes of severity, the refined cruelty and the tortures common to other nations of antiquity. It is one of their great excellences that they look beneath the outward act to its moral quality, the motive that prompted it. They know, for example, how to distinguish between murder and justifiable homicide; between stealing and an innocent harboring of another's goods; between an intentional and an accidental infliction of injuries on the person or property of others. Even in the Pentateuch there is prohibited one of the most common of ancient practices, the visitation by human authority upon an offender's family of the penalty which belonged only to him. " The fathers shall not be put to death for the children," says Moses in Deuteronomy, " neither shall the children be put to death for the fathers: every man shall be put to death for his own sin."[4] The mysterious influence of heredity is not

1 Ex. 21:23; Lev. 24:17, 18; Deut. 19:21.   2 Matt. 5:38, 39.   3 Matt. 5:17.   4 Deut. 24:16.

hereby denied. The inexorable law of cause and effect, by which the sins of the fathers are actually visited upon the children to the third and fourth generation, is not disputed or repealed. But to fallible men there is properly denied the right to trench upon the prerogative of the Almighty. The divine ways, as the prophet Ezekiel shows in speaking of this very matter, are equal; man's ways are unequal.[1]

20. CAPITAL OFFENCES.—By Hebrew law the penalty of death was prescribed for a greater number and variety of crimes than is now common in civilized countries. It is worthy of note, however, that it was never inflicted for wrongs committed simply against property. It was administered in an orderly, though a summary, way, no attempt being made to prolong the pain suffered or to render the culprit infamous. The motive assigned for a regulation in one of the minor forms of punishment seems to have pervaded, in spirit, all of them: that every thing should be avoided by which a "brother" would be rendered vile.[2] The barbarous cruelties inflicted in time of war, and sometimes by so representative a Hebrew as King David, are not to be charged against the divinely-sanctioned laws of the land.

Capital offences, according to Hebrew law, were willful murder;[3] the perjury of a witness by which the life of another was put in peril;[4] smiting or cursing one's parents, even persistent disobedience and rebellion on the part of a child;[5] man-stealing;[6] unfaithfulness in wedlock, as also unnatural sexual connections and the grosser forms of incest;[7] idolatry, witchcraft and the false assumption of prophetic inspiration;[8] sabbath-breaking;[9] and a refusal to submit to the decisions of the regularly-constituted legal authorities.[10] The heinousness of most of these offences consisted in the fact that they dishonored the people which had been chosen as God's heritage, and hence were calculated to destroy the foundations on which the theocracy rested.

21. PUNISHMENT, HOW ADMINISTERED.—Capital punishment was inflicted in a number of ways, though chiefly by stoning. When the life of the murderer was taken by the avenger of blood, it might be by means of a sword, spear, or any other weapon he chose. Those condemned to death by kings were ordinarily executed with the sword.[11] In the earlier periods the same was true under the law

---

[1] Ezek. 18 : 20.   [2] Deut. 25 : 3.   [3] Gen. 9 : 6; Ex. 21 : 12.   [4] Deut. 19 : 16–21.   [5] Ex. 21 : 15, 17; Lev. 20 : 9; Deut. 21 : 18–20.   [6] Ex. 21 : 16; Deut. 24 : 7.   [7] Lev. 20 : 10–21.   [8] Ex. 22 : 18; Deut. 13 : 5; 17 : 2–6.   [9] Ex. 31 : 14, 15; Num. 15 : 32–36.   [10] Deut. 17 : 12, 13.   [11] 1 Sam. 22 : 17; 2 Sam. 1 : 15; 4 : 12; 1 Kings 2 : 25.

when on account of the large number executed, or for any other reason, death by stoning was impracticable.[1] Even when the sword was resorted to the method was not beheading. This was sometimes practiced in time of war, but not as a punishment for crime before the Roman period.[2] A condemned criminal who was to be stoned was taken outside of the camp or city.[3] The witnesses threw the first stones, having first laid off their outer clothing and placed their hands on the culprit's head as a symbol that he was to bear his guilt.[4] In the talmudic times a stupefying drink, composed of myrrh and frankincense, was previously administered to him. After the witnesses, the whole community participated in the execution.

Of two other forms of capital punishment known in the East, strangulation and burning, the former is not mentioned in the Bible. It is thought by some that it is always meant when the form of the death penalty is not otherwise specifically mentioned. But there is no positive evidence that it was ever in use among the Jews before the times of Herod. Burning was prescribed in the Mosaic law as the punishment for certain gross forms of sexual immorality; but it seems most likely that in all cases it followed death by stoning, as we know it did in some cases.[5] The talmudic practice was to put to death by strangulation and to burn afterwards. The burning, however, among the later Jews consisted only in inserting a lighted wick in the dead man's mouth. Since bodies were sometimes, as an added indignity, burned after death, so they were sometimes suspended on a tree or gibbet after death for the same reason.[6] Impaling was a common punishment in Persia.[7] It was one of the provisions of the Deuteronomic law that a body hanged must be removed and buried before nightfall of the same day, on the ground that otherwise the land would be defiled.[8] Reference is made to this fact in Galatians 3 : 13, where it is said of Christ that he became a curse for us: " for it is written, Cursed is every one that hangeth on a tree."

22. CRUCIFIXION.—Crucifixion was the most degrading, inhuman and painful of all the forms of ancient punishment. It is not certain that any examples of it occur in the Old Testament.[9] In New Testament times it was practiced by the Romans in the case of slaves and such as were guilty of rebellion or highway robbery. It was

[1] Deut. 13 : 15.   [2] 1 Sam. 17 : 51; Matt. 14 : 10; Acts 12 : 2.   [3] Lev. 24 : 14; Num. 15 : 35; 1 Kings 21 : 10; Acts 7 : 58.   [4] Lev. 24 : 14; Deut. 13 : 9; 17 : 7; Acts 7 : 58.   [5] Gen. 38 : 24; Josh. 7 : 15.   [6] Deut. 21 : 22; 2 Sam. 4 : 12; Josh. 10 : 26.   [7] Ezra 6 : 11; Esth. 5 : 14; 7 : 9.   [8] Deut. 21 : 23.   [9] But cf. Gen. 40 : 19; Num. 25 : 4; Deut. 21 : 22, 23; Josh. 8 : 29; Ezra 6 : 11; Esth. 2 : 23. In all these cases impaling is probably referred to.

ordinarily preceded by scourging; in our Saviour's case it was attended by other brutalities. Although there are different forms of crosses, it is conceded that the one used in the crucifixion of our Lord consisted of one plank or beam crossing another at right angles near its top. This cross was laid upon the condemned to be borne

Three Forms of the Cross.

by him to the place of execution.[1] Arriving there his garments were stripped off and a stupefying drink usually administered. This drink was refused by Jesus.[2] The condemned was then nailed to the cross by nails passing through the hands and feet. Whether this was done before or after placing the cross in the ground, it is not possible to say; probably both methods were in use. Though exposed to the most excruciating pains, the poor victim often failed of relief by death for many hours; even sometimes, it is said, until the third day. It was a source of wonder to Pilate that our Lord expired so soon.[3] As a concession to Jewish custom, the Romans permitted the bodies of Jewish criminals to be buried at nightfall of the same day.[4] Hence death was hastened by other violence.[5] Could the divine abhorrence of sin have been expressed in a more emphatic way than by permitting Jesus Christ, his eternal Son, to be crucified? " Him who knew no sin he made to be sin on our behalf; that we might become the righteousness of God in him."[6]

23. PECULIAR TREATMENT OF THE HOMICIDE.—The provision for the punishment of murder is so peculiar as to deserve special notice. It is a restriction and a regulation of the old custom of blood revenge. By this custom the next of kin to the murdered man slew the murderer wherever found. This was naturally the occasion of many abuses, the innocent often suffering for the guilty. Moses provided for six cities of refuge, three on each side of the Jordan, to any one of which a person suspected of murder might flee. Having here a safe asylum, a judicial inquiry was instituted into his case. If he were found guilty of the crime charged, he was delivered over to the avenger of blood for execution. If acquitted of the crime of actual murder, but still chargeable with some form of homicide, he was compelled to remain where he was until

---

[1] John 19:17. [2] Mark 15:23. [3] Mark 15:44. [4] Deut. 21:23. [5] John 19:31.
[6] 2 Cor. 5:21.

the death of the high priest. He might then return unmolested to his own home. The later rabbins applied this law only to the case of Hebrews killed accidentally or otherwise. They reasoned that a stranger resident among them being so killed, would have no one to avenge him; hence the internment of the murderer was unnecessary. Other laws of the Pentateuch must be depended on to right the wrong.

The importance of this law is shown in the fact that while the subject is kept in view in the earliest phases of the pentateuchal legislation its particulars are not settled till the later. In harmony with the law, too, we find in the historical portions of Deuteronomy Moses designating three of the cities of refuge while leaving the other three, which lay in the still unconquered territory, for Joshua to select. The concession is also here added that, if the people by their obedience and faithfulness should come into possession of the whole region originally promised to Abraham, three other cities might be named, making nine in all. Such an enlargement of area came for a brief period in David's reign; but the people of Israel never really occupied the new district.[1]

24. MUTILATION.—Next to the infliction of the death penalty, punishment by mutilation was perhaps the most severe of any known to Hebrew criminal law. It was a very common form of penalty in antiquity; but unless we are to take the so-called *lex talionis*, an eye for an eye, a tooth for a tooth, literally, which is unlikely, there is only one instance where it is enjoined. For a gross form of immodesty a woman was liable to have her hand cut off by the public executioner.[2] No case of the infliction of such a punishment occurs in the biblical books.

25. FLOGGING.—Punishment by flogging, very common in later times, seems not to have been so widely in use among the earlier Hebrews. In the form of a correction for servants and children, however, there are frequent references to it in the Bible.[3] In some instances also it is prescribed in the Mosaic code as a penalty for wrong-doing.[4] Possibly, as the most natural method of punishment and one well known in Egypt, it is meant to be applied in some cases where the law is silent concerning the penalty. Doubtless, too, a Hebrew judge had the prerogative to order it though not specifically enjoined. The guilty person in an assault or altercation was flogged; and, in addition to a fine, flogging was enjoined for a man who made

---

[1] Gen. 15:18; Ex. 21:13; Num. 35:1-34; Deut. 4:41-43; 19:1-13.   [2] Deut. 25:11,12.
[3] Deut. 21:18; 2 Sam. 7:14; Prov. 13:24; 23:13.   [4] Lev. 19:20; Deut. 22:18; 25:1-3.

a false charge touching the fidelity of his young wife. The mode of inflicting the punishment is definitely laid down in Deuteronomy. The instrument used seems to have been either a rod or a whip made of leathern thongs. At a later period we read of a number of ingenious contrivances to render the lash more effective in giving pain.[1]

Roman Scourging.

It is a fact of value as confirming the Mosaic origin of the Deuteronomic code that the order of procedure it enjoins is like that used in Egypt as illustrated on the monuments. The culprit was made to lie flat on his face, and while his hands and feet were held, the blows were laid on his bare back. The course adopted by the Jews of a later time, on the other hand, was to tie the culprit to a stake by his hands. He was then stripped to the waist and the blows were inflicted by a servant of the court. The rabbins prescribed flogging for offences against the ceremonial law, for refusing to obey the Sanhedrin as well as for teaching doctrines not approved by them. The smaller judicial bodies and even the ruler of the synagogues had authority to impose this punishment;[2] and it is a marked illustration of their scrupulosity respecting the law rather than their humanity that they always stopped short with thirty-nine strokes, though the code allowed them forty.[3]

26. THE FINE.—Another form of judicial punishment known to the Hebrews was the fine. It was appointed, for the most part, for offences against property.[4] The fines did not accrue to the benefit of the state, but were paid over as compensation to the person aggrieved. What is said in Amos 2 : 8 of designing priests to whose advantage fines which they had imposed were used is clearly exceptional and illegal, as was much else that was allowed in the kingdom of the ten tribes. Fines ranged from one hundred shekels to thirty shekels or less. If an ox were stolen and disposed of, the

1 Judg. 8 : 7, 16 ; 1 Kings 12 : 11, 14 ; Isa. 10 : 26.   2 Matt. 10 : 17 ; 23 : 34 ; Mark 13 : 9 ; Acts 5 : 40 ; 16 : 22 ; 26 : 11.   3 2 Cor. 11 : 24.   4 Cf. Deut. 22 : 29.

offender was obliged to restore fivefold, and fourfold for a sheep. If, however, in either case the animal was still in the hands of the thief, that is, if he had not yet arrived at the point of parting with it for his own benefit, he was required to restore it and one more besides.[1] Were the thief unable to make restitution he might be sold as a slave, but (as Josephus asserts) only to the man whom he had defrauded.[2]

A thief discovered breaking into one's premises at night might be killed with impunity.[3] It was otherwise if the act took place in the daytime. The owner of an ox goring a person to death always suffered the loss of the ox. Its flesh might not be eaten. If the owner had been aware of the animal's evil propensity and had not used due precautions, he was obliged to pay, in addition, whatever sum was laid upon him, "for the redemption of his life."[4] If the person gored were a servant, the one entitled to his services was paid thirty shekels.[5] Where a person obtained property by fraud, suppression of the truth, retaining what had been found, or by false swearing, if he were found out, or subsequently repented of the act, he was fined one-fifth of the value of the property and required to present a ram as a guilt-offering before the Lord.[6] One having the property of another temporarily in his hands was expected to make restitution if it was lost or stolen. Should it be torn in pieces by wild beasts, evidence of the fact was sufficient. This requirement seems to have been an unwritten law in the patriarchal period;[7] at least we find Jacob going even beyond it in his dealing with Laban.

In Proverbs 6 : 31 a sevenfold restitution is spoken of. But seven is probably used here in the sense of a great deal, or as much as possible. Zacchæus, on the other hand, who lived in New Testament times, was thinking of the requirements of Roman law when he said, " Behold, Lord, the half of my goods I give to the poor; and if I have wrongfully exacted aught of any man, I restore fourfold."[8] This was the amount of restitution demanded by Roman law in such cases. The difficulty, however, was that the Roman law was very seldom executed save in cases like that of Zacchæus, where it was done voluntarily. As already noted above, the stealing of a person for the purpose of selling him was punishable under Hebrew law by death. It made no difference whether the sale was actually consummated or not. The Deuteronomic form of the law is either a modification of the other in the interests of mercy or is intended to put upon it its proper limitation.[9]

[1] Ex. 22:1, 4. [2] Ex. 22:3; Josephus, *Antiq.* 4, 8:27. [3] Ex. 22:2. [4] Ex. 21:28-30. [5] Ex. 21:32. [6] Lev. 6:1-7. [7] Gen. 31:39; Ex. 22:12. [8] Luke 19:8. [9] Ex. 21:16; Deut. 24:7.
15

27. IMPRISONMENT.—The earliest Hebrew laws knew nothing of imprisonment as a punishment for crime. Even in Genesis and Exodus we read of persons in Egypt who are imprisoned; but even here they are only such as are temporarily detained until they have

Inner or Lower Prison.

been tried or are executed.[1] Hebrew criminal law in its fundamental ideas seems out of harmony with such a custom. Simply to deprive a person of his liberty and support him at the expense of the state was punishment neither in the form of retaliation nor compensation. Detention in a city of refuge was not properly speaking imprisonment; nor was such occasional limited restraint as was put upon individuals for the prevention of evil, or in time of war.[2] The imprisonment of the prophets, especially of Jeremiah, was of a similar extraordinary character.[3] It was used by unscrupulous rulers as a means of checking their activity when it was considered hostile to the government. It is not until after the Babylonian exile that we find imprisonment resorted to as a punishment for crime real or supposed. Authority for this purpose was given to Ezra by the Persian monarch.[4] At the beginning of the Christian era we find the Sanhedrin, by Roman custom and authority, making use of the same means in their treatment of Christians.[5] The case of imprisonment for debt mentioned in Matthew is to be explained in the same way.[6]

As places of incarceration, cisterns were sometimes used. In certain instances, even where other places were at hand, partially-filled cisterns were preferred for the sake of enhancing the punishment. This was not-

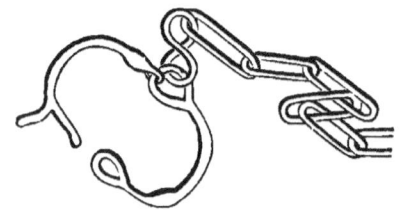

Roman Chain for Binding Prisoners.

ably true when Jeremiah was let down with cords into the cistern of "Malchiah the king's son."[7] Buildings intended for prisons

---

[1] Gen. 39: 20; 40: 3, 20; 42: 17, 19.   [2] 1 Kings 2: 36.   [3] 2 Chron. 16: 10; Jer. 20: 2; 29: 26; 32: 2; 33: 1.   [4] Ezra 7: 26.   [5] Acts 4: 3; 5: 18; 8: 3; 9: 2; Heb. 10: 34.   [6] Matt. 18: 30. [7] Jer. 38: 6, 7.

or houses of detention were known in Egypt at an early period.[1] In Ahab's time a part of the governor's house was so used.[2] There was also in the same period a similar place in connection with the temple.[3] The use of manacles and fetters was also common in the earliest times.[4] Samson was thus bound by the Philistines.[5] Among the Greeks and Romans blocks of wood were used for confining the feet of prisoners. Paul and Silas on one occasion were cast into the inner prison at Philippi and their feet made "fast in the stocks."[6] The neck was also confined in the same way at times. This was one of the indignities which Jeremiah was obliged to suffer.[7] Our Lord's words in Matthew 25 : 36 imply that prisons might be visited

Punishment by Stocks.

by the friends of those confined there. It seems to have been true at all periods.[8] The apostle Paul at Rome, even while chained to a soldier, was otherwise comparatively free, dwelling in his own hired house, and employing himself much as he saw fit.[9] In his case, however, the rigors of imprisonment were much lightened from the fact that he was a Roman citizen.

28. THE BAN.—A singular punishment known as the ban was a feature of Jewish law from the earliest times. It was applicable not only to persons but also to things. The New Testament term for the ban is anathema. A person or thing under the ban was understood to be devoted to God, originally in the sense that it was to be given up to destruction. In the time of the conquest almost everything found in Canaan was so devoted. Likewise the apostasy of a person, or even of a whole Israelitish city, to idolatry, exposed them to this fate. Indestructible things, like silver and gold, subject to the ban, were generally confiscated for the uses of the sanctuary.[10]

At the time of the exile the principle of the ban was somewhat modified. It became a form of punishment which was directed against anything seeming to threaten the existence of the theocracy; while for persons the penalty was no longer death, but excommunication. Ezra, for example, threatened it against any who failed to appear at a public assembly called to consider the subject of mixed marriages; all his substance was to be forfeited (devoted), and he

[1] Gen. 39 : 20; 40 : 3.   [2] Jer. 37 : 15, 20.   [3] Jer. 20 : 2; 29 : 26.   [4] 2 Sam. 3 : 34; Job 36 : 8; Ps. 149 : 8; Jer. 52 : 11.   [5] Judg. 16 : 21.   [6] Acts 16 : 24.   [7] Jer. 29 : 26 (margin).   [8] Jer. 32 : 8.   [9] Acts 28 : 16, 23.   [10] Deut. 13 : 16; Judg. 20 : 48; 21 : 10.

himself separated from the congregation of the captivity.[1] It is in
the form of excommunication, and particularly as a punishment for
alleged heresy or a refusal to appear before the ecclesiastical authorities, that the ban appears in the New Testament.[2] According to the
Talmud there were two forms of excommunication—a lighter and
a heavier. The former did not necessarily exclude from the public
services of the synagogue, but only from certain privileges. It lasted
for thirty days. During this time the excommunicated person was
obliged to enter the synagogue by a certain door, leave his hair
untrimmed, and might approach no Jew, except of his own family,
within four cubits. The heavier excommunication excluded from
every kind and degree of intercourse with the Jewish community.
The apostle Paul makes a number of allusions in his epistles to this
peculiar ordinance of the later Judaism;[3] and it would seem that
the earlier Christian communities were not uninfluenced in their
rules by it.[4]

29. LAWS CONCERNING PROPERTY.—The subject of property
among the Hebrews has been already treated to some extent in connection with other topics. In the Hebrew commonwealth, where the
political and social factors in the matter of property, as in other
things, were so intimately blended with the moral and religious, it is
not always easy to determine to what special category, technically
considered, a series of laws belongs. It is certain that no laws better represent the characteristic principles of the Mosaic legislation
or serve more to separate the Hebrews from all other nations of antiquity than those relating to property.

The Hebrew property laws were peculiar in the first instance from
the fact that they were intended to be largely an agricultural people.
The son of Sirach, doubtless referring to Genesis 2 : 15, speaks of
husbandry as " appointed by the Most High."[5] Throughout Hebrew
history we see among its foremost characters those engaged in such
pursuits. Moses in early life, like David, followed the flock. Elisha
was called to the prophetic office from the plough ; and Amos from
his cattle and the dressing of sycomores. The most common images
of earthly prosperity in the Old Testament and the most attractive
pictures of the Messianic future are drawn from the labors, the joys
and the hopes of the husbandman.

Previous to the occupation of Canaan we naturally hear little of
rights in land. As far as such rights were acknowledged they con-

---

[1] Ezra 10 : 8.   [2] John 9 : 22; 12 : 42; 16 : 2; cf. Luke 6 : 22.   [3] Rom. 9 : 3; 1 Cor. 16 : 22;
Gal. 1 : 8.   [4] 2 Thess. 3 : 11; 2 John 10.   [5] Ecclus. 7 : 15.

sisted simply in a tacit understanding that land anywhere found unoccupied might be used for pasturage. As soon, however, as the people of Israel had, by divine command, dispossessed the original inhabitants and gained a sufficient foothold in Canaan to justify the proceeding, the whole land was divided among the twelve tribes according to their relative numbers. To each family in a tribe, in fact, was assigned some proportionate part of the inheritance as its own. On this land the family planted itself and from it was expected to gain its subsistence. In the course of time the trades, a limited commerce, and other pursuits of a more complicated civilization, sprang up to occupy the attention of considerable numbers of the people. But at first they settled in Canaan as a nation of agriculturists.[1] If the historical parts of the Pentateuch did not assure us of this, it might be almost as safely inferred from its laws. Claiming to originate in this period and to be intended for the new nation in its new land, they are stamped throughout with allusions to agricultural pursuits. They assume everywhere the fact that each man is a holder of land. Critics, accordingly, who would transfer large portions of this legislation to periods long subsequent to the age of Moses have this indisputable fact to reckon with.

30. In the Mosaic laws two great principles are made to underlie the ownership of land. First, such ownership, as far as it existed in any tribe or family, could not be permanently alienated or lost; while secondly, and most important, it was authenticated by God himself in whom the real proprietorship inhered. A family once put in possession of a tract of land was insured that possession as long as the Hebrew commonwealth existed. It might voluntarily dispose of it by gift, exchange or sale; it could not do so beyond the year of jubilee. An interesting case is recorded in Numbers where special regulations are made by Moses for the purpose of securing the provisions of this law. The daughters of a man who had died without leaving a son to be his heir appeal to Moses for the property. Their request is granted; but subsequently, at the instance of relatives, they are prohibited from marrying outside their own tribe, lest the property into whose possession they had come should be alienated. [2]

The forfeiture of property for political offences in Ezra's time is exceptional, as in the case of Mephibosheth whose possessions David gives to Zeba.[3] Many facts in Israelitish history, on the other hand,

---

[1] Lev. 25: 23; Num. 26: 54, 55.   [2] Num. 27: 4; 36; cf. Josh. 17: 3 f.   [3] 2 Sam. 16: 4; 19: 29; Ezra 10: 8.

show how sacredly this law was guarded and how great was its political and moral significance.[1] It contributed perhaps as much as any other to the stability of the Hebrew people, a matter of no small difficulty in the ancient times: a matter of prime importance when their providential mission is considered. It contributed powerfully also to consolidate the nation and to give a special emphasis to its community of interest.

31. BEARINGS OF THE YEAR OF JUBILEE.—The limitations put upon a landed proprietor by the sabbatical year have been already considered ; those connected with the year of jubilee may be noticed here. The year of jubilee followed the seventh successive sabbatic year, that is, was celebrated every fifty years. The law for it is found in Leviticus.[2] The question of the actual year meant to be observed, whether the last of seven sabbatic years, that is, each forty-ninth year, or the year following, that is, the fiftieth, has been much discussed. The letter of the law plainly supports the latter view, and the sole objection to it is the supposed infelicity of having a year of jubilee follow immediately a sabbatic year. We find a precisely similar arrangement, however, in the sabbatic weeks of the ordinary year preceding pentecost. It was the fiftieth day after the beginning of harvest, and was the concluding festival of it, as the passover had marked its beginning. The year of jubilee seems to have been looked upon as a pentecostal year ; in other words, was meant to have the same relation to the several years preceding it that pentecost held to the several sabbatic weeks.

On the year of jubilee, as on sabbatic years, the land was left uncultivated, that which it spontaneously produced being free to all. At this time, too, any Israelite who had been in bondage was set free, unless he had become so already through another regulation.[3] Such a law as the latter might have been expected, as at this time every Israelite was permitted to "return to his possession and to his family." Since most of the servitude in Israel was brought about by pecuniary indebtedness, it naturally terminated at a period when debtors were again put in possession of the land which had originally been allotted to them. The value in money of any piece of land was reckoned with reference to its greater or less distance from the year of jubilee, the use of the land alone, as already intimated, being at the disposal of its original owner. It was a privilege, moreover, that was accorded to him or the next of kin, to recover a piece of

[1] Ruth 4:3; 1 Kings 21; cf. 2 Kings 8:3; Jer. 32:7; Ezek. 7:12, 13; 46:16.　[2] Lev. 25:8-16, 23-55; 27:16-25; cf. Num. 36.　[3] Ex. 21:2-6; Deut. 15:12-18.

land temporarily alienated, by paying to the temporary proprietor a sum corresponding to that which he had given, less the number and value of the crops he had taken from it. A more equitable arrangement could scarcely have been thought of.

Real estate in walled towns was made an exception to this law. An owner who had sold was permitted to redeem his property provided he did so within a year, but not afterwards. Levitical cities, on the other hand, as well as all the property in them, came under the provisions of the general law, reverting back to their original owners in the year of jubilee. Land in the suburbs of such cities could not be disposed of, or traded with in any manner. In case a man dedicated property to the Lord he was permitted to redeem it provided he added to it one-fifth of its value as reckoned by the number of crops it would produce before the year of jubilee, and provided, also, he redeemed it before that period. If not then reclaimed, or before that period, it was understood to be devoted forever.[1] The details of these exchanges of property probably varied at different times. Josephus informs us that the temporary proprietor of a piece of land made a settlement with its owner at the year of jubilee on the following terms: After making a statement of the value of the crops he had obtained from the land and of what he had expended upon it, if his receipts exceeded the expenses the owner got nothing; but if the reverse was true, the latter was expected to make good the loss.[2]

32. OWNERSHIP OF LAND.—The other fundamental principle of the Hebrew constitution with respect to property in land, that the real owner is God, is, as we have said, even more important in its political and moral scope.[3] In the New Testament it perpetuates itself in the teaching of more than one of our Lord's parables and in the universal point of view from which all property is regarded. Man is looked upon as a steward only of that which he is said to possess. The real proprietor is the world's Creator and Governor. So it was in early Hebrew history. Tribe and family received whatever rights they had in property from him. They were simply his tenants on the land they improved. For this tenancy acknowledgment was due. And here it is that we find the occasion and ethical relevancy of such laws, among many others, as those of the sabbatic year; the first fruits; the generous provisions made for the poor, everywhere represented as the wards of God; and for the priests and Levites, whose portion is directly declared to be that

[1] Lev. 27 : 19-25.   [2] Josephus, Antiq. 3, 12 : 3.   [3] Lev. 25 : 23.

which otherwise would have fallen to him.[1] The Bible doctrine concerning rights in landed and other property, as thus defined, it is needless to say gives no encouragement to those of modern communists. Their purpose rather was to secure such rights inalienably, under certain restrictions, to individuals, not to ignore or deny them. Above all their purpose was to make God's will and government supreme in human affairs.

33. Originally business transactions involving the transfer of property were carried on orally between the parties concerned, either by themelves or in the presence of witnesses.[2] In some cases a symbolical form, like drawing off the sandal, walking over the property, or giving a present, was used.[3] But even in the days of Jeremiah we begin to read of written contracts.[4] They were prepared in duplicate at the time of sale, and signed not only by the principals but also by witnesses. One of these was carefully sealed and preserved as an official document. The other was retained for use.

34. SECURITY OF PROPERTY.—For the security of property, there are to be found a considerable number of laws in the Pentateuch besides those already mentioned. The removal of landmarks, for example, was looked upon as a peculiarly heinous offence.[5] An adequate recompense was required in case a field or its products had been injured by the trespassing of another's cattle. The same was true of a fire causing damage, whether maliciously set or not.[6] Grain or other produce of a neighbor's field might be taken for immediate use, but nothing carried away.[7] Equitable provision was made for instances where money, goods or animals entrusted to another were stolen or in some way injured or lost.[8] Anything found, the finder was compelled by law to restore to its owner, including cattle gone astray. The fact that the owner was a personal enemy was not allowed to interfere with the practical working of the law.[9] A person injuring or killing another's cattle was expected to make full restitution.[10] If he had dug a pit and had failed to cover it, satisfaction was demanded for any trouble caused by his neglect.[11] Of a somewhat different character, but governed by the same general principle, is the law in Deuteronomy demanding care in building a house, so that lives may not be imperilled.[12]

35. Both humane and economic principles ruled in the Mosaic laws respecting the treatment of animals. Cross-breeding was forbidden,

---

[1] Num. 18 : 20.　[2] Gen. 21 : 28–30; 23 : 3–18.　[3] Deut. 11 : 24; Ruth 4 : 7; Ps. 60 : 8.　[4] Jer. 32 : 1–15; 1 Macc. 14 : 48.　[5] Deut. 19 : 14; 27 : 17; Job 24 : 2; Prov. 22 : 28; 23 : 10; Hos. 5 : 10.　[6] Ex. 22 : 5, 6.　[7] Deut. 23 : 25; Luke 6 : 1.　[8] Ex. 22 : 7–15.　[9] Ex. 23 : 4; Deut. 22 : 1.　[10] Lev. 24 : 19–21.　[11] Ex. 21 : 34.　[12] Deut. 22 : 8.

as well as ploughing with an ox and an ass yoked together.[1] Oxen
while threshing were not to be muzzled.[2] Dam and offspring might
not be killed on the same day, or the young removed from its mother
before the end of a week, or be cooked in its mother's milk at any
time.[3] A sabbath of physical rest was accorded to the laboring
beast.[4] An animal fallen down under its burden was to be helped
to its feet, no matter whose it was.[5] A law prohibiting the return
of foreign slaves seeking asylum in Israel is especially noteworthy.
They were allowed to dwell unmolested, wherever they chose,
within the bounds of the Holy Land.[6] Near this time Rameses II.
made a treaty with the Hittites especially stipulating that such
slaves should be restored to their Egyptian masters.[7] Here, too, the
Lord put a difference " between Egypt and Israel."[8]

[1] Lev. 19:19; Deut. 22:10.   [2] Deut. 25:4.   [3] Ex. 23:19; Lev. 22:27, 28.   [4] Ex. 20:10;
23:12; Deut. 5:14.   [5] Ex. 23:5; Deut. 22:4; cf. 1 Cor. 9:9, 10.   [6] Deut. 23:16.   [7] Rec.
of the Past, iv. p. 31.   [8] Ex. 11:7.

Coin of Antiochus Epiphanes.

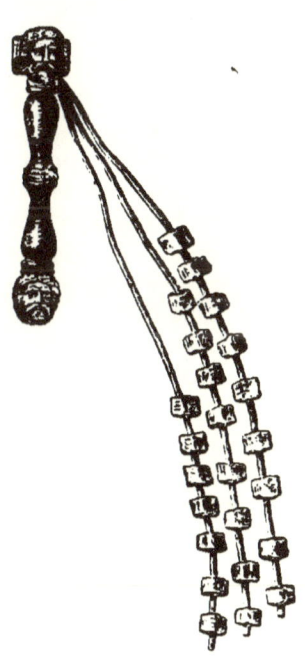

Flagellum or Roman Scourge.

Putting Out the Eyes of Captives.
(*From Assyrian Tablets.*)

CHAPTER X.

1. It is sometimes said that the Hebrews were a warlike people. It would be more correct to say that their political constitution and laws were such as to make war for them often a religious duty. War is nowhere represented in the Bible as a good in itself. It was to be undertaken only on God's command, and only against such as had proved themselves incorrigible enemies of him and of his people. It was inaugurated with religious rites, was always subject to divine direction and was carried on under the strict rules of discipline. Such rules of discipline, moreover, were not left to the moment of action or the arbitrariness of a casual leader. They were written down in detail among the perpetual statutes of the nation before any war was entered upon. It is worthy of attention, too, that while there is a foreshadowing of future military operations in the earlier books of the Pentateuch, it is in the book of Deuteronomy that we chiefly find reference to them. This book is largely made up of addresses by Moses delivered in the land of Moab just before the Jordan was crossed and the holy crusade against the idolaters of Canaan entered upon. What was more natural than that, to a considerable degree, they should be occupied with military affairs? The matter thus exactly fits the circumstances under which the discourses purport to have been uttered.

The legislative portion of Deuteronomy opens with specific instructions concerning what was to be done the moment the people of Israel set foot upon the soil of Canaan. "Ye shall surely destroy all the places, wherein the nations which ye shall possess served their gods, upon the high mountains, and upon the hills, and under every green tree: and ye shall break down their altars, and dash in pieces their pillars, and burn their Asherim [images of Astarte] with fire; and ye shall hew down the graven images of their gods; and ye shall destroy their name out of that place."[1] Anything more thoroughgoing than this could not well have been written. And it ought not to be difficult to understand the spirit underlying such instructions, or to find grounds, in the character of the God revealed in

[1] Deut. 12 : 2, 3.

the Scriptures and in the circumstances of the Israelitish people, justifying them.

2. WAR AGAINST THE CANAANITES.—In the first instance, the war inaugurated in Canaan by the chosen people was a war of extermination ordained by Jehovah against heathenism in its most degraded and offensive form. It was directed against a certain limited class of persons only dwelling within a certain limited area. A different method was pursued with other peoples not properly coming under the designation of inhabitants of Canaan.[1] "But of the cities of these peoples," it is said, " which the Lord thy God giveth thee for an inheritance, thou shalt save alive nothing that breatheth: but thou shalt utterly destroy them; the Hittite, and the Amorite, the Canaanite, and the Perizzite, the Hivite, and the Jebusite, as the Lord thy God hath commanded thee."[2] This was the authorization; but the motive of the command is also given: "that they teach you not to do after all their abominations, which they have done unto their gods; so should ye sin against the Lord your God."[3] That is to say, in the second instance, the war inaugurated by Israel in Canaan was for the purpose of acquiring a land clear of idolaters as well as of idols. In the case of the Canaanites there was plainly but one alternative : either to destroy them utterly or to leave them in the land as tributaries. The latter course was obviously impossible if the divine purpose respecting Israel was to be carried out.

With the execution of Jehovah's ban on the seven nations, the war of conquest practically came to an end. Henceforth the military operations of Israel, even those of David and his successors, were of a defensive character. One of the severest judgments visited upon the nation appears to have been occasioned by a desire to enter upon offensive warfare with the surrounding peoples.[4]

3. ORIGINAL COMPOSITION OF THE ARMY.—The division of the people in the wilderness into companies of tens, fifties, hundreds and thousands, with rulers over each division, was no doubt originally intended as a convenience in the management of internal affairs. It had special reference to civil matters. These rulers were to be able men, such as feared God, men of truth, " hating unjust gain." Their business was to "judge the people at all seasons."[5] But, as we have already seen, these divisions, with their respective heads, were made to serve another purpose also. They became the basis and norm of a military organization. Somewhat later these very rulers are spoken of as " captains," " officers of the host," and we find them acting as

[1] Deut. 20 : 10–14, 19, 20. [2] Deut. 20 : 16, 17. [3] Deut. 20 : 18. [4] 2 Sam. 24. [5] Ex. 18 : 21, 22.

such in an engagement with Midian.[1]   At first, then, the whole people were understood to compose the army of Israel.   Afterwards, laws were made defining more exactly its limits and determining who might be excused in time of battle.

4. From Numbers 1:3 it would appear that the whole male population over twenty years of age, if capable of bearing arms, were liable to military duty.   They were expected to be present at the place of muster when summoned.   Complete lists of such persons were kept by the *shoterim*, or registrars.   We are not informed in the Bible concerning the limit of military age upward.   Probably it was fifty, in conformity with that of the Levitical service; but Caleb did not lay down his weapons until he was more than four score years of age.[2]   It was made the duty of the registrars, also, to address the assembled levies; retain or dismiss those whom they found eligible or ineligible for active service; divide them into companies and battalions; bring them into battle array in the presence of the enemy; and designate appropriate leaders for them.   They acted, however, to some extent under prescribed rules.   They probably respected as far as practicable the original division into tens, fifties, hundreds and thousands.   We are even informed on what principles they were permitted to excuse any from serving.[3]

5. A priest was also present at every such mustering of the host, one specially designated for the purpose, whose province it was to encourage the people, especially assuring them that it was the Lord their God who went with them to fight against their enemies, and that, accordingly, they should not fear, nor tremble, nor be affrighted. Phinehas acted in this capacity in the war with Midian just mentioned, "with the vessels of the sanctuary and the trumpets for the alarm in his hands."[4]   It is easy to see that such an arrangement as this can only have been an exceedingly primitive one.   In fact, it would have been possible only in the earliest stages of the commonwealth and before the rise of the empire.   It consequently offers one of the strongest of incidental proofs against the theory of some modern critics, who assign to the deuteronomic code a much later date than that commonly given it.

6. At first the Israelitish army was composed wholly of infantry. This is to be inferred from a passage in Deuteronomy where the people are exhorted not to be afraid, in time of battle, of chariots and horses.[5]   Such a charge would have been an anachronism in any

---

[1] Num. 31:14.   [2] Num. 14:38; 26:65.   [3] Deut. 20:5-9; cf. 24:5.   [4] Deut. 20:2-4; cf. Num. 31:6.   [5] Deut. 20:1.

period after Solomon.[1] Up to his time the use of horses had apparently been looked upon as prohibited by Mosaic law.[2] In fact, Joshua was directly commanded to cut the hamstrings of those taken in battle and to burn the chariots.[3] David was the first to make an innovation in this respect, reserving, on the occasion of a war with the Syrians, a hundred of the chariot-horses captured. After this time, too, the higher officials seem to have ridden, on some occasions, on asses and mules.[4] Solomon was the first Hebrew king to establish a distinct cavalry arm of the military service.

7. THE ISRAELITISH ARMY IN CANAAN.—Subsequent to the settlement in Canaan, the men of war were summoned by messengers sent throughout the country, by the blast of a trumpet, or by planting signal-flags on elevated spots.[5] Warlike expeditions were generally undertaken in the spring.[6] During the period of the judges, to repel an invasion, make a foray, or avenge a wrong, it was customary to call only on such a number of the men of war belonging to adjacent tribes as might be deemed sufficient. It is said, for example, of Ehud that he "blew a trumpet in the hill country of Ephraim, and the children of Israel went down with him from the hill country, and he before them."[7] Barak led forth, in the same way, the men of Naphtali and Zebulon against Sisera.[8] Gideon, in his battles, had soldiers belonging principally to the northern tribes; and Jephthah those dwelling east of the Jordan.[9] This method naturally gave occasion to no little tribal jealousy. We do not learn that the soldiers of this early period wore any uniform or were paid wages. The first intimation of anything like a commissariat appears in Judges 20 : 10; but it was probably only a temporary arrangement. There is one instance noted where provisions were sent from their home to soldiers in the field.[10] The high figures mentioned in connection with some of the armies of Israel need not surprise us when we consider that it was often a levy of the entire male population.

8. In the early times, before any military operations were undertaken, counsel was asked 'of God through the Urim and Thummim or of a prophet.[11] Sacrifices, also, were in some instances offered; and until David's time the ark of the covenant accompanied the army.[12] The first notice we have of anything like a standing army in Israel is in the time of Saul. He is said to have gathered a force

---

[1] 1 Kings 9:19; 10:26. [2] Deut. 17:16. [3] Josh. 11:6, 9. [4] 2 Sam. 13:29; 18:9. [5] Judg. 3:27; 6:34, 35; 7:24; 1 Sam. 11:7; 13:3; Jer. 4:5, 6; Ezek. 7:14. [6] 2 Sam. 11:1. [7] Judg. 3:27. [8] Judg. 4:5–10. [9] Judg. 6:34, 35; 11:5, 6. [10] 1 Sam. 17:18. [11] Judg. 20:27; 1 Sam. 14:37; 23:2; 1 Kings 22:6; 2 Chron. 18:4. [12] 1 Sam. 4:4; 7:9; 13:9; 14:18; 2 Sam. 11:11; Jer. 6:4 (margin); Joel 1:14.

of three thousand men. A part of them were taken directly from the different tribes, and were supplemented by volunteers.[1] This very procedure had been predicted by the prophet Samuel when the people demanded a king.[2] In fact, as things then were, a king could hardly dispense with a body of soldiers who should continually be at his call. David increased the comparatively small standing army of Saul a hundred fold; at least this would be the sum of the several divisions which are said to have served him month by month.[3] Besides this force, there was also in his time a royal body-guard—the Cherethites and Pelethites—and a life-guard, composed of six hundred picked men. In addition to the regular army there was, in time of war, a levy of troops made from the people according to the emergency. Rehoboam gathered a force of one hundred and eighty thousand men from the two tribes of Judah and Benjamin alone.[4] Armies twice, and even three times, as numerous are mentioned in the subsequent history.[5] It is to be inferred from several passages that some form of maintenance at the public expense was provided for Israelitish soldiers after the introduction of a standing army.[6] Notices occur, too, of public buildings answering the purpose of arsenals.[7]

9. THE ARMY IN THE ROYAL PERIOD.—In its general features, the organization of the army remained much the same in the royal period as it had been in the time of the conquest.[8] The tribes, while they existed, usually followed the tribal banner.[9] On the basis of these and the smaller divisions already spoken of, larger ones were formed, answering to the modern army corps, whose leaders acted with considerable independence in the discharge of appointed duties.[10] A commander-in-chief was over the whole. The hiring of foreign mercenaries for purposes of war was introduced by David, and occasionally imitated by succeeding kings. In the time of the Maccabees it greatly increased, and in that of Herod the Great the army was made up almost entirely of them. In case a people with whom Israel was in conflict and its property were under the ban, the booty secured was often a source of considerable income. This might, of itself, have been a sufficient inducement to secure the services of foreign soldiers. The rule of division that we find obtaining under David was that a certain fixed proportion belonged to the king.[11] One half of the remainder was allotted to the soldiers, and one half

---

[1] 1 Sam. 13 : 2; 14 : 52; 24 : 2.   [2] 1 Sam. 8 : 11, 12.   [3] 1 Chron. 27 : 1.   [4] 1 Kings 12 : 21.
[6] 2 Chron. 13 : 3; 14 : 8.   [6] 1 Kings 4 : 27; 2 Chron. 26 : 14.   [7] 1 Kings 14 : 28; Cant. 4 : 4.   [8] 1 Sam. 8 : 12; 17 : 18; 18 : 13; 22 : 7; 29 : 2; 2 Sam. 18 : 1; 2 Kings 1 : 9; 1 Chron. 12 : 14.   [9] Num. 2 : 1–34.   [10] 1 Sam. 11 : 11; 2 Sam. 10 : 9–14; 18 : 2.   [11] 2 Sam. 8 : 7.

Egyptian War-chariot. (*After Wilkinson.*)

Ancient Roman Sol-
dier, with Shield, Spear
and Sword.

Captives before a Medean King. (*From a Bas-relief at
Persepolis.*)

Impaling Captives; Warriors in Coats of
Mail, with Bows and Battering-ram, attacking a City. (*From a Tablet in Palace at Nimrúd.*)

Taking a City by Assault, with Scaling-
ladders. At foot: Captives led away. (*After
Layard ; Kouyunjik.*)

of it to the rest of Israel.[1] Of both, however, tribute was required for the priests and the services of the sanctuary.

10. THE ROMAN ARMY.—Light will be thrown on several passages of the New Testament from a few facts concerning the Roman army. It was made up of divisions called legions, each legion being under command of an officer called a chiliarch. The legion was subdivided into ten cohorts, the cohort into two maniples, and each maniple into two centuries, made up of a hundred men or less.[2] The officer known as centurion appears several times in the New Testament history.[3] A guard of Roman soldiers often consisted of four men, or a "quaternion." The hours for standing on guard were arranged according to the watches of the night. As reckoned by the Romans, there were four such watches; hence, sixteen men were required for the entire night.[4] An instance is mentioned where the guard on duty are stationed, a part outside, and a part inside, the prison where those were confined who were to be watched.[5]

11. PRELIMINARIES OF A BATTLE.—According to Hebrew law and usage, before an attack was made upon an enemy there was to be generally a preliminary conference looking to a peaceable settlement. If this failed, war was declared in a formal manner.[6] Here and there hints are given respecting the special preparations made for a conflict of arms.[7] The army was first put in order of battle. Just what this was we are not informed. A division into three columns, apparently for assailing the hostile force in its centre and on its two flanks, is several times mentioned; but also, one of two, and of four, divisions.[8] The rear was protected by a special guard. During the march its office was to pick up the stragglers.[9] The prophet Isaiah alludes in one passage to the "wings" of an army.[10] Bodies of soldiers represented on the monuments of Egypt appear in closed columns of eight ranks, with six, ten or more men in each rank. The same is true of the Assyrian army as far as it concerns the massing of men in compact ranks. A column advancing to conflict was preceded by two ranks of spearmen. Next to them was a rank of bowmen. Behind them were the slingers. Spies were often sent out in advance of movements to learn the strength and positions of the enemy.[11] Night attacks, with skillfully-divided forces, were not infrequent.[12]

---

[1] Num. 31:27; cf. 1 Sam. 30:24, 25.   [2] Acts 10:1; 21:31.   [3] Matt. 8:5; 27:54; Acts 10:22. [4] John 19:23; Acts 12:4.   [5] Acts 12:6.   [6] Deut. 20:10; Judg. 11:12; 2 Kings 14:8.   [7] Isa. 21:5; Jer. 46:3.   [8] Gen. 14:15; Judg. 7:16; 1 Sam. 11:11; 2 Sam. 18:2; 1 Kings 20:27; 2 Macc. 8:22.   [9] Gen. 49:19; Num. 10:25; Josh. 6:9, 13.   [10] Isa. 8:8.   [11] Josh. 2:1; Judg. 7:10, 11; 1 Sam. 26:4.   [12] Gen. 14:15; Josh. 10:9; 11:7; Judg. 7:16-18; 2 Sam. 17:1.

The beginning of an engagement was signalized by the blast of a trumpet,[1] accompanied by the shouts of the combatants.[2] Strata-gems of various sorts were resorted to, including the ambuscade, feints, and circumvention or attacks in the rear.[3] Settling ques-tions in dispute by a contest of chosen champions from either army seems to have been confined to the earlier periods.[4] Fighting in any case consisted mostly of hand-to-hand combat, where much depended on physical strength, agility, and swiftness of foot.[5] The recall, like the charge, was sounded by trumpets.[6] Deeds of valor were often highly rewarded by presents and personal honors, and a victory was celebrated with the greatest demonstrations of joy.[7] Captured weap-ons and other trophies were sometimes hung up as memorials in the sanctuary; at other times they were buried in their graves with the fallen heroes.[8]

12. TREATMENT OF PRISONERS.—The cruelties practiced in an-cient warfare are well known. The monuments of Egypt and As-syria abound with illustrations of them. The Assyrians were accus-tomed to collect the heads of all those slain in battle, and by the size of the pile estimate the extent of the victory. The Egyptians, in a similar way, cut off and numbered the hands of their slaugh-tered foes. At the same time, those taken prisoners were often sub-jected to the severest tortures. They were impaled, skinned alive, their tongues torn away and their eyes gouged out. No pain or in-humanity was too great to be inflicted on a captive taken in war. Those whose lives were spared, including women and children, were bound together like so many cattle, and driven off, scantily clothed, bareheaded and barefooted, to be held or sold as slaves. (See illus-trations, pages 233, 239.)

13. The Israelites, it must be remembered, lived in the midst of these barbarous surroundings. If they differed at all from their neighbors and those with whom they waged war, it was wholly due to the restraints which the spirit and letter of the Mosaic regulations imposed upon them.[9] The reasons justifying extreme measures with the seven nations and Amalek have already been given. It was in the last analysis a matter of duty and loyalty to Jehovah. Com-pare page 235, Sec. 2. The Mosaic statutes nowhere concede, even against Canaanites, the liberty of indulging in the refined cruelties

---

[1] Num. 10:9; 2 Chron. 13:12; 1 Macc. 16:8; 1 Cor. 14:8.   [2] Ex. 32:17; Josh. 6:20; 2 Chron. 13:15.   [3] Josh. 8:11-19; Judg. 7:16; 2 Sam. 5:23.   [4] 1 Sam. 17; 2 Sam. 2:14. [5] 2 Sam. 1:23; 2:18; 1 Chron. 12:8.   [6] 2 Sam. 20:22.   [7] Ex. 15:1-21; Judg. 1:12; 5; Josh. 15:16; 1 Sam. 17:25; 18:6; 1 Chron. 11:6.   [8] 1 Sam. 21:9; 31:10; 2 Kings 11:10; 1 Chron. 10:10; Ezek. 32:27.   [9] 2 Sam. 8:2; 2 Kings 6:22; 2 Chron. 28:8-15.

16

of which we have just spoken. As a matter of fact, the Hebrew
soldiery appears to have been noted for its exceptional humanity;[1]
and if the Bible records not a few examples of a contrary practice,
they are given as matters of truthful history, which the reader, with
the ethical standard even of the Old Testament before him, is expected to condemn. As already noticed, for warfare with other
than Canaanites definite rules are prescribed in the Pentateuch.
Wars of aggression are not, however, referred to. The Israelites
were not expected to engage in such wars; in fact, never did so.
They were wars undertaken in self-defence to obtain, or hold in peace,
the possessions which God had granted them. In Deuteronomy we
find a regulation concerning female captives taken in war. It is
characterized by a spirit of the utmost humanity and consideration.[2]

14. WEAPONS.—It is proper to suppose that the weapons of war
used by the Hebrews were in general like those of other ancient
nations. In both the Old and New Testament there are passages in
which a considerable number of them are named. For example, in
the account of Goliath of Gath we learn that he had a "helmet of
brass upon his head, and he was clad with a coat of mail; and the
weight of the coat was five thousand shekels of brass. And he
had greaves of brass upon his legs, and a javelin of brass between
his shoulders. And the staff of his spear was like a weaver's beam.
And his spear's head *weighed* six hundred shekels of iron: and his
shield-bearer went before him."[3] In like manner in the Epistle to
the Ephesians the apostle Paul makes incidental allusion to nearly
all the pieces of a Roman soldier's equipment: "Stand therefore,"
he says, "having girded your loins with truth, and having put on
the breastplate of righteousness, and having shod your feet with the
preparation of the gospel of peace; withal taking up the shield of
faith, wherewith ye shall be able to quench all the fiery darts of the
evil *one*. And take the helmet of salvation, and the sword of the
Spirit, which is the word of God."[4]   .

15. THE SHIELD.—Noting first the weapons of defence, the shield
is that most frequently mentioned in the Bible. It was of two kinds,
which are distinguished by separate words; a small and light one,[5]
and another of a size sufficient to protect the whole body.[6] In some
cases, notably in that of Goliath, an attendant bore the shield of
the warrior. Concerning the exact form of the shield borne by
Hebrew soldiers we are not informed in the Scriptures. The Egyp-

---

[1] 1 Kings 20: 31.   [2] Deut. 21: 10–14.   [3] 1 Sam. 17: 5–7; cf. 2 Chron. 26: 14; Neh. 4: 13,
16; Jer. 46: 3.   [4] Eph. 6: 14–17.   [5] 1 Kings 10: 16, 17; 2 Chron. 9: 16.   [6] Ps. 35: 2.

tian shield, as a rule, was oblong, rounded or pointed at the top, but with square corners at the bottom. It was carried by means of a handle near the centre of the side next the person. The Assyrian shield, on the other hand, was ordinarily round, though it also appears in other shapes on the monuments. In sieges, for example, Assyrian soldiers are represented as carrying large four-cornered shields with a sort of roof on the top for the protection of the head. The Roman shields were also of two kinds. One of them was small and round. The other consisted of a wooden frame protected above and below with iron, covered with hide, and had in the centre of the outside a rounded projection of iron.

Most ancient shields, including those of the Hebrews, were doubtless made in the same way, having a frame of wood or wicker-work which was covered with hide. We read, for example, of shields being broken and burnt, as also of their being anointed, that is, oiled, in order to make the leather that covered them supple and glistening, as well as to protect it from dampness.[1] Shields were also variously ornamented. It is likely that those mentioned by the prophet Nahum as " made red" were covered with copper or bronze.[2] This was common with the Jews of a later day, as it was with Homer's heroes.[3] Specimens of such bronze shields, from the ruins of Babylon, are now on exhibition in museums. In Isaiah we read of uncovering the shield.[4] When not in use it seems to have been protected by some light covering. In time of peace it was kept in an arsenal.[5] Troops garrisoning a fortress suspended their shields upon its outer walls, possibly in token of possession.[6] On great public occasions shields, as a symbol of power, were sometimes borne in procession. It was for this purpose that Solomon "made three hundred shields of beaten gold . . . and put them in the house of the forest of Lebanon."[7] The shields of gold taken by David from Hadadezer were probably few, and carried only by those in immediate attendance on the king.[8] Simon, one of the Maccabæan heroes, is said to have sent a golden shield of the weight of a thousand minas to "confirm the treaty with the Romans;"[9] and Judas the Maccabee adorned the front of the cleansed temple, after its profanation by Antiochus Epiphanes, with crowns of gold and with shields.[10] Both were doubtless symbolically employed.[11]

16. THE HELMET.—The helmet is rarely mentioned in the Old

---

[1] 2 Sam. 1:21; Ps. 76:3; Isa. 21:5; Ezek. 39:9.   [2] Nah. 2:3.   [3] Josephus, *Antiq.* 13, 12:5.   [4] Isa. 22:6.   [5] 2 Chron. 26:14.   [6] Cant. 4:4.   [7] 1 Kings 10:17; 2 Chron. 12:9. [8] 2 Sam. 8:7; 1 Chron. 18:7.   [9] 1 Macc. 14:24.   [10] 1 Macc. 4:57.   [11] Gen. 15:1; Deut. 33:29; Ps. 3:3; 7:10.

Egyptian Archer. (*Rosellini.*)

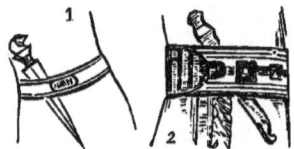

1, Egyptian, and 2, Assyrian Short Dagger. (*From Slabs in British Museum.*)

A Roman Centurion, with Helmet and Sword.

Egyptian Shields, Spear and Sword. (*After Rosellini.*)

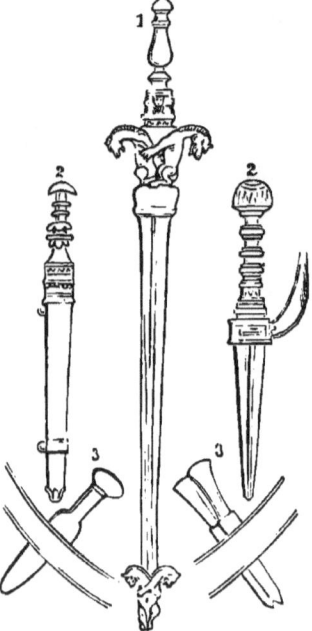

1, 2, Assyrian Swords, and 3, Daggers. (*From Nineveh Monuments.*)

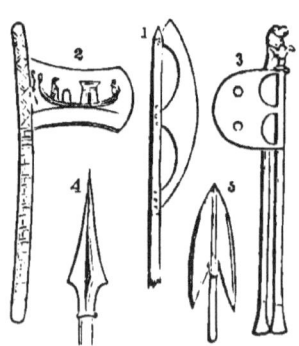

1, 2, 3, Egyptian Battle-axes, and 4, 5, Spear Heads. (*From Rosellini and Champollion.*)

Testament. It seems not to have been considered essential to a soldier's equipment in the earliest times. Uzziah was the first king of
Israel to provide helmets for his army.[1] Egyptian soldiers, moreover, of the monumental period, wore on the head only a close-fitting
cap of leather or of felt; though this was sometimes covered with
strips of metal. But in the seventh century B.C. they seem to have
adopted a more elaborate protection; at least Jeremiah's allusion to
them would suggest this.[2] With the Assyrians the case is different.
With the exception possibly of some of the light-armed troops, no
Assyrian warrior was considered fully equipped without the helmet.
It was of various shapes and materials, though generally consisting
of a round cap, either wholly of leather or of leather supplied with
iron bands. Sometimes it was entirely covered with metal. From
the apocryphal books we learn that the Syrian soldiers with whom
the Hebrews came in contact during the Maccabæan period were
also provided with metal helmets.[3]

17. ARMOR.—The coat of mail likewise was a device known to
the most ancient peoples. It is named in the Bible in connection
with Goliath.[4] The Hebrew for it there, literally rendered, would
be " breastplate of scales." The Egyptian and Assyrian monuments
represent their kings as protecting themselves in this way when in
battle. In later times a coat of mail appears to have been worn by
ordinary soldiers.[5] The most complete form of it was a garment
like a shirt, but longer and without sleeves, covered over with metal
scales. In this form it was probably worn only by kings and nobles.
The common soldier had either a simple jacket of the same material,
or protected himself by binding strips of leather, sometimes covered
with metal scales, around the more exposed parts of his body, always
excepting the arms, which were left free. Large quantities of metal
scales once used for armor have been found in the ruins of Nineveh.
Each scale is a separate thin piece of iron, from three to four inches
in length. At one end it is square, at the other round. The Hebrew
king Uzziah is said to have provided his soldiers with coats of mail;
but they were probably of the less elaborate sort.[6] Saul and Ahab,
on the other hand, would naturally have had the best which the skill
of the time could provide;[7] but this did not prevent the latter from
receiving his death-wound by means of an arrow, which entered between the lower armor and the breastplate.

18. Greaves, or armor for the legs, are mentioned in the Old Tes-

[1] 2 Chron. 26:11.   [2] Jer. 46:4.   [3] 1 Macc. 6:35.   [4] 1 Sam. 17:5.   [5] Jer. 46:4.   [6] 2 Chron. 26:14; cf. Neh. 4:16.   [7] 1 Sam. 17:38; 1 Kings 22:34; 2 Chron. 18:33.

tament only as a part of the equipment of Goliath. They were not very commonly used by soldiers in ancient times; not at all, as far as we know, by the Hebrews. The Assyrian heavy-armed soldier of a later day wore, beside the sandal, a sort of armored stocking or leathern boot, fastened by strings of the same material. In Isaiah 9 : 5 a literal translation of the Hebrew would be, "every boot of the booted warrior." The Romans, in the time of our Lord, wore only the ordinary sandal bound beneath the foot. This fact is suggested by the Greek in Ephesians 6 : 15, where the feet are spoken of as "shod," literally, "under-bound," "with the preparation of the gospel of peace."

19. The Bow.—The principal offensive weapons of the ancients were the bow and arrow, and sling, for fighting at a distance, and the sword, spear and lance, for hand-to-hand conflict. The bow was used not only by the common soldier, but by the charioteer and persons of the highest rank. Its possible effectiveness may be inferred from the fact that, in the history of Genesis, Esau needed no other weapon for the successful pursuit of the wild antelope.[1] In Assyria bowmen were sometimes mounted on horses, and the Scythians were noted for this kind of warfare. Among the Hebrews the Benjamites were especially skilled in the use of the bow.[2] Bows were made both of wood and of copper or bronze.[3] As it respects their form, the monuments show that they were sometimes long and slightly bent; sometimes short and curved to a half circle. The expression found in the Hebrew, "tread the bow," where the English is "bend the bow," has led to the supposition that bows of great size were in use among the Israelites as well as those of ordinary lighter form.

The strings were probably made from the intestines of animals, especially of the ox and the camel. The arrow was of polished wood and also, particularly in Egypt, of reeds, and was armed at the tip with metal or stone.[4] The Assyrians understood the process of feathering arrows to give them greater precision. Sometimes, also, they were poisoned or supplied with inflammable material, in order to work the greater mischief on the foe.[5] The quiver was carried, according to convenience, sometimes on the side, sometimes on the back. Their monuments show Assyrian soldiers carrying it suspended from the shoulders. It has been inferred from Habakkuk 3 : 9, "Thy bow was made quite bare," that, when not in use, the bow was kept in a case of some sort. As a matter of fact, the Egyp-

1 Gen. 27 : 3.   2 1 Chron. 8 : 40; 2 Chron. 14 : 8.   3 Job 20 : 24; Ps. 18 : 34.   4 Isa. 49 : 2; Jer. 51 : 11 (margin).   5 Job 6 : 4; Ps. 7 : 13; Eph. 6 : 16.

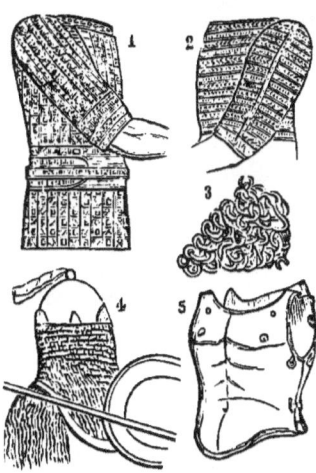

1, 2, Assyrian Mail. (*Nineveh Marbles.*) 3, Part of Chain Mail. (*From Kouyunjik.*) 4, Greek Cuirass. (*From Temple Collections.*) 5, Persian Mail.

Assyrian Archers with Spear behind a large Shield. (*From Nineveh Marbles.*)

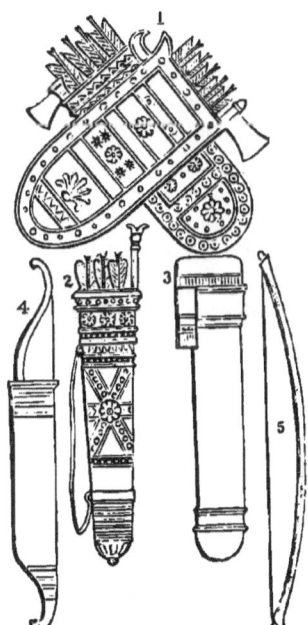

Assyrian Slinger.

1, 2, Assyrian Quivers and Case for Arrows and Bow. 3, 4, Egyptian Cases for Bows. 5, Egyptian Bow.

Roman Standards. (*After Fairbairn.*)

tians are represented as using such a covering for the middle part, where it would naturally be grasped in carrying.

20. THE SLING.—The use of the sling is first spoken of in the Bible in Judges 20 : 16. Here again the Benjamites are singled out for honorable mention as being able to " sling stones at an hairbreadth and not miss." How formidable this weapon might be in a practiced hand the history of David's combat with Goliath well shows.[1] The Israelitish army was provided with companies of slingers as early as the time of Elisha.[2] According to the monuments the sling was both an Egyptian and an Assyrian weapon, and it was used on both sides in the wars of the Romans against the commonwealth newly established by the Maccabees.[3] It consisted of a simple strip of leather or other strong material, wide in the middle and narrow at both ends. The method of swinging it appears to have been much the same as in modern times. Not only were smooth stones used for hurling, but balls made of burnt clay, of lead and various other hard substances.

21. THE SWORD.—The swords used by the ancients were, in form, both straight and curved ; and, in size, long, like those used in modern armies, and short, like a modern dirk or dagger. That the Hebrews had the straight sword might perhaps be inferred from passages where men are said to have fallen upon their swords ;[4] that they had the curved form, or scimeter, from the many that speak of smiting with the sword. We read also of a two-edged sword. This may have been simply the ordinary long sword sharpened on both edges. Ehud's double-edged sword, described as a cubit in length, seems to have been made shorter than usual. The material from which swords were made was generally iron ; although Egyptian swords of bronze are exhibited in the museums.[5] As a rule, the hilt seems to have been elaborately ornamented ; in Assyria, often with the head of some wild beast. The sword was carried in a sheath, most probably of leather, and worn on the left side.[6] The Persians wore the sword on the right side, while the Greeks and Romans carried it sometimes on one side and sometimes on the other. That the Hebrews followed the custom of the Egyptians and Assyrians in this respect may be inferred from the circumstance that it is stated that the reason why Ehud carried his upon the right side was that he was left-handed.[7]

---

[1] 1 Sam. 17 : 40.   [2] 2 Kings 3 : 25.   [3] Josephus, *Wars of the Jews*, 3, 7 : 18 ; 4, 1 : 3.   [4] 1 Sam. 31 : 5.   [5] 1 Sam. 13 : 19 ; Mic. 4 : 3.   [6] 2 Sam. 20 : 8 ; Jer. 47 : 6 ; Ezek. 21 : 3.   [7] Judg. 3 : 15, 16, 21.

22. SPEAR AND JAVELIN.—The second principal offensive weapon was the spear. It was carried alike by chiefs and common soldiers. All the men of war of the tribe of Naphtali were at one time armed with it.[1] The shaft was of wood and armed at one end with a sharp iron blade. The opposite end was usually pointed, making it also a formidable weapon in a strong hand, while it was thus fitted to be stuck in the ground when not in use.[2] There are two kinds of spear mentioned in the Bible and distinguished by different names in the Hebrew.[3] The practical difference seems to have consisted in the weight and length of shaft; the one being used for thrusting only, the other for hurling also. The translation "javelin," found in the Authorized Version, has been changed in some passages to "spear" by the revisers.[4] The javelin belonged to the same general class of weapons as the spear, but it was considerably lighter.[5] The spear spoken of in John 19 : 34 was the usual one carried by the Roman soldiers. In the time of the early emperors it was about six feet in length, the length being divided about equally between the shaft and the iron blade.

23. THE BATTLE-AXE, ETC.—The battle-axe was another weapon much used in antiquity. The Egyptian monuments have many representations of it in different forms; and it is known that the Assyrian armies not only made use of it in connection with their chariots, but independently. The prophet Jeremiah speaks of the Chaldæans as marching against Egypt with "axes as hewers of wood."[6] Different styles of hammers also were adopted as implements of war.[7] The "staves" spoken of in Matthew 26 : 47 as borne by those who arrested Jesus were probably nothing more than clubs which had been hastily caught up in the absence of other weapons. The same Greek word is used as in 2 Maccabees, where it is said, " But they seeing also the assault of Lysimachus, some of them caught stones, others clubs, . . . and cast *them* all together on the party of Lysimachus."[8]

24. THE CHARIOT.—Among ancient implements of war a special place is to be assigned to the chariot. The military strength of a people was often best indicated by the number of chariots it could put in the field. In the exodus period Pharaoh pursued after Israel with a force including six hundred of them.[9] It is an evidence of the great strength of some of the Canaanite nations with which

---

[1] 1 Sam. 18:10; 21:8; 1 Chron. 12:24. [2] 1 Sam. 13:19; 26:7; 2 Sam. 2:23. [3] Judg. 5:8; 1 Sam. 13:19. [4] 1 Sam. 18:11; 19:10. [5] 1 Sam. 17:45. [6] Jer. 46:22; cf. Ps. 74:5. [7] Prov. 25:18; Jer. 51:20; cf. Nah. 2:1. [8] 2 Macc. 4:41. [9] Ex. 14:7.

Egyptian Troops in Ranks, led by a Trumpeter.   (*From Monuments at Thebes.*)

Ancient Trumpets.

Assyrian Shields and Spears.

Arab with Sword.   General Form of Ancient Battering-ram.

Israel had to cope that Jabin, one of their kings, had nine hundred "chariots of iron" at his disposal.[1] In Solomon's time, as we have already noted, chariots and horses were imported into Palestine from Egypt at the price of six hundred and one hundred and fifty shekels, respectively.[2] Down to the time of the Seleucidæ they were in use among all the peoples with whom Israel had to do. In the New Testament, on the other hand, the only mention made of chariots is where they are used for peaceful purposes or in the symbolism of the Apocalypse.[3]

In Egypt chariots of war began to be used, it is thought, as early as B.C. 1530. They were two-wheeled and drawn by at least two horses. Whatever the number of horses, they were harnessed abreast. The form of the ancient war-chariot is well known from frequent representations on the monuments. They were low, and were entered from behind. The body was placed directly on the axletree, and often highly ornamented with leather and bright metals. On the sides were attached cases for weapons. From one to three persons occupied a chariot. The usual number was two, one acting as charioteer and the other as warrior. Jehu carried three in his chariot, the third being named in the English version "captain." In the Hebrew, however, he is the "third" (man).[4] The horses were richly caparisoned and provided with nets and other devices to protect them from flies and the heat. On the Assyrian monuments the trappings of the horses are represented as very ornate. They were also at times furnished with an armor of leather, which covered the whole body.[5] The form of the chariot was much the same throughout the East at all periods. The chariot of iron spoken of as in use among the Canaanites was probably only the ordinary chariot armed with scythes or sickles to make them more formidable.

25. SIEGE AND DEFENCE OF CITIES.—Since all cities in ancient times had walls, the art of war consisted largely in their siege and defence. The references in the Bible to this kind of warfare are very frequent. The walls of cities were often of great size and strength. Directly behind one wall was sometimes built a second and a third. They were of such thickness that large bodies of men could be massed upon them.[6] In addition to heavy two-leaved and iron-bound gates, the walls were provided with a parapet, and at regular intervals towers, from which the defence was conducted. A moat or ditch surrounded them, which, when filled with water, made

---

[1] Judg. 4 : 3.   [2] 1 Kings 10 : 29.   [3] Acts 8 : 28; Rev. 9 : 9.   [4] 2 Kings 9 : 25.   [5] Cf. Esth. 6 : 8; Ezek. 27 : 20.   [6] Neh. 12 : 31; 1 Macc. 13 : 45.

approach difficult. Advantage was often taken likewise of elevated spots of ground or high precipices, as in the case of Jerusalem itself, to render a city more impregnable to a hostile force. Besides such direct defences for cities, fortresses were frequently built in outlying districts, to serve the same general purpose for them and the otherwise unprotected villages and hamlets of the neighborhood. The land of Judah was especially provided for in this way.[1]

26. If a walled city refused to surrender when challenged to do so, it was either directly assaulted or siege laid to it. In the former case stratagem was often resorted to in order to induce the men of war to venture outside the walls. The device of Joshua before Ai will be recalled.[2] If this could not be effected, the walls were mounted by ladders or other means, and their defenders if possible overpowered. In such an assault heavy-armed soldiers were placed in advance, while bowmen and slingers sought to protect them from the missiles of the enemy. If it were found impracticable to carry a city by storm, and a regular siege was necessary, the first object was to cut off all communication with the surrounding country. This was sometimes done by surrounding it with a temporary wall or rampart. From this wall, which in places was carried near to that of the city and to the same height, offensive operations were carried on. Other means employed were undermining, the battering-ram and the movable tower.[3] There is evidence on the Assyrian monuments that the machine known as the catapult was early used. It was a contrivance on a large scale for casting stones and other heavy missiles. The variety of machines of this sort brought into use in the wars of the Maccabees may be gathered from a single passage relating to the operations of Antiochus Epiphanes. In an attack on Jerusalem it is said of him that he "set up towers for shooting and engines and machines for casting fire and stones, and scorpions to cast darts, and slings."[4]

27. On the approach of an enemy the defenders of a city prepared for a protracted siege. They strengthened their walls, stopped up or concealed the water-courses outside the town, and provided it, as far as possible, with the means of subsistence.[5] When attacked, they responded from the walls with showers of arrows, sticks of wood, boiling water or oil, and massive stones.[6] If strong enough they sallied forth to drive off the attacking party. Sieges often lasted for months and even years. That of Samaria by the Assyrians, for

[1] 2 Chron. 17:2.   [2] Josh. 8.   [3] Isa. 23:13; Jer. 51:58; Ezek. 4:2; 21:22.   [4] 1 Macc. 6:51.   [5] 2 Chron. 32:3, 4; Isa. 22:9.   [6] Judg. 9:53; 2 Sam. 11:20, 21, 24.

example, continued three years; that of Jerusalem by the Babylonians, a year and a half; that of Ashdod by Psammeticus of Egypt, twenty-nine years; that of Tyre by Nebuchadnezzar, thirteen years. Cyrus took Babylon only by turning the course of the Euphrates. Alexander, after a siege of seven months, finally captured Tyre, which was built on an island, by constructing a road to it from the main land.

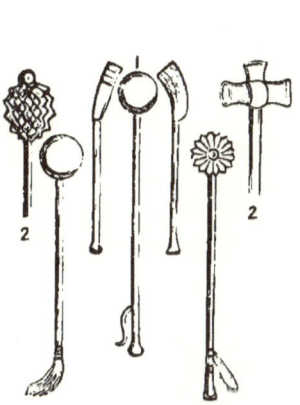

1, Egyptian Clubs and Maces.
2, Assyrian Mace, and Head of Staff.

Wall of Damascus, showing Houses built upon and over the Wall.

The Eastern Wall of the City of Jerusalem, showing Square Tower built into the Wall.
(*After a Photograph.*)

A General View of the Tabernacle and its Enclosure.

[The outer enclosure should have three more pillars represented upon the front side and one more upon the front end to make up the number to sixty.]

PART III.

SACRED ANTIQUITIES.

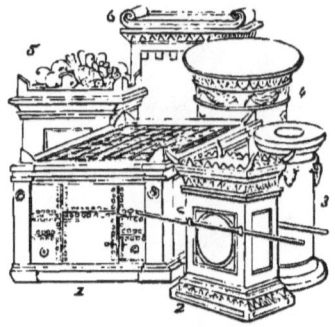

Forms of Ancient Altars.

1. Hebrew Altar of Burnt Offering. 2, Hebrew Altar of Incense. 3, 6, Roman Altars. 4, 5, Greek Altars.

Supposed form of the Golden Censer.

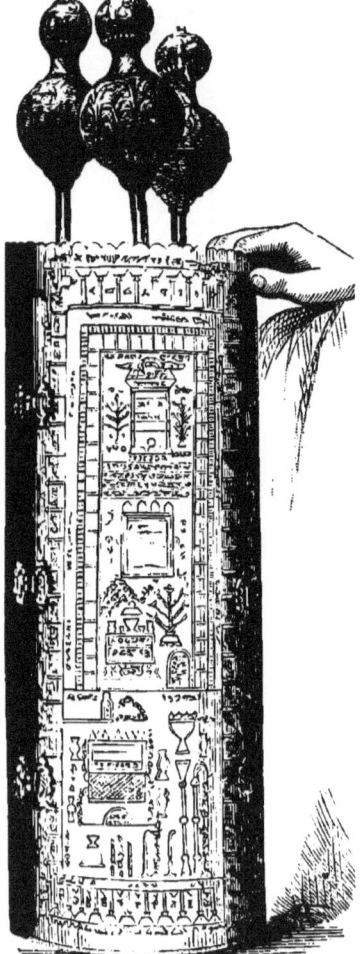

The Phylactery Worn by Pharisees.

High Priest.　　　Priest.

Showing the difference in dress. The Priest has a trumpet; the High Priest has on a breastplate and an ephod.

The Samaritan Pentateuch enclosed in its Cylinder, at Nablûs.

CHAPTER XI.

1. THE following passages of the Pentateuch treat of the annual feasts to be observed by Israel: Exodus 12 : 1–28, 43–51 ; 13 : 3–10 ; 23 : 14–19 ; 34 : 18–26 ; Leviticus, chap. 23 ; Numbers 9 : 5–14 ; chaps. 28, 29 ; Deuteronomy 16 : 1–17. When examined, they will be found to have an intimate connection with the history of the exodus, and just that outward historical connection with one another which might have been expected from their actual inner relationship and the order of the narrative in other respects. The series naturally starts with the passover and feast of unleavened bread, whose origin dates back to the beginning of the exodus, and whose inner ground and occasion are especially illustrated in the circumstances attending the departure from Egypt. Then follows, in the sinaitic legislation, the announcement that there are to be three annual pilgrimage feasts, known under the Hebrew name of "chaggim." They include besides the two already named, which being celebrated at the same time are regarded as one,[1] Pentecost or the feast of harvest, and Tabernacles or the feast of ingathering. These three feasts are distinguished from the others, the so-called "moadim," by the fact that they could only be observed at the central place of worship, where every male Israelite was obligated to appear to celebrate them.

In the third book of the Pentateuch, which is largely taken up with the details of that which is summarily stated in the legislation of Exodus, there is a list of all the festivals of the Hebrew year, with an account of the special ceremonies accompanying them ; while in Numbers we are informed what sacrificial offerings were appointed for each. In Numbers, too, on the occasion of the first repetition of the observance of a feast, we meet with one of the most marked characteristics of the Mosaic laws, that is, their journalistic form. All the regulations relating to a subject were scarcely ever made at one time. The circumstances of the people were largely allowed to shape the action of the lawgiver in this respect. Hence a considerable number of the laws were given piecemeal, here a part

---

[1] With Deut. 16 : 1 cf. v. 16.

and there its counterpart; here the body of the law and there other laws having a bearing on its practical operation. In Numbers 9 : 5–14, for example, where the historical record of the first observance of the passover is found, a regulation appears defining the relation of persons to it who, at the time, are providentially absent or are ceremonially unclean.

Finally, in Deuteronomy, which looks forward to the changed conditions of the people as settled in Palestine, no new point is made, but the old one is emphasized that there are three of the feasts requiring the presence of all male Israelites at the central sanctuary. That was the one circumstance most likely to be overlooked. Hitherto they had lived within sight of the tabernacle. Hereafter they might be separated from it by the length or breadth of the land. If so, it must not be urged as an excuse for not observing the old law of the passover, of pentecost and of tabernacles. Thus the harmony of these laws, as connected with the history of the exodus period and finding one and all their immediate occasion in it, is complete.

2. Another thing which modified the number, order and to some extent the character of these occasions was the agricultural year. The cycle began with the barley-harvest, with which the harvest season in Palestine opened; it ended with the fruit-harvest, with which the season of annual ingathering came to a close. In like manner pentecost was placed at the beginning of wheat-harvest, seven weeks after the passover. The reason why the sacred seasons of the Hebrews were thus closely connected with their agricultural year is not hard to find. Such an arrangement was adapted and designed to deepen on the part of the people their sense of dependence on God, as well as to stimulate their gratitude to him for the bounties of the earth and skies.

3. But with the institution of the Sabbath the Hebrew sacred festivals were even more closely united than with the agricultural year, or as related events in the history of Israel. In the passage where for the first time they are enumerated in consecutive order they are thus introduced: "The set feasts of the Lord, which ye shall proclaim to be holy convocations, even these are my set feasts. Six days shall work be done: but on the seventh day is a sabbath of solemn rest, an holy convocation; ye shall do no manner of work: it is a sabbath unto the Lord in all your dwellings."[1] This shows that the Sabbath was the norm by which the entire series of festivals was to be governed and characterized. The underlying motive for

[1] Lev. 23 : 2, 3.

its institution, the recognition of the divine claim to the whole life of the individual, was to be their motive also. Any theory of the Hebrew feasts which fails to note their essential connection and their connection throughout with the institution of the Sabbath will be vitally defective.

4. THE SABBATH.—The Sabbath, like the family, is one of the primitive institutions of the race. In its very ground it is of universal application. " The sabbath was made for man."[1] "And God blessed the seventh day, and hallowed it: because that in it he rested from all his work which God had created and made."[2] The later ceremonial observance of the Sabbath was a Hebrew institution ; the Sabbath in essence never was. It arose long before the rise of the Hebrew nation ; it did not pass away; its vital obligations and duties did not cease when that nation's principal mission came to an end with Jesus Christ.

The recognition of definite periods of seven days previous to his time is positive evidence that the Sabbath existed, at least in idea, before Moses.[3] The term " week," also indicated by a specific Hebrew word, is a strongly confirmatory fact in the same direction.[4] That, however, the Sabbath was particularly observed by Israel before the exodus the limited records of the Bible furnish no convincing evidence. We know that the patriarchs worshipped by means of sacrifices, and that they knew of the weekly period and reckoned by it. We are not expressly told that they kept the seventh day religiously. The monuments of Assyria, however, so far supply our lack of information on this point as to show that long before the time of Moses, even before Abraham left Ur of the Chaldees, a seventh day was set apart from ordinary occupations by an eastern people. Among Assyrian scholars opinions differ concerning the kind of observance by which the seventh day was distinguished as well as the reasons for it. The fact that it was more or less widely signalized by abstinence from work is, we believe, undisputed.

As it respects Israel, the same fact might be inferred from the manner in which the subject is introduced when our attention is first called to it.[5] The new reason assigned in the decalogue why the people should keep the Sabbath holy—because Jehovah had brought them out of the land of Egypt—was simply putting a national or provisional stamp upon the institution. It was of the same nature as the additional sacrifices ordered for the day. It

[1] Mark 2 : 27.   [2] Gen. 2 : 3.   [3] Gen. 7 : 4, 10; 8 : 10, 12.   [4] Gen. 29 : 27, 28.   [5] Ex. 16 : 5, 22–30; 20 : 11.

abrogated nothing which had been previously fixed, but simply built upon it.

Ethically speaking, the thread of connection which united the other festival days with the Sabbath was that both were designed to recognize the supreme claim of God. But the obligation faithfully to observe those other than the Sabbath was, no doubt, meant to be especially enhanced by the consideration that to such an extent they were based on a primitive divine institution of so fundamental a character as this. The cycle of the week, having its climax in the seventh day, was made the basis of the system. It was used as the unit of measure, to give a sacred character to every other division of time. As the seventh day was sacred, so was the seventh month. During that month occurred no less than four of the seven national feasts. The seventh year marked a similar bound. And so again the fiftieth year, which followed seven cycles each of seven years, was a still more sacred sabbath, a year of jubilee.

Not only were the feasts as a whole arranged with reference to the cycle of the week, or the recurrence of the Sabbath, but the same was true of them individually. The feast of unleavened bread and that of tabernacles, for example, each lasted seven days. Each began on the fifteenth of the month, that is, at the expiration of two cycles of weeks and when the moon was full. Pentecost, too, was celebrated on the fifteenth of the month, and began fifty days after the presentation of the first fruits, that is, the day following 7 × 7 weeks. And the whole series of yearly festivals was brought to a close by a special one at the end of the feast of tabernacles. It was like a final solemn sabbath of the year after its week of festival days had passed.

"The sacred seasons form thus a complete and symmetrical scheme, giving proper and balanced expression to the leading ideas of Israel's religion, and especially adjusted to their relation to God as their Creator, Benefactor and Sanctifier. It is a natural, if not a necessary, conclusion that this is no accidental conglomerate. It is not the long accretion of ages, a body of laws aggregated in the course of time under varying and contingent circumstances. It is just the consistent unfolding of one definite scheme of thought, and as such bears the stamp of one reflecting and constructive mind, by which it has been carefully elaborated and adjusted into correspondence with certain dominant ideas."[1]

5. THE PASSOVER.—As already noted, the opening festival of the

---

[1] Green, *The Hebrew Feasts* (New York, 1886), p. 50.

Jewish ecclesiastical year was the passover. It was appointed for the fourteenth of Nisan, otherwise known by the old Hebrew name of Abib, corresponding nearly to April in our calendar. Historically, it was intimately connected with the exodus from Egypt. When the angel of death went forth to destroy the first-born of the Egyptians, he passed over the Israelites, on the lintel of whose doors the blood of a lamb had been sprinkled; hence its name passover, which answers in sense to the Hebrew word used on that occasion. "And the blood shall be to you for a token upon the houses where ye are: and when I see the blood, I will pass over you, and there shall no plague be upon you to destroy you, when I smite the land of Egypt."[1]

Origanum maru, or supposed Hyssop.

The observance was of the nature of a feast. On the tenth day of the month a lamb was to be selected by each family in Israel. If the family was too small to require a whole lamb, two or more contiguous families were to unite in the celebration. "According to every man's eating" they were to make their "count for the lamb."[2] An unblemished male of a year old was required, but it might be taken from the sheep or the goats indifferently. It was to be killed on the evening of the fourteenth, literally, "between the evenings," and consumed the same night. The flesh was to be roasted, not eaten raw, or boiled, and not a bone of the animal was to be broken. Along with it, unleavened bread and bitter herbs might be used, but nothing more. Whatever portions were not needed for food were to be destroyed the same night by burning. "And thus," the instructions ran, "shall ye eat it; with your loins girded, your shoes on your feet, and your staff in your hand: and ye shall eat it in haste: it is the Lord's passover."[3] This observance was to be for Israel a memorial, to be kept as a feast to the Lord throughout their generations. Foreigners were not allowed to participate unless they had been circumcised; nor could any part of the animal be carried outside the house where the celebration occurred.

6. In the nature of the case, there were some things distinguishing the first observance of the passover from all others that succeeded it. The original injunction that it should be eaten by households

[1] Ex. 12:13.   [2] Ex. 12:4.   [3] Ex. 12:11.

at home, with the loins girded, was essentially modified even in the sinaitic and deuteronomic laws. They look forward to a settlement in the land of Canaan, and it is prescribed that all males at least shall go up to the central place of national worship to eat the passover. Moreover, they were to take with them some additional offering, "according to the blessing of the Lord."[1] Again, in the first celebration alone the blood of the slain animal was sprinkled by means of a "branch of hyssop" on the lintel, or upper casing, of the door of each house and its two posts, where the ceremony took place. According to later custom the blood was sprinkled on the altar, where also the fat was consumed. In the first celebration a journey was entered upon on the following day. In subsequent times it was regarded as holy, and kept with the sacredness of a sabbath. Still further, the injunction that the company should be made up of one's own household and his nearest neighbors was so far disregarded in the later practice that friends were invited indiscriminately. "Between the two evenings," the time when the animal was to be slain, is understood by the Samaritans, the Karaite Jews and some modern commentators to mean the time between sunset and dark. But Jewish authorities generally, including Josephus,[2] refer it to the whole of the afternoon before sunset. This was doubtless the understanding in our Lord's time, as it was that of the Talmudists. In fact, considerable time was required for the slaughter of so many animals and other needful preparations.

7. The only historical references to the keeping of the passover that we have in the Hexateuch are in Numbers 9 : 1-5, which was the second year of the exodus, and in the book of Joshua.[3] This is not strange, especially in view of the circumstance that the sinaitic legislation itself, as we have seen, looks forward to its celebration only in the land of Canaan. Its observance is four times mentioned in the later historical books.[4] It is significant that in the first of these instances advantage was taken of permission given in the law to keep the festival a month after the usual time. Subsequent to the Babylonian exile we find the Levites assuming the right of slaying the animal, which in the original law was assigned to the whole congregation. Even in the prophecy of Ezekiel the important typical bearing of the passover is more than foreshadowed; while the apostle Paul especially emphasizes it in the words, "For our passover also hath been sacrificed, even Christ: wherefore let us keep the

---

[1] Ex. 34 : 18-20; Deut. 16 : 2, 16, 17; cf. 1 Sam. 1 : 3-7; Luke 2 : 41, 42.   [2] Josephus, *Wars of the Jews*, 6, 9 : 3.   [3] Josh. 5 : 10.   [4] 2 Kings 23 : 21; 2 Chron. 30 : 15; 35 : 6; Ezra 6 : 19.

feast, not with old leaven, neither with the leaven of malice and wickedness, but with the unleavened bread of sincerity and truth."[1]

8. LATER USAGE.—The importance of this feast in the history of our Lord's time and life, especially its bearing on the crucifixion, will justify particular notice of New Testament references to it. When our Lord was upon the earth, the number of people who went up yearly to Jerusalem to keep the passover might have been reckoned by hundreds of thousands. The hospitality not only of the city but of the surrounding country was severely taxed. Entertainment was essentially gratuitous, although it is stated that guests left to their hosts the skins of the passover lambs, together with the vessels used in the festivities. As every male representing a family was expected during his stay in the city, in addition to the passover, to offer a burnt offering to the Lord, it can be readily conceived that the concourse of people and their activity in the vicinity of the temple were extraordinary.

The special preparation for the passover began with the evening of the thirteenth of Nisan, when all leaven was scrupulously removed. Unleavened cakes were also then baked, and by Jewish regulations might be made of the flour of wheat, barley, spelt, oats or rye, but mixed with water only. The whole of the fourteenth of Nisan was, to a large extent, regarded as a holiday. The regular evening sacrifice was offered an hour earlier than usual to allow time for killing the passover lambs. If this date fell on Friday, that is, the day before the Sabbath, it was offered two hours before the ordinary time, or at about half past one in the afternoon. Following this was the ceremony of slaying the lambs in the court of the temple. It is claimed to have proceeded in this way: The people entered by divisions, not less than thirty at a time. Two rows of priests, each priest holding a bowl, stood between the altar of burnt-offering and the place of slaughter. One of them handed up the blood, which was sprinkled at the altar's base; the other passed back the empty bowls. The animal was slain by the man who brought it. The remaining work, skinning and cleansing the animal, the separation of the fat and preparing it for the altar, was done by attendants. During the entire ceremony what was called the Hallel[2] was chanted by a choir of Levites, others present joining in the responses.

The paschal lamb was roasted whole on a spit, extreme care being taken that it did not come in contact with the oven. The meal at

1 Ezek. 9:4–6; 1 Cor. 5:7, 8; cf. Rev. 7:2, 3; 9:4.   2 Pss. 113–118.

which it was eaten was regarded as, in every sense, a festive one.
The guests were brightly clothed and reclined at the table as at ordinary meals. Although not enjoined in the original institution of
the passover, four times during the progress of the repast they partook of wine. There is no evidence that the wine used was unfer-
mented. Mixing it with water was invariably practiced, and this
would imply the contrary. Everything about the meal was suggestive of joyousness. The lamb was a symbol of deliverance from
death. The unleavened bread betokened a similar hasty deliverance
from the hard bondage of Egypt. The bitter herbs reminded of a
bitterness already past. By Jewish law they might be lettuce, endive, succory, horehound or what is called charchavina. Succory
and horehound are given only as probable renderings of the rabbinical Hebrew words employed.

The supper began with a prayer of thanksgiving and drinking the
first cup, after which the hands were washed. The bitter herbs,
moistened in salted water, were thereupon eaten, and, the dishes
being removed, the second cup was filled. Before drinking it, passages of Scripture, embracing the early history of Israel, were recited
or read, in obedience to the command found in the original law of
the passover. Following this the first part of the Hallel was sung,
the second cup drunk and the hands again washed; the last ceremony being accompanied, as in the former instance, by a brief
prayer. The lamb was then carved and eaten, the third cup drunk,
followed soon after by the fourth, and the singing of the second part
of the Hallel, Pss. 115–118.

9. THE PASCHAL CONTROVERSY.—The purposes of the present
work would be little subserved by entering, to any great extent, into
the paschal controversy which, since the second century, has divided
the wise and good of the Christian Church. It is well known that
there is lack of agreement on the question whether the evening of
Thursday, on which, as all concede, our Lord instituted his supper
and was betrayed, was that of the fourteenth of Nisan, the regular
time for slaying the paschal lamb, or that of the thirteenth. If it
was the latter, as many hold, then our Lord anticipated in the meal
he instituted the regular passover feast by one day, and was crucified
at or near the time when the passover offerings were slain in the
court of the temple. At first thought this would appear more fitting,
in view of the purpose for which he gave himself up to a sacrificial
death. But when all the circumstances, including the several statements of the evangelists, are considered, we have the greatest diffi-

culty in believing that such was the case. At the start, the apparent relevancy of our Lord's being crucified at the very time when the paschal lamb was offered is offset by the equally apparent infelicity of his celebrating with the apostles what is called " the passover" a day before the usual time. The passover proper, it is admitted, it could not have been. Had such an observance, out of its proper time, been possible in other respects, slaying a lamb in the temple for such a purpose would have been out of the question.

The discussion would doubtless never have arisen had we simply before us the accounts of the so-called synoptic, that is, the first three, gospels. They agree perfectly in characterizing the meal spoken of as the passover.[1] If their language is to be taken in its most natural sense, there is no escape from the conclusion that, according to them, our Lord kept the passover with the twelve on the fourteenth of Nisan, the same night on which it was observed by the Jews generally. There are not a few, however, who maintain that the Gospel of John and many incidental circumstances are directly opposed to such a result. These show, they think, that it was only a quasi-passover, a special meal in connection with the institution of the Lord's Supper, that is referred to by the synoptists, and that it took place on the evening of the thirteenth of Nisan.

John 13 : 1, for example, is cited, where this supper is spoken of as having occurred " before the feast of the passover ;" also John 13 : 28, 29, where Judas Iscariot is understood by some of the disciples to have been instructed to make preparations " for the feast." But in both these instances the feast of the passover is joined in conception with that of unleavened bread, which immediately followed it. This was no unusual thing either before or at this time.[2] The same is true of John 18 : 28, where it said of the Jews that they did not enter into the palace or prætorium of Pilate, " that they might not be defiled, but might eat the passover." That the passover proper cannot be here meant is evident from the fact that it was not eaten until after sunset, while the defilement incurred would only have lasted until the evening. On the other hand, if they had entered the Roman prætorium on the night of the fourteenth, it would really have prevented their partaking of the *chagigah* or peace offerings, which at that period were offered on the first day of the feast of unleavened bread.

---

[1] Matt. 26 : 2, 17; Mark 14 : 12–16; cf. Matt. 26 : 18, 19; Luke 22 : 7, 8.   [2] Deut. 16 : 2; 2 Chron. 30 : 21–24; 35 : 8; Josephus, *Antiq.* 14, 2 : 2; Josephus, *Wars of the Jews*, 5, 3 : 1; Mark 14 : 1; Luke 22 : 1.

Again, the apostle John, it is said, speaks of the Friday on which our Lord was crucified, once, as the "preparation of the passover," and at another time as the "preparation," and that this is inconsistent with the theory that he was crucified on the fifteenth of Nisan.[1] But here, as before, the "passover" means the whole series of feasts extending through the seven festival days which were connected with it, and the "preparation" referred to is the preparation for the sixteenth, which the apostle himself characterizes as a "high day." It was the day on which the first sheaf of barley was presented in the temple.

It has been still further urged, as favoring the view that Jesus was crucified on the fourteenth of Nisan, that what is said to have been done on that day, the buying of the fine linen, the preparation of the spices and the ointment, and the like, are incompatible with the theory that it was on the fifteenth, which was a day of festive rest.[2] To this it may be replied that while the fifteenth of Nisan, the day immediately following the eating of the passover, was a day of festive rest, it had not the same sanctity as the Sabbath. Besides, according to the Talmud, it was entirely lawful, even on the Sabbath, to perform the usual offices for the dead.

10. On the other hand, were it to be admitted that the crucifixion took place "between the evenings" of the fourteenth of Nisan, which was the time for slaying the passover lamb, we should be shut up to several unsatisfactory or impossible conclusions. In the first place, at this solemn moment, when it might be supposed that the attention of the entire people would be directed to what was going on in the court of the temple, we should find the multitudes following the Roman soldiers to witness the crucifixion. Not only so, but each of the four evangelists records that the chief priests and scribes were also there. How can this be harmonized with any right conception of the duties of these officials on the afternoon of the fourteenth of Nisan?[3] It is the apostle John, moreover, who reports that Joseph of Arimathæa and Nicodemus, both members of the Sanhedrin, busied themselves with the matter of obtaining the body of Jesus and making provision for its burial at this same time.[4] For these and other reasons we are forced to the conclusion that the evangelists meant to represent that our Saviour ate the real passover with the twelve on the night of his betrayal, and that it was at the close of his last celebration of this historic institution, and as a Christian substitute for it, that he established his own supper.

[1] John 19: 14, 31.   [2] Mark 15: 46; Luke 23: 56.   [3] Matt. 27: 39, 41; Mark 15: 29, 31; Luke 23: 35; John 19: 21.   [4] John 19: 38, 39.

11. The Feast of Unleavened Bread.—As already noted, the feast of unleavened bread followed directly on that of the passover. In fact the paschal lamb was eaten at the beginning of the first day of the former feast, the fifteenth of Nisan; the Hebrew day being reckoned from evening to evening. It was this circumstance that gave rise to the custom of calling both feasts by the same name. The law for the observance of the feast of unleavened bread is found in several passages of the Pentateuch.[1] Certain critics of our day, on the basis of the theory that the Pentateuch is made up of various documents, which they profess to be able to discriminate and to separate from one another, discover a want of harmony between the law of the feast in the other books and what is said in Deuteronomy. They allege that while in Exodus two days of holy convocation are spoken of, the first and the seventh, in the latter book we hear of but one. It is true that the account as found in Deuteronomy is peculiar in many respects, especially in merging together what in Exodus and Leviticus is kept apart. But it is to be remembered that the book of Deuteronomy appears to be simply a repetition, for purposes of instruction, of matters previously given. That its author knew of the two peculiarly holy days of the feast, though speaking of but one, is evident from the fact that in the context he refers to a ceremony of great importance, the waving of the sheaf of barley, that occurred only on that day.

As might be naturally inferred, the feast of unleavened bread derived its name from the circumstance that only bread of this sort was allowed to be eaten during it, that is, from the fifteenth to the twenty-first of the month Nisan. The additional characterization, "bread of affliction," found in some passages,[2] is not given to it because in itself this bread was disagreeable to the taste. It was used simply as a symbol of what Israel had suffered in the bondage of Egypt and of the haste with which deliverance had been effected. The whole feast, like that which preceded it, was of a joyous character. Though calling attention to thralldom, it signalized manumission. The ritual to be observed on each day of the feast is definitely prescribed in the book of Numbers.[3] A burnt offering was required, consisting of two young bullocks, a ram, and seven he-lambs of the first year, all without blemish, together with their meal offering, fine flour mingled with oil. Besides these sacrifices, which were made for the congregation as a whole, individuals were

[1] Ex. 12: 15-20; 13: 3-10; Lev. 23: 6; Num. 28: 17; Deut. 16: 8. [2] Deut. 16: 3. [3] Num. 28: 19-24.

expected to bring others on the first day or the following days, in obedience to the injunction that they were not to appear before the Lord "empty."[1] These were mostly peace offerings, and were accompanied with festive meals.[2]

The first day of the feast, as we have already noted, was to be kept as especially sacred, all servile work being given up, and the title "sabbath" being given to it. The fact that the fifteenth of Nisan is called a sabbath is quite analogous to biblical usage with respect to the other feasts.[3] Overlooking this circumstance, some have misunderstood the language of Leviticus 23 : 11, where instructions are given concerning what is to be done on that day, supposing the weekly Sabbath to be meant. It is the first day of the feast of unleavened bread, as a uniform Jewish tradition agrees (the fifteenth of Nisan, that is so named, on whatever day of the week it fell). It was on the day following it that a sheaf of barley was waved in the sanctuary to indicate the formal opening of the harvest season. Before this ceremony took place all harvesting of grain was unlawful. "And ye shall eat neither bread, nor parched corn, nor fresh ears, until this selfsame day, until ye have brought the oblation of your God : it is a statute forever throughout your generations in all your dwellings."[4]

The Talmud contains minute instructions on the method of procedure, in the later time, in cutting and waving the barley. Originally, doubtless, the ceremony was of a much simpler character. The place whence it was to be taken was first carefully selected by a delegation from the Sanhedrin. It must be an ordinary field, and one on which only ordinary cultivation had been bestowed. The grain was cut on the evening of the fifteenth of Nisan by three persons commissioned for the purpose, and to an amount that would produce about three pecks of grain. It was then threshed, parched, ground, and mixed with oil and frankincense. Only a small part of it was actually used as a wave offering. The rest was given to the officiating priest.

12. THE FEAST OF WEEKS.—The second great pilgrimage feast of the Jews, counting the passover and the feast of unleavened bread as one, was the feast of weeks, or pentecost. Other names applied to it are the "feast of harvest" and the "day of first fruits." It came exactly fifty days after that of unleavened bread, or after 7×7 weeks, counting from the presentation of the sheaf of barley. Hence we get the names "pentecost," meaning fifty, and "weeks,"

---

[1] Ex. 23 : 15.   [2] Cf. 2 Chron. 35 : 13.   [3] Lev. 19 : 3, 30; Ezek. 20 : 12, 20.   [4] Lev. 23 : 14.

when the intervening sabbatical cycle is especially in view. When called the "feast of harvest," the fact was emphasized that the wheat harvest, and with it the whole harvest of grain, approximated its close. The title "day of first fruits" refers to an offering of bread from the new wheat enjoined in the law for this feast. After the destruction of the Herodian temple, pentecost was observed by the Jews also in commemoration of the giving of the sinaitic covenant, whose anniversary it was held to be. There is no direct support for such a tradition in the Old Testament.[1]

The special offerings required on the day of pentecost were two young bullocks, one ram, and seven lambs of the first year, with their appropriate meal offerings, and a kid of the goats for a sin offering. These were not only additional to the usual daily sacrifices, but also to those made in connection with the presentation of the new flour.[2] The latter was what peculiarly distinguished the day as a festival. The presentation was in the form of two wheaten loaves or cakes. They were made from two tenths of an ephah of fine flour.[3] At a later time the Talmud exactly prescribed their size. In length they were to be seven, and in width four, hand-breadths, and four fingers high. The accompanying sacrifices were seven lambs of the first year, one young bullock and two rams, for a burnt offering, along with their appropriate meal offering; a kid of the goats for a sin offering, and two lambs of the first year for a sacrifice of peace offerings. It will be seen that the number and richness of the offerings at the feast of pentecost considerably exceeded those of the sixteenth of Nisan, when the sheaf of barley was waved. The one indicated only the beginning of the harvest season, the other its fullness. Each of the offerings had a special significance. The burnt offering was a recognition of the universality of the divine claim. The sin offering expressed the longing that the sins committed during the season now closed might be wiped out. And the peace offerings symbolized a renewal of fellowship with the Creator and Benefactor.

The wave loaves of the feast of pentecost were leavened. Such was the case with all bread offered in connection with thank offerings. The principal reason for this doubtless was that they were intended to represent the ordinary food of the people, the daily bread, for whose provision they hereby expressed their gratitude. Another reason also has been assigned: "Let it be remembered that these two loaves, with the two lambs that formed part of the same

---

[1] Cf. Ex. 19.   [2] Num. 28: 26-31.   [3] Lev. 23: 17-20.

wave offering, were the only public peace and thank offerings of
Israel ; that they were accompanied by burnt and sin offerings ; and
that, unlike ordinary peace offerings, they were considered as ' most
holy.' Hence they were leavened, because Israel's public thank offerings, even the most holy, are leavened by imperfectness and sin, and
they need a sin offering."[1]

Of the wave loaves and lambs, they being public offerings, one of
each was given to the high priest; the rest fell to the other priests
officiating at the sanctuary. The fat of both the lambs was consumed on the altar. The remaining flesh was eaten at a sacrificial
meal within the precincts of the temple. None of it might be left
over beyond the following midnight. The presentation of public
sacrifices on this and succeeding days was followed by the more
private ones. Many were the thank offerings kept for such occasions, the presentation of them in the sanctuary being followed by
festive meals occupying the afternoon and evening. This feast, too,
and that of tabernacles, would naturally be the most appropriate
time for individual offerings of the first fruits. The law requiring
such offerings did not specify the time.[2] Among other things, for
example, a cake of the first dough might then have been brought
as a heave offering to the Lord ;[3] or a basket of miscellaneous first
fruits have been presented at the altar in connection with the interesting formula recorded in Deuteronomy 26 : 2–11. The three
thousand souls added on the day of pentecost to the Christian Church
were also " first fruits," and first fruits of a more glorious harvest
which from that day to this has not ceased to be gathered.

13. We need not wonder that the one day prescribed in the law
for this feast was, in later times, found too short, and that other days
were set apart to it. In fact, later Judaism made a change in this
respect in all the leading feasts excepting only the day of atonement,
devoting, instead of one day, two days to them. This they did, as
a primary reason, on account of the uncertainty attaching to their
method of reckoning time, especially the observations of the moon's
phases. Pentecost, whose exact date was dependent on the first observation of the new moon of Nisan, would naturally be kept on the
sixth of Sivan, which was the sixty-fifth day after that event ; but
to guard against mistake the seventh day was likewise celebrated.
The only reference to pentecost found in the historical books of the
Old Testament is an incidental one in 2 Chronicles 8 : 13. It is
three times mentioned in the New Testament ; and as the day when

---

[1] Edersheim, *The Temple*, p. 230.   [2] Ex. 22 : 29; 23 : 19; 34 : 26.   [3] Num. 15 : 19, 21.

the Holy Spirit descended as the gift of the risen Saviour, is signally honored. The account in Acts informs us that there were then "dwelling at Jerusalem . . . devout men, from every nation under heaven. . . . Parthians and Medes and Elamites, and the dwellers in Mesopotamia, in Judæa and Cappadocia, in Pontus and Asia, in Phrygia and Pamphylia, in Egypt and the parts of Libya about Cyrene, and sojourners from Rome, both Jews and proselytes, Cretans and Arabians." [1] Josephus speaks of the number attending in his day as a "great many ten thousands." [2] It is probable that while not so many Jews from Palestine would be present at this feast as at the passover or the feast of tabernacles, those of the dispersion were even more generally represented. It was the time of year when it would have been easiest for them to visit the mother city.

14. THE FEAST OF TABERNACLES.—The feast of tabernacles closed the pilgrimage feasts of the Hebrew calendar, and was to them also of the nature of a climax. As the feast of "tabernacles" or booths, it recalled as perhaps nothing else could do the ancient history of the covenant people and God's providential dealing with them in the wilderness. As the feast of "ingathering," another of its names, it signalized the conclusion of a year which had been crowned with the divine goodness. So transcendent was its importance in the eyes of Old Testament writers that it was called by them "the feast" and "the feast of Jehovah." [3] Like the passover and the accompanying festival of unleavened bread, it lasted seven days, from the fifteenth to the twenty-first of Tishri, the seventh month of the Jewish ecclesiastical year. [4] An eighth festival day followed, but it took on a different character and had a different meaning from the preceding feast. The people no longer dwelt in booths; and the offerings, as well as the ritual of temple service, were altered. It is only in the more detailed legislation of the middle books of the Pentateuch that this eighth day is mentioned. So close was its connection with the feast of tabernacles with respect to time, that at a later period the latter was sometimes spoken of as a feast of eight days. [5] Still, they are carefully distinguished in their original institution, and the eighth day is looked upon as the closing day, not simply of the feast of tabernacles, but of the whole cycle of yearly festivals.

The feast of tabernacles was not only, like the passover and pen-

---

[1] Acts 2:5, 9-11; 20:16; 1 Cor. 16:8.   [2] Josephus, *Antiq.* 14, 13:4; 17, 10:2.   [3] Lev. 23:39; 1 Kings 8:2; 2 Chron. 5:3; 7:8, 9.   [4] Lev. 23:36, 39; Num. 29.35-38.   [5] 2 Macc. 10:6; Josephus, *Antiq.* 3, 10:4.

tecost, a highly-joyous occasion, but this element seems to have been meant, as it related to the people, especially to dominate in it. The law of its institution reads, "Howbeit on the fifteenth day of the seventh month, when ye have gathered in the fruits of the land, ye shall keep the feast of the Lord seven days: on the first day shall be a solemn rest, and on the eighth day shall be a solemn rest. And ye shall take you on the first day the fruit of goodly trees, branches of palm trees, and boughs of thick trees, and willows of the brook; and ye shall rejoice before the Lord your God seven days. And ye shall keep it a feast unto the Lord seven days in the year: it is a statute forever in your generations: ye shall keep it in the seventh month. Ye shall dwell in booths seven days; all that are homeborn in Israel shall dwell in booths: that your generations may know that I made the children of Israel dwell in booths, when I brought them out of the land of Egypt: I am the Lord your God."[1]

15. A discussion arose at an early day on the question whether the branches of trees spoken of, the willow, the palm, etc., were to be used in the construction of the booths or to be carried about in the hand. The latter view, which is probably the correct one, was adopted by the Pharisees, the former by the Sadducees. It is certain that when this feast was celebrated in the time of Nehemiah, the Jews, in building their temporary abiding-places, did not think it necessary to use the trees mentioned in Leviticus;[2] and in our Lord's day, the Pharisaic tradition was exclusively followed. Originally, perhaps, willow and palm branches served a double purpose: they were borne in the hand during the festivities and were also used to ornament the otherwise plainly-constructed booths.

16. As the feast of tabernacles was specially characterized by the booth and other mementos of by-gone days, so it was distinguished by the number and variety of sacrifices required during its celebration. Each day had its burnt offering and sin offering. The former had the peculiarity that, from the first day to the last, the number of bullocks offered was to be one less each day, while the number of lambs and rams of a year old was to remain the same. On the first day, for example, there were sacrificed thirteen bullocks, two rams and fourteen lambs, together with the appropriate meal offerings. On the second day there were sacrificed twelve bullocks, the number of the other animals remaining the same. On the third day, eleven bullocks were offered up, and so on. This singular arrangement has never been satisfactorily explained. It is noticeable, however, that

[1] Lev. 23: 39-43; cf. vs. 33-36; Num. 29: 12-38. [2] Neh. 8: 15-18.

the closing number on the seventh day would be seven, the sacred number; and it has been pointed out that the whole number of burnt sacrifices during the week is exactly divisible by seven, as is also the sum of each of the several kinds of sacrifices. Of the bullocks there were seventy, of the rams fourteen, and of the lambs ninety-eight. These offerings, as was the case in the other feasts, were in addition to the daily morning and evening sacrifice, and on the sabbath to the burnt offering, with the meal and drink offering, designated for that day. On the eighth day of the festival, as on the first and tenth days of this month, the sacrifice consisted, in addition to the sin offering, of only one bullock, one ram and seven he-lambs. All the sacrifices throughout the joyous week were accompanied, at least in later times, not only by trumpet-blasts[1] on the part of the priests, but by the singing of the so-called Hallel,[2] with musical accompaniment by the Levites and responses from the people.

17. The first historical reference to the feast of tabernacles is apparently found in the book of Judges.[3] Processions and diversions of various sorts accompanied it at this time. While celebrated at the national sanctuary, the unsettled character of the times prevented the widest participation of the people. It is otherwise after the completion of Solomon's temple.[4] So popular did the feast of tabernacles and the other pilgrimage feasts then become that, after the separation of the ten tribes, Jeroboam expressed the fear, "If this people go up to offer sacrifices in the house of the Lord at Jerusalem, then shall the heart of this people turn again unto their lord, even unto Rehoboam king of Judah."[5] This king, accordingly, made the golden calves, and placed them, one at Dan and the other at Bethel, and even had the temerity to change the date of the feast of tabernacles from the fifteenth day of the seventh month to the fifteenth day of the eighth, a date, according to the sacred historian, "which he had devised of his own heart." Subsequent to the Babylonian exile, as might be expected, the concourse of people attending the national festivals and their scrupulosity in observing them greatly increased. It is said, for instance, of an observance of the feast of tabernacles in the time of Nehemiah that "since the days of Jeshua the son of Nun unto that day had not the children of Israel done so."[6] It is worthy of note, too, that besides the seven days of the festival proper, the eighth day was kept by the returned exiles, in apparent consciousness of its true import as the closing day of the

---

[1] Num. 10:10.　[2] Pss. 113-118.　[3] Judg. 21:19 ("the feast").　[4] 1 Kings 8:2, 65; 9:25; 2 Chron. 5:3; 7:8; 8:13.　[5] 1 Kings 12:27-33.　[6] Neh. 8:17.

18

whole series of yearly festivals. The record is, "they kept the feast seven days; and on the eighth day was a solemn assembly [closing festival], according unto the ordinance."[1] The only other reference in the historical books to the observance of the eighth day is found in 2 Chronicles 7 : 9, where it is said of Solomon that he held a "solemn assembly" [closing festival] upon it.

18. The feast of tabernacles underwent some important changes at the hands of the later Jews. For example, the most minute regulations were made concerning the structure of the booths, and, except in the case of heavy rains, all Israelites were expected to make them their only habitation for the space of seven days. The "fruit of goodly trees" mentioned in the Pentateuch was definitely interpreted as meaning the citron; and the "boughs of thick trees" were myrtle boughs. All worshippers at the feast, even children, were required to provide themselves with branches of the poplar, myrtle and willow, and to interweave them to form what was known as the *lulav*. The custom can be historically traced to the time of the Maccabees.[2] This *lulav* was carried daily, and in the left hand, in the processions that marched to the temple. Reaching the temple the crowds surrounded the altar of burnt offering, waving the boughs and shouting hosannas. On the seventh day they encompassed the altar seven times.

19. A second principal peculiarity of the post-exilian celebration of this feast was the ceremony of bringing water from the pool of Siloam. A festive procession, headed by a priest bearing a golden pitcher, started for the purpose at the time of the offering of the daily morning sacrifice. The return was so timed that the priest re-entered the so-called "water-gate" before the drink offering which accompanied the sacrifice was made. He was received in the forecourt of the temple with trumpet-blasts. A second priest there took the pitcher from his hands, with the words of Isaiah 12 : 3 : "Therefore with joy shall ye draw water out of the wells of salvation," mingled the water with the wine of the drink offering, and poured the whole into a silver receptacle on the southeast corner of the altar. From here it was carried, by means of a subterranean channel, into the Kedron valley. More than one of the prophets was supposed to make allusion to this ceremony.[3] It has been thought that it was in particular reference to it that on "the last day, the great *day* of the feast, Jesus stood and cried, saying, If any man thirst, let him come unto me, and drink."[4] The origin of the rite is uncertain; but it

---

[1] Neh. 8 : 18.   [2] 2 Macc. 10 : 7.   [3] Ezek. 47 : 1; Joel 2 : 23; Zech. 14 : 8, 17.   [4] John 7 : 37.

was especially favored by the Pharisees. During the high-priesthood of Alexander Jannæus (B.C. 104–78), who with his court belonged to the Sadducæan party, this ruler, while officiating at the altar on an occasion of this kind, instead of pouring the water into the receptacle set apart for it, contemptuously threw it on the ground. So enraged were the spectators at this act of apparent sacrilege that they mercilessly pelted Jannæus with the citrons which they held in their hands, and would have put him to death had it not been for the interposition of his guard.

20. Another change introduced into the feast of tabernacles in the later times was an illumination, on the evening of the first day, of the court of the women with golden candelabras. At the same time also a torchlight procession, with music and dancing, was conducted by leading Israelites known as "chassidim" and "men of deed." Throughout the whole night the festivities were continued. Israelites living at too great a distance from Jerusalem to make it convenient for them to be present at the feast, especially those in foreign lands, were allowed to observe it in their local synagogues. Prayer and the reading of the law, in such cases, took the place of the more elaborate ritual of the temple.

21. THE NEW MOON.—Besides the four festivals already noted there were two others provided for in the Mosaic laws: that of the new moon and the atonement. The latter was more properly a fast, and the only one enjoined in the ancient law. The custom of celebrating the reappearance of the moon probably originated before the time of Moses. It was at least widely prevalent with eastern peoples in antiquity. Among the festivals of the Jews it always held a prominent place. With the exception of the new moon of the seventh month, the law enjoined only the offering of special sacrifices and the blowing of trumpets on this day; but it seems to have been generally kept by the people as a full holiday, with voluntary abstinence from servile labor. On the new moon of the seventh month, the number of offerings, like the blowing of trumpets, was considerably increased. Although the feast is sometimes called "the feast of trumpets," the blowing of trumpets was by no means peculiar to it. The original law on this point reads: "Also in the day of your gladness, and in your set feasts, and in the beginnings of your months, ye shall blow with the trumpets over your burnt offerings, and over the sacrifices of your peace offerings; and they shall be to you for a memorial before your God."[1] That is to say, the

_____
[1] Num. 10 : 10.

trumpets on all these occasions were appointed for rallying the people anew to Jehovah's standard and to a public acknowledgment of loyalty to him.

22. The observance of the first day of the lunar month began to take on a new character soon after the Babylonian exile. The tendency to exaggerate its importance, however, showed itself in a much earlier period. On this day, for example, we find King Saul making a state banquet, and the family of David offering up a special annual sacrifice.[1] Even in the kingdom of the ten tribes the prophets are able to utilize the larger assemblies on these occasions for religious instruction.[2] But, from the time of the exile, the festival began to assume the character of a new year's celebration. It was on the first day of the seventh month that the returned exiles resumed the regular services of the sanctuary.[3] In the Jewish ecclesiastical year, as we have seen, much depended on the correct determination of the appearance of the new moon. How it was effected in the times before the exile it is not possible to say. After the rise of rabbinism definite rules were laid down. On the thirtieth day of each month, if it were found necessary, an all-day session of the Sanhedrin was held. The fact of the moon's appearance was learned by actual observation and not by astronomical reckoning. The latter method was not adopted until two centuries after the destruction of the second temple.

Trustworthy witnesses were encouraged to bring the news at any expense, and, if necessity required it, to travel on the Sabbath for the purpose. A banquet was specially provided in Jerusalem for this class of persons. As soon as, in the judgment of the Sanhedrin, the fact was established, the words "It is sanctified" were spoken and the feast began. Signal-fires kindled on the Mount of Olives and other heights spread the information to the extremities of the Holy Land. If cloudy weather made an observation of the new moon impossible, the old month was reckoned as one of thirty days, and the new one began with the evening of the following day. On the other hand, if the new moon was seen on the thirtieth, within certain limits it was counted as the first day of a new month, and the preceding month reckoned one of twenty-nine days. The New Testament contains no reference to the celebration of this feast by our Lord in Jerusalem. This is not strange, since it might have been just as properly observed in any one of the many synagogues of Palestine.

---

[1] 1 Sam. 20:5, 6, 24, 29. [2] 2 Kings 4:23; Isa. 1:13; Ezek. 46:1; Hag. 1:1. [3] Ezra 3:6; Neh. 8:2.

23. THE DAY OF ATONEMENT.—The tenth day of the seventh month was observed as the day of atonement. At this time atoning sacrifices were offered for the sins and uncleannesses of the people of Israel as a whole, and for the purification of the temple in all its parts and appurtenances. At each of the great yearly assemblies—indeed on almost every day of the year—special offerings were made either for the sins of individuals or of the community; but they did not suffice to make the requisite impression even of the necessity of the remission of sin, much less to restore the sinful to his lost place in the theocracy or visible kingdom of God. Beyond this the blood of bulls and goats could never go, so cleansing the offerers that there should be "no more conscience of sins." But to go even so far—to make a due "remembrance of sins" year by year, and bring the people into outward harmony with their institutions—the solemn rites of the day of atonement were needful.

Accordingly it was not without reason that one entire day of each year was solemnly set apart for the purpose of humiliation and confession. It was the more marked that it stood by itself, the sole fast enjoined amongst a number of joyous festivals. In all its appointments, moreover, it was peculiar and designed to attract attention and awaken serious thought. On this day alone the services of the sanctuary extended into the holy of holies. On other days of the year the high priest might participate in the public services of God's house, or might not; on the tenth of Tishri he alone could officiate, other priests acting simply as his assistants. On this day, also, he was obliged, in certain ceremonies, to put off his ordinary golden vestments and clothe himself from head to foot in garments of white linen. We might wonder that a day so important as this in the Jewish ecclesiastical year does not stand at its close. Why does it precede rather than follow the feast of tabernacles, whose festivities begin on the fifteenth of the same month? The day of atonement in some sense was a preparatory occasion for the feast of thanksgiving, the closing festival of the year. It did all that the ceremonial law could do to bring the individual and the nation into harmony with God, and effect that peace of conscience without which true joy of heart was impossible.

At all the sacrifices offered on the day of atonement the high priest officiated. In addition to the daily morning and evening offerings, there was a burnt offering of a ram, which was presented in behalf of the priesthood; a young bullock, a ram and seven lambs of the first year, with their meal offering, in behalf of the

people ; a kid of the goats for a sin offering ; and, finally, the purely
expiatory sacrifices of the day,—a young bullock for the priesthood,
including the high priest, and two goats for the people.[1]   One of the
goats was killed and its blood sprinkled on the altar ; the other,
bearing symbolically the sins of the people, was sent into the wilderness.   In form the latter ceremony resembled that for the purification of a leper.[2]   Doubtless, also, it represented the same idea
ceremonially.   One of the goats was understood to atone for the
people by its blood ; the other, which was said to be " for Azazel "
(dismissal), showed the effects of such atonement—symbolized the
total removal of guilt.   By their union they represented more perfectly him who, as the " Lamb of God,"[3] "taketh away the sin of
the world ;" being made sin for us " that we might become the righteousness of God in him."[4]

24. The order of services on the day of atonement, at the time
of our Lord, was established by rabbinical law.   The high priest
began his preparations for it seven days before, taking up his abode
in the temple for that purpose.   In view of the possibility of his
becoming disabled, a substitute was appointed to take his place in
such an emergency.   The whole week was given up to participation
in the daily sacrifices and to rites of purification.   Since the duty
of offering the fifteen sacrifices of the day of atonement rested solely
upon him, he made sure that he understood the ritual.   A kind of
rehearsal seems to have taken place on the evening of the ninth
of Tishri.   At that time the Sanhedrin, fearing undue Sadducæan
influence, bound the high priest by solemn oath to introduce no
change into the accustomed service.

On the tenth, public services began at early dawn.   The high
priest put on his official garments, washed his hands and feet in a
golden vessel, and offered the morning sacrifice.   Five times during
the day it was incumbent on him to bathe, and ten times to wash
his hands and feet.   The traditional order of service allowed the
offering of some parts of the burnt sacrifices of the day immediately
after the morning sacrifice ; but this does not accord with the instructions given in Leviticus.[5]   The most peculiar rite of the day, the
offering of the expiatory sacrifices, was preceded by another change
of raiment, the high priest now clothing himself wholly, even to his
girdle, in white ; then, with his hands on the head of the bullock,
he made confession for himself and for his brethren of the house of

---

[1] Ex. 30: 10; Lev. 16: 1-34; 23: 26-32; Num. 29: 7-11.   [2] Lev. 14: 1-7.   [3] John 1: 29.
[4] 2 Cor. 5: 21.   [5] Lev. 16.

Aaron. At every mention of the name of the Lord the people near by bowed themselves, while the more remote made praiseful response. Next, it was determined by lot which of the two goats was to be offered upon the altar and which was "for dismissal." The bullock presented as a sin offering for the priests was thereupon killed and its blood caught in a vessel prepared for it. Following this act, the high priest entered the holy of holies with a censer of live coals and incense in his hand, the people meanwhile remaining silent and in worshipful attitude. Within the holy of holies he placed upon the coals the incense he had brought, and offered a brief prayer of supplication. Returning after a little, he received from an attendant the vessel of blood—which, to prevent coagulation, had been continually stirred—and, re-entering the holy of holies, sprinkled it in the direction of the supposed mercy-seat, once upward and seven times downward. Going back again to the holy place, he deposited the bowl of blood on a golden stand before the vail and killed the one of the two goats designated for sacrifice. With its blood he entered once more the most holy place and sprinkled it, as before, eight times in the direction of the mercy-seat. Coming again into the view of the people, he placed the bowl by itself on another stand before the vail. Taking then the bowl of bullock's blood, he sprinkled in the same manner with it eight times in the direction of the vail, and afterwards other eight times with the blood of the goat. Following this, he thoroughly mixed together the blood of both which remained and sprinkled with it the horns and top of the altar. Forty-three times in all he made this sign of cleansing, taking care always that none of the blood lighted upon his garments. What remained of it at the conclusion of the ceremonies he poured out at the base of the altar. Thus, according to the law, he made atonement for the holy sanctuary, the tabernacle of the congregation, for the altar, for the priests and for all the people.[1]

25. For Azazel.—One thing more the Mosaic law required in this impressive ceremony of expiation: to send off into the wilderness the remaining goat, the sins of the people having first been placed symbolically upon its head. Rabbinical law demanded that the goat should not simply be driven into the wilderness, but be hurled backward into an abyss. The spot selected for the purpose is said to have been a rocky place east of Bethany. The moment of its accomplishment was signalled to the worshippers at the temple by means of flags. Meanwhile the carcass of the sin offering had

[1] Lev. 16 : 33.

been removed outside the city limits and burnt;[1] the high priest
had read in the "court of the women" such passages of the Pentateuch as bore on the observance of the day, interspersing the
reading with appropriate confessions and supplications, and the
remaining sacrifices of the day, including the evening sacrifices,
were offered. The evening of the day of atonement, in the time
of our Lord and later, was given up to festivities. Modern Jews
keep the day by abstinence from labor and a rigid fast. The rules
of the synagogue do not allow one to put on his "shoes" (sandals)
or wash himself. Young children and the sick alone are exempt
from the obligation.

26. Much has been made, by some modern critics, of the circumstance that the historical books of the Old Testament never speak
of the observance of the day of atonement.[2] But the same is true
of the feast of the new moon; and that of Pentecost is only incidentally alluded to in 2 Chronicles 8 : 13. In the Pentateuch there
is a fourfold presentation of the law respecting the day of atonement, and the institution stands most intimately connected with
others about whose historical reality there can be no dispute. In
fact, the whole Mosaic system of laws is permeated by its spirit and
formally bound to it by many indirect references. The day of
atonement, indeed, holds as central a place among the institutions
of Judaism as does the fact of atonement among the doctrines and
religious teachings of Christianity. Every allusion to the ark, for
example, carries with it a tacit recognition of this day; for the title
"mercy-seat" is based both formally and morally on the act of the
high priest in sprinkling there the blood of the atonement. Moreover, the second temple—for which the critics referred to suppose
the rites of the day of atonement were specially invented—was without the ark. The high priest could only sprinkle the blood near
the spot where he might suppose the ark originally stood.

27. PURIM.—In this connection two important post-Mosaic festivals claim attention—purim and the feast of dedication. The
first, called also, in 2 Maccabees 15 : 36, "the day of Mordecai,"
fell on the fourteenth and fifteenth of Adar, the last month of the
Jewish ecclesiastical year.[3] It was established by Mordecai, and
commemorated the deliverance of the Jews from the destruction
threatened by Haman, prime-minister of the Persian empire in the
reign of Xerxes. Two days were devoted to the feast, since the
Jews of Susa had needed two days to complete the overthrow of

<hr>

[1] Heb. 13 : 11-13.   [2] See Ecclus. 50 : 5; Acts 27 : 9.   [3] Esth. 9 : 17.

their enemies. The name purim, meaning "lots," was given to the feast in irony. It was by lot that Haman had decided to destroy the Jews on the thirteenth of Adar.[1] A root similar to this has been found in the later Persian; though the word might be derived from the Hebrew *pur*, meaning to separate.

Originally the feast consisted of a social meal combined with various festivities and the sending of portions to others.[2] There is a bare intimation in the book of Esther that the thirteenth of Adar was also observed, and in a somewhat different manner from the other two days.[3] After the ninth century of our era there is historical evidence of such observance, but not earlier; though the tradition that the feast began with a fast is widespread. From the first book of Maccabees we learn that from about B.C. 161 the thirteenth of Adar was kept as Nicanor's day, that being the date of his defeat by Judas the Maccabee.[4] This circumstance, joined with the fact that the Jews in Babylon were unfavorable to this fast, renders its genuineness doubtful. The early observance of purim itself—that is, the fourteenth and fifteenth of Adar—is vouched for both by the second book of Maccabees and by Josephus.[5] Both recensions of the Greek additions to Esther also bear witness to the same effect.[6] These additions arose not later than B.C. 52, and may have originated as early as B.C. 181–145, during the reign of Ptolemy Philometer. Among the Jews of a later day it was customary to read, some time during this feast, the whole of the book of Esther. It might be read in any language. In modern times the occasion has degenerated to one of great and often immoderate hilarity. It is generally supposed that the "feast of the Jews" mentioned in John 5 : 1 as having been attended by our Lord was this purim feast.[7] It may have been, however, the feast of dedication, although in other cases where the latter feast is mentioned its full title is given to it.

28. The Feast of Dedication.—The feast of dedication dates from the reconsecration of the altar and temple at Jerusalem after their defilement by Antiochus Epiphanes.[8] It lasted eight days, beginning on the twenty-fifth of Chislev, corresponding to December. In its ceremonial it somewhat resembled the feast of tabernacles, in that branches of trees were carried about the streets, the temple was illuminated and the Hallel daily chanted. This resem-

---

[1] Esth. 3 : 7, 13; 9 : 24, 27.   [2] Esth. 9 : 17–19, 22.   [3] Esth. 9 : 18; cf. 4 : 16.   [4] 1 Macc. 7 : 48, 49.   [5] 2 Macc. 15 : 36; Josephus, *Antiq.* 11, 6 : 13.   [6] Add. 7 : 10.   [7] See also John 4 : 45; 6 : 4.   [8] 1 Macc. 4 : 52.

blance was doubtless intended, since we read in 2 Maccabees,[1] "And they kept eight days with gladness, in *the feast* of tabernacles, remembering how not long before, during the feast of tabernacles, they had dwelt in the mountains and in the caves like beasts." Another circumstance serving to give this form to the feast was that Solomon in the first dedication of the temple clearly had the feast of tabernacles in view.[2]

The second book of Maccabees is introduced by two letters purporting to be sent by the Jews of Palestine to those of Egypt, which recognize the observance of this festival.[3] In the time of Josephus it had considerably changed its character, having become a day of general rejoicing. After speaking of the institution of the day by Judas the Maccabee, this writer goes on to say: "And from that time to this we celebrate this festival and call it 'lights.' I suppose the reason is because this liberty beyond our hope appeared to us; and that from this the name was given."[4] By the later Jews fasting and mourning were forbidden during this season. Each night it was expected that at least one oil lamp would be lighted outside every door, even that of the poorest family. It was regarded as highly meritorious if as many lamps were lighted as there were members of the household; and better yet if that number were doubled through every night of the eight.. This custom was rabbinically explained as arising from the fact of a miracle by which Judas had been supplied with oil for the lamps of the sanctuary. Most likely, however, it had its origin from the custom of illuminating the temple at the feast of tabernacles. The feast of dedication and that of our Saviour's birth have both, it is true, the same date; but the Christmas tree, with its many lights, had another origin.

[1] 2 Macc. 10:6.   [2] 1 Kings 8.   [3] 2 Macc. 1, 2.   [4] Josephus, *Antiq.* 12, 7:7.

TABLE OF HEBREW FESTIVALS AND FASTS.

MONTH.	DAY.	FESTIVAL.	REMARKS.
Nisan (Abib)=April (approximately).	. 1	New Moon ("Trumpets").	
"	. 14	Slaying of Passover. . . .	Passover was eaten on the following evening.
"	. 15–21	Feast of Unleavened Bread.	
"	. 16	Waving of sheaf of new barley.	Barley harvest began on 17th.
Iyar (Ziv)=May .	. 1	New Moon.	
"	. 15	"Second Passover". . . .	See Num. 9:5–14.
Sivan=June	1	New Moon.	
"	. 6	Pentecost.	Fifty days from the Passover.
Tammuz=July	1	New Moon.	
"	. 17	Fast.	Taking of Jerusalem (on the ninth by Nebuchadnezzar) by Titus.
Ab=August	1	New Moon.	
"	. 9	Fast.	Destruction of temple. See Jer. 52:12, 13.
"	. 15	Feast of "Wood Offerings."	See Neh. 10:34; 13:31.
Elul=Sept..	1	New Moon.	
Tishri (Ethanim)=Oct.	1	New Year's Feast.	
"	3	Fast.	Murder of Gedaliah (Jer. 41:20).
"	10	Day of Atonement.	
"	15–21	Feast of Tabernacles.	
"	22	Closing festival of the year.	
Marcheshvan (Bul)=Nov.	1	New Moon.	
Chislev=Dec..	1	New Moon.	
"	. 25	Feast of Dedication.	
Tebeth=Jan.	1	New Moon.	
"	. 10	Fast.	Siege of Jerusalem (Jer. 39:2).
Shebat=Feb.	1	New Moon.	
Adar=March	1	New Moon.	
"	. 13	Fast of Esther.	
"	. 14, 15	Feast of Purim.	The more strict Jews of our Lord's time observed Monday and Friday of each week as a private fast. See Luke 18:12.

CHAPTER XII.

1. The tabernacle was Israel's first historic sanctuary. In leading them out of Egypt God had manifested himself to them in the pillar of cloud and of fire. Wonderful and condescending as was this means of communicating with his people, it was only the first stage in that series of divine manifestations which culminated in the incarnation. At Sinai, accordingly, Israel was commanded to prepare a place for God that he might dwell among them. At a later period he is pleased to speak of this place as having been his dwelling-place: "I have not dwelt in an house since the day that I brought up the children of Israel out of Egypt, even to this day, but have walked in a tent and in a tabernacle."[1] The various names applied to the tabernacle serve to show the purposes for which it was intended. It is called, for example, a "tent," to show its movable and transitory character. It is called the "tent of meeting" and the "tent of witness," to signify that here, by special appointment, God met and communed with his people, and that here, within the ark, were the tables of stone, Jehovah's testimony to Israel respecting what he required. It is called also an "abode," a "sanctuary," as being the place where the holy presence of Jehovah was to be specially manifested, in distinction from the infrequent and transitory theophanies of the past. For much the same reason it was sometimes known as a "palace" or "temple."[2]

The work of erecting the tabernacle was planned, as we are informed, immediately after the first group of laws was given from Sinai and the covenant established with Israel. The gross defection that took place in the matter of the golden calf seems to have delayed its execution. In answer to the prayer of Moses, however, a sanctuary was temporarily provided by the erection of a tent for the purpose just outside the camp. Apparently it was the one that had hitherto served as the tent of the leader of the host. It was pitched without the camp as a sign that Jehovah held in abhorrence that spirit of idolatry which had recently been manifested. The record of the actual carrying out of the plan of building the taber-

---

[1] 2 Sam. 7 : 6.   [2] Ex. 25 : 22; 29 : 42-46; 1 Sam. 1 : 9; 3 : 3; 1 Chron. 29 : 1, 19; Ps. 5 : 7.

nacle—the details of which are given in Exodus, chapters 25–31—
is found in the same book, chapters 35–40. At God's command the
materials were provided by the people, and the work was executed
under the direction of Bezaleel, of the tribe of Judah, and Oholiab,
of the tribe of Dan.[1]

2. The court of the tabernacle was rectangular in form. Its
length was one hundred cubits and its breadth fifty cubits; the cubit
being equivalent here, as we may suppose, to about one foot and a
half. It was enclosed by a row of wooden pillars on which was
suspended a canvas screen. Each of the pillars was five cubits in
height, and the space between them was also five cubits. It has
been found puzzling by some to place sixty pillars (the number
given in the Bible) around this court with twenty on each side and
ten on each end. The difficulty will disappear if it be remembered
that after placing twenty pillars on the side, but nineteen spaces
would be inclosed, hence the first pillar on the end should be placed
in the same line with those on the sides; and in order to inclose ten
spaces on the end, the first pillar on the second side should be on a
line with those on the end. By this arrangement, in the first corner
would be number twenty-one of the pillars; in the second, number
thirty-one; in the third corner, number fifty-one; and the last pillar
placed, number sixty.

The pillars had sockets of bronze or copper at the base, and at
the top a capital which was overlaid with silver. The screen was
made of fine twined linen. It was attached to the pillars by means
of rods which extended from one pillar to another and by hooks,
both of silver. This screen was unbroken except at the entrance
on the eastern side. Here was a curtain, twenty cubits wide, of
more elaborate workmanship, being the "work of the embroiderer
of blue, of purple, and scarlet, and fine twined linen." It was of
the same breadth as the screen. Within this court—which formed,
as will be noticed, a double square—was placed, first, toward the
east and directly in front of the entrance, the altar of burnt offering; a little further on, the laver; and finally the tabernacle proper
with its furniture. These articles may be described in their order.

3. THE ALTAR OF BURNT OFFERING.—The altar of burnt offering was a square, hollow structure, each side measuring five cubits
and the height being three cubits. It was built of planks of acacia
wood, which were overlaid with what is called in our English versions "brass;" but bronze or copper is probably intended, as in

[1] Ex. 35: 30–35.

other places where this term is used in the Old Testament. The altar had horns at each upper corner, and they were of one piece with the rest of the structure. No steps being allowed,[1] the altar was approached by means of an inclined plane, probably of earth. The inside was most likely filled with the same material when it was stationary and in use.[2] It was provided with rings on two of its sides and with staves plated with brass for carrying it. Halfway between the bottom and top was a projection or ledge, and beneath

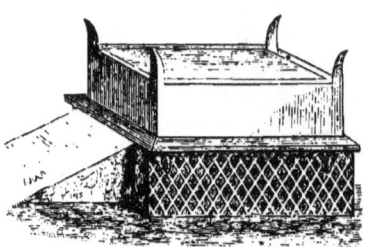

Supposed form of the Altar of Burnt Offering in the Tabernacle.

Supposed form of the Altar of Burnt Offering in the Temple. (*From Suren-husius's Mishna.*)

this a brazen netting extending around the four sides of the altar. The rings just mentioned were placed at the point where this netting met the projection. It seems likely also that the inclined plane of earth or other material extended upward to this projection on the altar. The distance to its top would still be about two and one half feet. The instruments and vessels belonging to the altar are described as "pots" (for the ashes), "shovels," "basins," "flesh-hooks" and "fire-pans." All of these were of brass.

4. THE LAVER.—The laver was apparently a round brazen vessel. It stood, as we have said, between the altar of burnt offering and the tabernacle proper. The water was used by the priests in cleansing themselves before entering the holy place or offering sacrifice. It may also have served for washing the flesh of the animals offered in sacrifice. It was made of the brass obtained from the mirrors presented for the purpose by the women of Israel.[3] It rested on a base or on feet of the same material.

5. THE TABERNACLE.—The tabernacle itself was a rectangular structure thirty cubits long, ten cubits wide and ten cubits high. These dimensions are not directly given in the Bible, but may be safely inferred from statements it does make, the same being supported by Josephus,[4] and by the corresponding dimensions of Solomon's temple. The sides of the tabernacle were composed of

Ex. 20 : 26.   [2] Ex. 20 : 24, 25.   [3] Ex. 38 : 8.   [4] Josephus, *Antiq.* 3, 6 : 3.

boards of acacia wood, forty-eight in number. Forty were used on the north and south sides and eight on the west side. Each of these boards was provided at the bottom with a couple of tenons of silver which fitted into a silver socket of the weight of a talent, or nearly a hundred pounds. The boards were also gilded. To hold them together, they had rings, apparently on the outside, through which gilded bars were passed, five in number for each of the three sides,— one of the bars or series of bars extending along, continuously as we may suppose, the centre of the boards. Whether it was one continuous piece or made up of several pieces, the end of one piece being thrust into that of the next, as Josephus alleges,[1] it is not possible to say. That acacia boards of the size of those here described might have been made of trees to be found at this time on the sinaitic peninsula there is no good reason to doubt.

Form of a Brazen Laver on Wheels.

The two corner boards on the back side of the tabernacle are described as "double beneath, and in like manner they were entire unto the top thereof unto one ring."[2] It has been thought by some that the Bible represents that in width each of the boards on the west end was like those on the two sides, that is, one and a half cubits wide. In that case we should have as the outside width of the entire structure twelve cubits. We must, then, understand the dimensions given by Josephus as being those of the inside. And further, we should be compelled to believe that the planks were of extraordinary thickness,—rather beams than planks or boards. But neither of these inferences is necessary or probable. The Bible, while giving the width of the planks in general, expressly excepts those of the two corners where the planks are joined to form an angle or post; the two together being, as we may accordingly infer, in this case one cubit in width. Of the space inclosed within this structure now, one third (that on the west side) was set apart for the so-called holy of holies. It contained only the ark with its furniture, the mercy-seat, and the tables of the law. In form it was

[1] Josephus, *Antiq.* 3, 6 : 3. [2] Ex. 36 : 29.

A Front View of the Tabernacle with its Tent. For description, see pages 286-295.

Form of Golden Candlestick carried in Triumph by Titus at Rome, after the Capture of Jerusalem. (*From the Arch of Titus.*)

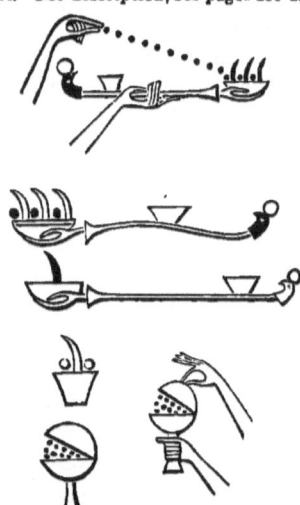

Forms of Ancient Egyptian Censers, found on the Monuments. (*Wilkinson.*)

Ancient Egyptian Winged Cherubs, protecting the figure of a god. (*From the Monuments.*)

Supposed form of the Molten Sea, or Great Laver, made by Solomon for the Temple.

exactly a cube, being ten cubits broad, long and high. The other two thirds of the space of the tabernacle formed what was known as the holy place. It was twenty cubits long by ten cubits wide and high. In it was placed on one side the golden candlestick, opposite to it the table of shew-bread, and between them, but nearer to the holy of holies, the altar of incense.

6. THE HOLY OF HOLIES.—The holy of holies was separated from the holy place by a "vail of blue, and purple, and scarlet, and fine twined linen: with cherubim the work of the cunning workman."[1] It was hung by golden hooks on four pillars of acacia wood, overlaid with gold and standing in sockets of silver. A screen separated also, in part, the front of the tabernacle from the outer court. It is described in the same terms as the vail before the inner sanctuary, excepting that it was not the work of a "cunning workman," and did not have the cherubim ; it was suspended also on five golden pillars instead of four, and their sockets were of brass. The suggestion of one commentator that one post, the middle one, was higher than the rest, and formed one of the supports for a ridge-pole, over which the tent covering was placed, must be regarded as, in the circumstances, somewhat extravagant. It is more likely to have had something to do with the different arrangement of the curtains, which is also suggested by the diverse description of these pillars as having "chapiters" and "fillets," that is, capitals and rods. It would at least have been desirable in the case of this much-used curtain that, unlike that of the holy of holies which was suspended on hooks, it might be easily moved to one side. The extra pillar would on this supposition have been advantageous in giving support to the rod. The distance between the pillars would still have been three feet.

7. The covering of the tabernacle was of four kinds.[2] That which was laid on first, and directly over the tops of the planks forming the enclosure, is called "the tabernacle." It was in two parts, each twenty cubits wide and twenty-eight long. These two parts were severally made up of five smaller pieces fastened (probably sewed) together, and then the two in turn were joined by means of fifty loops in their respective borders and by golden clasps. The material of this covering is described as of "fine twined linen, and blue, and purple, and scarlet, with cherubim ;" that is, with figures of cherubim embroidered upon the stuff. Supposing that, when completed, it was laid evenly on the structure, it would have fallen over the

---

[1] Ex. 26 : 31.   [2] Ex. 26 : 1, 6, 7 ; 36 : 8, 14.

19

two ends five cubits, and on the sides would have failed to reach the ground only by one cubit. It was enjoined, however, that it should be put on in such a manner that the line of division between the two curtains should coincide with that separating the holy place from the inner sanctuary.[1] On the back side, accordingly, the covering would nearly have reached the ground.

A second covering, intended to be a "tent over the tabernacle," was of goat's hair, a common material for tent-cloth. It had two parts like the preceding, one of them being composed of five pieces, thirty cubits long by four wide, the other of six, of the same size. The two were coupled together like the first two. Supposing that when united it had been laid over the structure in such a manner that the place of coupling corresponded with that of the first covering, there would be one breadth of four cubits to hang over the front, besides a sufficient amount to cover the whole of the back and two sides down quite near to the ground. Such an arrangement conforms exactly to the directions given in Exodus.[2] By such an arrangement, too, the inside covering, as was probably intended, would be completely protected by the outer one. Moreover, it is not unlikely that the second covering was provided with cords and fastened, like the ordinary tent, to the ground with pins. We at least read of the pins of the tabernacle as distinct from the pins of the court.[3]

8. But what is to be said of the two other coverings of which we read in Exodus 26 : 14? "And thou shalt make a covering for the tent of rams' skins dyed red, and a covering of sealskins above." If they were to be put on as the others were, would there not seem to be an excess of this kind of covering? Instead of keeping out dampness from the interior in the case of rain, would they not have had a tendency to produce it, besides being highly inconvenient in other respects? And where, in that case, would be the tent form from which the whole structure had its name? Happily we are not restricted to this method of putting on the additional coverings. As far as the Bible is concerned the matter is left entirely open. While the form, measurement and method of placing the other two coverings are stated in detail, here it is simply said that a covering is to be made for the "tent," that is, the second covering, and the materials of which it is to be made are indicated.

What we should most naturally think of would be an actual tent overspreading the remaining structure and reaching out some dis-

[1] Ex. 26 : 33.   [2] Ex. 26 : 9, 12, 13.   [3] Ex. 27 : 19; 35 : 18.

tance into the court. In the preparation of this tent dyed rams' skins and the skins of seals might be employed in ways that would easily suggest themselves to persons who were continually using skins for this purpose. It is an interesting confirmation of the view here taken that the word rendered covering in our passage is not the same as that used for the other two coverings of the tabernacle, but is that used of the roof of the ark which Noah built.[1] And while Moses is spoken of as "erecting" the tabernacle, he is said to have "spread" the tent, that is, the second covering, over the tabernacle, and to have put the covering of the tent, that is, the tent of rams' skins, etc., "above upon it; as the Lord commanded Moses."[2] The Hebrew used is peculiar and makes the impression that the covering of skins was of the nature of a roof somewhat elevated above the others. The matter has been more fully discussed because of the confusion of ideas prevailing upon the subject.

9. THE ARK.—The articles of furniture contained in the tabernacle have already been enumerated. Within the inner sanctuary, or the holy of holies, was the "ark of the covenant." It was so called on account of the two tables of stone which were there placed.[3] In form it was a simple chest of acacia wood, in width and height one cubit and a half and in length two cubits and a half. It was overlaid throughout with gold. Rings were placed at the four corners and fitted with staves for carrying it. Around the top was a gilded rim or moulding, and the lid, which was called the "mercy-seat," was of solid gold. On each end of this lid, and of one piece with it, was set the figure of a cherub, made from beaten gold. The two cherubim faced inward and covered the mercy-seat with their wings.

Supposed form of Ark of the Covenant.

The "Mercy-seat" was the lid, or cover; the winged figures are to represent the cherubim. For other forms, see p. 288.

This was the most holy place of the sanctuary. The high priest alone could enter it once in the year, and then only amidst clouds of incense. "There," said Jehovah, "I will meet with thee, and I will commune with thee from above the mercy-seat, from between the two cherubim which are upon the ark of the testimony, of all things which I will give thee in commandment unto the children of Israel."[4] Besides the tables of stone there were at

[1] Gen. 8 : 13.   [2] Ex. 40 : 19 ; cf. Num. 4 : 25.   [3] Ex. 25 : 10, 16.   [4] Ex. 25 : 22.

one time by the ark a pot of manna and Aaron's rod that budded.[1] All except the first were lost, as it would seem, while the ark was in the possession of the Philistines, or earlier. The ark itself was probably burnt when Nebuchadnezzar took Jerusalem.[2]

10. THE ALTAR OF INCENSE.—Nearest the veil, outside the holy of holies, was the altar of incense.[3] Its position is not without sig-

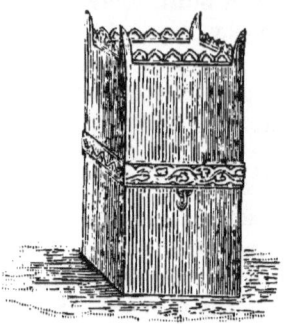

nificance.[4] From the fact that it was overlaid throughout with gold it received also the name of the "golden altar." Like the ark, it had a gilded moulding about the top, beneath which, on two of its sides, the four rings were found by which it was borne. It was a cubit long and broad and two cubits high. The original altar was made of acacia wood; that of Solomon of cedar. The only religious service which took place specially at this altar

Supposed form of Altar of Incense, or Golden Altar.

was the offering of incense made there each morning and evening, and the sprinkling of it with blood on the day of atonement. An altar of incense is spoken of in Revelation as a part of the furniture of the heavenly temple.[5]

11. THE TABLE OF SHEW-BREAD.—The table of shew-bread also was made of acacia, or shittim, wood.[6] In form it was like ordinary tables, excepting the rings on the two sides and the inserted staves which were never removed. It was two cubits long, a cubit in breadth, and a cubit and a half high. It had "a border of an handbreadth round about" and "a golden crown to the border." This "border" appears to have been a framework somewhat below the upper surface of the table, and intended as a support for it. The "crown" (rim) of the border and the "crown" of the table are clearly distinguished. The former was a

Supposed form of the Table of Shew-bread.

moulding intended principally for ornamentation. That on the surface of the table would also be of use. The table was plated over in every part with gold. On it were to be found at all times "dishes,"

---

[1] Ex. 16:33; Num. 17:10; Deut. 31:26; Heb. 9:4.　[2] 1 Kings 8:1,9; 2 Chron. 35:3. [3] Ex. 30:1-10, 34-38.　[4] 1 Kings 6:22; Heb. 9:4.　[5] Rev. 8:3,4.　[6] Ex. 25:23.

"spoons," "flagons" and "bowls." We may infer that the dishes were for the bread; the spoons for the frankincense; and the flagons and bowls for the drink offerings. Every Sabbath twelve loaves of bread, covered with frankincense, called "shew- [Heb. "presence"] bread" were placed upon the table. On the following Sabbath they were removed and others substituted. The old frankincense was at the same time burned upon the altar and the bread eaten in the sanctuary by the priests.[1] At a later period the name given to the bread was "array-bread" or "row-bread."[2] In Solomon's temple, too, instead of the one provided for in the original law there were ten tables. In the representation of the table of shew-bread on the arch of Titus at Rome the two borders plainly appear. The lower one is around the middle of the legs. It supports the two silver horns of the priests. And instead of being borne by means of staves extending through rings this table is carried from the base on men's shoulders.[3]

12. THE CANDLESTICK.—The only remaining article of furniture in the tabernacle was the golden candlestick or candelabrum.[4] The principal part of it, the lamp proper, consisted of an upright shaft resting on a pedestal, and having a cup at its top which, when provided with oil and a wick, served for a lamp. From this central shaft proceeded six others, three on each side, all being on the same plane, and all probably extending upward to the same level. The candlestick stood opposite the table of shew-bread, on the south side of the tabernacle. It was made throughout of beaten gold, a talent in weight being required for the purpose. Tradition gives its height as five feet and its extreme breadth as three and a half feet. It was ornamented along its several shafts with flower cups, the main shaft having four and the others three. Their form was that of the calyx of the almond blossom. The top of each shaft was surmounted by a ball-like protuberance, from which sprang a flower, and in this flower was found the cup containing the oil. (See illustration, p. 288.) The immediate object of the candlestick, the holy place being without natural light, was to give light to the priests in the performance of their duties. But it was doubtless intended to have also a symbolical significance.[5]

It was one of the duties of the priests to fill the cups of the candlestick with the finest oil every evening, and to trim the wicks every morning, using golden snuffers and dishes provided for the purpose.[6]

[1] Lev. 24:5-9 ; cf. 1 Sam. 21:3-6.   [2] Neh. 10:33 (Hebrew).   [3] Josephus, *Antiq.* 3, 6:6.
[4] Ex. 25:31-40.   [5] Ps. 36:9; 104:2; Isa. 10:17; Zech. 4:1-6; John 8:12; 1 Tim. 6:16.
[6] Ex. 27:20.

They appear to have been kept burning day and night, although in the time of Josephus but three were burnt during the day (*Antiq.* 3, 8 : 3). As Solomon placed ten tables of shew-bread in the temple which he built, so he had made for it ten golden candlesticks.[1] His object in both instances seems to have been to add to the glory of the building. In the second temple there was but one candlestick.[2] This was removed by Antiochus Epiphanes, but restored by Judas the Maccabee.[3] It was most likely this candlestick of Judas which Titus afterwards carried to Rome, and that is represented now on the arch erected in Titus' honor. It resembles in its general outline the one described in the Pentateuch. The eagles and sea monsters engraved upon it were doubtless the work of later pagan hands.

13. The historical reality of the Mosaic tabernacle has been severely assailed by certain modern critics. But it is supported not alone by one portion of the Pentateuch, but almost equally by every part into which these critics arbitrarily partition it.[4] And this testimony the following history abundantly confirms. It was a singular act of David to erect a tent on Mount Zion for the ark which he had brought from Kirjath-jearim, considering especially its more recent history and the demands of his own times.[5] It would be well-nigh inexplicable without the Mosaic precedent for it. The assumption that the Israel of the exodus had not the requisite skill to execute a work of this kind is rapidly disappearing before the remarkable archeological discoveries of modern times. The objection that this people was not provided with the requisite means for transporting through the trackless wastes of the sinaitic peninsula such a mass of material is equally wide of the mark.

It is nowhere stated in the Pentateuch that the six wagons and twelve yoke of oxen at the service of the Levites for carrying purposes were all the means at hand for this object.[6] It was to the family of Merari that the transportation of the heavier parts of the tabernacle was assigned. According to the record it formed an army of thirty-two hundred able-bodied men, between the ages of thirty and fifty years. This should have been found an amply sufficient force, on any reasonable theory of the structure of the tabernacle. The objection that the Pentateuch recognizes a two-fold tabernacle has been already touched upon. It could never have been urged except on the theory that the five books of the Pentateuch are a

---

[1] 1 Kings 7 : 49.   [2] Ecclus. 26 : 17.   [3] 1 Macc. 4 : 49.   [4] Ex. 33 : 7-11; Lev. 17; Num. 10 : 35; 11 : 16; Deut. 10 : 1-5; 31 : 14.   [5] 2 Sam. 7 : 2.   [6] Num. 7 : 8, 9.

patchwork of different and often conflicting documents. After the tabernacle was planned the defection of Israel made its immediate erection inexpedient. In the interval, the leader's tent, pitched for a special reason outside the camp, was used as the " tent of meeting."[1] It was not the tabernacle proper; for the Levitical institutions had not yet been established.

14. The tabernacle, in the nature of the case, was not intended to be a permanent sanctuary. Its history subsequent to its dedication, in the second year of the exodus, runs parallel with that of Israel until the entrance into the promised land. Afterwards, for a considerable period, it seems to have remained at Gilgal, the headquarters of Joshua and the Israelitish army.[2] Following the conquest, it was for a long time at Shiloh.[3] Here in fact it appears to have remained during the whole period of the judges. While at Shiloh the tabernacle is called a "house," and again a "palace" or "temple," of Jehovah. It is also spoken of as having door-posts and the like.[4] From this language it has been assumed by some that it had altogether changed its character, and become a building instead of a tent. But such a supposition directly contradicts other passages which presuppose its tent form at this period.[5] The probable harmony of the two classes of references lies in the supposition that the tabernacle, while at Shiloh, had a temporary enclosure built around it, to which reference is sometimes made as though it were the tabernacle itself.

When the ark was taken by the Philistines[6] the tabernacle naturally lost much of its glory and became less permanent. We hear of it at Nob during the reign of Saul, whence it was removed to Gibeon.[7] Here, as we learn from the books of Chronicles,[8] it divided the honors for a time, as the sanctuary of Jehovah, with the tent which David erected for the ark on Mount Zion.[9] Zadok, of the family of Eleazar, ministered at the former, and Abiathar, or his son Abimelech, at the latter.[10] This dualism, possible only during the transition state through which Israel was now passing, ceased in Solomon's day, with the defection and deposition of Abiathar.[11] We have no information concerning the removal of the tabernacle from Gibeon. The "tent of meeting" which was deposited in the temple may well have been that which David originally erected on Mount Zion.[12] Without the ark, the tabernacle was but the shell from which

[1] Ex. 33:7–11: Num. 10:33; 12:5; 14:14. [2] Josh. 4:19; 5:10; 9:6; 10:6; 14:6. [3] Josh. 18:1, 10; 19:51; 22:12,19,29. [4] Judg. 18:31; 19:18; 1 Sam. 1:7,9,24; 3:3, 15. [5] 1 Sam. 2:22; Ps. 78:60. [6] 1 Sam. 4:11. [7] 1 Kings 3:4. [8] 1 Chron. 16:39–42; 21:29; 2 Chron. 1:3–6, 13. [9] 2 Sam. 6:17; 1 Chron. 15:1. [10] 1 Chron. 16:39; 24:3. [11] 1 Kings 2:26, 27. [12] 2 Chron. 5:5.

the fruit had disappeared. With the temple immediately in view, it is not strange that it was overlooked and forgotten.

15. TEMPLE OF SOLOMON.—The gathering of materials for the projected temple was mostly the work of David. He himself, as a man of blood, was not permitted to build it; but it was promised him that a son of his should have that honor.[1] Solomon began its erection in the fourth year of his reign, which, according to the received chronology, was B.C. 1012, and four hundred and eighty years after the exodus from Egypt. He had the special assistance of Hiram king of Tyre, who had been the warm friend of his father. The temple was built on Mount Moriah, which lay eastward from Mount Zion and originally outside of the city's walls. It was completed in seven years and dedicated with great pomp. In its ground plan the structure closely resembled the tabernacle, but with double its dimensions.[2] The main building was similarly divided into the holy place and the holy of holies, the former measuring twenty cubits each way, the latter forty cubits by twenty. In height, however, the temple was thirty cubits. Along the front side extended a porch having the width of the main building and being ten cubits deep.

The height is not given in the book of Kings, but it cannot well have been greater—it may have been less—than that of the principal part. The statement in 2 Chronicles 3 : 4 that it was one hundred and twenty cubits high seems to rest on a corrupt text. It is called a "porch." If it had been a hundred and twenty cubits high, its title would have been more properly "tower." And it is scarcely probable, moreover, that so striking a feature of the building, had it existed, would have been overlooked in the book of Kings. It is true that the porch of Herod's temple was wider and higher than the main building, and that Josephus makes Herod say that the temple then before him, the one built by the exiles from Babylon, lacked sixty cubits of being as high as that of Solomon.[3] But it is likely that the dimensions of Solomon's temple were taken from this passage in second Chronicles.

16. Solomon's temple was entered from the east between two massive pillars called respectively Jachin, "he shall establish," and Boaz, "in it is strength" (?)—the former standing on the right. The dimensions of these pillars are variously stated; but the account in the book of Kings seems the most trustworthy, which gives the height as eighteen cubits and the circumference as twelve cubits.[4] Upon

---

[1] 2 Sam. 7:13; 1 Kings 5:1; 1 Chron. 22.　　[2] 1 Kings 6; 2 Chron. 2–4; Josephus, *Antiq.* 8, 3:3.　　[3] Josephus, *Antiq.* 15, 11:1.　　[4] 1 Kings 7:15; 2 Chron. 3:15.

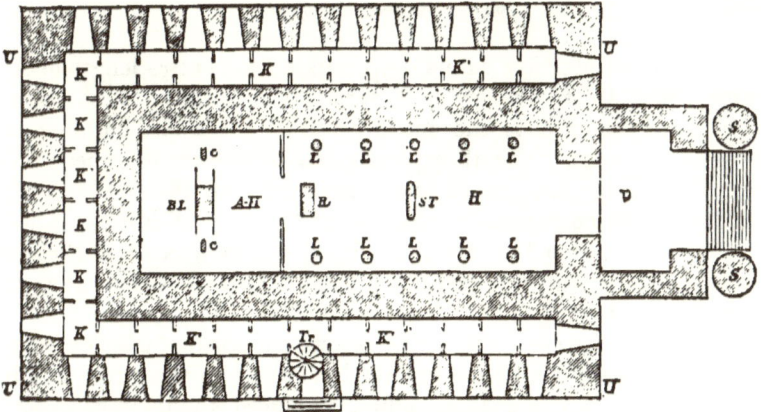

Ground-Plan of Solomon's Temple.

A–H, The Most Holy Place.
H, The Holy Place.
V, The Entrance-Hall or Porch.
K and K', Side Chambers.
U, U, U, U, Corner-stones.
S. S, The Two Pillars, Jachin and Boaz.
B L, The Ark of the Covenant,

c. c, The Cherubim.
L, L, L, The Ten Golden Candlesticks and the Ten Tables.
R, The Altar of Incense.
Tr, The Winding Stair to the Stories in the Side Chambers.
T, Table of Shew-Bread (but see 2 Chron. 4 : 8),

The Scene from the Arch of Titus, Rome, representing bearing in triumph the Golden Candlestick and Table of Shew-Bread. The figures are partially defaced.
(After a Photograph.)

each was a chapiter five cubits deep, making the entire length of the pillar about thirty-five feet. A series of chambers, three stories high, were attached to the outside wall of the main building on three of its sides. The theory that the chambers described were rather receding galleries of increasing width, in the inside of the building, finds no support in the text of the book of Kings. These chambers were each five cubits in height; but on account of the fact that the temple wall was less thick and receded as it went upward, they differed in width, the lower being five cubits, the second, six, and the third, seven. The cedar beams supporting the floor were not let into the walls of the temple, but rested on what is called in architecture a scarcement or offset, produced by their successive diminution upward.

These chambers, supposing the foundation and floors required three cubits, would be altogether eighteen cubits high, reaching three cubits above the centre of the main building. The upper stories were reached by means of staircases from the lower ones. The text of the book of Kings is obscure at this point. It says: "The door for the middle side-chambers was in the right side of the house: and they went up by winding stairs into the middle *chambers*, and out of the middle into the third." The right side, looking toward the east, would be the south side. The first word rendered "middle" is translated "lowest" by the Septuagint and Targums. But the Hebrew text may still be correct, the sole end being to show how the middle and third stories were reached; it being understood that the first one would have a door. According to Josephus, there were thirty chambers on each of the floors.

17. The temple, and as we may suppose its surrounding chambers, had a series of windows; but in the former they were for the purpose of ventilation rather than light. Light was obtained by means of the golden candelabrum. It is said, moreover, that the apertures were closed with "fixed lattice work," that is, they were not intended to be opened. The construction of the temple, as was doubtless designed, made windows in the oracle or holy of holies impossible. The number, form and position of the windows mentioned is not given; but it is likely that those of the temple extended around the upper part of the wall on all sides except the front.

The temple, like the tabernacle, had an enclosure or court around it which, in the book of Kings, is called the "inner court," and of which it is said that it was built of "three rows of hewn stones, and a row of cedar beams." It is implied that there was also an outer court, and the fact is directly stated in other parts of the Old Testament.[1] The first court is elsewhere called the "court of the priests" and the "upper court."[2] The outer court, like the inner, was surrounded by a wall. Josephus gives the height of these walls as three cubits. They may well have been ten cubits, corresponding to the dimensions of the temple in other respects as compared with the tabernacle. The row of cedar beams is to be thought of as laid on the wall horizontally and forming for it an ornamental coping. Nothing is said directly in the Bible concerning gates for these enclosures. From incidental passages, as where priestly gate-keepers are spoken of as forming three divisions, and a third entrance to the house of the Lord is named,[3] it may be safely inferred that there were three such. Both courts were paved with stones. The size of the courts can only be guessed. If the inner one was double that of the tabernacle, it would measure two hundred cubits in length by one hundred in breadth.

18. The walls of the temple were built of stone, Josephus says of "white stone;" and they may have been taken from a quarry which still exists near the Damascus gate. They were "made ready at the quarry: and there was neither hammer nor axe nor any tool of iron heard in the house, while it was in building."[4] The thickness of the walls is not given, but must have been considerable, judging from their great diminution as they went upward, and from what we know of the palace of Solomon, where "stones of ten cubits" and "stones of eight cubits" were made use of.[5] The roof was made of beams and boards of cedar. Whether it was flat or gabled is not said, but most likely the former, and that it was provided with a balustrade.[6] The interior walls were wainscoted with boards of cedar, beautifully ornamented with carvings of cherubim, palms and flowers, and overlaid with gold. We may suppose that while the figures were in bas-relief, their outline was sunken, so that their upper surface did not extend beyond the surface of the boards; at least this is the most common form of engraving found on the Egyptian monuments. The floor was of cypress wood, and, like the walls and ceiling, was overlaid with gold.

19. The oracle was separated from the holy place by a partition of cedar boards, which were doubtless ornamented like the rest of the temple's interior. It was entered by a two-leaved door of olive wood which turned on golden hinges. "The lintel *and* door posts

[1] 2 Kings 21 : 5; 23 : 12; 2 Chron. 33 : 5.   [2] 2 Chron. 4 : 9; Jer. 36 : 10.   [3] 2 Kings 25 : 18; Jer. 38 : 14; 52 : 24.   [4] 1 Kings 6 : 7.   [5] 1 Kings 7 : 10.   [6] Deut. 22 : 8.

were a fifth part *of the wall.*" The door of the holy place was made of fir, the posts only being of olive wood. It was in two parts, each part, in turn, having two leaves. The whole door with its casing took up a fourth part of the wall, as that of the oracle had required a fifth. In addition to the door entering the oracle, we learn from 2 Chronicles 3 : 14, a statement which is supported by Josephus[1] and the practice of the second temple, that there was also a vail of "blue, and purple, and crimson, and fine linen," with figures of cherubim embroidered upon it. Josephus says that the curtain was before the door. We may suppose, accordingly, that the door swung inward, and that the curtain was intended to protect the oracle from the curious gaze of the priests and others on the day of atonement and at other times when the door was opened. It is a singular fact that this vail is not mentioned in the book of Kings. Some have supposed that the perplexing passage in 1 Kings 6 : 21, where we read, "and he drew chains of gold across before the oracle," originally read, "and he drew the curtain provided with golden chains across before the oracle."

The dimensions of the holy of holies upward is given as twenty cubits, while the height of the holy place is thirty cubits.[2] It is probable that in 1 Kings 6 : 2 the exterior of the temple alone is described. Externally, it is likely, the whole building was covered by one roof. This would leave a vacant space ten cubits high by twenty cubits long and broad above the oracle. It was shut off from the holy place by the partition of cedar boards before referred to. It is impossible to say for what purpose such a space was reserved. In Chronicles, also, we read of certain upper chambers of which elsewhere no information is given. Possibly only the upper tier of side-chambers may be here meant, or some that were made over the porch. It has been conjectured that the tent used by David for the ark, or possibly the relics of the ancient Mosaic tabernacle itself, were deposited over the holy of holies. The theory is attractive, but has absolutely nothing to support it; besides, in that case there would have been necessary a strong floor above the holy of holies. This could hardly have been secured across a space of thirty feet without beams. The beams, in turn, would need to be let into the temple walls, which would be contrary to the structure of the building in other respects. Moreover, if this upper chamber were visited, another aperture through the wall, for a door, would have been needed. More likely than any of these hypotheses is the supposition

---

[1] Josephus, *Antiq.* 8, 3 : 3 and 7.   [2] 1 Kings 6 : 2, 16, 20.

that the object of shutting off the space was to make the dimensions of this oracle in all respects double that of the tabernacle.

20. THE FURNITURE.—The furnishing of Solomon's temple needs to be described only so far as it differs from that of the tabernacle. In the oracle were placed two additional cherubim of olive wood. The wood was carved ("image work") and overlaid with gold. When spread, the wings of the cherubim were each five cubits long, and altogether they required the entire space that made up the western wall of the sanctuary. Their height was ten cubits.[1] It has already been noticed that the one table of shew-bread had been increased to ten in Solomon's temple, as had also the one candlestick to ten candlesticks. They were ranged on the two sides of the holy place, five on each side. In two passages of the historical books but one table is spoken of in connection with this building.[2] This fact has been regarded by some as indicating diversity of authorship and date. But it is more probable that in these instances the one table is referred to on which the bread was actually placed; for it cannot well have been distributed on all of them. Moreover, by a well-known idiom of the Hebrew language the article is frequently used to distinguish one of a class.

In place of the much smaller brazen altar of the tabernacle, the one in Solomon's temple was twenty cubits square by ten high.[3] The tabernacle, too, had but a small laver for the use of the priests. Solomon supplanted it by what is called a molten sea. This was a receptacle for water, manufactured from melted copper or bronze, and was ten cubits in diameter and five cubits deep. The rim was highly ornamented, and the whole supported on the backs of twelve brazen oxen, standing together in groups of three, with their faces turned outward toward the several points of the compass. According to the book of Kings, it had a capacity of two thousand baths—a bath being equal to about eight gallons. In Chronicles the capacity is stated as three thousand baths.[4] The difference may be due to a corruption of the text of Chronicles; or, in one case the actual capacity may be given, in the other the amount of water usually found in it. As even two thousand baths of liquid would more than fill a vessel of these dimensions if it were hemispherical in shape, most likely this was spherical. The predilection of the Scriptures for round numbers and their avoidance of fractions is illustrated here in the fact that while they make the circumference

---

[1] 1 Kings 6 : 23–28 ; 2 Chron. 3 : 10–13.   [2] 1 Kings 7 : 48 ; 2 Chron. 29 : 18.   [3] 2 Chron. 4 : 1.
[4] 1 Kings 7 : 23, 26 ; 2 Chron. 4 : 2, 5.

of this receptacle thirty cubits, the diameter is said to have been ten cubits. It is well known that the exact diameter of a circle holds the relation to its circumference of 1 to 3.14159.

The laver of the tabernacle was designed to provide a place where the priests might make their ablutions. Having supplied this want by the molten sea, Solomon had ten lavers made, corresponding to the ten candlesticks and ten tables of shew-bread, that the flesh to be offered on the altar of burnt offering might be cleansed in them.[1] These lavers were placed on brazen pedestals, four cubits square by three cubits high, five on each side of the holy place. Each one held forty baths; they must, accordingly, have been of considerable size, and the water drawn from them, as from the molten sea, have been taken from beneath. The only indication of their dimensions is in 1 Kings 7 : 38, where each one is said to have been four cubits. The depth of the bowl is probably referred to.[2]

21. The temple of Solomon stood about four hundred years. It was destroyed by the army of Nebuchadnezzar, under Nebuzaradan, in the eleventh year of the reign of Zedekiah, having previously been plundered.[3] Comparing 2 Kings 25 : 8 with Jeremiah 52 : 12, an apparent discrepancy in dates is discovered.[4] The one gives the day of the burning of the temple as the seventh of the fifth month; the other, as the tenth of that month. It is most likely, as the Talmud asserts, that between these two dates the capture, plundering and destruction of the temple are all included. The one account dates from the time the temple was taken; the other, from that of its final overthrow.

22. TEMPLE OF ZERUBBABEL.—Of the external appearance of the so-called temple of Zerubbabel, built by the exiles who returned from Babylon, the Bible furnishes little information. It was finished and solemnly dedicated in the year B.C. 516. It doubtless occupied the same site as the structure erected by Solomon. It may have been of equal size, since it was not necessarily because of its inferiority in this respect that the fathers, who had seen the glories of the original temple, wept at the sight of this one.[5] That, on the other hand, it was larger than Solomon's temple cannot be fairly inferred from Ezra 6 : 3, where Cyrus is said to have ordered that its height should be sixty cubits, nothing whatever being said of its length.[6] This same kind-hearted monarch directed that the "ex-

[1] 1 Kings 7 : 27-39; 2 Chron. 4 : 6.   [2] Cf. 1 Kings 7 : 27, 32, 35.   [3] 2 Kings 25 : 8, 13; 2 Chron. 36 : 18; Jer. 52 : 12, 17.   [4] See Baruch 1 : 2; Josephus, *Antiq.* 10, 8 : 5; Josephus, *Jewish Wars*, 6, 4 : 5.   [5] Ezra 3 : 12; Hag. 2 : 3.   [6] Josephus, *Antiq.* 15, 11 : 1.

penses" of the building should be given out of the king's house. We have no evidence that either of the directions was actually carried out. There were special reasons why the inner dimensions of the second temple should not essentially differ from those of the first, in which the norm furnished by the tabernacle was carefully followed. We may therefore look upon those given by Cyrus as referring to the temple externally, if adopted at all, the additions included; or as simply meant to carry the idea that the Jews might not only rebuild the temple, but build it, if they chose, to twice its former size.

23. From the first book of Maccabees we learn that both the oracle and the holy place were provided with curtains.[1] Josephus states that the former was quite bare of any furnishing.[2] According to the Talmudists, however, there was a stone set up in the place where the ark formerly had been. On this stone, once in the year, the high priest sprinkled the blood of the sin offering. On the other hand, the second temple had but one candlestick and one table of shew-bread. It had also the altar of incense overlaid with gold;[3] while its altar of burnt offering retained the size of that of Solomon's temple.[4] A reservoir for water is likewise mentioned in Ecclesiasticus.[5] The last passage might lead one to infer that previous to the high-priesthood of Simon there had been no provision of this kind in the temple of Zerubbabel, or, if any, an inferior one. We are told incidentally, in the books of Nehemiah and Ezra, that the courts of this temple were supplied with depositories, and with cells or cloisters for the priests.[6]

24. This temple was captured and plundered by Antiochus Epiphanes B.C. 168, who also celebrated idolatrous worship in it. Retaken by Judas Maccabæus, it was restored, cleansed and rededicated exactly three years after its profanation. The golden crowns and shields with which this hero ornamented the front of the restored temple were less in harmony with its objects and history.[7] While Alexander Jannæus was high priest, he had built, for his own protection, a wooden partition around the altar and that portion of the temple which it was lawful only for the priests to frequent.[8] Pompey captured, invaded, but did not sack, the building, when he took Jerusalem, B.C. 63, during the consulate of Marcus Tullius Cicero. It was recklessly plundered of its treasures, however, by Crassus,

[1] 1 Macc. 4:51. [2] Josephus, Wars of the Jews, 5, 5:5. [3] 1 Macc. 1:22; 4:49. [4] Josephus, Against Apion, 1, 22. [5] Ecclus. 50:3. [6] Ezra 8:29; 10:6; Neh. 3:30; 10:37; 12:44; 1 Macc. 4:38, 48. [7] 1 Macc. 4:52, 54, 57. [8] Josephus, Antiq. 13, 13:5.

who from B.C. 54–53 ruled in the province of Syria.[1] It greatly
suffered also on the capture of Jerusalem by Herod, and the sacred
precincts were stained with the blood of its many defenders.[2]

25. TEMPLE OF HEROD.—The so-called temple of Herod deserves
a fuller description than can well be given in these pages. No doubt
personal ambition and a desire to ingratiate himself with the Jews
were the principal motives influencing this monarch in entering upon
so difficult and costly an undertaking. To allay natural suspicion,
Herod employed a thousand priests, specially trained for the purpose, in building the fore-court and the temple proper. For the
same reason he agreed to take down no part of the old temple until
the material was prepared to restore it immediately in larger pro-
portions and in surpassing grandeur. He was willing, at the outset, that his work should appear as one of restoration and enlargement. As a matter of fact, the whole building was transformed in
the process. Still he helped to maintain the identity of the old with
the new. It continued to be called the "second" temple.

The work began in the eighteenth year of Herod's reign, B.C. 20–
19. It was not completed until the time of the procurator Albinus,
A.D. 62–64. When it is said, therefore, in the Gospel of John,[3]
"Forty and six years was this temple in building," it is simply
meant that so long a time had been already spent upon it, B.C. 19–
A.D. 28. We are dependent for information concerning the great
work mostly on Josephus and on a tract of the Talmud which is
exclusively devoted to the subject. Happily, in this case both may
be relied on, in respect to their general statements, with great con-
fidence. In entering upon the undertaking, the site of the old temple on Mount Moriah was greatly enlarged by means of immense
sub-structures. It formed, according to Josephus, a rectangular space
equivalent to a stadium square, that is, a little more than six hundred English feet.[4] The Talmud makes the area considerably larger,
and modern investigations tend to confirm this view. It seems to
have been longest from north to south. The whole was surrounded
by a high and massive wall capable of military defence. This wall
was broken on the west by four gates, and, as it would appear, on
the south by two gates, and on the east and north respectively by
one gate. On the northwest corner, and only a little way removed,
frowned the strong citadel of Antonia. Steps from the court led

---

[1] Josephus, *Antiq.* 14, 7 : 1; Josephus. *Wars of the Jews*, 1, 88.   [2] Josephus. *Wars of the Jews*,
14, 16 : 2.   [3] John 2 : 20.   [4] Josephus, *Antiq.* 15, 11 ; *Wars of the Jews*, 5, 5 ; Talmud, Tract
Massecheth Middoth.

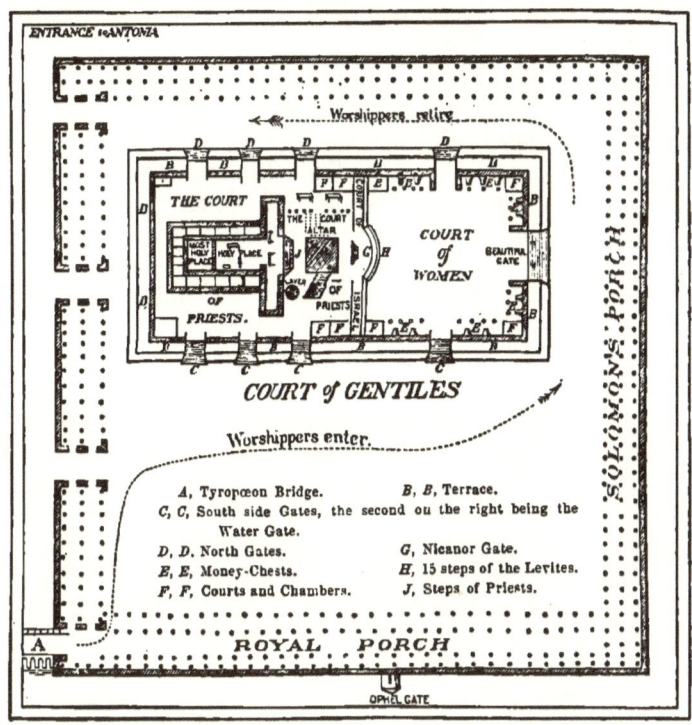

Herod's Temple: Ground-Plan, with Courts, Gates, Porches, etc.

Ruins of a Synagogue at Kefr-Bir'im, near Kadesh in Galilee.
(By Permission from *Pal. Memoirs.*)

directly up to it. Paul was once carried as a prisoner up these steps, and on the way was allowed to pause and address the excited throngs assembled in the court below.[1]

26. Coming within the wall one found himself at once in the outer court of the holy place. It was also called the "court of the Gentiles," because other than Jews were admitted to it. Beyond this, however, strangers were warned by notices on suspended tablets that on pain of death they should not venture. A tablet of this sort, in the Greek language, has been recently unearthed at this spot. It was because it was supposed that Paul had transgressed such an ordinance that the uproar took place recorded in Acts 21 : 28. This court was paved throughout with variegated marble, and surrounded with a magnificent colonnade, forming what are called in our English Bibles "porches," that is, porticoes. A double row of Corinthian pillars, thirty-seven and a half feet high, each formed from a single piece of marble, extended around the entire outer wall. They were covered by a highly-ornamented roof of polished woods. The "porch" on the east side was known as Solomon's porch; that on the south as the royal porch. The latter exceeded all the others in grandeur. Instead of three rows of marble columns it had four, forty pillars standing in each row. The two middle rows were twice as high as the other two, and the space between them twice as wide. This porch is supposed to have occupied the site of the royal palace of Solomon. From its top one could look into the valley of the Kedron, four hundred and fifty feet below. It has been supposed by some that this was the "pinnacle of the temple" referred to in the account of our Lord's temptation.[2]

It is easy to understand how such a place as this "court of the Gentiles" would be one of common resort for the people of Jerusalem. It was here, in Solomon's porch, that our Saviour was walking when the Jews came about him and asked, "How long dost thou hold us in suspense?"[3] It was here that he overthrew the tables of the money-changers. It was in the same place that Peter and John healed the lame man who had been laid at the temple gate, and we read that, as he held the apostles, "all the people ran together unto them in the porch that is called Solomon's, greatly wondering."[4] Good authorities maintain that, besides apartments for priests and Levites, there were also to be found in this court and probably on the west side, near the gate that leads to the upper city, the "council chamber," in which the Sanhedrin was wont to meet. The temple

---

[1] Acts 21 : 35, 40.   [2] Matt. 4 : 5.   [3] John 10 : 24.   [4] Acts 3 : 11.

did not lie in the centre of the court, but somewhat nearer to the
northern and western sides.

27. Passing inward, now, from the "court of the Gentiles," one
came first to a low wall which marked its boundary on three sides.
On this wall, at intervals, were placed the marble tablets before
mentioned, warning against a further approach those who were not
Jews. Within this wall rose the terrace on which the temple stood.
It was about fifteen feet from the first-named wall to that of the
outer court of the temple proper. Steps led up to the latter on every
side but the west. There were nine series of them, leading to as
many gates, the principal one being of course on the east, where was
the gate called "Beautiful." From the "court of the Gentiles" the
ascent to this gate, according to Josephus, was by fourteen steps.
The Talmud gives the number as twelve. The gate itself was of
Corinthian brass, and so massive that it is said to have required the
united strength of twenty men to open and close it.

28. Entering the temple precincts from the east, one found himself in the so-called "court of the women." It was so named not
because of its exclusive use by women, but because women were
not allowed to proceed further except for the purpose of sacrifice.
Jewish authorities assure us that the place was frequented by all
classes of worshippers, the women occupying raised galleries on three
sides of it. There was also a colonnade on three sides of the court.
At one point of it were found, it is probable, the thirteen trumpet-
shaped receptacles for contributions; each one being marked with
the object for which the money was given. Nine were for legal dues
and four for free-will offerings. Here we may suppose our Lord saw
the poor widow cast her two mites into the "treasury."

Fifteen steps, in the form of a half circle, led up from the "court
of the women," through another magnificent gate, into the "court
of Israel." It was on these steps that the Levites were accustomed,
at the feast of tabernacles, to sing the fifteen psalms of degrees.
Some have even supposed that the title of these psalms arose from
this circumstance, but it is not probable. The "court of Israel"
was really one with that of the priests, the latter being simply a
little higher than the former, the ascent to it being by two steps.
The line of division between them was marked by an ornamental
stone balustrade. According to the Talmud, the "court of Israel"
was only a narrow strip of about eleven cubits, in front of the "court
of the priests," and having the width of the temple area. Josephus[1]

[1] Josephus, *Wars of the Jews*, 5, 5:6.

claims that it extended to this depth around the entire temple. Beyond this boundary priests alone could ordinarily go. In case of sacrifice, where the laying on of the hands of the person presenting the victim was required, admission to the "court of the priests" was of course allowable even to the laity.

29. The "court of the priests" encompassed the temple on all its four sides. Inclusive of that of Israel, it measured one hundred eighty-seven cubits from east to west, and one hundred thirty-five from north to south. Access to it for priests, as we have seen, was not simply through the "court of the women," that is, from the east, but also by three gates on the north and south sides respectively. Chambers and depositories were built in convenient places along the inner walls. On the west side of the space and on still higher ground stood the temple. The open space in front of it was occupied by the huge altar of unhewn stones, not less than forty-eight feet square at the base, decreasing as it went upward to thirty-six feet, and, inclusive of the horns, fifteen feet high. An inclined plane forty-eight feet long by twenty-four broad approached it from the south. A careful system of drainage carried from its southwest corner the refuse of the altar into the Kedron valley. Twice in the year, at the passover and the feast of tabernacles, the stones of the altar were whitened. On the north side of the altar were all the needed requisites for the sacrifices: rings for binding the victims to be slain, eight marble-covered tables for their flesh, and columns provided with hooks for suspending it. Nearer the temple, but toward the south, was a colossal brazen reservoir for water, supported on the backs of twelve immense lions. The reservoir was filled anew each day by machinery. The aqueduct that brought water to the temple had a total length of forty miles. From the "court of the priests" to the temple proper there was a flight of twelve steps.

30. The grandeur of this structure, built entirely of white marble and lavishly gilded, must have been indeed imposing. Josephus alleges that the stones of its foundations were solid marble blocks measuring sixty-seven and a half by nine feet. The figures seem extraordinary; but stones measuring forty feet in length, and weighing over one hundred tons, have already been excavated from its ruins. The temple was entered through a porch. It was broader than the main building, extending beyond it thirty feet on each side. Altogether, it was one hundred and fifty feet broad and of the same height, standing thus like a gigantic wall sixteen and a half feet thick in front of the temple. Josephus states its thickness as twenty

cubits, possibly confounding it with its excess of width over that of
the temple on each side. The entrance, which was not provided with
a door, was sixty feet high and thirty broad. Josephus, who is here
less trustworthy than the Talmud, makes the figures in this case also
greater. The gateway and adjoining walls were covered with ele-
gant carvings and gold leaf. A golden eagle, which Herod originally had placed above it, was some years later torn down by an
infuriated mob of Jews.

31. Passing through the porch, an ornamental door, covered on
the inside by a curtain, led into the interior of the temple. The
measurement of the temple within, including the holy place and the
oracle, was ninety feet in length by thirty broad, and sixty feet high.
The oracle occupied, as in the earlier sanctuaries, one third of the
space. The holy place was furnished with the customary articles:
the table of shew-bread, the golden candlestick, and the altar of
incense, the latter being between the other two and the candlestick,
on the south side. A wooden partition, as some maintain, separated
one part of the temple from the other. A vail hung over the door
which admitted to the oracle—the vail that was rent in twain at the
death of our Lord. It is minutely described in the Talmud, and is
said to have been so heavy that three hundred priests were required
to hang it. Other authorities hold that there were two vails suspended here, a cubit apart, and that there was no other partition.
In the oracle there was to be found nothing except the large stone
before mentioned, near which, once in the year, the high priest performed the rites of the day of atonement.

32. Like the temple of Solomon, this one had a series of chambers
built against the outer walls on three sides. They were thirty-eight in
number and three stories high. Fifteen were on the north and south
sides, respectively, and eight on the west side. One could easily pass
from one to another of the rooms, as also, by means of winding staircases, from one story to another, and to the roof. The principal
entrance to the side chambers was on the northeast corner of the
temple. Their roof was sixty feet from the ground. Above the
temple proper, also, there was built a large room having the same
length and breadth as the main building, and being sixty feet high.
As the porch was but one hundred and fifty feet high, this addition
on the top of the temple, reckoning in the thickness of the floors,
did not fall so far short of it as is commonly supposed. The whole
temple, excepting the porch, was surmounted by a gabled roof of
cedar wood armed with golden spikes, and surmounted by a magnif-

icent balustrade. The room over the temple was entered through a door that opened upon the roof of the southern tier of side chambers.

33. The government of the sanctuary was entirely in the hands of priests and Levites. At their head stood the "captain of the temple," of whom we several times hear in the Acts.[1] His position was regarded as only second to that of the high priest. Under him were others having the same title, but subordinate in authority.[2] The duties of the officers of the temple were manifold. Sentries composed of Levites were stationed at twenty-one different points, mostly at the gates; and in three places there were guards of priests. The temple watch was changed at noon each day. It cannot be wondered at, in view of what has been said of this remarkable structure, that the disciples of our Lord, as they lingered on one occasion on the sides of Mount Olivet and looked down upon it all aglow with the rays of the setting sun, desired to call his special attention to it.[3] Strange as his sad prediction concerning it may have then appeared, its essential fulfillment was witnessed by some of those very disciples. In A.D. 70 Roman soldiers, under the command of Titus, applied the torch that reduced to blackened ruins this last and most splendid of the Jewish temples.

34. THE SYNAGOGUE.—The synagogue was an institution that arose after the return of the Jews from the Babylonian exile. Once started, a natural effort was made to show that it had its basis in the earliest history of the people. Two of the Targums actually represent Jacob and Rebekah as worshipping in a synagogue. Such passages as Isaiah 55 : 6 and Psalm 82 : 1, containing not the remotest reference to such institutions, were, by a rabbinical exegesis, made to apply to them. The word synagogue is to be found, it is true, in our English Bibles as early as Psalm 74 : 8, "They have burned up all the synagogues of God in the land." But it would now be generally conceded that, if the reference be to synagogues in the ordinary sense of that term, it would be a pretty conclusive proof that this psalm arose after the Babylonian exile. There is no trace of the institution in the law or the prophets. The rise of it, on the other hand, may be readily discovered in the history of the exiles before spoken of, especially in connection with the efforts made among them to become indoctrinated in the book of the law.[4]

One of the fundamental characteristics of the synagogue was that it was a place of instruction.[5] It was instituted and maintained

---

[1] Acts 4 : 1; 5 : 24, 26.   [2] Luke 22 : 4, 52.   [3] Matt. 21 : 1, 2.   [4] Neh. 8 : 8.   [5] Josephus, *Against Apion*, 2, 17.

less for purposes of worship, although the simpler forms of worship were observed in it, than to communicate, and keep fresh among all classes of the people, a knowledge of God's will as contained in the Old Testament. And it was because this end seemed so pre-eminently important to post-exilian Judaism, and so essential to the right exercise, and even the continued existence, of its institutions, that it endeavored to find a historical basis for it in earlier practice. The synagogue was especially adapted to the Jews of the dispersion. It found a speedy welcome among them. In the time of our Lord there were few communities of these Jews in any part of the world that did not enjoy a synagogue, to say nothing of the multitude that were planted in Palestine. We read of them as found not only in such small places as Nazareth,[1] but also in Damascus,[2] in Salamis on the island of Cyprus,[3] in Iconium,[4] in Thessalonica,[5] in Berœa,[6] Athens,[7] Corinth[8] and Ephesus.[9] In a council held at Jerusalem to consider certain points in dispute among early Christians, it is said, " For Moses from generations of old hath in every city them that preach him, being read in the synagogues every sabbath."[10]

35. The synagogue proper is not to be confounded with another somewhat similar institution to which reference is made in Acts 16 : 13. Places were sometimes extemporized under the open skies where meetings for worship might be held. Generally they were to be found on the sea-coast or a river's bank, because of the frequent lustrations required by the Jewish ceremonial law. Ten men in any community, who were so disposed, were a sufficient number to form a synagogue. In a large city like Jerusalem or Rome there were many of them.[11] They exercised not only religious but also, to some extent, civil jurisdiction over their membership. In purely Jewish communities, as in some parts of Palestine, the entire civil authority was vested in them. A distinction, however, is to be made between the elders of a Jewish community, in whose hands were its civil and religious administration in general, and those who took part in the public services of the synagogues. The latter did not form a permanent class. Any competent member of the community was eligible to officiate in turn in the exercise of these functions: read passages from the Scriptures, offer the usual prayers and benedictions, and make remarks upon the selections of Scripture read. Numerous

---

[1] Matt. 13 : 54.   [2] Acts 9 : 20.   [3] Acts 13 : 5.   [4] Acts 14 : 1.   [5] Acts 17 : 1.   [6] Acts 17 : 10.   [7] Acts 17 : 17.   [8] Acts 18 : 4, 17.   [9] Acts 18 : 19, 26.   [10] Acts 15 : 21.   [11] Acts 6 : 9.

are the instances where we find our Lord taking advantage of this
privilege, and there is no recorded instance where it is disputed.[1]

There were, it is true, officers of the synagogue; but their business
consisted simply in keeping order and seeing to it that the required
services went on in the usual way. This was especially the case with
the so-called "ruler of the synagogue," of whom we read in several
passages.[2] He attended also, it is likely, to all matters that concerned
the building and its furnishing. Each ordinary synagogue, it would
appear, had but one such ruler or president. In Antioch, on the
other hand, there were several of them. We are told but little concerning this officer, and know nothing of the class to which he belonged, or on what terms or for what period he held the office. It
is to be assumed that he was a prominent person in the community,
and most probably belonged to the body of elders to which the
management of its affairs in general was committed. Besides the
"ruler of the synagogue," there were connected with each institution of this kind a number of minor officials, answering somewhat to
deacons in the Christian church. It was their business to keep the
building clean; open and close it for worship; during the services
to hand the roll of the Scriptures to the person called upon to read
them; assist in the execution of sentences there pronounced; collect
and dispense alms, and the like.[3]

36. The word synagogue is of Greek origin, and literally means a
gathering together. Like the word church the term was used to designate both an edifice and the people accustomed to meet in it. Ruins
of ancient synagogues are still to be found in the Holy Land, especially in Galilee. They date back to the second or third century
of our era. It has even been supposed, though the matter is in dispute, that the ruins of the very building in Capernaum to which
allusion is made in Luke 7 : 5 have recently been unearthed. In
selecting a site for a synagogue, the principle seems to have governed,
to get the highest and most conspicuous point of land in the place.
Probably the passage in Isaiah[4] that speaks of the house of the Lord
as being established "in the top of the mountains" had something
to do with the custom. If such a site were impracticable, the place
of greatest resort was sought for the building, and a pole was often
attached to it in order that it might be higher than those in its
neighborhood.[5] (See illustration, page 305.)

---

[1] Matt. 4 : 23; 9 : 35; 12 : 9; 13 : 54.   [2] Mark 5 : 22; Luke 13 : 14; Acts 13 : 15; 18 : 8, 17.
[3] Matt. 6 : 2; 10 : 17; 23 : 34; Mark 13 : 9; Luke 21 : 12.   [4] Isa. 2 : 2.   [5] Prov. 1 : 21; cf.
Matt. 6 : 5.

The most common form of the synagogue on the inside was a rectangular space with single or double colonnades. The amount of carving and other embellishment depended on the skill of the builder or the pecuniary ability of the community. The space was divided much on the same principle and in the same manner as that of the tabernacle and temple. The part of the building nearest the door corresponded to the "court of the women," the separation of the women being observed in the worship of the synagogue as in that of the temple, the rabbis basing the practice on Zechariah 12 : 11–14. The inner and higher portion, which began near the centre, represented the sanctuary proper, and contained the so-called ark with the rolls of Scripture. It was not absolutely essential that worship in order to be legitimate should be conducted in a building specially set apart for the purpose. In cases of necessity rooms in private houses were used. In harmony with this practice was that of the early Christians in their worship.[1]

Synagogues were so constructed that on entering them the worshipper faced toward Jerusalem. In the front and centre of the elevated platform stood the reading-desk, where the Scriptures were read and addresses delivered.[2] The ark or chest containing the rolls was near the posterior wall. Before it was drawn a vail answering to that of the holy of holies, and above it was suspended a lighted lamp, which was never allowed to go out. A candlestick with eight branches stood at one side, that was lighted only at the feast of dedication. While the congregation generally sat, or stood, facing the ark, the more distinguished members of the community were accommodated with seats which faced the congregation. These were considered the "chief seats of the synagogues," and were coveted by those who sought glory of men.[3] Possibly the same custom was carried over, in some degree, into the Christian church, and it may be this which we find so forcibly rebuked in the epistle of James.[4]

37. Every Sabbath day the Jews were accustomed to assemble in their synagogues for prayer and the reading of the Scriptures. The service of song was unknown to them. The public services were introduced by two benedictions recited by all. A sort of creed followed, based on several passages from the Pentateuch.[5] Then came another benediction if it were a morning service, two of them if it were an evening service, the last being a form of evening prayer. Next followed a more formal prayer made up, at least in part, of the

---

[1] Acts 2 : 46; 5 : 42.   [2] Neh. 8 : 4.   [3] Matt. 23 : 6.   [4] James 2 : 2, 3.   [5] Num. 15 : 37–41;
Deut. 6 : 4–9; 11 : 13–21.

eighteen (now nineteen) so-called "eulogies," still extant in the Talmud. It was offered just in front of the ark, as the former part of the service had been conducted at the reading-desk. The leader was some person selected from the congregation for the purpose, and he prayed standing. The congregation also stood, although in the temple they were accustomed to prostrate themselves, and at close of the several prayers responded with an "amen."[1]

The same person who conducted the devotional part of the services led also in the reading of the law. Others, to the number of at least seven, assisted him in it. The reading was begun and closed with a benediction. In the earlier times the entire Pentateuch was so divided into sections that the whole of it could be read through in three, or, as others say, three and a half, years. At present it is divided into fifty-four sections, and, allowance being made for intercalary months, the whole is read in a single year. The reading of a section from the law was followed by that of one from the prophets.[2] Under the head of prophets, the historical books of Joshua, Judges, Samuel and Kings were included. The prophetical portions might be read by a single person. As the reading was in Hebrew, which had already become a dead language two centuries before Christ, an interpreter stood by to interpret the law verse by verse. The prophets, on the other hand, might be interpreted three verses at a time.

The reading of the prophets was, or might be, followed by an address based on the passages read. It could be made by any mentally-competent person present. In the light of these facts new interest is given to the record of our Lord's words in the synagogue at Nazareth when "he began to say unto them, To-day hath this scripture been fulfilled in your ears. And all bare him witness, and wondered at the words of grace which proceeded out of his mouth."[3] The reading was done standing. The address was made in a sitting posture. The right of private members of the synagogue thus to speak, conceded in the time of our Lord, ceased in the second century, when it was limited to the eldership. The order of service just given was that for the Sabbath; a simpler form was in use for week days (Mondays and Thursdays), when also regular assemblies for worship were held. A portion only of the law was read on these occasions, and the reading might be participated in by three persons instead of seven. Similar gatherings, moreover, took place on the great festival days, when passages of Scripture specially selected for the purpose were read.

[1] Matt. 6:5; Mark 11:25; Luke 18:11.   [2] Acts 13:15.   [3] Luke 4:21, 22.

CHAPTER XIII.

THE PRIESTHOOD.

1. IF Israel had been fitted for the privilege, the whole nation, instead of a single tribe, might have enjoyed the prerogatives of the priesthood. To this effect were the words addressed to Moses on Mount Sinai just before the giving of the law: "Thus shalt thou say to the house of Jacob, and tell the children of Israel; Ye have seen what I did unto the Egyptians, and how I bare you on eagles' wings, and brought you unto myself. Now therefore, if ye will obey my voice indeed, and keep my covenant, then ye shall be a peculiar treasure unto me from among all peoples: for all the earth is mine: and ye shall be unto me a kingdom of priests, and an holy nation."[1] This may be said to have been the ideal toward which the divine institutions in the Mosaic period pointed. And even in the lowest stages of moral corruption to which it sunk, Israel was never permitted to lose sight of its high destination. For this purpose it was that through circumcision every male Israelite bore in his flesh the sign of his consecration; and through another divine appointment carried on his ordinary dress a badge to indicate that he belonged wholly to God.[2]

The people of Israel came far short, it is true, of reaching the mark of their high calling. Still, it was of unspeakable value during the time of preparation, especially as an educating influence, that there should be a standard of this sort. It was needful to show that the law could make nothing perfect; that it was necessary to bring in thereupon "a better hope." The apostle Peter, addressing his Christian brethren, tells them that they have attained that which was ever the goal of the chosen people: "But ye are an elect race, a royal priesthood, a holy nation, a people for *God's* own possession."[3]

2. Hence the setting apart to divine service, in the priesthood, of one tribe of Israel in place of twelve was for the time, so to speak, a needful expedient. It was the best means of finally attaining that which was at present unattainable. A direct historical occasion for such consecration was offered during the exodus from Egypt. In the last fearful plague which came upon the Egyptians, when the

---

[1] Ex. 19 : 3-6.   [2] Num. 15 : 37-40; Deut. 22 : 12.   [3] 1 Pet. 2 : 9.

315

firstborn of man and beast were slain, Israel, as usual, had escaped. For this act of mercy God justly claimed recognition. He said to Moses: "Sanctify unto me all the firstborn, whatsoever openeth the womb among the children of Israel, both of man and of beast: it is mine."[1] Subsequently it was enjoined that in place of the firstborn of all the tribes, the whole tribe of Levi, with its cattle, should be given up to Jehovah for special service. As, however, they did not number as many as the firstborn of all the tribes, it was required that for the remaining two hundred and seventy-three, five shekels apiece should be paid to the priests, that is, to the sanctuary. Ever afterwards this sum continued to be the price paid for the redemption of the firstborn of man or beast.[2]

Within the tribe of Levi which had thus been divinely set apart for the service of the sanctuary a marked distinction was at once made. A part of it, Aaron and his sons, was designated for priests, the rest to be their attendants and ministers. It was a divine arrangement throughout. "No man," says the epistle to the Hebrews, "taketh the honor unto himself, but when he is called of God, even as was Aaron."[3] The special duties of the Levites, in distinction from the priests, are laid down in the following passages: Numbers 3:6-10; 18:2-6. During the sojourn in the wilderness, for example, it fell to them, when required, to take down and put up the tabernacle; to transport it on their shoulders, or in wagons provided for the purpose, and, when at rest, to take care of it; provide the shew-bread, the means for the ordinary offerings; and perform other similar services that the priests might demand of them as their assistants.

3. The ceremony of consecration for the Levites was much simpler than that for the priests.[4] The "water of expiation" was first sprinkled upon them. Their clothing was then washed and their persons bathed and shaved. Following this, the congregation of Israel, through their representative, laid its hands upon their heads, and Aaron offered them "for a wave offering before the Lord;" that is, led them toward the altar and back again. The ceremony was concluded with an offering of consecration consisting of two young bullocks, the one being for a sin offering and the other for a burnt offering.

4. PREREQUISITES FOR THE PRIESTHOOD.—Aaron, who was designated for the high-priesthood, was an elder brother of Moses.[5]

[1] Ex. 13:2.   [2] Num. 3:11-51; 8:14-18; cf. Ex. 32:26.   [3] Heb. 5:4.   [4] Num. 8:6-21.
[5] Ex. 28:1.

His sons, who were appointed to the office with him, along with their male descendants, were Nadab, Abihu, Eleazar and Ithamar. Of these sons the first two were early put to death for the crime of offering false fire before the Lord.[1] Of the remaining two, Eleazar succeeded to the priesthood on the death of his father.[2] After him came Phinehas his son.[3] At a later period, for some reason unrevealed, we find Eli, a descendant of Ithamar, holding the position.[4] At the time of Solomon, during the high-priesthood of Zadok, the succession again reverted to the line of Eleazar.[5]

· Descent from Aaron gave only a hereditary right to the office of priest. Certain other qualifications were also essential. Nothing is said in the Bible concerning the age of a candidate; but it is not unlikely that the law for the Levites was here, too, considered binding which placed the age of service at twenty-five or thirty years.[6] It was probably fixed for the Levites at thirty, during the more trying period of the sojourn in the wilderness. Tradition, however, fixes the legal age for entering upon the duties of the priesthood at thirty. The law for the priesthood, moreover, required that one should be free from any serious physical defect, like blindness, lameness and others fully detailed in Leviticus 21 : 17–23. Physically-incapable priests were provided for out of the common fund, but might not officiate at the altar. The Talmud enumerates no less than one hundred and forty-two blemishes which disqualified from the priesthood. While officiating at the sanctuary priests were not allowed to indulge in wine or strong drink. Except in the case of near relatives, they were not permitted to defile themselves by touching a dead body or even to disfigure themselves in their mourning. Even the rending of the garments and the neglect of any public duty was prohibited to them on such occasions.[7] It was further required of a high priest that he should only marry a virgin of Israel, and, in later times, that he himself should not have had for a mother one who had been a captive.[8]

5. CONSECRATION.—All priests, at least in the first instance, were solemnly set apart to their office by a special ceremonial. The details of it are given in Exodus 29 : 1–44; Leviticus 8 : 1–36; cf. Exodus 40 : 12–15. It took place at the door of the tent of meeting, in the presence of the entire congregation. The bodies of the candidates were first bathed with water and invested with the holy gar-

[1] Lev. 10:2.　[2] Num. 20:26.　[3] Num. 25:11-13; Judg. 20:28.　[4] 1 Sam. 14:3; cf. 1 Sam. 2:9.　[5] 1 Kings 2:27; 1 Chron. 24:3.　[6] Num. 4:3; 8:24, 25.　[7] Lev. 21:1-6, 10-15.　[8] Josephus, Antiq. 3, 12:2.

ments. Next followed the anointing with a composition specially prepared for the occasion and used nowhere else. It was made up of myrrh, cinnamon, cassia and calamus mingled with the purest olive oil. This ointment was poured on the head. The ceremony of anointing was followed by sacrifices in which it was not Aaron and his sons, but Moses, who officiated. They consisted of all the three kinds recognized in the law: the sin offering, the burnt offering and the peace offering. Along with the last a peculiar ceremony took place. When Moses had slain the victim, he took of its blood, "and put it upon the tip of Aaron's right ear, and upon the thumb of his right hand, and upon the great toe of his right foot." The same was also done in the case of Aaron's two sons. It was a most impressive symbol of the completeness of the consecration required of them. The ceremonies of the first day were concluded by Moses sprinkling the blood of this victim, commingled with the anointing oil, on the garments of Aaron and his sons.

It was held by the rabbins that the ordinary priest at his first consecration was simply touched on the forehead with the anointing oil. The same opinion has been adopted by not a few modern critics and commentators; some, however, holding that the only anointing they had was the sprinkling with oil and with the blood of the sacrifice offered at the close of the first day. But it is clear from numerous passages that the ordinary priest was also regularly anointed at this time.[1] It might be inferred, too, from the fact that he was treated in the same way as the high priest in the subsequent use of the oil.[2] The fact that the high priest alone was called the "anointed priest" had its sufficient basis in the circumstance that, subsequent to the first anointing, it was repeated only for him and not for the ordinary priest. There is no evidence that in the period of the exile or afterwards the high priest himself was anointed.

Seven entire days were devoted to the services of consecrating Aaron and his sons to the priesthood. Those of the first day have been already described. On the second and each of the five others the same sacrifices were offered.[3] During the whole period Aaron and his sons were obliged to remain in their places before the tent of meeting. The rabbinical tradition is that, in addition to the sacrifices, the candidates were also each day anointed. The Scriptures do not affirm this; but it is certain that the altar was daily anointed.[4] On the eighth day, the ceremonies of consecration being over, the

---

[1] Ex. 28:41; 30:30; 40:15; Lev. 7:36; 10:7; Num. 3:3.   [2] Lev. 14:18.   [3] Ex. 29:35; Lev. 8:33.   [4] Ex. 29:36.

newly-anointed priests entered upon their service by first offering a sin and a burnt offering for themselves; and the same, together with a peace and meal offering, for the people.[1]

6. DUTIES OF THE PRIESTS.—As a matter of course, the duties of the priests were mostly in connection with the tabernacle and temple. No others were competent to offer sacrifices at the altar. It was specifically forbidden to the Levite to "come nigh unto the vessels of the sanctuary and unto the altar [that is, in the way of public service], that they die not." It was the province of the priests to mediate between God and his people, receiving from the latter's hands the offerings they brought, and blessing them in the name of the Lord.[2] It was their duty to offer incense, morning and evening, in the holy place; to cleanse the golden candlestick and provide it with oil; and, each Sabbath, to remove the shew-bread from the table and put fresh bread in its place. It was incumbent on them, too, to keep the interior of the sanctuary clean; furnish a guard at its entrance; and during the sojourn in the wilderness, on breaking camp, to wrap up the sacred utensils in such a form that they might be carried by the Levites.[3] It was for them to see that a fire was kept continually burning on the altar of burnt offering, and that it was freed from ashes and other refuse.[4] Here also, morning and evening, they offered the burnt offering with its meal offering for the congregation; and on the occasions of the various feasts, such other sacrifices as were specially appointed for them.

For such offices as these the priesthood was made wholly responsible. Nor was this all. To them was intrusted the oversight of the Levites;[5] the duty of determining the worthiness or unworthiness of animals offered for sacrifices; as well as the value of objects presented to be redeemed for the uses of the sanctuary.[6] Every leper in Israel came to the priests for examination and instructions.[7] It was they who prescribed the services required in all cases of ceremonial purification taking place at the sanctuary, as in discharging from vows, and for wives suspected of unfaithfulness. They held also the office of teachers, as it respected all the statutes that the Lord had given "by the hand of Moses." The rolls of the law were expressly put in their charge by the lawgiver.[8] They had a duty to do, moreover, as judges. All controversies were peremptorily settled by their verdict. "The man that doeth presumptu-

---

[1] Lev. 9: 1-5.   [2] Lev. 9: 22; Num. 6: 22-27; 18: 3.   [3] Num. 3: 38; 4: 5-16; 2 Kings 12: 9; 25: 18; 2 Chron. 29: 16.   [4] Lev. 6: 8-13. .   [5] Ex. 38: 21; Num. 4: 28, 33; 7: 8.   [6] Lev. 27. [7] Deut. 24: 8.   [8] Deut. 31: 9.

ously"—so runs the law—"in not hearkening unto the priest that standeth to minister there before the Lord thy God, or unto the judge, even that man shall die."[1]

7. To the high priest the whole priestly service stood open. He might do as little or as much of it as he chose. It was customary for him to leave all of it to others, except on the Sabbath and other festival days. There were for him, however, special obligations. Besides the oversight of the sanctuary and its worship,[2] no one but he, as we have already seen, could officiate on the day of atonement.[3] And it was his duty, unless he specifically delegated it to others, to present, morning and evening, the daily meal offering appointed on the occasion of the installation of Aaron and his sons.[4] Josephus informs us that this was done by him "of his own charges."[5] In later times, at least, the high priest had a dwelling in the temple besides one in the city of Jerusalem. During the day he was usually to be found in the former.

8. CLASSES OF PRIESTS AND LEVITES.—From the books of

A Levite.

Chronicles we learn that David divided the priesthood into twenty-four classes, each class representing a family.[6] Their respective heads formed a titled order. Sixteen of the families were from the line of Eleazar and eight from that of Ithamar. The order in which they performed their duties was determined by lot. This arrangement, inaugurated by David, was adopted also by his successors. Each of the classes remained on duty at the temple one week, that is, from one Sabbath to the next.[7] At the same time that David introduced this system for the priests, he likewise divided the Levites into twenty-four classes.[8] In addition to the duties incumbent on them before, others were imposed by him and the kings that followed him. They acted, for example, as singers and musicians; as porters; as trustees of sacred funds and as secretaries.[9] But by far the greater number still remained simple assistants of the priests.

[1] Deut. 17 : 12; 19 : 17; 20 : 2–4.   [2] 2 Kings 12 : 7; 22 : 4.   [3] Lev. 4 : 5; 16 : 16.   [4] Lev. 6 : 20.   [5] Josephus, *Antiq.* 3, 10 : 7.   [6] 1 Chron. 8 : 14; 23 : 16; 24 : 1–18; 31 : 2; 35 : 4. [7] 2 Chron. 23 : 4.   [8] 1 Chron. 23 : 4, 28.   [9] 1 Chron. 15 : 23; 25 : 6; Neh. 12 : 44.

The duties of the Levites in the temple of Herod seem to have been much the same as in that of Solomon and of Zerubbabel. They had in charge the sacred vestments and utensils; the various depositories and their contents; the provisions for the meal and incense offerings; and they acted also as the temple police under the direction of the priests. Other books of the Old Testament, while not directly supporting the statements derived from Chronicles respecting these matters, do so at least by implication.[1]

Of the priests who returned from the exile only four of the twenty-four classes were represented; and there was a still smaller proportion of Levites.[2] In order to restore the original classification of priests, these four, according to the Talmud, drew lots for the rest, and those chosen assumed the names originally borne by the respective classes. It is certain that they were early restored; though at first there were but twenty-two of them.[3] As it concerns the manner of the restoration, it seems quite likely that it was gradually brought about, possibly by the later return or discovery of other priests belonging to these classes, or by the selection, in some way unknown to us, of representative men in their places. It is generally assumed that the twenty-four classes that existed in the time of our Lord still bore the ancient names. It can be actually affirmed, however, only that those mentioned in the later times do bear the names given to them in the period of the exile.[4] Each of the twenty-four courses was made up of a certain number of families, and the services of the week were divided among them according to their number. If there were more families in a course than there were days in the week, they were associated together. On the Sabbath the whole course was expected to be present. At the national festivals priests of any course might join in ministering at the altar; and at the feast of tabernacles all the courses were expected to hold themselves in readiness for service. While one part of a course was on duty at the temple, the rest of it was put under certain restrictions as being liable to be called upon to share in it.

9. DRESS OF THE PRIESTS.—When engaged in service the priests, including the high priest, wore an official costume. This was not required of Levites. The costume of the ordinary priest consisted of four specified articles: a tunic, trousers, a girdle and a turban.[5] The material and color of these articles are particularly named.

---

[1] 2 Kings 11:18; 12:2; 19:2; 22:4; 25:18; Isa. 37: 2; Jer. 19:1; 20:1; 29:26; 52:24.
[2] Ezra 2:36–39.　[3] Neh. 12:1–7.　[4] 1 Macc. 2:1; Luke 1:5.　[5] Ex. 28:40; cf. 29:8; 39:27; Lev. 8:13.

21

The material was byssus (*shesh*), by which cotton may have been meant; or, if not cotton, a fine quality of linen.[1] Why this was enjoined may be inferred from the fact that for a warm climate this material, as compared with goods made from wool, would be both

Dress of the Priest.

suggestive of cleanliness and helpful to it. The color was white; doubtless as symbolical of the personal purity demanded of one who officiated as priest.[2] The tunic was of woven work and was made from one piece. According to Josephus, who, however, probably only represents the customs of his own times, it fitted close to the body, reached to the feet and had sleeves; while the opening for the neck was provided with cords, by which it might be made large or small at pleasure.[3] The trousers seem to have been of the same material as the tunic, but covered only the middle part of the body, reaching from the loins to the thighs, "to cover the flesh of their nakedness" when they went into the tent of meeting, or came near the altar "to minister in the holy place."[4]

Of the material and form of the priest's girdle nothing appears to be said in the Bible. Josephus, probably basing his opinion on Exodus 39 : 29, affirms that the material was of byssus, and that it was embroidered with blue, purple and scarlet, the three colors of the curtains of the tabernacle.[5] He may have correctly stated what was the custom of his own day, and this would most likely have been in general harmony with tradition. In the meantime the text in Exodus seems to refer, though, it must be confessed, not with absolute clearness, to the girdle of the high priest only. We are accordingly left to infer that that of the ordinary priest was of the same stuff and color as that of the rest of his costume. His official

---

[1] Ex. 39 : 28 ; cf. 28 : 42 (in the Hebrew).   [2] Ezek. 44 ; 17.   [3] Josephus, *Antiq.* 3, 7 : 2.   [4] Ex. 28 : 42, 43.   [5] Josephus, *Antiq.* 3, 7 : 2.

dress was completed by the turban. It also was of byssus, and, if we may judge from the Hebrew word used, was of the form of the inverted calyx of a flower. A noun from the same root means a hill. The turban was bound upon the head. Josephus makes no special distinction between the turban of the ordinary priest and the high priest's mitre, except that the latter, according to him, had over it another one of a blue color and embroidered.[1] This cannot well have been the practice in the earliest times. Jewish authorities inform us that when the clothing of the ordinary priest became soiled it was not washed for further use, but torn up and made into wicks for the lamps of the temple.

10. That the clothing of the priests did not remain the same in all periods of Israelitish history, conforming in this respect to the laws given on the subject in the Pentateuch, has been inferred from 1 Samuel 22 : 18.[2] It is there represented that the priests in the tabernacle at Nob wore linen ephods, and this has been supposed to be the very article of dress which in the Pentateuch is accorded solely to the high priest. The ephod of the high priest, however, is never said, in the original Hebrew, to have been of linen, but of "fine linen" (byssus), an entirely different article. Besides, the high priest's garment, as we shall hereafter see, was embroidered. We have no warrant for assuming, moreover, that the priests of Nob, who, on his summons, appeared before Saul at Gibeah, came in their official dress. We should expect the contrary. The linen ephods which they wore may have been a sort of undress uniform, which would have been eminently suitable for them in view of their ordinary apparel. In any case this passage in Samuel does not state that the linen ephod was an official costume of the priests, or that it formed any part of it. The priesthood went barefoot during the discharge of their duties in the sanctuary; at least sandals are never mentioned in such a connection, and their use would have been out of harmony with Oriental ideas of propriety.

11. DRESS OF THE HIGH PRIEST.—The official dress of the high priest differed in several important respects from that of the priest. The close-fitting tunic with sleeves and the short trousers were the same. The girdle, on the other hand, as we have reason to suppose, was originally the one described in Exodus 28 : 39; 39 : 29; although, as we have seen, Josephus makes this also the girdle of the ordinary priest. On a ground-work of white byssus were embroidered the other three colors of the sanctuary, blue, purple and scarlet.

[1] Josephus, Antiq. 3, 7 : 3; cf. Ex. 39 : 8.   [2] Cf. 1 Sam. 2 : 18.

The covering for his head, too, is called in our text by a name different from that applied to the turban of the priest. It seems to have been made of a long strip of byssus or linen, which was wound around upon itself until it took the shape of a very high conical figure. It was doubtless meant to be an essential mark of dignity.[1] Besides these four articles of dress which the high priest had in common with the rest, there were four others in which he was peculiar.[2]

Dress of the High Priest.

12. Over the close-fitting tunic of byssus he wore, first, what is known as the "robe of the ephod," since it was never worn without the ephod. It also was of byssus, but blue in color, without sleeves, and reaching, apparently, only to the knees. It had an opening, provided with a strongly-protected border, "a binding of woven work round about," through which the head was thrust. The lower edge was highly ornamented. Alternating with figures of pomegranates, embroidered in blue, purple and scarlet, there were little golden bells, as the rabbins affirm, seventy-two in number. The object of these bells, according to the Scriptures, was that their sound might be heard when the high priest went into and came out from the holy place before the Lord, that is, the inner sanctuary, on the day of atonement. Some have supposed that the bells, like those used at the mass among Roman Catholics, were to call the attention of the people to the different stages of the ceremony. It seems more probable that they were intended to act as a restraint upon the high priest, and to be a reminder to the people, and as it were to Jehovah himself, that the appointed mediator was there to mediate for Israel.[3]

[1] Ezek. 21 : 26; Zech. 3 : 5.   [2] Ex. 28 : 1–43; 39 : 1–31.   [3] Ecclus. 45 : 9.

13. The second peculiar feature in the high priest's dress was the ephod. Its material was byssus. Into this were wrought threads of gold, blue, purple and scarlet, "the work of the cunning workman." Respecting its form there has been considerable dispute, as the directions given in Exodus are at present not very clear. Following rabbinical precedent, the general opinion has been that it consisted of seven principal parts. There were, first, two pieces to cover the front and back of the body, reaching from the shoulders to the middle of the thighs. Then there were two shoulder-strips, by means of which the front and back portions were connected above. On each of these two strips there was placed an onyx stone (margin of the Revised Version, "beryl") set in gold. The two together had engraved on them the names of all the tribes of Israel. Finally, there was a girdle, "the cunningly woven band," attached to it, and of the same material and workmanship as the ephod, by whose means the latter was held firmly to the body. Another representation of the matter is regarded as more satisfactory by some critics. They would make the two shoulder-pieces considerably wider, and suppose that when they were joined together in front they had the appearance of a narrow cape. The lower part of the ephod, on the other hand, according to them, was a sort of waistcoat or jacket, without sleeves, reaching from below the arms to the waist, and firmly bound about the body by the band already described. Between the shoulder-pieces or cape and the jacket, the blue robe would thus be somewhat visible. Josephus gives still another description, but it cannot be harmonized with the text of the Pentateuch.

14. The breastplate of the high priest, the third peculiar article of his costume, is thus described in the Bible: "And thou shalt make a breastplate of judgment, the work of the cunning workman; like the work of the ephod thou shalt make it; of gold, of blue, and purple, and scarlet, and fine twined linen [byssus], shalt thou make it. Foursquare it shall be and double; a span shall be the length thereof, and a span the breadth thereof." On the breastplate thus made there were placed, in golden setting, four rows of precious stones, three in each row, and on the stones were engraved the names of the twelve tribes of Israel. In what order the stones were placed it is not stated. It was further provided, in its two upper corners, with two gold rings, by means of which it was attached by golden chains ("wreathen work"), passing across the breast, to the setting of the precious stones in the shoulder-pieces. To bind it still more closely to the ephod there were two other gold

rings attached to its two lower inside corners, through which passed strips of blue lace to two rings placed in the lower front edge of the shoulder-pieces underneath. In this way Aaron was to "bear the names of the children of Israel in the breastplate of judgment upon his heart," when he went into the holy place, "for a memorial before the Lord continually."[1]

15. URIM AND THUMMIM.—Again, there were to be put in, or assigned to, the breastplate of judgment the Urim and Thummim,

Egyptian Light and Truth.

literally, "the Lights and the Perfections," that they might be upon Aaron's heart when he went before the Lord, and that Aaron might ever "bear the judgment of the children of Israel upon his heart before the Lord." In some way to us unknown divine decisions respecting Israel were reached by means of the Urim and Thummim. In the history of the people up to the time of Solomon, when both name and function disappear, we find them used in this way.[2] But concerning what they were and how they were used no one has been able to give a satisfactory answer. Josephus supposed that they were not distinct objects, but were identical with the stones of the breastplate, which in some supernatural manner indicated the will of God. Philo conjectured that they were two symbolical images of light and truth which had been worked into the material of the breastplate. Others have thought that they were simply some provision, possibly a couple of precious stones, for casting lots, through which a divine decision was given. It is at least true that in certain instances where we might suppose that the Urim and Thummim would be consulted, we find what appears to be the use of the lot.[3] And if it were permitted to trust the version of the Septuagint, in 1 Samuel 14 : 41, which reproduces, somewhat freely it would appear, the original of an obviously corrupt passage, a direct support would be found for the theory. It reads as follows: "And Saul said, O Lord God of Israel, wherefore is it that thou hast not answered thy servant to-day? If the wrong is in me, or in my son Jonathan, O Lord God of Israel, show light [the Urim], [but if, on the other hand, it be] in thy people Israel, then show right [the Thummim]."

16. The fourth peculiar article belonging to the high priest's cos-

[1] Ex. 28 : 29.   [2] Num. 27 : 21; Judg. 1 : 1, 2; 20 : 18, 23; 1 Sam. 23 : 2, 4, 6, 9-12.   [3] 1 Sam. 10 : 19-22; 14 : 37-42.

tume was the golden plate worn on the front of the mitre and inscribed "Holy to the Lord."[1] It was of pure gold and attached to a strip of blue lace just above the forehead. The object of it is said to be to show that the high priest is to "bear the iniquity of the holy things," that is, to be held responsible if they are not holy, and to make the needful atonement by which they shall be rendered acceptable, when offered by the people. It was a conspicuous object and one of the most suggestive in the whole attire of the chief priest. It has been argued by some that, like a crown, it symbolized the high position, the almost royal dignity, of this official. But in that case it would probably have been of a different form; at least, differently inscribed. It was in another way, according to the book of Zechariah, that this thought was symbolized by the high priest Joshua, namely, by actual crowns of gold and silver.[2]

17. In the time of the Maccabees, however, a crown along with a purple robe was actually presented to the high priest Jonathan, by Alexander Epiphanes, as insignia of office;[3] and Josephus, in describing the costume of the chief priest in his day, speaks of a polished golden crown, of three rows, one above another, out of which there arose a cup of gold.[4] It is probable that the novelty first arose with the Maccabæan Jonathan. It does not appear that even in Josephus's time the crown displaced the simple inscribed plate of earlier days. It has already been stated that the high priest had another costume, wholly white, which he wore while offering the expiatory sacrifices on the day of atonement. In distinction from this and from the dress of the ordinary priest, the other was spoken of as "the finely wrought garments," and in the Talmud as "the golden clothing."[5] The articles were costly and regarded with no little reverence. Until the reign of Hyrcanus, B.C. 135–105, when not in use they were kept in the temple; after this, until the time of Herod the Great, in the adjacent citadel of Antonia, whence they were allowed to be taken on the occasions of the three great pilgrimage festivals and on the day of atonement. After A.D. 36 they were again put wholly within the custody of the priesthood. One high priest received them from another, and, as we have seen, during the whole period of the existence of the second temple, investiture rather than anointing was the ceremony indicating the assumption of office.

18. A fact that should not be overlooked is that the historical

[1] Ex. 28:36; 39:30; Lev. 8:9. [2] Zech. 6:11. [3] 1 Macc. 10:20. [4] Josephus, *Antiq.* 3, 7:6. [5] Ex. 31:10; 35:19; 39:1, 41.

books of the Bible mention a secondary high priest, a personage quite unknown to the Pentateuch. He is called both "second priest" and "ruler."[1] In the Talmud he was known as the "sagan" (sagen, segan), and it was made his duty to officiate when, for any reason, the high priest was incapable. He acted, in general, as assistant to the high priest, and, next to him, exercised control over the remaining priests.

19. MAINTENANCE OF THE PRIESTS AND LEVITES.—The physical maintenance of the numerous priests and Levites was at all times a matter of great importance. It was by no means left wholly to the generosity of their brethren of the other eleven tribes, but express provision was made for it in numerous laws. The principle on which such support was required was not simply that the priests and Levites were performing services in their behalf as their appointed representatives. It was a still higher and more fundamental obligation. All owed tribute from their substance to God. That tribute God relinquished in favor of the tribe of Levi, including Aaron and his sons, to the end that they might devote themselves wholly and untrammelled to the service of their brethren at the sanctuary. Again and again this fact is repeated and impressed upon the children of Israel, and rehearsed, for their encouragement, to the Levites themselves. On this account the latter were not to share with their brethren in the inheritance of the land of Canaan. A tithe, that is, tenth, of their income was to be sacredly set apart by all the remaining Israelites for their maintenance.[2] This was their principal means of support. Outside of it they had, as will be hereafter noted, places to dwell in assigned them, and participated to the amount of one one hundred and fiftieth part in the spoils of war.

From their tithe the Levites were required to give, in turn, a tithe to the priests.[3] It was to be reckoned to them "as though it were the corn of the threshing-floor, and as the fullness of the wine-press." They were to have the privilege, in other words, to be, in so far, themselves almoners of the bounty of God. The tithe they received from their brethren consisted of one tenth part of all the products of the soil, of fruit trees, and of cattle. In the case of land products, if a man chose to pay in money rather than in kind, he could do so by adding one fifth the money value of the tithe.[4] The tithe of flocks and herds was not redeemable. Every tenth one, good or bad, passing under the rod, was the Lord's. If any attempt were made to ex-

---

[1] 2 Kings 25 : 18; 2 Chron. 31 : 13; Neh. 11 : 11; Jer. 52 : 24.   [2] Num. 18 : 20, 21; cf. Deut. 10 : 9; 18 : 1, 2; Ezek. 44 : 28.   [3] Num. 18 : 26-32.   [4] Lev. 27 : 31.

chang it for another less desirable, both were forfeited. It is set down to the credit of Hezekiah that he so stimulated the people of his time to discharge faithfully their duty in the matter of the tithes that additional rooms were necessary in the temple in which to store them.[1]

20. A second tithe was enjoined in Deuteronomy, but it had only indirectly to do with the support of the sanctuary.[2] In the earlier legislation instructions had been given that three times in the year every male Israelite should appear at the sanctuary.[3] This legislation, like that of Deuteronomy, obviously looked forward to a permanent settlement in Palestine. The deuteronomic law, accordingly, made provision for the normal expenses to be incurred on these pilgrimages to the central place of worship. After a tenth of one's income had been given to the priests, a second tenth, that is, a tenth of the remaining nine tenths, was to be carried, either in kind or its value in money, to the sanctuary, and there expended in festive meals. Strict injunctions are given that the Levites are not to be overlooked in such meals.[4]

It is assumed by certain modern critics that what we have here called a second tithe was not really such, but only another, and in fact the earlier, form of the legislation found in the book of Numbers. The latter, as an alleged later development, they thus bring into antagonism with it. Such a theory, however, takes no account of the form of the deuteronomic law, which makes a direct reference, as it would seem, to that of the book of Numbers.[5] A new regulation permitting the slaying of animals for food at home instead of at the sanctuary, as had been required in the wilderness, diminished by so much the former perquisites of the priests. Partly, at least, to compensate for this loss, as we may suppose, the law in Deuteronomy respecting the second tithe was framed.[6] It reads: "And this shall be the priests' due from the people, from them that offer a sacrifice, whether it be ox or sheep, that they shall give unto the priest the shoulder, and the two cheeks, and the maw. [And in addition to] the firstfruits of thy corn, of thy wine, and of thine oil, and [also] the first of the fleece of thy sheep, shalt thou give him."[7] The additions made in the brackets simply serve to show the relation which this law holds to that of Numbers. There, the firstfruits had already been assigned to the priest. Here, the fact is recalled in order to add to what is there said of this new source of income, the first fleece of the sheep.

---

[1] 2 Chron. 31:11.   [2] Deut. 14:23-27.   [3] Ex. 23·14, 17; cf. Deut. 12:18.   [4] Deut. 12:19; 14:27-29; 16:14.   [5] Deut. 18:2; cf. Num. 18:20, 21.   [6] Deut. 12:15.   [7] Deut. 18:3, 4.

The parts of the animal set apart in the later legislation as the portion of the priest are also additional to those given in connection with the peace offerings in the other form of the law.[1] Along with the stomach, which, on account of its fatness, was regarded as a particularly choice morsel, they are here given the shoulder and the two cheeks. There, it is the "wave breast" and "heave thigh." And while, in the earlier legislation, only the peace offerings were included, in Deuteronomy all sacrificial meals made at the sanctuary are indicated, and those in its vicinity. That a second and additional tithe is really referred to in Deuteronomy is confirmed by Jewish usage and tradition. The apocryphal book of Tobit, for example, puts into Tobit's mouth the words, "The tenth part of all increase I gave to the children of Levi, who ministered at Jerusalem; and the second tenth part I sold, and went and spent it every year in Jerusalem; and the third [tenth] I gave *unto them* to whom it was meet." The testimony of Josephus supports the same view.[2]

21. In addition to these two tithes, a third, as already intimated in the quotation from the book of Tobit, was also required. It came, however, only once in three years, and had but an indirect relation to the support of the Levites. The law, found only in Deuteronomy, reads as follows: "At the end of every three years thou shalt bring forth all the tithe of thine increase in the same year, and shalt lay it up within thy gates: and the Levite, because he hath no portion nor inheritance with thee, and the stranger, and the fatherless, and the widow, which are within thy gates, shall come and shall eat and be satisfied; that the Lord thy God may bless thee in all the work of thine hand which thou doest."[3] Some commentators have supposed that this tithe was not additional to the second, but that a special use of the latter was required for the third year. But, as far as the letter of the law is concerned, the same reasoning that would substitute it for the second tithe on the third year would require its being substituted also for the first, and this cannot by any means be admitted.

22. The priests, besides a tithe of the tithe given them by the Levites, were entitled by the Mosaic legislation to receive in the way of support, among other things, the firstborn of men and animals and the firstfruits.[4] These were regarded as sacred to God, and his right in them, as far as they constituted a pecuniary resource, was transferred to the priests. Clean animals, that is, such as might properly

[1] Lev. 10:15.   [2] Tobit 1:7; cf. Josephus, *Antiq.* 4, 8:8.   [3] Deut. 14:28, 29; cf. 26:12.
[4] Lev. 27:26, 27; Num. 18:17, 18; Deut. 15:19, 20.

be offered upon the altar, were presented for that purpose, and sacrificed as peace or as thank offerings. The fat was consumed on the altar; but the " wave breast," the " heave thigh," the shoulder and the two cheeks, with the stomach, fell to the priests. The remainder of the animal, it would appear, was eaten by the owner and his friends at a festive meal. If such animal had blemishes unfitting it for sacrifice, it was redeemed at a specified sum; otherwise it became entirely the property of the sanctuary. No animal could be presented at the altar before it was a month old. The firstborn of ceremonially unclean animals, like the ass and camel, was either redeemed or had its neck broken.[1] The latter alternative was probably resorted to only when, for some other reason, the animal was regarded as comparatively worthless. For the firstborn of an ass a lamb might be brought,[2] which was no inconsiderable concession. The price paid in redeeming an animal was one fifth more than its estimated market value.

23. As already remarked, the so-called firstfruits were also a source of income to the priests.[3] They were of three classes. There was, first, the sheaf of barley that was waved before the Lord as the introduction to the barley-harvest. Having been threshed, a part of the grain was burned on the altar in the form of a meal offering; the rest was the portion of the priests.[4] Again, there was the offering of the firstfruits of the wheat-harvest. It consisted of two wheaten loaves made from two tenths of an ephah of fine flour. After being waved before the Lord, the loaves came into the possession of the priests officiating at the ceremony.[5] Still further, it was made the duty of every tiller of the ground to select from the products of his land and his fruit trees some part to present at the sanctuary. The Talmud named the fruits as wheat, barley, grapes, figs, pomegranates and olives. Honey was also included, and custom admitted lemons. These products having been presented at the altar became the property of the priests, and might be eaten or disposed of in any other way they saw fit. The amount to be presented by any person was left to his own sense of propriety.[6] Again, under certain circumstances land was confiscated to the sanctuary, that is, inured to the benefit of those officiating there. If, for example, a person had consecrated to Jehovah some part of his hereditary estates, it was within his power to redeem it by adding one fifth to the estimated value of its yield before the year of jubilee. If

[1] Lev. 27:27; Num. 18:15. [2] Ex. 13:13. [3] Num. 18:13. [4] Lev. 23:9-14. [5] Num. 15:19, 21. [6] Ex. 23:19; Num. 18:13; Deut. 26:2.

he did not redeem it, or if he sold his interest in it, it fell to the priests at that time.[1] Moreover, the priests received a part of many of the offerings which were presented at the altar. Among these the shewbread may be included. After remaining one week, that is, from one Sabbath to the next, on the table in the sanctuary, it might be eaten by the priests. From the offerings proper there fell to them from the whole burnt offering only the skin of the animal.[2] From the meal offering, which always accompanied the burnt offering, they had that which was left over after the sacrifice. From the rest of the meal offerings they might appropriate whatever remained, excepting that which the priests offered for themselves; that was wholly consumed. What was not used of the log of oil that the leper brought for the ceremony of his purification belonged to the priests.[3] From the thank offerings he first received the breast and the thigh. To these parts, as we have noted above, there were afterwards added the two checks, the shoulder and the stomach. These offerings included all sacrifices made at the sanctuary, or in its vicinity, which were attended by a festive meal.[4] In the case of the sin offering the whole animal, excepting the fat burned on the altar, was set apart as the food of the priests.[5] The same was true of the trespass or guilt offering. Of certain of these offerings, such as were termed "most holy," only priests could partake.[6] Of the rest, their families, including in some instances servants born in the house, might eat. In no case could a stranger or a hired servant eat of flesh any part of which had been offered on the altar as a sacrifice to Jehovah.[7]

24. LEVITICAL CITIES.—The law provided, in addition to these incidental and more precarious means of support, that after settlement in the land of Canaan there should be assigned to the whole tribe of Levi, inclusive of priests and Levites, forty-eight cities among the possessions of the different tribes. Of these thirteen were afterwards allotted to the priests, and six, three on either side of the Jordan, were set apart as cities of refuge.[8] In this allotment, besides the city proper, there was to go with it a tract of land around it for the purpose of pasturage. The property within the cities was the inalienable right of the Levites. If for a time they parted with it, they were at liberty to redeem it whenever they chose. In any case it reverted to them on the year of jubilee. The out-lying pasture lands, on the other hand, they were not permitted to part with on any terms or for any period. These cities, however, being within

[1] Lev. 27 : 16-21.   [2] Lev. 7 : 8.   [3] Lev. 14 : 10.   [4] Lev. 7 : 34; Deut. 18 : 3.   [5] Lev. 6 : 26-28.   [6] Lev. 6 : 29.   [7] Lev. 22 : 10.   [8] Num. 35 : 1-34; Josh. 11 : 4; 21.

the bounds of the other tribes, might be inhabited to some degree by members of these tribes.

The amount of land actually given for the maintenance of flocks and herds is not certain. The matter is stated in these terms: "And the suburbs of the cities, which ye shall give unto the Levites, shall be from the wall of the city and outward a thousand cubits round about. And ye shall measure without the city for the east side two thousand cubits, and for the south side two thousand cubits, and for the west side two thousand cubits, and for the north side two thousand cubits, the city being in the midst. This shall be to them the suburbs of the cities." To some commentators the conditions in the second of these verses seem to be out of harmony with those of the first. They conjecture, therefore, that in the first instance pasture lands only are referred to; while in the second an additional one thousand cubits for gardens and vineyards are conceded. But the second of the two verses seems rather to describe how the one thousand cubits of land allotted for pasturage are to be measured. The line is to extend from the wall of the city one thousand cubits. Hence, measuring from one corner to another, it would be two thousand cubits more than the length of the city wall on that side. In general terms this is probably what was meant. It is by no means necessary to suppose that the Bible intends to represent that all the Levitical cities were surrounded with walls exactly square, or that the walls ran precisely north and south and east and west.

25. As part of a widespread effort to show that the history and institutions of the Jews are a purely natural development, it has been maintained that such development is particularly illustrated in the case of the Levitical priesthood. But this can only be shown by refusing to accept the biblical record as genuine and authentic. As already noted, the anointing of the high priest was an important part of his induction to office, according to what purports to be a Mosaic law. At the time of the Babylonian exile, however, when, according to the critics referred to, the institutions of Judaism reached their culmination, such a practice of anointing had already ceased, and it is never heard of afterwards. Again, the Urim and Thummim, according to the same Mosaic law, were an essential part of the high priest's furnishing; but after the time of Solomon they wholly disappear from the biblical history. To the whole tribe of Levi there are assigned in the Pentateuch forty-eight cities, thirteen of them being allotted to the priesthood. But on the return from the Babylonian exile the priests actually outnumbered those who

served technically as Levites. How is it possible that there should
be so great a disparity between the history of the later times, in
these and many other respects, and the alleged institutions of those
times, if they really arose in them?

There is nothing whatever in the Old Testament to encourage the
hypothesis of a priestly assumption of prerogatives to which they
were not entitled by law and precedent. The priests were never
anything more than representatives of the people whom God chose
to be to him a kingdom of priests. Their influence during the
period covered by the biblical books was always relatively small,
especially when compared with that of the prophets. Outside the
sanctuary they were not only deprived of their official dress but
were subject to not a few civil restrictions. Their income, at its best,
was not at all extravagant. We have little reason to suppose that
it ever reached the limits prescribed by law. No penalties were provided in the law itself for violations of its injunctions in this particular. The actual receipts of the priests for their maintenance, accordingly, depended largely on the generosity and religious fidelity
of their countrymen. How unnatural is it, therefore, to find in the
Levitical legislation anything like the programme of a later priestly
class whose demands grew ever greater as their power increased!
How impossible is it to do this when it is made a condition that we
deny the authenticity and genuineness of the documents from which
we get all our information on the subject!

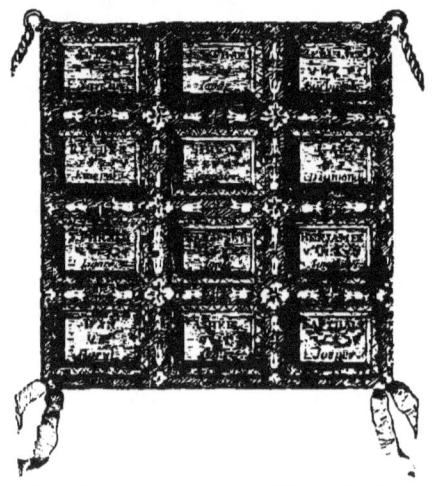

THE BREASTPLATE OF THE HIGH PRIEST.
Indicating the probable arrangement of names of tribes and the stones.

CHAPTER XIV.

1. THE most common way of giving expression to religious feeling in the patriarchal period seems to have been by animal and other sacrifices. The Scriptures represent them as among the earliest acts of men. "Cain brought of the fruit of the ground an offering unto the Lord. And Abel, he also brought of the firstlings of his flock and of the fat thereof."[1] It is not said in the Bible that God at this time, or earlier, himself instituted a system of offerings. If he had done so, the importance of the matter, in view of subsequent laws, would seem to have called for a declaration to that effect. And the reason why he accepted the offering of Abel in preference to that of Cain does not appear to be because the former was from the "firstlings of his flock and of the fat thereof." It was the spirit of the giver more than the gift that he considered. The one was careful to choose the best; the other took, apparently, what first came to hand. It is true that Abel's offering happens to correspond, to some extent, with that which the Levitical laws afterwards prescribe; but the language of the narrative makes it clear that there is here no reflection backwards of a later ritual. The fat spoken of in connection with Abel's sacrifice is not that which in the Mosaic legislation is ordered to be burned upon the altar.

2. Moreover, the Hebrew word used for the offering itself is one that in the Levitical laws never represents animal sacrifices. The whole account is simple narrative. Still it is highly significant as showing how our first parents—for Cain and Abel can have been only imitators—but recently driven from Eden, felt toward God. They were conscious of their dependence; they recognized the divine claim upon them; they desired to propitiate the divine favor. When, at a later period, this childlike symbolism was made the medium of instruction, a vehicle of grace, and it was sought, by its means, to deepen man's sense of dependence and need until the coming of the one true Sacrifice, there was simply done in this case what was done in many another of the Mosaic institutions. Moses was supernaturally led to make use of an ancient custom, correct it where it

[1] Gen. 4: 3, 4.

335

needed correction, curtail it or build upon it as the case might be, and make it a divine law for Israel. The sacrifices of the Old Testament were clearly never intended to be an ultimate means of restoration to God. As a shadow of good things to come, however, as a present resource for setting forth man's relations to his Maker, especially as prefiguring the mystery of the cross, they must be pronounced exceedingly well chosen.

3. The practice of human sacrifices was widely prevalent among the nations of antiquity. It is not strange that it should have been so. It has been thought by some that young children were sometimes sacrificed upon the altar by the Israelites during their sojourn in the wilderness. The inference is drawn principally from the strong prohibitions of such sacrifices in the Mosaic laws.[1] There was a sufficient ground for such prohibitions, however, in the known customs of the Canaanitish and other neighboring peoples.

4. Sacrifices permitted to Israel were animal and vegetable, or bloody and unbloody. The former were naturally regarded as by far the more important. The latter were generally presented as accompaniments of the former; although in a few instances offered independently.[2] The range of objects allowed by the Mosaic ritual to be sacrificed was considerably less than was customary among other nations. For the bloody sacrifices only such animals were taken as were most common with the people, and were, generally speaking, the most useful to them. The same was true of the vegetables used. Besides cattle, sheep and goats, of both sexes, pigeons and turtle-doves were permitted. In cases of extreme necessity the last two might be substituted for the others.[3] The birds used in the ceremony for the purification of a leper were not, properly speaking, sacrifices.[4] It was essential that whatever was offered in sacrifices should be without blemish, and, if an animal, be at least eight days old. It was one of the duties of the priests to make a thorough examination of all animals presented at the altar.[5] The prophet Malachi, accordingly, was justified in exclaiming against the derelict priesthood of his day, "And when ye offer the blind for sacrifice, it is no evil! and when ye offer the lame and sick, it is no evil! Present it now unto thy governor; will he be pleased with thee? or will he accept thy person? saith the Lord of hosts."[6]

5. WHAT THE VEGETABLE OFFERINGS INCLUDED.—The vegetable offerings consisted of roasted ears or heads of grain, fine flour

---

[1] Lev. 18: 21; 20: 2; cf. Ez k. 20: 26.   [2] Lev. 5: 11; 7: 12; Num. 5: 15.   [3] Lev. 5: 7; 12: 8.   [4] Lev. 14: 4.   [5] Lev. 22: 20–24, 27.   [6] Mal. 1: 8.

(or the latter baked into cakes without leaven), oil, wine and frank-incense.[1] They included, besides the ordinary meal and drink offer-ing, the first sheaf at the passover, the shew-bread and the pente-costal loaves. The object here, as in the case of animal offerings, seems to have been to require that which was best known and most used by men and most valuable to them. It was common in Egypt to make offerings of fruits and flowers. They appear to have been excluded from the Mosaic ritual on the ground that they were pro-ductions of the earth which might be obtained without special cost to the offerer. Among the Israelites it was essential to the idea of a sacrifice to Jehovah that it should be property owned by him pre-senting it; that it should be worth something; and that it should be a perfect specimen of its kind. In the later times there was a dis-pute between the Pharisees and Sadducees, in which the former main-tained against the latter that whatever was offered by the nation as a whole should be purchased with funds taken from the revenues of the temple and those voluntarily contributed.

Leaven, as inducing corruption and as a symbol of it, was not used in connection with the vegetable offerings.[2] In the same con-nection with this prohibition (v. 11), and doubtless on the same gen-eral ground, the use of honey as an offering was forbidden. It is true that the two loaves of bread offered at pentecost were leavened, as were also the cakes waved in connection with the peace offerings;[3] but they were simply consecrated by the act, not brought upon the altar. In the latter case, as the context plainly shows, they must have been unleavened. For the same reason that leaven was not used with the meal offerings they were always salted. In the later times the practice prevailed of salting all sacrifices, animal as well as vegetable, and even the incense, the drink offerings and the wood upon the altar.[4]

6. ANIMAL SACRIFICES—HOW PRESENTED.—In the ritual of animal sacrifices five things were generally regarded as essential: the presentation of the victim; the laying on of hands by the offerer; the slaying; the sprinkling of the blood; and the burning of some portion of the animal upon the altar. The Bible neither enjoins nor forbids the ornamentation of animals brought to be sacrificed. It seems quite unlikely that it was practiced by the Israelites, although the Talmud allowed it in a single instance. It was customary among other peoples. In most cases of animal sacrifices the imposition of

---

[1] Lev. 2:1, 4, 14. [2] Lev. 2:11. [3] Lev. 7:12, 13. [4] Cf. Matt. 16:5-12; Luke 13:21; 1 Cor. 5:6.

22

hands was enjoined, as in that of the burnt offering, the peace offering and the sin offering, when private persons were concerned. It is likely that it took place in the case of the trespass offering. When a sin offering was made for the entire congregation, the ceremony of the laying on of hands was performed by the elders as its representatives. At a later period three delegates from the Sanhedrin officiated in this capacity on the day of atonement. The rite obviously presupposes substitution. The desire or purpose of the individual or community was thereby symbolically transferred to the victim. It was not simply sins that were so transferred, but, through the different species of offerings, the act of expiation, of thanksgiving and of self-surrender. In the case of burnt or peace offerings for all Israel there was no laying on of hands, and the same was true in such private offerings as the passover lamb, the firstborn, the tithes of animals, and when doves were presented. It was omitted also in the daily offerings of the sanctuary. The rite itself was a most impressive one; perhaps it might be called the climax of the whole sacrificial ceremony. The Talmud provided that both hands of the offerer should be laid between the horns of the animal. When it was a sin offering, it was made to stand, during the rite, facing somewhat toward the west of north. The offerer approached it from the east and stood at its side, not in front, as he laid his hands upon it. A ceremony somewhat similar in meaning to that of the laying on of hands was that of waving or heaving (elevating) an object presented at the altar. It took place in some of the animal sacrifices, but especially in connection with the vegetable offerings. In the former class of objects the waving was horizontal; in the latter, perpendicular. The rite came into use for the most part only when a small portion of what was presented was intended for the altar.

7. The slaughter of the animal designed for private sacrifice was generally left to the one offering it, except in the case of birds.[1] In public sacrifices, as well as in those for the leper, the animal was slain by the priests. The burnt, sin and trespass offerings were placed, during the ceremony of slaying them, on the north side of the altar. The life was taken in order to obtain the blood. This was carefully drawn by a priest into a cup, which being pointed could not be set down, and sprinkled, according to the nature of the offering, around the base of the altar, on its horns, or before the vail in the holy place.[2] Once in the year only, as we have seen, it was carried into the holy of holies. This use of the blood was based on representa-

---

[1] Lev. 1:15.   [2] Lev. 4:6, 17, 30, 34; cf. Gen. 9:4; Ex. 12:13; Deut. 21:1-9.

tions often found in the Pentateuch and expressed in the words,
"For the life of the flesh is in the blood: and I have given it to you
upon the altar to make atonement for your souls: for it is the blood
that maketh atonement by reason of the life."

After the sprinkling of the blood followed the process of skinning
the animal, dividing it into its several parts and cleansing them.
This duty was done by priests, whose number varied according to
the animal sacrificed. It was made a rule by the rabbis that eight
priests should officiate at the slaughter of a sheep or goat, and the
preparation for the accompanying meal and drink offerings; twelve
in the sacrifice of a ram; and twenty-four in that of a bullock.
When otherwise prepared, the different parts of the animal were
salted and placed upon the altar. A piece once put there could not
be withdrawn. It was sanctified by the altar.[1]

8. The idea of using fire for the destruction of the object sacrificed
was not that it was given over to the consuming anger of God. On
the contrary, as the Hebrew word employed shows, it was simply a
method of bringing it before God and rendering it acceptable to
him. The fire was not "strange fire," but something which God had
originally provided for the purpose.[2] The principal part of the
victim, besides the blood which had been offered in another way,
ascended as a "sweet-smelling savor to God." When fire was needed
for the altar of incense it was not kindled anew, but taken from that
of the burnt offering. This would not have been the case if the fire
used there had been looked upon as a symbol of the divine wrath.
The entire sacrificial code is full of the idea of the satisfaction which
God derived from the burnt sacrifices of his people when rightly
offered.[3]

9. Of the different kinds of sacrifice all were offered either on the
ground of communion with God or with the desire to restore such
communion when broken. To the former class belonged the burnt
and peace offerings; to the latter the sin and trespass offerings. The
burnt offering has in the Hebrew the significant name of *olah*, that
is, that which ascends; referring to the fact that it was wholly consumed upon the altar. It was sometimes named *olah kalil*, that is,
a "whole burnt offering;" in Greek, "holocaust."[4] It symbolized
entire surrender. There is one passage, it is true, where the idea of
atonement is connected with it; for it could not be offered without
the shedding of blood.[5] But it presupposes atonement rather than

[1] Cf. Ex. 29:37; Matt. 23:19. [2] Gen. 8:21; Lev. 1:9; 4:31. [3] Ex. 29:18; Lev. 2:2, 9,
12; 3:5, 6; 4:31; Num. 15:3, 7, 10, 13; 18:17; cf. Eph. 5:2. [4] 1 Sam. 7:9. [5] Lev. 1:4.

looks forward to it. It was one of the most common of sacrifices. A principal part of the daily morning and evening service in the sanctuary was the offering of the burnt offering. None of the great national festivals could be celebrated without it. Even if other animal sacrifices were offered they were regarded as incomplete without this one. It has been questioned whether in cases where the sin and burnt offering were offered at the same time the former always preceded. It seems likely that the practice was not uniform. In instances where the idea of atonement or purification predominated, especially on the day of atonement, the sin offering preceded, in the ritual, the burnt offering; in others, where that which characterized the whole series of offerings was rather adoration and praise than confession, the burnt offering came first. In the case of the discharge of the Nazarite from his vow, the sin offering preceded.[1]

10. THE BURNT OFFERING.—For the burnt offering an unblemished male animal was necessary. It might be a bullock, ram or goat. In the case of poor people, as already noted, turtle-doves, or the young of tame doves, were accepted. These might be of either gender. The blood of the victim was thrown on the altar below the red line, which in the last temple was drawn around it five cubits from its base. If an animal, it was afterwards skinned, the skin becoming the property of the officiating priest. The stomach, the entrails and the "sinew[2] of the hip" were then carefully removed, the carcass divided into sections corresponding to the structure of the animal, washed and salted, and laid upon the fire of the altar. In later times it was customary for the priest first to lay on the head, the rump pieces and fat. He then took the remaining parts, the legs and inwards, which in the meantime had been cleansed by their owner, and placed them above the others.

When birds were offered the officiating priest pinched off the head, allowing the blood to fall upon the sides of the altar. Before it was put on the fire the feathers of the body and wings, the crop, and the entrails with their contents were separated from it. The wings were rent without being removed from the body. The carcass was placed on the altar in other respects entire, the head being burned with the rest. Subsequent to the Babylonian exile it was allowed, on occasions, to offer whole burnt offerings for others than Jews.[3] The emperor Augustus, we are told, had a daily burnt offering, consisting of two lambs and a bullock, presented in the temple of Herod.

[1] Lev. 5:7; 12:6,8; Num. 6:14,16; chaps. 28, 29.   [2] Gen. 32:32.   [3] Ezra 6:10; cf. Ex. 18:12.

Afterwards, when this concession was thought to carry with it a recognition of civil headship, it was refused by the Jews.[1]

11. The Peace Offering.—Another form of sacrifice among the Hebrews was the peace or thank offering. The Hebrew word commonly used for it is *shelamim*, which is a plural, the singular being found only in Amos 5 : 22. The double title arose from the usage of the old versions by which our own was modified. The Latin Vulgate, following the Septuagint, is authority for the name "peace offering." Luther's German version, on the other hand, adopted for the original word the rendering "thank offering." The former title corresponds better with the original word, which carries with it the idea of fellowship and communion with God. Still another name, *zebach*, that is, "slaying" (with the added idea of its being in some sense a sacrifice), is also found in the Pentateuch.[2] In the peace offering only the choicest part of the animal came upon the altar. The thing chiefly emphasized was the accompanying sacred meal. In it God was regarded as the guest of the individual or the community. It prefigured, indeed, the state of things so beautifully set forth in that familiar passage of the Apocalypse, "Behold, I stand at the door and knock: if any man hear my voice and open the door, I will come in to him, and will sup with him, and he with me."[3] The flesh of the animal was symbolically divided between God and his servants the priests, on the one hand, and the owner, with his family and friends, on the other. That which was placed on the altar, the fat of the animal—that is, the fat adhering to the inwards—was for God.

To the priests, as already stated, were given, after they had been waved, the breast, shoulder, two cheeks, stomach and right thigh. The remainder belonged to the offerer, who made a sacrificial meal of it for his friends, including the Levites, strangers, orphans and widows.[4] The skin in this case fell to the person or persons bringing the sacrifice. The blood of the animal, as in the case of the burnt offering, was thrown around the base of the altar. Animals brought as peace offerings might be of either gender; but doves, as being insufficient to furnish a common meal, were excluded. In certain kinds of them, animals having blemishes were accepted, as long as there was nothing in them unfitting them for food.[5] There were two principal forms of peace offerings, public and private. The lambs presented at pentecost, for example, were a public peace offering.

[1] Josephus, *Wars of the Jews*, 2, 17:2.   [2] Gen. 31:54.   [3] Rev. 3:20; cf. Gen. 18:1-10.
[4] Lev. 7:30-32; Deut. 18:3, 4.   [5] Lev. 22:23.

They were regarded as "most holy," and accordingly were slain on the north side of the altar, and their flesh, the fat having been burned, was eaten only by the officiating priests in the holy place.[1] The remaining public peace offerings were regarded simply as "holy," being slain on the south side of the altar; and the designated parts having been severally offered, or given to the priests, the rest was eaten by the offerers, at the sanctuary or anywhere in Jerusalem.

12. As it respects the private peace offerings, it has been too hastily inferred from Leviticus 7 : 11–21 that there were but three kinds (those there specified), and that they were entirely distinct from one another. They may be more properly divided into two classes : such as were legally binding and such as were purely voluntary. To the former class belonged solely the peace offering of the Nazarite.[2] Among the voluntary peace offerings may be distinguished, first, those made because of a vow. They were promised, and subsequently brought to the Lord either in view of past deliverances or for the purpose of securing present divine interposition. There was, secondly, the spontaneous peace offering, which depended on no previous vow or promise, but was the result of a simple prompting of the heart.[3] Thirdly, there was a special sort offered in token of thanksgiving. It might be either a voluntary offering or one that the offerer had taken upon himself as an obligation. It differed from the other two in that in connection with it there was required a meal offering. A shorter time, too, was allowed for the consumption of this species of peace offering ; in other words, it was regarded as more sacred than the others.[4]

13. THE SIN OFFERING.—It is a noteworthy fact that the word used in Hebrew for sin offering is the same as that for sin. It shows that in the Hebrew mind there was a close ethical connection between the two ideas. This kind of offering undoubtedly comes nearest to representing the underlying idea of all bloody sacrifices, and in the list of those legally appointed it stands pre-eminent. In other sacrifices the notion of atonement is merely incidental ; in the sin and trespass (or guilt) offering it is central. And the principal difference between the last two is that the one looks more to satisfaction and restitution, the other to expiation. The one considered chiefly the offence, the other the offender. The ritual of the sin offering was of a much more rigid and serious character than that of the trespass offering. The latter was always accompanied with

<hr>

[1] Lev. 23: 20.   [2] Num. 6: 13, 14.   [3] Lev. 7: 28–34.   [4] Lev. 7: 12 16.

the making of amends; the sin offering sufficed of itself. The trespass offering was of a private and individual character. The sin offering might be for a community or the whole people. The one was brought on festival occasions, the other never. The sin offering was brought in connection with other sacrifices, the trespass offering only by itself, except in a single instance—the cleansing of a leper. In the case of the latter the blood was cast against the sides of the altar; in the other, there was a variety of solemn ceremonies prescribed. With these distinctions there was certainly room for both among Mosaic institutions, and the theory of some critics that the trespass offering is but a later subordinate development from the sin offering has as little biblical as logical support. The only historic basis for it is the fact that in one instance the ram of the trespass offering is called a "sin offering."[1] But as matter of fact, in underlying idea both are sin offerings—that is, offerings for sin. The probable reason why all mention of the trespass offering fails in the pre-exilian history, with the exception of 2 Kings 12 : 16 and notices in Ezekiel,[2] is that it was a purely private offering and never presented for the whole community.

14. As it respects the occasions when sin offerings were brought, they were offered for the whole community at all the great festivals: that of the new moon, the passover, pentecost, new year's day and the day of atonement.[3] In these cases the idea of the offering was purification for past offences. Sin offerings for individuals, on the other hand, might be brought at any time. They were, first, such as were brought without reference to specific transgressions, but had regard to those defilements of the body which directly suggested a corrupt nature: as in the case of one purified after childbirth; the cleansing of the leper; for the Nazarite after the expiration of his vow, and some others.[4] Secondly, they were such as were offered for those who had unwittingly incurred guilt. The law made no provision for persons sinning presumptuously, or with "a high hand," except punishment by death or removal from the congregation. The rabbis, however, greatly extended the list of sins committed "through ignorance." In the earlier practice, doubtless, there were many mitigating circumstances admitted, which brought the more overt transgressions into the class of offences for which atonement might be made.

Some peculiarities of the sin offering, in distinction from the tres-

<hr>

[1] Num. 5 : 8; cf. 2 Kings 12 : 16. [2] Ezek. 40 : 39; 42 : 13; 44 : 29. [3] Num. 28; 29 : 5, 11, 16, 22, 31. [4] Lev. 4 : 4, 14, 23, 28; 5 : 1, 2, 4, 6; 12 : 6-8; 14 : 19; 15 : 15; Num. 6 : 10, 14.

pass offering, have been noted.   Others distinguishing it from other
offerings may also be mentioned.   Only in this was the ceremony
practiced of moistening the horns of the altar of burnt offering
with the blood of the victim.   It was done with the finger.   In the
case of the sin offering alone is it definitely said that the blood remaining after the other rites were finished shall be poured out at
the base of the altar, although, according to tradition, it was actually
done in every instance where animals were sacrificed.[1]   Again, in
certain instances the blood of the sin offering was sprinkled abroad.
This was true when the high priest brought one for himself.   Carrying the blood into the holy place he sprinkled it several times in the
direction of the curtain of the oracle and moistened with it the
horns of the altar of incense.   A similar sprinkling of the blood
took place when a sin offering was brought for the entire people.[2]
The fat adhering to the inwards of the victim, it being a bullock
in these cases, having been burnt on the altar, the rest of the animal
was consumed in some clean place " without the camp."[3]

A plain object of all these rites was to set forth impressively the
fact of uncleanness and the necessity of atonement for it.   How
seriously they were meant to be regarded may be inferred from a single
circumstance.   If in the course of his administration a drop of the
blood of one of the sin offerings fell upon the garment of the priest,
it was to be washed in a ceremonially-clean place.   The earthen vessel also in which the flesh, in the case of some of them, was cooked
for the priests was broken in pieces; if it were of metal it was rinsed
and scoured.[4]   Only the flesh of those sin offerings whose blood was
carried neither into the holy place nor the oracle was eaten by the
priests.   That of the others was burned; because, in these cases, the
priests were among those for whom the sacrifices were offered.   Lit-
urgically speaking, it was this fact that divided the sin offerings into
two distinct classes; though the eating in the one case symbolized
the same thing as the burning in the other—the divine acceptance
of the offering.[5]

The animals presented as sin offerings differed according to circumstances.   In the case of the high priest it was invariably a bullock; for the congregation it was either a bullock or a male goat;
for a " ruler," a male goat; for a private person, a female goat, or
a kid of the same gender and one year old, or a lamb.   In cases of
extreme poverty, two turtle-doves or young pigeons might be sub-

---

[1] Lev. 4: 17, 18.   [2] Lev. 4: 13-21.   [3] Lev. 4: 8 12; cf. Heb. 13: 11-13.   [4] Lev. 6: 27-30.
[5] Lev. 10: 17.

stituted for the lamb; or even one tenth of an ephah of fine wheat flour, without the usual oil and frankincense.[1]

15. THE TRESPASS OFFERING.—As in the case of the sin offering, the same Hebrew word is used to indicate the trespass offering and the trespass for which it was brought. In no other way, perhaps, could the fact have been more forcibly expressed that immediate interposition was necessary to prevent evil consequences. Guilt and the punishment of guilt to the Hebrew mind were thus made inseparable ideas. Like the burnt and sin offering, the trespass offering belonged to those reckoned as "most holy;" that is, such part of it as did not come upon the altar was eaten exclusively by priests in the fore-court of the sanctuary. All such sacrifices, too, were slain on the north side of the altar of burnt offering. "And he shall kill the he-lamb in the place where they kill the sin offering and the burnt offering, in the place of the sanctuary: for as the sin offering is the priest's, so is the guilt [trespass] offering: it is most holy."[2]

Certain correspondences and differences between the sin and trespass offering have already been noted. Still others remain. As it respected the kind and number of animals offered, there was greater limitation here than in the case of the sin offering. More freedom was allowed in the latter because the sin offering was a more fixed and continually-recurring rite, and was an obligation on persons in the greatest variety of circumstances. For the trespass offering, on the other hand, a ram or a he-lamb was alone required. Beyond them, indeed, no choice was permitted, whether the person were poor or rich. In the use of the blood, moreover, as already intimated, the trespass offering corresponded to the other animal sacrifices rather than to the sin offering. In one case only was the blood of the trespass offering differently applied. On the occasion of the cleansing of a leper it was put by the priest on the leper's right ear and toe and the thumb of his right hand.[3]

16. The cases for which the trespass offering was legally prescribed were seven. Those mentioned in Leviticus 5 : 1–6, though sometimes reckoned in this category, really required a sin offering. The first is noticed in Leviticus 5 : 15, 16. It is that of a person sinning unwittingly in the "holy things." The reference is to an improper rendering of the tithes, firstlings and the like. One who by mistake had defrauded the sanctuary was permitted to make restitution by offering an unblemished ram, of a certain fixed valuation, as a

[1] Lev. 4 : 24, 28, 32; 5 : 7, 11; Num. 15 : 24, 27.   [2] Lev. 14 : 13; cf. 1 : 11; 7 : 2.   [3] Lev. 14 : 14.

trespass offering, and restoring the thing withheld, together with one fifth of its value in money. The second case follows in the immediate context.[1] It concerns one who, without direct intention, had transgressed some command of God, which, if wittingly done, would have been punished by death or exclusion from the congregation. The third instance has to do with a man who has dealt falsely with his neighbor in a matter of deposit or of bargain, or has oppressed him, or has found that which had been lost and dealt falsely therein, and sworn to a lie.[2] In such transgressions the man had first to make restitution in full, adding to the same one fifth of the value of the object in money. Secondly, he had to bring a trespass offering to the Lord. It is worthy of notice that the acceptance of the offering is made dependent on repentance, as shown by a voluntary pecuniary satisfaction previously rendered.[3]

A fourth instance where a trespass offering was required was that of criminal intercourse of a man with a betrothed maid.[4] Death was the penalty affixed to this crime in the case of a free woman. Here it is looked upon rather from the Old Testament point of view that another had property rights in the bondmaid. A remark of Delitzsch in this connection will be generally approved: "The Old Testament law makes here a distinction in classes which Christian morality cannot allow." Fifthly, a trespass offering was called for in the ceremony for purifying a leper.[5] It was on the ground that the Jewish community had been unwittingly injured in its standing as well as its support. The offering, however, was not, as in other instances, a ram but a he-lamb; that is, in so far there was a letting up from the full requirements of the law. In like manner and for much the same reason, a Nazarite who had defiled himself by coming in contact with a dead body was obliged to bring a trespass offering.[6] He had been thereby not only interrupted in the fulfillment of his vow, but the time already spent in its fulfillment passed for nothing. He must begin again. On this account some restitution to the sanctuary was considered essential. The pecuniary burden upon him, however, was made as light as possible.

Finally, we read in the book of Ezra of certain men who had married foreign wives that "they gave their hand that they would put away their wives; and being guilty, *they offered* a ram of the flock for their guilt." Their guilt consisted in doing what the law had not indeed directly prohibited—for it had only forbidden inter-

---

[1] Lev. 5: 17–19.   [2] Lev. 6: 2, 3.   [3] Cf. Num. 5: 5–8.   [4] Lev. 19: 20, 21.   [5] Lev. 14.
[6] Num. 6: 6–12.

marriages with Canaanitish peoples—but that which was clearly against the spirit of the law, and brought the little community recently returned from exile into the greatest moral peril. Although the trespass offering is so infrequently mentioned in the Bible after the Mosaic period, when it does appear here in the time of the exile it is as a legal obligation well known and generally recognized.

17. A principal idea underlying animal sacrifices was the childlike one of a meal which the offerer prepared for God. In such a meal vegetables, with bread and wine, might not ordinarily fail; hence the so-called "meal" or vegetable offerings not only accompanied all the burnt and peace offerings, but were often presented independently. In several passages the material of this offering is specifically called "the bread of God."[1] In the case of animal offerings, the animal brought, except it were the first born, might be one which had been reared by the offerer or one bought with his money. In vegetable offerings, on the other hand, only that which the offerer had produced on his own land, and in some of them had prepared in his own house, was admissible. The salt that was added to them, as to all other sacrifices, had a similar meaning, setting forth the idea of friendship and fellowship. No doubt it tended to prevent corruption and rendered the food more palatable. But custom, from the most ancient times, had established that to eat bread and salt with a person was to enter into friendly relations with him, a bond, indeed, which death alone should break.[2]

18. There were certain offerings required which were really vegetable offerings and yet were not technically classed among them. Such was the so-called second tithe described in Deuteronomy 14: 22–27. It was to be eaten "before the Lord," that is, at his sanctuary. Such, too, was the third tithe. A festival was provided from it at home; but none the less was it looked upon as a sacred meal, to which the wards of Jehovah, the Levites, were to be specially welcomed.[3] The first tithe, likewise, which was wholly devoted to the support of the Levites, is definitely named "a heave offering" unto the Lord.[4] In each of these cases the presentation to the Lord is regarded as an essential part of the transaction. The sheaf waved in the sanctuary on the sixteenth of Nisan was a similar offering; also the offering of firstfruits, whose ceremonial is given in Deuteronomy 26: 1–11; the offering of the first of the dough, mentioned in Numbers 15: 20, 21; and the two wave loaves of the day of

---

[1] Lev. 21: 6, 8, 17.   [2] Num. 18: 19; 2 Chron. 13: 5.   [3] Deut. 14: 28, 29.   [4] Num. 18: 24.

pentecost.[1] The last even take the name of "meal offering." The shew-bread, moreover, placed anew on the table every Sabbath was an offering of this sort, as well as the parched grain of the firstfruits spoken of in Leviticus 2 : 14. The last, in fact, marks the point of transition from the vegetable offerings in the broad sense to those employed and spoken of in the narrower technical sense.

19. CLASSES OF VEGETABLE OFFERINGS.—The vegetable offerings proper may be divided, for convenience, into two classes: those

which were brought independently and those which were brought as accompaniments to other offerings. Again, the former class may be divided into those a portion of which was given to the officiating priest and those which were wholly consumed. No part of these offerings was ever eaten by the persons bringing them. They were regarded, in this respect, as "most holy." To the independent meal offerings of the first class was reckoned, first, the presentation of raw wheat flour, mixed with oil and frankincense, described in Leviticus 2 : 1–3.[2] A handful of the mixture was burnt on the altar; the rest was for " Aaron

Supposed Frankincense (*Boswellia Thurifera*).
(*After Dr. Birdwood.*)

and his sons." To the same category belonged, second, the oblation described in the immediate context, consisting of oven-baked unleavened cakes and wafers mixed with oil;[3] also, third, similar cakes baked in a pan and broken up into convenient morsels; and, fourth, what is called a meal offering of the frying-pan.[4]

In each of these instances a " memorial" only was burnt upon the altar. What was left was the priest's. The fifth independent meal offering, that of the firstfruits, has already been described above. It was composed of " corn in the ear parched with fire, bruised corn of

[1] Lev. 23 : 17; cf. Ex. 31 : 22.   [2] Cf. Ex. 29 : 2.   [3] Lev. 2 : 4.   [4] Lev. 2 : 7.

the fresh ear," mingled with oil and frankincense.[1] Sixth, a meal offering was necessary in case a man would put a suspected wife on trial for infidelity to him. It was of barley meal and prepared without oil or frankincense, being a "meal offering of jealousy . . . bringing iniquity to remembrance."[2] All these meal offerings were private and purely voluntary; the last one, however, only in the sense that it was wholly at the option of the husband to subject his wife to trial or not. There was still another which was not voluntary but enjoined by law, where but a part of the material came upon the altar: it was that which was accepted for a sin offering in cases of extreme poverty. It is the sole instance where the idea of atonement is connected with the meal offering.[3]

20. Of the class of independent meal offerings, the whole of which was consumed upon the altar, there were but two: that brought by the high priest at his consecration and daily afterwards,[4] and that required in the ceremony for the purification of a leper.[5] The passage Leviticus 6:20-23 was interpreted by the later Jews to mean that from the time of the first anointing of the high priest he was daily to bring a meal offering. The practice in the time of our Lord was to bring one half of it with the morning, and the other half in connection with the evening, sacrifice. An ordinary priest, however, might represent the chief priest on such occasions; and this, perhaps, met sufficiently well the original law which made the observance binding on "Aaron and his sons."

The meal offerings which accompanied most of the burnt and peace offerings were originally appointed only for the period following the conquest of Canaan.[6] There were certain burnt offerings,[7] as also peace offerings—the two lambs offered at pentecost—which were supplemented by no meal offering. The latter, whenever brought in conjunction with animal sacrifices, and at no other time, had associated with it a drink offering. According to the practice of the Jews, no part of the wine of which it was composed was considered a perquisite of the priests, although the law is silent concerning the matter.[8] It was wholly poured out, it would appear, at the base of the altar. In the Hebrew ritual, as was not the case in heathen religions, wine was never offered by itself.

The law required a meal offering with the daily morning and evening sacrifices, as well as with the additional daily ones appointed for the various festivals, including the Sabbath;[9] with the burnt offer-

[1] Lev. 2:14.　[2] Num. 5:15.　[3] Lev. 5:11-13.　[4] Lev. 6:23.　[5] Lev. 14:10, 20.
[6] Num. 15:2-4.　[7] Lev. 12:6.　[8] Ecclus. 50:15; Josephus, *Antiq.* 3, 9:4.　[9] Num. 28, 29.

ing brought on the presentation of the firstfruits at the passover[1] and at pentecost;[2] with the burnt and sin offerings made for the congregation when it had sinned unwittingly;[3] and with those of the Nazarite when he had completed his vow.[4] In three instances the accompanying meal offering consisted of flour baked in some form: the daily offering for the high priest, the peace offerings brought as a special thanksgiving, and those of the Nazarite.[5] The meal offerings requiring oil and frankincense were those where unbaked fine flour was used; when the same was baked in a pan, a frying-pan or oven; the wafers; the high priest's daily offering, and the flour made from the passover sheaf. The meal offerings requiring only oil were those accompanying a burnt or peace offering. That requiring only frankincense was the shew-bread. Those where neither oil nor frankincense was necessary were the two pentecostal loaves, that made by a jealous husband, and that which was substituted for a sin offering.

The proportion of flour, oil and wine used in the different meal offerings was as follows: In conjunction with a sheep, one tenth of an ephah of flour, one fourth of a hin of oil and one fourth of a hin of wine. With a ram, two tenths of an ephah of flour and one tenth of a hin of oil and wine respectively were required. With a bullock, the amount of flour was three tenths of an ephah, and of oil and wine one half a hin. In the voluntary meal offerings the limit downwards was one tenth of an ephah of flour, and wine and oil in proportion. This amount might be increased to six ephahs of flour, but not beyond; this being the largest amount used in the public meal offerings at the feast of tabernacles.[6] In the case of baked meal offerings the material was brought in the form of ten cakes, except in that of the high priest, when the number was twelve with reference to the twelve tribes of Israel. The latter were broken each into two parts; twelve parts being offered at the daily morning, and twelve at the evening, sacrifice.

21. THE DAILY SACRIFICES.—The daily sacrifices in the sanctuary consisted, first, of a burnt offering of a lamb with its appointed meal offering. This was followed by the meal offering of the high priest. Then came the offering of incense at the altar of incense, and, succeeding this, the drink offering for the previous meal offering, the pouring out of which was accompanied by the blast of trumpets and chanting by a choir of Levites not less than twelve in

---

[1] Lev. 23:13.   [2] Lev. 23:18.   [3] Num. 15:24.   [4] Num. 6:15.   [5] Ex. 29:40; cf. Lev. 8:26; Lev. 7:12-15; Num. 6:15.   [6] Num. 15:1-12.

number. In the second temple forms of prayer were occasionally used. In case of absence from the sanctuary these prayers were repeated by the priests at their homes. On the Sabbath two lambs were offered as burnt offerings, with the appointed meal and drink offerings.[1]

22. Certain modern critics, already several times referred to as a class, profess to find evidence of a prolonged development in the system of Levitical sacrifices extending far beyond the period of the exodus. Such evidence, however, rests largely on a more or less arbitrary division of the material of the Pentateuch into inharmonious documents, and is further supported by an appeal to facts and customs of Israelitish history which are mostly exceptional and abnormal. A certain degree of development in all institutions of the Pentateuch is to be admitted. It was more than a step from the primitive customs of the patriarchs to the sinaitic legislation. It was a very important step from the period of sojourn in the wilderness to that of settled life over a wide extent of territory in Canaan. The legislation of Deuteronomy, promulgated on the eve of the conquest, indicates this advance. It insists, as is done nowhere else, on the centralization of worship: all sacrifices are still to be brought and only brought to one central altar. This may be said to be a distinguishing peculiarity of the deuteronomic form of the law as far as it relates to worship. Worship at a plurality of altars had indeed never been conceded by statute, though the contrary has been alleged, principally on the basis of Exodus 20 : 24. In the wilderness, with the congregation gathered about the tabernacle, there was no need of emphasizing the matter of worship at one altar; but when Israel was about to cross the Jordan there was a special call for it, and it was done.

23. Two considerations are particularly urged against the Mosaic origin of the Levitical system of sacrifices: first, the practice of the Israelites down to the time of David and even afterwards; and second, the alleged attitude of the earlier prophets. Respecting the first point, it is to be admitted that there was much in the practice of Israel during the period mentioned which was not in harmony with the Levitical code. But the modern critic was not the first to discover this. It is either noticed on the spot and stamped as transgression by the historians who communicate the fact; or it occurred in a time of general lapse, like the hundred years immediately following the capture of the ark by the Philistines, when the people

provoked God " to anger with their high places," and he was wroth
with his inheritance, "so that he forsook the tabernacle of Shiloh,
the tent which he placed among men."[1] During this time statute
law largely gave place to common law, and the Israelites fell back
to customs which had ruled before the time of Moses. Even prophets
like Samuel and Elijah, though doubtless under divine direction,
sacrificed at places where the tabernacle was not.[2] This widespread
lapse, with its inevitable consequences of social and political degen-
eracy, was not without its compensations. Israel learned the serious
lesson which needed to be learned, that without Jehovah it could not
prosper. The season of discipline through which it passed prepared
the nation, as perhaps nothing else could have done, to understand
the significance and appreciate the privileges of the temple at Jerusalem.

Respecting the second point, it may be said that there is no valid
evidence that the prophets ever showed any antagonism to the custom of animal sacrifices. When, for example, Jeremiah represents
God as saying, " For I spake not unto your fathers, nor commanded
them in the day that I brought them out of the land of Egypt, concerning burnt offerings or sacrifices,"[3] he cannot have meant to intimate that the sacrificial code of the Pentateuch did not exist, or that
it was not of Mosaic origin or of divine authority. He meant just
what he did in another place when he said, " To what purpose
cometh there to me frankincense from Sheba and the sweet cane
from a far country? your burnt offerings are not acceptable, nor
your sacrifices pleasing unto me."[4] He meant that the Israelites
of his time were building on the outward rite instead of the inward
spiritual fact symbolized by it. These texts can be used against the
existence of Levitical institutions and their acknowledged authority
in Jeremiah's time only so far as they are used to show that the
prophet was hostile to all kinds of sacrifices. But the latter is impossible. He was a loyal Israelite and himself a priest. He elsewhere speaks of animal sacrifices as a crowning blessing of the hap-
pier future before his people.[5]

Jeremiah was a contemporary and coadjutor of Josiah, who was
one of the most zealous of the reforming kings of Israel. He meant
precisely what Samuel meant when he said to the recreant Saul, who
had sought to compensate for deliberate transgression by a public
sacrifice, " Behold, to obey is better than sacrifice, and to hearken

[1] Ps. 78:58-60.   [2] 1 Sam. 7:5-10; 10:8; 11:14,15; 16:2; 1 Kings 13:30-38.   [3] Jer.
7:22; cf. Amos 5:22.   [4] Jer. 6:20.   [5] Jer. 33:18, 21.

than the fat of rams."[1] He meant what the prophet Hosea did when, in rebuke of the gross externalism of his day, he declares as the mind of the Lord, "For I desire mercy, and not sacrifice; and the knowledge of God more than burnt offerings."[2] What was objected to was not the act of sacrificing, above all, not sacrificing in harmony with the Levitical ritual, but spiritual misdirection; a habit of worship which ended with itself and carried with it no submission of the will.

24. CEREMONIAL PURIFICATIONS.—The subjects of purifications and of vows have a close relation to that of sacrifices, and may accordingly be treated here. The Israelitish laws of purification were of a ceremonial nature, and belonged to those "rudiments of the world" which, from the Christian point of view, may well seem "beggarly."[3] Nevertheless they fulfilled an important function in the education of the covenant people, especially in the direction of awakening a consciousness of sin and in preparing the way for the revelation of the one great sacrifice for sin. It is to be noted at the outset that the Hebrew conception of ceremonial cleanness and uncleanness was by no means conterminous with that of sin and holiness. The symbolism was often in danger of being mistaken for the thing symbolized; but in the representations of the Scriptures they were kept invariably apart. Being clean in a ceremonial sense, according to them, indicated simply a state of fitness to be in a certain place and to participate in certain privileges; in other words, that one was in good standing as a member of the Jewish communion. It was otherwise in some ancient religions, as, for instance, the Zend, which showed no capacity thus sharply to distinguish between the real and the apparent.

It is proper to remark also that the Levitical codes do not confound ceremonial with mere physical cleanness, although water played an important part in the rites of purification. They had only this in common, that the one was regarded as becoming in a person's intercourse with God, as was the other in his intercourse with men. As it would have been a mark of disrespect to appear in the presence of an earthly king with an untidy person or a disordered dress, so it was regarded as derogatory to the majesty and purity of Jehovah for one ceremonially unclean—a state symbolical of moral uncleanness and to a certain extent synonymous with physical uncleanness—to appear before him. Hence it was that, before entering

---

[1] 1 Sam. 15 : 22. [2] Hos. 6 : 6. [3] Gal. 4 : 3, 9; Col. 2 : 8, 20; cf. Matt. 15 : 11, 17; Acts 10 : 15; 15 : 9.

23

upon any important public transaction in which Jehovah was especially to have part, as in the giving of the law on Sinai, the people
were commanded to sanctify themselves.[1] This included, besides
certain forms of abstinence, the bathing of their persons and washing of their garments. How closely associated ceremonial cleanness
was with cleanliness is even more strikingly seen in the case of the
priests and Levites. They were required to bathe their persons not
only at the time of their consecration, but it was regarded as a
strictly necessary preparation for the daily sacrifices of the temple.[2]
It is well known that the later Jews made extravagant applications
of the Mosaic laws respecting purifications, besides adding largely
to them. How our Lord regarded all such works of supererogation
may be learned from his rebuke of a Pharisee who had blamed him
for not observing them.[3]

25. Three classes of ceremonial impurities required animal sacrifices as a means for their removal: that arising from contact with
the dead of men or animals; that from leprosy in men, houses or
clothing; and that caused by the morbid fluxes of the human body.
In all these cases that from which purification was really sought was
the corruption induced by death in some of its forms or symptoms.[4]
When viewed in this light the matter assumes a far more serious
aspect than when, as superficially treated by some, it is looked upon
as a social, sanitary or merely ecclesiastical arrangement of the Jewish priesthood. It was for this reason, doubtless, that the defilement
caused by coming in contact with a dead body was regarded as the
worst of all, and that the ceremony appointed to relieve from it was
of so peculiarly solemn a nature. This species of defilement lasted
seven days. It extended not alone to persons who had actually
touched a corpse, but to the place where it had lain, to open vessels
in the vicinity, to those entering such places, even to such as partook
of a feast for the dead, or touched the grave or bone of a dead person in the field.[5] Moreover, those becoming thus unclean commun-
icated their uncleanness to everything they touched.

26. Purification in cases of this sort was effected by the ceremony
of sprinkling with water which had been mingled with the ashes of
a red heifer burned as a sin offering "without the camp." The
sprinkling in the case of unclean persons took place on the third and
seventh days of their uncleanness. At the latter period they were
to bathe and wash their clothing in water. In the case of vessels

¹ Ex. 19 : 10, 11, 15.   ² Ex. 29 : 4; 40 : 12; Lev. 8 : 6.   ³ Luke 11 : 37–40.   ⁴ Gen. 2 : 17.
⁵ Num. 19 : 11–16, 18, 22 ; 31 : 19.

one sprinkling, combined with washing, was sufficient. The ceremony as originally appointed is described in detail in Numbers 19: 1-22. Why the ashes of a red heifer were required it is not possible to say with certainty. It may have been simply to enhance the symbolical import of the rite as a sin offering, red being the color of blood. According to the Mishna two white or black hairs springing from the same follicle rendered the animal unfit. As in other sacrifices, the animal was to be without blemish, one that had never borne the yoke, and, as later custom demanded, between the years of one and five. The cedar wood, hyssop and scarlet used for the sprinkling had each a symbolical meaning. They formed together a sort of brush, the stick of cedar serving as the handle, and the scarlet wool being used to bind the twigs of hyssop upon it.

The ashes of one heifer, as thus used, lasted a long time. It was a tradition of the Jews that not more than nine had been necessary from the days of Moses. It being a public necessity, the expense of it was borne by the temple treasury. In the light of these facts, it is with new interest that one reads the references to this ceremony found in the epistle to the Hebrews: " For if the blood of goats and bulls, and the ashes of a heifer sprinkling them that have been defiled, sanctify unto the cleanness of the flesh : how much more shall the blood of Christ, who through the eternal Spirit offered himself without blemish unto God, cleanse your conscience from dead works to serve the living God ?" In the case of persons who had become unclean by coming in contact with the carcass of an animal, the disability lasted but for a single day. Washing the garments was a necessary condition for its removal.[1] Things which had been thus defiled were also cleansed with water, excepting earthenware, which was broken.

27. The second species of ceremonial defilement was that arising from the leprosy. The law concerning it is given at length in Leviticus, chapters 13 and 14. Leprosy was understood to defile not only the person afflicted with it but any one touching him. If a person entered a house which had been pronounced leprous by the priest, he was made unclean thereby for one day. The rabbins reckoned the leper as among the dead. This thought also appears in the prayer offered by Aaron for Miriam when so visited by a special providence: " Let her not, I pray, be as one dead, of whom the flesh is half consumed when he cometh out of his mother's womb."[2] The law regulating intercourse with others under these

---

[1] Lev. 11 : 24, 32, 33, 40.   [2] Num. 12 : 12.

circumstances was of the strictest character. A person who had been officially pronounced a leper was obliged to go about with his clothes rent, his hair loose, his upper lip covered, and on the approach of any one to cry out, "Unclean, unclean." His dwelling-place was to be alone and "without the camp." The last expression was understood by the later Jews to mean, in the case of walled towns, outside the walls. On pain of forty stripes the leper was forbidden to go beyond the bounds set for him. He was admitted, however, to a certain portion of the synagogue on condition of his entering it and going from it at a different hour from the rest of the congregation. Thus excluded from the society of others he naturally sought it in the company of those afflicted like himself.[1]

Purification of the Leper.

The question whether persons or things were actually affected by the leprosy was left to the decision of the priests. Regulations of the most minute character concerning the matter, in addition to those of Leviticus, are to be found in one of the tracts of the Talmud. The process of purification was as follows:— Persons or things showing symptoms of the disease, but authoritatively pronounced free from it, were cleansed by washing in water. Garments found to be really infected with it were burnt, and houses torn down. A leprous person who had recovered and been declared convalescent by a priest was required to present himself at the entrance of the camp, or the gates of the city, for the rites of purification. They consisted of two stages, and lasted altogether seven days. First, the candidate brought to the priest two ceremonially-clean birds; the rabbins say sparrows were generally used for the purpose.

[1] 2 Kings 7 : 3; Luke 17 : 12.

One of the birds was killed and its blood caught in a vessel in which was "living water." The other bird was dipped into this liquid along with cedar wood, hyssop and the crimson thread which bound the two together. With this bunch of hyssop the leper was sprinkled, whereupon the living bird was loosed to fly away. Finally, the leper washed his clothing, shaved off all the hair of his body, and bathed his person.

The second stage of the ceremony began on the seventh day, until which time the leper was not allowed to return to his family. Now he appeared at the sanctuary. Again his clothing was washed and his body bathed and shaven. On the eighth day he brought the appointed sacrifices, consisting of two male lambs as a burnt and trespass offering, respectively, and a ewe lamb as a sin offering. The burnt offering was accompanied by a meal offering. In case of poverty he might bring, in place of the lambs, two turtle-doves or two young pigeons. A log of oil—less than a pint—was also required in the ceremony, the leper being anointed with it, as also with the blood of the trespass offering, on the tip of his right ear, the thumb of his right hand and the toe of his right foot, while a portion of it was poured on his head. There can be little doubt that the Psalmist refers to this impressive ceremony when he says, " Purge me with hyssop and I shall be clean ;"[1] and a new significance is given, in view of it, to the numerous references that occur in the Gospels.[2]

28. The third species of ceremonial defilement was that arising from morbid fluxes of the sexual organs. These, too, were looked upon as the more or less remote results of death. They were clear disturbances of natural functions. Such disturbances, as the consequence of sin, were regarded as having not simply a physical, but also a *quasi* moral, quality. Hence the necessity of ceremonial purification, especially in connection with that part of man's physical nature where he was most. exposed to sin. The mere act of giving birth, or the normal and legalized communion of the sexes, are nowhere represented in the Scriptures as evil. It is certain that the accompanying conditions, what were abnormal and sickly, were so treated. Gonorrhœa not only rendered the person afflicted with it unclean, but, for a more limited time, whatever such person came in contact with or spit upon.[3] The same was true of involuntary nocturnal emissions. It has been thought by some that, under Levitical law, ordinary conjugal intercourse also rendered ceremonially unclean. This was the opinion of the later Jews. But

[1] Ps. 51 : 7.   [2] Matt. 8 : 2; 10 : 8; 11 : 5; 26 : 6; Mark 1 : 40; Luke 17 : 12.   [3] Lev. 15 : 1-12.

the original phrase rendered "with whom"[1] means here, it would
seem, "beside whom," as in Leviticus 15 : 24, where the former meaning appears to be excluded by 20 : 18. Other passages quoted in
support of the contrary view, when correctly interpreted are not
found to be really so.[2]

A woman's monthly sickness rendered her unclean for seven days,
and whatever she touched was made unclean until the evening.[3] The
husband who lay beside his wife was subject to the same disability.
If the bloody flux continued and assumed the form of a disease, the
ceremonial impurity lasted as long as the sickness. This seems to
have been the trouble from which the woman suffered who is spoken
of in the Gospels.[4] The purification enjoined in the last-mentioned
cases were of a simple character. A man or woman having an issue
was required, when it ceased, after waiting seven days, to wash the
garments and bathe the body in living water. For a sacrifice there
were brought on the eighth day two turtle-doves or young pigeons,
one of which was offered as a sin offering, the other as a burnt offering. Those indirectly affected were required simply to bathe their
bodies and wash their clothing. Vessels involved, if of wood, were
cleansed with water; if of earthen ware, were broken. The uncleanness induced by nocturnal emissions could be cleansed after
the lapse of a day by a bath and washing the soiled clothing.

In the case of childbirth the ritual of purification was more elaborate.[5] The woman was held to be ceremonially unclean for forty
or eighty days, according as she had borne a male or a female child.
At the expiration of this period she brought to the sanctuary a
turtle-dove or young pigeon, as a sin offering, and for a burnt offering a lamb of one year old. If too poor to provide a lamb she was
permitted to bring a dove or young pigeon in its place. It will be
recalled that the mother of our Lord availed herself of this privilege when she came to present him in the temple.[6] It was on this
occasion, too, that the devout Simeon took the babe in his arms and
exclaimed, "Now lettest thou thy servant depart, O Lord, according
to thy word, in peace; for mine eyes have seen thy salvation."[7]

29. RELIGIOUS VOWS.—In one of their two principal classes of
positive and negative vows, the religious vows of the Israelites held
an intimate relation to the Levitical system of sacrifices. A positive
vow was one in which some designated object or person was dedicated
to Jehovah. A negative vow was one of abstinence from certain de-

[1] Lev. 15 : 18.   [2] Ex. 19 : 15; 1 Sam. 21 : 5; 2 Sam. 11 : 4; 1 Cor. 7 : 5.   [3] Lev. 15 : 19-24.
[4] Matt. 9 : 20-22.   [5] Lev. 12 : 1-8.   [6] Luke 2 : 22-24.   [7] Luke 2 : 29.

fined privileges or enjoyments for the alleged purpose of doing honor
to Jehovah. These two species of vows are distinguished by different
words in the Hebrew. The first vow of which we have record in the
Scriptures, that of Jacob at Bethel, was one of the former class.[1]
The vow of the Nazarite was one of the latter.

Vows are nowhere enjoined, they are simply recognized and regulated, in the Bible. The Levitical law concerning them was made,
and apparently with design, an appendix to the main body of Levitical laws.[2] It had to do simply with a prevailing custom. It was
something which could scarcely be looked upon as a constituent part
of the Israelitish religion. The Mosaic laws in the main concerned
themselves with what Jehovah required or forbade. Vows had relation to that which, outside these laws, one voluntarily took upon
himself. But though a person might venture beyond the positive
requirements of the sinaitic code, it was certainly wise to make provision that in no case should he find himself outside its regulative
precepts.

30. Accordingly we find the matter incidentally treated in the
Pentateuch, and always in harmony with its own fundamental principles. If, for example, one had made a vow he was held to be
legally bound to discharge it to the letter.[3] It was not at his option,
moreover, in making a vow to disregard prior and more imperative
obligations. He might not assume to devote anything to Jehovah
in the way of a vow which the law already demanded of him, nor
anything not properly his own. This was a perversion of right principles which our Lord denounced. In his time children, in plain
disregard of the fifth commandment, were accustomed to evade the
duty of supporting their parents by saying that the means necessary
for it had been devoted to God.[4] In the case of unmarried daughters, as also of married women, the validity of a vow was made dependent on the consent of father or husband. They were obliged,
however, to object, if at all, at once on hearing of the matter. A
vow to have legal force must be freely made, made audibly, and,
where others were concerned, in their presence.[5] According to rabbinical law one might not dedicate a portion which on the contin-
gency of his death would fall to his widow ; or, in vows of abstinence,
pledge himself to anything which interfered with the preservation
of life or the rights of those dependent on him. Outside of these
limitations, and two others named in Deuteronomy 23 : 18, a person

---

[1] Gen. 28 : 20–22.   [2] Lev. 27 : 1–33; cf. Lev. 26 : 46.   [3] Num. 30 : 2; Deut. 23 : 21–23.   [4] Matt.
15 : 4–6.   [5] Num. 30 : 3–12.

was at liberty to present to the Lord any article of property, animals clean and unclean, houses and lands (until the year of jubilee), and even himself, his wife, his children and servants.

31. Inasmuch as such presentation, excepting only animals which could be sacrificed, was necessarily formal rather than literal, the objects might be redeemed by the giver by paying into the treasury of the sanctuary a sum amounting to one fifth more than their estimated value. For men from twenty to sixty years of age the price for redemption was fifty shekels; for women of the same age, thirty shekels. Between the ages of five and twenty the price was twenty shekels for men and one half that for women. From the age of one month to five years the price of redemption was five shekels for a male and three for a female; for those over sixty the price was fifteen shekels for a male and ten for a female. The priest was at liberty, however, in cases of poverty to accept a much smaller sum.[1]

Unclean animals were either redeemed by adding a fifth to their appraisement or sold at that valuation and the money paid to the sanctuary. Houses and lands were treated in the same way; the estimated products of the latter before the year of jubilee being, however, alone exchangeable. If one subsequently sold land which he had dedicated to Jehovah, the buyer remained in possession until the year of jubilee; the land was then forfeited to the sanctuary and could not be redeemed. On the other hand, if one bought a piece of land and dedicated the same to Jehovah, he was at liberty to redeem it provided he did so at once. In any case, in the year of jubilee it reverted to the original owner or his family.[2] The form of positive vow known as *cherem*, a term applied to objects placed under a ban, has already been noticed. Other notable instances of positive vows mentioned in the Scriptures, in addition to that of Jacob, are the tragic one of Jephthah, that of Hannah, and those of the sailors who threw overboard the prophet Jonah.[3] Examples of negative vows are those of Samson, the prophet Samuel, and John the Baptist; all of whom were Nazarites.

32. THE NAZARITE.—The Levitical law relating to Nazarites presupposes their existence as a class.[4] It contemplates, as in the cases just noted, nothing more than to regulate customs so as to make them conform to what was fundamental in the Israelitish religion. As the name in the Hebrew implies, the Nazarite was a dedicated

[1] Lev. 27: 11–27, 33.　[2] Lev. 27: 20, 22–24.　[3] Judg. 11: 30–40; 1 Sam. 1: 11; Jon. 1: 16.
[4] Num. 6: 1–21.

person, separated, for the time being, in a special sense unto Jehovah. One had power not only to become himself a Nazarite, but parents could bind their children to his rules of abstinence. Besides a heightening of the ordinary obligations of life, the Nazarite was especially bound to two things: to abstain, for a time or for his entire life, from wine and strong drink and from cutting the hair. The former particular was what essentially characterized the class; the latter was a kind of badge of it. What his regalia was to the priest, that his flowing locks were to the Nazarite. He was, in fact, looked upon as a sort of priest whose obligations were the more sacred that they were self-imposed and did not come by inheritance.

Abstinence from the fruit of the vine was absolute. It extended "from the kernels even to the husk."[1] If, however, the Nazarite's obligation had ended with this, he would have been only so far a Rechabite. The Rechabites were prohibited the use of wine along with the building of houses and the cultivation of land. But with the Nazarite the unchecked growth of the hair was a second distinction. In the later time, along with other perversions, it became the chief distinction. The Levitical law was so interpreted that other wines than grape wine and other kinds of spirituous liquors were allowed to the Nazarite; but not even a comb might touch his hair. A distinction, however, was made in this respect between what was called "a Samson Nazarite" and "a perpetual Nazarite." The former was permitted, on certain conditions, to clip his hair and defile himself by the dead. But the concession was probably more theoretical than practical, and arose from an effort to justify the otherwise illegal conduct of Samson. As already intimated, the vow of the Nazarite was for a limited period or for life. By rabbinical law it could not be for a less period than thirty days. If no period were stated, the shortest allowable was understood. In case of defilement by coming in contact with a dead body, even of the nearest relative, the Nazarite was obligated anew for the whole period, if it had been limited, and in all cases to special rites of purification.[2] In talmudical times willful transgression of the Nazarite's vow was punishable with stripes.

33. The ceremonies at the expiration of the period were of a peculiar character.[3] They took place at the door of the sanctuary. First, a male lamb of the first year was brought as a burnt offering, a ewe lamb of the first year as a sin offering, and a ram as a peace offering. All must be without blemish. In connection with the first

---

[1] Num. 6:4.   [2] Num. 6:9-12.   [3] Num. 6:13-21.

there were to be provided also appropriate meal and drink offerings, besides a basket of unleavened bread, cakes of fine flour mingled with oil, and unleavened wafers similarly treated. According to rabbinical practice the unleavened bread was baked in the form of ten cakes and ten wafers, with which one fourth of a log of oil was used. The whole was offered in one basket. During the later history of the second temple there was a special room reserved for Nazarites in the so-called court of the women. At the conclusion of the above-named sacrifices in his behalf, the Nazarite went to this chamber, kindled a fire, cooked the portions of the peace offering remaining, and burned the hair of his head. In the original legislation the burning of the hair was appointed to be done at the door of the tabernacle. In later usage it was permitted to cut it previous to the Nazarite's appearing at the sanctuary for the rites of purification; but it was regarded as essential that it should be consumed there. This may throw some light on the conduct of Paul, who is said to have shorn his head at Cenchreæ because he had a vow.[1] It might have been so if he had previously taken the vow of the Nazarite and had there reached its limit. Following this ceremony, the priest waved the boiled shoulder of the peace offering together with one unleavened wafer and one unleavened cake, putting his hands for the purpose beneath those of the Nazarite. The remaining bread and flesh, after those portions to which the priest was legally entitled had been given to him, were then eaten by the Nazarite and his friends.

There is an intimation in the law that when the Nazarite was able so to do he brought other offerings of his free will besides those mentioned.[2] As was natural to expect, an institution of this kind was liable to great abuses. One such was making a merit of being a Nazarite, an evil, moreover, against which the law had, in some particulars, provided.[3] The class seem to have been very common at the beginning of our era and shortly after, and they were supposed to be able to transfer the merit obtained from their abstinence to others. Hence persons often shared with them the expense attendant on their absolution, with the understanding that they shared also in their good works. It is related of King Agrippa that he once did this in order to propitiate public favor.[4] On the other hand, the object Paul had in view, in assuming on one occasion the charges of four impoverished Christian Nazarites, is said to have been the eminently worthy one of conciliating Jewish brethren who were extremely "zealous for the law."[5]

[1] Acts 18:18.   [2] Num. 6:21.   [3] Lev. 27:9, 10; cf. Prov. 22:26, 27.   [4] Josephus, *Antiq.* 19, 6:1.   [5] Acts 21:23, 24.

CHAPTER XV.

1. THE origin of idolatry is a question much discussed. Those who accept the hypothesis of a purely natural development of the Israelitish religion generally hold that monotheism was a somewhat late development from polytheism, the latter, according to them, being the original form of religion among men. From a deification of the objects of nature there was a gradual advancement, especially forwarded by the prophets, to the conception of a supreme Being, who is Creator, Preserver and Governor. It is needless to say that this is not the teaching of the Bible, from which we get all the information that we have on the subject. It teaches that God created man in his own moral image and with a knowledge of himself as the one God. Whatever else may be meant by the "tree of knowledge of good and evil" and man's relations to it, it certainly implies an original state of innocence in which obedience to God was regarded as the highest duty and intelligent, childlike communion with him as the highest boon. That the temptation and fall of man were historic facts, and that it was this original lapse from God which lay at the basis of all his subsequent sin and misery, the Bible everywhere assumes. Knowing God, men "glorified him not as God, neither gave thanks; but became vain in their reasonings, and their senseless heart was darkened."[1]

/ Idolatry arose from the attempt of fallen man to form, first inwardly then outwardly, a conception of the invisible God. Originally the human soul itself reflected the divine image. As long as it was unfallen the worship of more than the one God was impossible. When that image was defaced and man's "senseless heart was darkened," polytheism and idolatry were sooner or later inevitable. Accordingly, to keep alive a knowledge of the one God, his being and claims, a revelation was needful. That revelation is given in the Scriptures. The best results of archæological research confirm the teachings of the Bible that monotheism was an original possession of man, and that in the history of the patriarchs, from Adam to Noah and from Noah to Abraham, we have a true account of the manner in which the primitive religion was preserved and transmit-

[1] Rom. 1:21.

ted in the early times. It is no sufficient objection to this represent-ation to say that the people of Israel showed for so long a time a powerful tendency toward polytheism, at least toward worship by means of images. There are examples enough of such a tendency in human history to fall away from a higher to a lower intellectual and spiritual plane. There are few instances where peoples have risen from a lower to a higher stage of intellectual and moral cul-ture; none at all of their emergence from polytheism to the worship of one God, except as that God first interposed to provide the requi-site impulse and to direct the consequent development.

2. THE TERAPHIM.—The first form of idolatrous worship of which the Bible gives us any information is that by the use of teraphim.

It was practiced by the ancestors of Abraham.[1] It is a singular fact that it was also the last form of idolatry to which the people of Israel clung after their return from the Babylonian exile.[2] The ter-aphim seem to have been images having the form of a man, though not always of his full size.[3] Their name would indicate that they were looked upon as having to do with the support of life, and they ap-pear to have served simply as household gods, like the penates of the ancient Romans. The word is always found in the plural. This probably indicates not a plurality of images, or a plurality of deities; but like *Elohim*, the Hebrew word for God, either a combination of divine attributes, or it is the so-called plural of eminence.

There is no evidence that before the time of the judges the teraphim were ever consulted as oracles.[4]

Teraphim.

Subsequently, however, this form of idolatry seems not to have been altogether unknown in Israel.[5] From the prophet Ezekiel it is learned that the Babylonians were familiar with it. He says in one place, "For the king of Babylon stood at the parting of the way, at the head of the two ways, to use divination: he shook the arrows to and fro, he consulted the teraphim, he looked in the liver."[6] There is no evidence that the teraphim were ever directly worshipped. La-ban, like his ancestors, was acquainted with the true God. The same, no doubt, was true of the Micah mentioned in the book of Judges. It is safe to infer, therefore, that, at least among the Israelites, their

---

[1] Josh. 21: 2, 11; cf. Gen. 31: 19, 53 (margin); 35: 2.   [2] Zech. 10: 2.   [3] Gen. 31: 34; 1 Sam. 19: 13, 14.   [4] Judg. 17: 5.   [5] Hos. 3: 4.   [6] Ezek. 21: 21.

use was a corruption of the true religion rather than an abandonment of it. Divine aid was sought by this means. It is clear, too, that there was always a strong public sentiment against this perversion of the worship of Jehovah.[1]

3. THE GOLDEN CALF.—Another form of idolatrous worship practiced by the Israelites was that of the golden calf. The first time that it is mentioned in the Bible is during the Israelitish sojourn at Mount Sinai.[2] On account of the long absence of Moses and the consequent withdrawal of the visible presence of Jehovah in the pillar of cloud, the people lost heart and said to Aaron, "Up, make us gods, which shall go before us; for as for this Moses, the man that brought us up out of the land of Egypt, we know not what is become of him." In compliance with this demand Aaron prepared from the golden ornaments of the people a "molten calf," fashioning it with a "graving tool." Judging from the language used and from what is known was the later custom in like cases, it is to be inferred that the image was made of wood and covered over with plates of gold which had been cast for the purpose. The people accepted the image as a representative of Jehovah who had brought them out of Egypt, and Aaron had an altar built, and allowed burnt offerings and peace offerings to be brought before it.

Bronze Figure of the Egyptian Apis or Bull. (*Wilkinson.*)

It has been generally supposed that the idea of such an image was suggested by what was known of Egyptian idolatry, live bulls being worshipped in Egypt: one under the name of Apis at Memphis, and another under the name of Mnevis at Heliopolis. This is extremely improbable, for many reasons. In that case one might have expected that they would take a live animal instead of the image of one. Moreover, there is no evidence that out of Egypt the Israelites ever showed any tendency to adopt Egyptian idolatrous usages.[3] It would, least of all, have been expected of them at this time. It is more likely that the image, while called a calf, really had the form of a cherub so common in the East, especially in the land from which the Israelites originally came. The cherub had the body of a bull but the head of a man. It was also provided with wings. Of such an image as this, with which, it is probable, they had always

[1] Gen. 35 : 2.   [2] Ex. 32 : 1–6.   [3] Josh. 24 : 14; Ezek. 20 : 8; 22 : 3.

been familiar, it is easier to think of its being said, "These be thy gods, O Israel, which brought thee up out of the land of Egypt." The destruction of the image by Moses and the judgment visited upon the people in consequence of it did not prevent a recurrence of this form of idolatry at a later period. After the division of the kingdom, Jeroboam, though perhaps with more of a political than a religious aim, made two calves of gold, setting up one in Bethel and

The Egyptian Gryphon.

the other in Dan. And to the inhabitants of the northern kingdom he said, "It is too much for you to go up to Jerusalem; behold thy gods, O Israel, which brought thee up out of the land of Egypt."[1] As in the first instance, it is probable that Jeroboam simply meant to offer the people a visible representative of Jehovah; but, as in the first instance, the unwarranted and forbidden device was the source of incalculable evil to Israel.

4. THE HIGH PLACES.—A third form of illegalized worship in the earlier times was that of the "high places." Originally this term was applied to hill-tops which were favorite spots for offering sacrifices; but later it came to have, in biblical language, a technical meaning, referring to worship at forbidden places instead of that enjoined at the sanctuary. During the patriarchal period worship was offered when and where occasion called for it, especially where there had been a theophany or God had definitely appointed it. Elevated places were not excluded, neither were they exclusively chosen. In the sinaitic legislation, however, a law was given which enjoined sacrifice at one central altar only, or at such other places as God by special revelation might indicate. Doubtless the object of the law was to prevent Israel from doing what the surrounding heathen nations, the Moabites and Canaanites, were accustomed to do, and to secure unity and purity of worship. There is abundant evidence in subsequent history that this statute was not very faithfully kept; but there is no sufficient evidence that, as some have alleged, even for the mass of the people much less for the leaders, it had no existence, or that it was understood in a different sense from the one explained.

1 1 Kings 12:28.

Exceptions to its observance are generally characterized as such in the Scriptures, and are never spoken of with approval.[1] Solomon, for example, is said to have erected a high place to Chemosh; but in the same breath it is called the "abomination of Moab."[2] For about a century, reckoning from the time when the ark was captured by the Philistines, this sacred object lost its historic and accustomed position. It was kept in a private house and furnished no place of public resort. During this anomalous period, as already noticed, Jehovah, for purposes of chastisement, withdrew from Israel, and the "tabernacle of Shiloh, the tent which he placed among men."[3] The people consequently returned, to a considerable extent, to the customs which ruled before the sinaitic law was given. Worship on high places prevailed, though not to the extent that any one place more than another became a sanctuary. The worship at these places was by no means purely idolatrous. It was often conducted by Levitical priests, and nominally was the worship of Jehovah only.[4] After the reinstatement of the ark in its former position there was no worship of this kind, unless exceptionally offered and enjoined, like that of Elijah on Mount Carmel, which was not looked upon with disfavor by those who represented the best religion of Israel. The writer of the books of Kings is of one mind here with the writer of the books of Chronicles, as well as with all the poets and prophets of Israel whose works we have. There were good kings, like Asa and Jehoshaphat, who tolerated high places in their reigns; but they were regarded as coming so far short of doing all that loyalty to Jehovah required of them.[5]

5. THE BRAZEN SERPENT.—During the sojourn in the wilderness Moses, at God's command, had a brazen serpent prepared as a means of restoring such as had been bitten by the deadly fiery serpents. The passage reads: "And Moses made a serpent of brass, and set it upon the standard: and it came to pass, that if a serpent had bitten any man, when he looked unto the serpent of brass, he lived."[6] This image was long preserved, probably in the tabernacle, and naturally was regarded with a reverence bordering on superstition. Nothing, however, is heard of it until the reign of Hezekiah. Of him it is said, "He removed the high places, and brake the pillars, and cut down the Asherah: and he brake in pieces the brazen serpent that Moses had made; for unto those days the children of Israel did burn incense to it; and he called it Nehushtan," that is,

[1] Judg. 8:27.   [2] 1 Kings 11:7.   [3] Ps. 78:58–60.   [4] 2 Chron. 33:17.   [5] 1 Kings 15:14; 18:36; 19:14; 22:43.   [6] Num. 21:9; cf. John 3:14; 1 Cor. 10:9.

the brass thing.[1]   Some, for insufficient reasons, have supposed that
the original brazen serpent was left in the wilderness, and that this
one was introduced by Ahaz.   It is more likely that from the wilderness period it had continued to be, to some extent, an intermediate object of worship, Jehovah being invoked through it.   Whatever
may have been true in this respect, the wise Hezekiah properly
judged that its value as a relic was not sufficient to compensate for
the harm it was likely to do in leading the people into idolatry.

6. In the instances hitherto noticed idolatry has appeared in its
mildest form, that is, in the form of divine worship through representative images.   Jehovah might be the one worshipped in such
cases or he might not.   In any case, such worship had been strictly
prohibited in the decalogue.   The second commandment was always
in more danger of being broken by Israel than the first.   Both were
continually and persistently transgressed during the first thousand

years of their history. Peculiarly incon-
sequent, accordingly, is the reasoning so
common among a certain class of biblical
critics who maintain that the failure to
execute an alleged law is pretty con-
clusive evidence that the supposed law
was not yet in existence as statute law.
That the decalogue forms a part of the
earliest documents of the Bible is well-
nigh universally conceded.

Baal side of a great Altar in a Temple
near Kunawat (*Canatha*), east of the
Jordan.

7. BAAL.—The worship of Baal was a
far grosser departure from the right way
than any hitherto noticed. The teraphim,
the brazen serpent and the symbolic cherubim, although illegal, might
have been employed without the direct intention of renouncing loyalty
to Jehovah.   The same was true, in general, of worship at the high
places.   But to adopt rites of worship peculiar to heathenism and
to employ them in the worship of a heathen deity was another thing.
It is not to be denied that in the case of Israel the name Baal may
have been sometimes used where Jehovah was meant; but it was a
kind of mixing of terms that was attended with the highest peril
and most generally led to a total lapse from the true religion.   The
worship of Baal, under some one of his many names, was the most
widespread of any throughout the East.   He represented the powers
of nature, especially of the sun.   The most notable gods known to

[1] 2 Kings 18: 4.

the Phœnicians and Canaanites were Baal and Ashtoreth (plural, Ashtaroth), a female deity corresponding to him. Under the different names of Phtah, Tum and Amun Ra, Baal was also honored in the several districts of Egypt. Besides the famous temple erected to him at Heliopolis in that land, there was another at Baalbek, in Cœle-Syria. The oldest Akkadian hymns are addressed to Baal as the god of the sun. The word Bel, title of the principal deity of ancient Babylon, is likewise only another form of the name Baal. So, too, the title Molech (sometimes written Moloch, Milcom, Malcom), the national divinity of the Ammonites, simply stood for Baal; and the same is true of Chemosh, the abomination of the Moabites.

Baal was regarded as a being having universal and absolute authority. His worship was almost exclusively inspired by fear. That of Ashtoreth, his counterpart, often degenerated into the grossest sensual indulgence. Baal was honored with the greatest pomp and the most ornate ceremonial. It is said in condemnation of King Ahab that he "reared up an altar for Baal in the house of Baal which he had built in Samaria." The images that served to represent this god were often made in the human form, in which he appeared as a haughty monarch, sceptre in hand and clothed with all the insignia of power. Pillars also were erected to him to which the name *chammanim*, "sun images," was given. They are several times referred to in the Scriptures.[1] The ritual at his shrines consisted of sacrifices offered to him, including incense, dancing and wild revelling around his image.[2] His votaries sometimes so far lost control of themselves in their frenzy as to inflict the severest injuries upon their persons.[3] The monuments show that there was also a custom of carrying images of the god around in procession, while the people prostrated themselves in the dust before it.[4] Besides the ordinary animal sacrifices, game was brought to the altars of Baal, with the various grains and fruits, and especially cakes made from raisins. The offering of young children in his honor, both male and female, was considered particularly meritorious.[5]

The priests of Baal were also his prophets. They wore a peculiar official dress, for the preservation of which houses were erected.[6] The first mention of this form of idolatry in Israel is during the period of the exodus.[7] Bitterly as the covenant people were punished on this occasion, it did not deter them from the same transgression

---

[1] Lev. 26:30; 2 Chron. 14:5; 34:4; Isa. 17:8; 27:9; Ezek. 6:4, 6.   [2] Jer. 7:9; 11:13; 32:29.   [3] 1 Kings 18:26-29; cf. 1 Kings 18:19.   [4] Epist. of Jeremias, vs. 3-6.   [5] Lev. 18:21; 20:2-5; Hos. 3:1.   [6] 2 Kings 10:22.   [7] Num. 25:3; Deut. 4:3.

24

in times not long subsequent.[1] After the period of Samuel it was renounced for a time, but only to be taken up again with new zest under the kings of the divided kingdom. To what extent it was sometimes carried may be judged from the fact that eight hundred and fifty priests of Baal and Ashtoreth were maintained at the table of Jezebel.[2]

8. In two instances Baal is used in the Old Testament as the name of a man.[3] It is often found in compound words, either as the name

of a place or person or to indicate some special feature of idolatrous worship. Baal-berith was the covenant-Baal, that is, not the one who watched over the sacredness of covenants, but the one who entered into covenant with his votaries.[4] Baal-gad, a city mentioned in the book of Joshua,[5] probably derived its name from the fact that Baal was there honored as the god of fortune. Baal-zebub was the name which Baal bore in Ekron, one of the five cities of the Philistines. It means "Baal of the fly," or "lord of the fly." The expression seems not to have been used in derision, but to indicate that Baal's protection might be invoked against the pest of insect life.[6] Baal-peor is the name of the place where the Israelites were first seduced to the worship of this god.

Assyrian Ishtar, the Astarte of the Greeks and Ashtoreth of the Phœnicians.

The name is generally supposed to imply that the rites of worship in this instance were of a specially-licentious character.[7] The name Baal is found in the Bible uniformly joined with the article. In the Septuagint and the New Testament the article is sometimes found in the feminine gender.[8] In these cases it is not, as might be supposed, Ashtoreth that is referred to. The article rather belongs to a Hebrew word left out, meaning shame. So strong was the dislike among the later Jews for this species of idolatry that, instead of calling this idol "the Baal," it was called "the shame," and this word being feminine the word Baal itself was given the feminine article. When found with it, accordingly, the whole means "the shameful Baal."

9. ASHTORETH.—As already observed, Ashtoreth was the female counterpart of Baal, the plural, Ashtaroth, being a plural of em-

[1] Judg. 2 : 11–13 ; 6 : 25, 26 ; 8 : 33.   [2] 1 Kings 18 : 19.   [3] 1 Chron. 5 : 5 ; 8 : 30.   [4] Judg. 8 : 33 ; 9 : 4.   [5] Josh. 11 : 17 ; 12 : 7.   [6] 2 Kings 1 : 2, 3, 16.   [7] Num. 25 : 3.   [8] Hos. 2 : 8 ; Zeph. 1 : 4 ; Rom. 11 : 4.

inence, or referring to the various modifications under which the idol was worshipped. Others hold that the plural is used for the abstract, that is, points to the abstract meaning of the word, and that there is no real difference of meaning between the singular and plural forms. In the earlier books of the Bible the plural alone is used. This goddess is one with the Ishtar of the Assyrian pantheon and Astarte of the Greeks and Romans. The word Asherah, falsely rendered "groves" in the "authorized" English version, is sometimes used for the name of the goddess, as appears from Judges 3 : 7, where Baalim and Asheroth, the plural of Asherah, are used in parallelism.[1] Asherah, however, is ordinarily used to designate the image under which the goddess was worshipped. It was of wood, and had, apparently, the form of a tree whose branches perhaps had been trimmed so that there was a resemblance to the human figure. It is enjoined in Deuteronomy, "Thou shalt not plant thee an Asherah of any kind of tree beside the altar of the Lord thy God, which thou shalt make thee."[2]

The Bible says nothing of any image of this goddess in human form; but she so appears on the Assyrian and other monuments. On the latter, the more usual representation of her is of a majestic crowned figure standing on the back of a lion. Prostitution both of men and women was one of the most common forms of offering made to Ashtoreth.[3] The prophet Jeremiah refers to this goddess under the title "queen of heaven." He says,[4] "The children gather wood, and the fathers kindle the fire, and the women knead the dough, to make cakes to the queen of heaven, and to pour out drink offerings unto other gods, that they may provoke me to anger." As Baal was the sun-god, so Ashtoreth was the corresponding moon-goddess. In Genesis 14 : 5 a city is spoken of by the name of Ashteroth-karnaim—that is, Ashteroth of the two horns. The title refers to the figure of the goddess in which she appears with a crescent-moon upon her head. It is improbable that any radical distinction is to be made between the Ashtoreth of the Zidonians, whose worship Solomon introduced into Jerusalem, and the Syro-Phœnician idol of the same name.[5] Like Baal, the corresponding female idol was honored under a great variety of names, with widely-dissimilar rites in different places and at different times.

10. CHEMOSH.—Chemosh was the national god of the Moabites, and, as already remarked, is identified in general with Molech

---

[1] Cf. Judg. 6 : 28; 1 Kings 18 : 19; 2 Kings 23 : 4.   [2] Deut. 16 : 21.   [3] Deut. 23 : 17.   [4] Jer. 7 : 18; cf. 44 : 19.   [5] 1 Kings 11 : 5; cf. 1 Kings 16 : 32; 18 : 19.

and Baal.[1]   On the Moabite Stone this idol is recognized as the one
through whom calamity had come upon the people and by whose
power deliverance from the Hebrews, if it came, was to be effected.
The father of the king of Moab who had this inscription prepared
was called Chemosh-gad in honor of the idol.   That Chemosh and
Molech were essentially the same god under two names appears from
the fact that the Molech of the Ammonites is once directly called
Chemosh;[2] and while Solomon is said to have erected high places to
the gods of the Moabites and Ammonites, as well as to Ashtoreth,
the names only of Ashtoreth and Molech (Milcom) appear in the
context.   The worship of both these idols was accompanied by the
most cruel and licentious rites.   Human offerings were looked upon
as especially pleasing to them.   When Mesha king of Moab was
defeated by the united forces of Judah and Israel, it is recorded of
him that he offered up his son that "should have reigned in his
stead" as a burnt offering.[3]   The prophet Amos also charges the
crime of human sacrifices upon the Moabites.[4]   There are several
specific injunctions in the Pentateuch against this form of idolatry,
especially against passing children through the fire to Molech;[5]
and as it concerns the sensuality of the Moabitish idolatry, it is significant that the only other name given to Chemosh in the Old Testament is Baal-peor.[6]   Obscene figures of a female divinity corresponding to Chemosh, as Ashtoreth did to Baal, have been recently
discovered in the land of Moab.   On the brow of one is the inscription "Divinity of [sexual] association."

11. TAMMUZ.—Tammuz was the supposed divinity for whom the
prophet Ezekiel says he saw, in vision, Israelitish women weeping at
the north gate of the temple in Jerusalem.[7]   The word is found only
in this passage; and as the Targums and ancient versions, excepting
the Vulgate, simply transfer without translating it, expositors have
been left largely to conjecture concerning its meaning.   The fact
that it is also the post-exilian name of a month corresponding nearly
to July added still more to the complexity of the problem.   Jerome,
Cyril of Alexandria and others identified Tammuz with the Phœnician Adonis.   In a note on the passage in Ezekiel where the word
occurs, Jerome explains that the name Tammuz was given to the
month in which Adonis was slain, that being the time when he was
first bewailed by the women and afterwards greeted by them with
song as having come to life again.   It is unlikely that originally

---

[1] Num. 21:20; Jer. 48:7, 13, 46.   [2] Judg. 11:24.   [3] 2 Kings 3:27.   [4] Amos 2:1.   [5] Lev.
18:21; 20:2-5; Deut. 12:31; 18:10.   [6] Num. 25:1-9; cf. Ps. 106:28.   [7] Ezek. 8:14.

this was anything more than a conjecture, which in Jerome's time had become a tradition. The sole ground for the conjecture may have been that the women wept for Tammuz and that that was the name of a month. Possibly, however, Adon—that is, lord—may have been one of the titles given to Tammuz. This would have still more strongly suggested the Greek fable of Adonis. According to the best authorities, Tammuz is the name of an Assyrian and a Babylonian deity of Akkadian origin. The word in its Assyrian form means "son of life," and in its original spelling—*Dumuzi*—is not very unlike its Hebrew derivative.

12. RIMMON.—Rimmon was a Syrian divinity to whom a temple was erected in Damascus. As in the case of Tammuz, there is but one mention made of this god in the Bible.[1] Naaman's request of Elisha after his healing will be recalled: "In this thing the Lord pardon thy servant; when my master goeth into the house of Rimmon to worship there, and he leaneth on my hand, and I bow myself in the house of Rimmon, . . . the Lord pardon thy servant in this thing."[2] Rimmon is doubtless the Assyrian *Ramanu* or *Rammanu* whose name is found as that of a deity on the monuments. The word appears to have no connection with the Hebrew word for pomegranate, with which it has sometimes been associated. In Assyrian it means either "the exalted one" or, as derived from another root, "the thunderer." As a matter of fact the god Ramanu was the god of the air in the Assyrian and Babylonian pantheon, and sometimes was definitely named "the god of thunder and lightning."

13. DAGON.—Dagon was the national god of the Philistines. The name occurs several times in the biblical history of Israel.[3] In form the idol was represented with the hands and face of a man and the body of a fish. A female deity corresponding to him was called Atargatis. The word occurs in the Bible only in the apocryphal books of Maccabees;[4] but it is likely that it might properly be substituted for Ashtaroth in 1 Samuel 31 : 10. Among the more famous temples to Atargatis were those of Ascalon and

The Fish-god. (*From a Bas-relief from Khorsabad. Botta.*)

Hierapolis. Another one, at Karnion, was destroyed by Judas the Maccabee. The fact that Karnion is the Ashteroth-karnaim of Genesis 14 : 5 suggests an essential harmony between the two deities

---

[1] 2 Kings 5 : 18.   [2] 2 Kings 5 : 18.   [3] Judg. 16 : 23; 1 Sam. 5 : 2; 1 Macc. 10 : 83; 11 : 4.
[4] 2 Macc. 12 : 26; cf. 1 Macc. 5 : 43, 44.

Ashtoreth and Atargatis. The latter word, in fact, is held by some critics to be the Aramaic form of the other; but this is doubtful. Traces of the worship of Dagon are found among the Phœnicians as well as the Philistines. Originally, it would appear, both Dagon and Atargatis were honored as deities not alone on the coast of the Mediterranean, but the latter, at least, in Syria also and the former throughout eastern Asia. On the Assyrian monuments the word Dagon appears as *Dakan;* on the Babylonian as *Dagan.* The monuments

preserve also somewhat numerous representations of the idol, generally in the form described above. There were temples of Dagon at Gaza and Ashdod. The one at Ashdod was destroyed by Jonathan, one of the Maccabæan brothers.

14. NEBO.—Nebo was the title of an idol named in connection with Bel or Baal in the prophecy of Isaiah.[1] In the Assyrian and Babylonian pantheon he was the fifth in the list of planetary divinities, and corresponded both in name and alleged attributes with Hermes of the Greek and Mercury of the Roman mythology. He is described on the monuments as the "god of knowledge" and recognized as the inventor of the wedge-shaped system of writing. His symbol was the wedge or arrowhead. He seems to have been much more honored among the Babylonians than the Assyrians. The

Nebo. (*From a Statue in the British Museum.*) proper names Nabonassar, Nabopolassar, Nebuchadnezzar and many others are compounds, with the word Nebo as one of the elements. The temple of Nebo at Borsippa was rebuilt by his devotee Nebuchadnezzar. Statues of the god have been found at Nineveh, and a fine example of one of them has been transported to London and may be seen, as appears above, in the British Museum.

15. REMPHAN, ETC.—Remphan (Revised Version, Rephan) is the name of an idol mentioned in the address of Stephen recorded in the Acts.[2] It is doubtless equivalent to the Chiun of Amos 5 : 26, and the one word may be a corruption of the other. Chiun is referred to by the prophet as having been honored by the Israelites as a god during their sojourn in the wilderness. As the monuments show, both names were used by the Assyrians and Babylonians as titles of the god Saturn, a planetary deity like Nebo. He

[1] Isa. 46 : 1.   [2] Acts 7 : 43.

was honored as a fire-god, and human sacrifices were presented to him. The Assyrian Adrammelech, whom the Assyrian colonists from Sepharvaim in Samaria worshipped, is but another name for the same idol. The word means "Adar is king." In Babylonian and Assyrian the simple title Adar is used. Anammelech ("Anu is king") was another of the gods honored by the Sepharvites. The statement that Anammelech represented the female power of the sun, as Adrammelech did the male power, is not borne out by the most recent investigations. Anammelech, whose name is simply Anu on the monuments, was one of the three highest gods in the Babylonian pantheon after Il, the other two being Bel and Nisroch. Anu stood at the head of the triad. He had a female counterpart whose name was Anath. It has been supposed that this word appears in certain proper names of the Old Testament.[1]

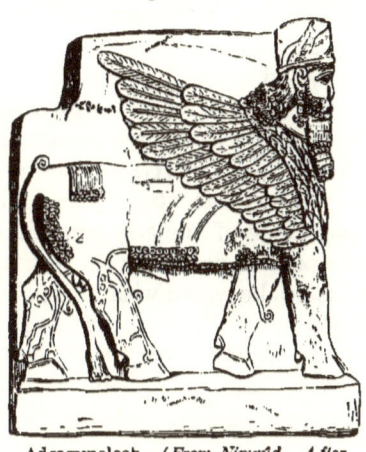

Adrammelech. (*From Nimrûd. After Layard.*)

Other gods worshipped by Samaritan colonists were called severally Succoth-benoth, Nergal, Ashima, Nibhaz and Tartak. The first named it is likely is the same as Zirbanith, who was honored in Babylon as the wife of Merodach. Nergal was the Assyrian and Babylonian god Nirgal. As a planetary divinity he represented Mars. Of Ashima nothing further is known. The same is true of Nibhaz and Tartak, unless the latter word be a form of Itak, which was the name of one of the gods of Assyria and Babylon. There were two idols worshipped by apostate Israelites in Babylon under the titles Gad and Meni.[2] In the revised English version the words have been translated, respectively, "Fortune" and "Destiny." Whether they are meant to represent distinct deities, or the words are to be taken in a more general sense, it is not possible to say with certainty. The fact that Baal was sometimes recognized as the god of fortune—Baal-gad—is significant.

16. JUPITER AND MERCURY.—Jupiter (Greek, Zeus), the chief Olympian deity, is twice referred to in the New Testament.[3] Mythology represented him as at once the everlasting god of gods of whom

---

[1] Josh. 15:59; 19:38; Judg. 1:33.   [2] Isa. 65:11.   [3] Acts 14:12; 19:35.

it could be said, "Zeus was, Zeus is and Zeus shall be," and also, most inconsistently, as a being subject to the ordinary human passions and necessities. It was not looked upon by the heathen as impossible, it would seem, even in the first century of our era, that their deities should appear among them. The reason why the inhabitants of Lystra thought especially of Jupiter and Mercury in connection with the miracle wrought by Barnabas and Paul is not far back. It was these two gods, as Ovid alleged, who had been entertained by Philemon, and Baucis his wife, in the neighboring Phrygia; while Jupiter was the tutelary divinity of Lydia, and divine worship was regularly paid to him there.

On the same occasion on which Barnabas was superstitiously looked upon as Jupiter, Paul was named Mercury, "because he was the chief speaker." Mercury (Greek, Hermes) in the Roman and Greek mythology was an incarnation of the divine intelligence. He was regarded as spokesman of the gods, especially of Jupiter. He was generally represented in art as a robust, bearded man, clothed with a mantle and his head covered with a travelling-cap. As the ideal of youthful strength and skill, his statue was frequently found in the ancient gymnasiums. There occurs in 2 Maccabees[1] the expression "brought

Figure of the Temple of Diana.
(From an old Coin.)

under a hat." The hat of Mercury is meant, and the expression implies initiation into the sports of the gymnasium, repudiated by the strict Jews as a heathen custom.

17. DIANA.—Diana was the goddess specially honored at Ephesus, of which city she is represented as the patron divinity. A magnificent temple for her worship existed there in ancient times. It was centuries in building, and was looked upon as one of the seven wonders of the world. The edifice was burned B.C. 356. Of this temple and its enshrined goddess diminutive models were still made and sold in great numbers at the beginning of the Christian era. It was the fear that the success of Paul would interfere with this trade that led Demetrius the silversmith and others of his craft to oppose the apostle's ministry.[2] Diana was looked upon as the moon-goddess, corresponding in general to the Greek Artemis, sister of Apollo and a favorite child of Zeus. In art she was represented as a spotless maiden, of stately and beautiful form but of great mod-

[1] 2 Macc. 4 : 12.   [2] Acts 19 : 23-41.

esty.   Among the Ionian Greeks, notwithstanding her maidenly purity and chastity, she was regarded as the patron deity of children and of motherhood.   Elsewhere she was held to be goddess of the chase as well as of the life of the earth generally, both vegetable and animal.   In this case she was mostly honored by her votaries with invocations in the spring, her worship being accompanied with extravagant and fanatical rites.

18.   MAGICAL ARTS.—The practice of magic was one of the most widespread forms of idolatry in the East in biblical times.   The fact is strongly marked by the numerous laws in the Pentateuch concerning it.[1]   There is not one of them that does not adjudge so fundamental a departure from the principles of the theocracy as worthy of death.   The different phases of the laws present a noticeable gradation in the emphasis they put upon the matter, that of Deuteronomy being the fullest and most emphatic of all.   In Exodus reference is made only to the female magician.   In Leviticus five different sorts of magic come under consideration.   Deuteronomy, while taking note of all these, adds the names of three other kinds, and says of the evil that it is an "abomination unto the Lord," and that "because of these abominations" Jehovah was now about to drive out the Canaanites before Israel.   It enjoins, accordingly, that there shall not be found among the latter "one that useth divination, one that practiceth augury, or an enchanter, or a sorcerer, or a charmer, or a consulter with a familiar spirit, or a wizard, or a necromancer." These epithets presuppose a familiarity with what is known as the "black art" which is surprising.   A brief notice of each of these several forms of magic, and of a few others mentioned elsewhere in the Bible, is all that can be here attempted.

19.   Divination is a generic term which covers all the others.   The root underlying the word in Hebrew means to cut, divide, hence, figuratively, decide.   It is only used in a bad sense in the Scriptures, and is never applied to the utterances or acts of the prophets of Jehovah.   Augury is apparently used in Deuteronomy also in the general sense of any occult art.   The original word means to act covertly, and hence to use magic, to conjure.   It is, however, possible that it may come from another root which would imply that the conjurer found his omens in the color, shape or movements of the clouds. An "enchanter," if we follow the root-meaning of the term, was one who whispered, hissed or, in other words, used the arts of divination professionally.   The word for serpent comes from the same root,

<hr>

[1] Ex. 22:18; Lev. 19:26, 31; 20:6, 27; Deut. 18:9-14.

and it has been supposed by some that the form of divination referred to is what is called ophiomancy or divination by means of serpents. But this is not its meaning in Genesis 44 : 5, where it is used of the divination said to have been practiced by Joseph. He is assumed to have used a cup for the purpose. Still there is evidence in the Scriptures that serpent-charming was not unknown.[1]

The term "sorcerer" seems also to be of a more or less general character. The original word means to mutter, and in one of the intensive forms of the verb, to mutter charms, practice magic. It is the same root-word that is used when the "sorcerers" and "magicians" of Egypt are spoken of as attempting to imitate Moses and Aaron "with their enchantments."[2] The "charmer" was one, literally, who bound knots or charms. This was one of the most common devices of magicians. Numerous references to the use of the magic knot for exorcism and other purposes have been found on the monuments of the East. In a papyrus manuscript now in the British Museum power is ascribed to the book of which it once formed a part as follows: "This hidden book triumphs over enchantments, connects ligatures, prepares ties, destroys the (door) lock. Life and death proceed from it."

The "consulter with a familiar spirit," according to the Hebrew, was an inquirer of an ob or python. The word ob meant originally a leathern bottle; then the belly of a conjurer in whom the python or conjuring spirit was supposed to dwell. It is also sometimes used for the spirit itself. Ventriloquism seems to have been employed by magicians of this sort to aid the deception and heighten the impression they desired to make. This was the form of magic professed by the so-called "witch of Endor." She is called "mistress of an ob," that is, she was thought to have power over spirits, and even to awaken the dead. Undoubtedly, however, she was more surprised than Saul at the appearance of the prophet Samuel in response to her incantations. The "wizard" was, literally, the "knower" or wise man. He who could foretell the future above all others was naturally considered as the wise man. The "necromancer," as the word itself suggests, was one who was supposed to have power to commune with the spirits of the deceased, and by that means learn the secrets concealed from the living.

20. A few other forms of divination are mentioned in the Old Testament. In Ezekiel, as noted above, it is said of the king of Babylon that he "stood at the parting of the ways, at the head of

---

[1] Ps. 58: 4, 5; Jer. 8: 17.   [2] Ex. 7: 11.

the two ways, to use divination : he shook the arrows to and fro, he consulted the teraphim, he looked in the liver."[1] He wished to have it determined for him whether he should march against Jerusalem or Rabbah. Whether inscribed arrows were used as lots, or they were simply allowed to drop on the ground and to give in that way an indication of the supposed will of the unseen powers, it is not possible to say. The inspection of the entrails of sacrificial victims in order to discover supernatural intimations was very common. The liver was specially prized for this purpose. The prophet Hosea charges a peculiar form of superstition on the Israelites of his day. He says, speaking in the name of the Lord, " My people ask counsel at their stock, and their staff declareth unto them."[2] What is referred to seems to have been a species of rhadomancy in which rods were allowed to fall, and the divine will, as was thought, was intimated by the direction in which they fell.

21. A noticeable thing in the scriptural treatment of all these diverse superstitions is that they are regarded as a class. The terms employed originally referred to distinct forms of superstitious arts. At the time when the Bible takes them up they have so far already developed what is at their basis that one term suffices to cover the most of them. To inquire of an ob, for example, indicated as well the rites of necromancy. The corrupt tree was one though it might have many branches. And, again, it is worth noticing that the Scriptures simply assume without argument the falseness and worthlessness of all such methods of discovering future events and seeking protection from impending evils. They are characterized as abominations hateful to God and to be abstained from totally. The right of inquiry on such themes is not denied. The desire for more knowledge is not rebuked. In direct connection with the passage in Deuteronomy which has just been considered the promise is uttered, " The Lord thy God will raise up unto thee a prophet from the midst of thee, of thy brethren, like unto me; unto him ye shall hearken."[3]

[1] Ezek. 21 : 21.　　[2] Hosea 4 : 12.　　[3] Deut. 18 : 15.

CHAPTER XVI.

1. JUDAISM as a divinely-ordained system of civil and religious government had no place for and offered no encouragement to sectarian division. Judaism as modified and developed under the influence of the scribes was extremely favorable to it. Samaritanism was the only sect which arose before the exile, and its origin was in a political rather than a religious movement. Moreover, it was less a division among the Jews themselves than an excrescence from without which unsuccessfully attempted to fasten itself upon the Jewish polity.

2. SAMARITANISM.—The name Samaritan is derived from the city of Samaria, the metropolis of the region inhabited by the Samaritans. It was situated in the midst of Palestine, west of the Jordan and about thirty miles directly north of Jerusalem. The district bearing the name was bounded on the north by Galilee and on the south by Judæa. In the time of our Lord it covered a space about forty miles square, being somewhat larger than the province of Galilee. The Bible informs us that in the place of the Israelites whom the king of Assyria deported from this region he brought men "from Babylon, and from Cuthah, and from Avva, and from Hamath and Sepharvaim, and placed them in the cities of Samaria instead of the children of Israel: and they possessed Samaria, and dwelt in the cities thereof."[1] This language leads to the inference which the monuments confirm, that the number and variety of heathen colonists was very great. They were able to "possess" Samaria and its cities.

Led by their superstitious fears, these Babylonian colonists asked of the king of Babylon that they might be instructed in the religion of the Jews. He granted their request, and is said to have sent them an Israelitish priest from among the exiles in Babylon.[2] How small was the influence he exerted appears from the fact that the colonists kept up their idolatrous practices. "They feared the Lord, and served their own gods, after the manner of the nations from among whom they had been carried away." What the priest spoken.

---

[1] 2 Kings 17:24; cf. v. 6 and 18:11.   [2] 2 Kings 17:26, 27.

of was unable to effect seems to have been brought about, to some degree, through the influence of the Israelites who continued to dwell in the land; at least a marvellous change took place. There were no less than nine different nationalities represented among the colonists,[1] and they greatly outnumbered, it is likely, the original inhabitants left among them. Still, Samaritanism, which accepted the Pentateuch as its book of religion, developed institutions not so wholly unlike those of the Jews, and continues yet to exist, was the product of the strange amalgamation.

3. On the return of the Jews from the Babylonian exile the Samaritans requested that they might join them in the erection of the temple at Jerusalem. For obvious reasons this was refused. At the same time a son-in-law of Sanballat, their "Horonite" leader, was banished from Jerusalem for refusing, being himself a Jew, to break off his connection by marriage with Sanballat. He was a grandson of Eliashib, the high priest, and was received by the Samaritans, who smarted under the rejection of their proposals, with open arms. A rival temple was soon afterwards built on Mount Gerizim, and Manasseh, the exile from Jerusalem, was made its high priest. It was a bold undertaking, and it can only be ascribed to the high place the Samaritans ascribed to the Mosaic law that it succeeded so well. It was a very pertinent question in itself which the Samaritan woman put to our Lord at Jacob's well: "Our fathers worshipped in this mountain; and ye say, that in Jerusalem is the place where men ought to worship."[2] The temple on Gerizim was destroyed by the Jews under John Hyrcanus B.C. 135–105. The Romans were always disposed to treat the Samaritans mildly; but a revolt that occurred in the time of Vespasian was the occasion of the death of more than eleven thousand of them. Since A.D. 1517 they have been under Turkish rule.

4. In belief the modern Samaritans are strict monotheists. They hold to a resurrection of the dead, a day of judgment and everlasting rewards and punishments. The Messiah, who, according to them, was to appear on earth six thousand years after the creation, is already secretly here. They look for speedy manifestations of his power in great political and moral revolutions, culminating in the universal conversion of men to the Samaritan faith. The last judgment they suppose will come seven thousand years after the creation. They observe the seven national feasts of the Jews, the passover with great solemnity. On the last day of it—that is, of the feast of unleav-

[1] Ezra 4 : 9.   [2] John 4 : 20.

ened bread—they march in procession to Mount Gerizim. They
keep the Sabbath also with great sacredness, and recognize the law
of release on each seventh year and on the year of jubilee. Every
male over twenty years of age pays a yearly tax equivalent to one
half a shekel, a census being taken annually to determine their
number. The rite of circumcision on the eighth day is also practiced.

5. The language at present used by the Samaritans is the Arabic.
The Hebrew, however, remains for them the sacred tongue, being
that of the law. Their pronunciation of the Hebrew differs somewhat from that of others, being characterized principally by the
omission of the guttural sounds. The square letter in use for the
Hebrew since the second century B.C. the Samaritans have never
adopted. They employ one of their own which has a close resemblance to the Phœnician. There is also a distinct Samaritan language in which there are some remains of ancient literature. Among
them are what is known as the *Samaritan Chronicle*, or an unauthen-
tic book of Joshua, and the *Chronicles of Abul Fath*. Neither of
them arose, it is likely, before the thirteenth century of our era.
They have, besides, ten prayer-books, two collections of hymns,
fragments of commentaries on the Pentateuch, etc. The Samaritan
Pentateuch is the Pentateuch according to the present Hebrew text,
but appearing in the Samaritan character. It is of considerable
value, though on the whole inferior to the Masoretic or usual Hebrew
text. The so-called Samaritan version, on the other hand, is simply
a translation of the Pentateuch into the Samaritan language. It
arose after the beginning of the Christian era. A second version
was made into Arabic in the eleventh or twelfth century.

6. THE SCRIBE.—The two factors most potent in the life of Israel
before the exile were the priests and prophets. They were essentially one in their influence. The efforts made by some critics to
show a marked antagonism between them as classes have not been
successful. These two classes being in harmony, there was no occasion or encouragement, as already remarked, for sectarian divisions.
The principal division which the Israelitish history shows in this
period, excepting always tribal differences, is that between the more
and the less faithful Israelites; between the evil and the good as
measured by the standard of the Mosaic laws. After the exile and
the disappearance of prophetical activity the case was otherwise.
In the place of the prophet there arose the scribe. At first he was
nearly identical with the priest. In the gifted Ezra the offices were
actually united. A little later, however, they gradually separated

from one another, until in the time of the Maccabæan struggle they
stood over against one another as avowed antagonists. This serves
to explain better than almost anything else the origin of the two
principal divisions in post-exilian Judaism. The party of the Pharisees sprang out of that of the scribes; the party of the Sadducees
out of that of the priests. Neither was ever numerically identical
with the body from which it arose; but the spirit and tendencies of
the priesthood, in the later times, were always best represented by
the Sadducæan party, while the Pharisees answered, as the flower
to the seed, to the principles and aims of the powerful class of
scribes.

7. The first object of the scribe was to honor the Mosaic law and
make its precepts the rule of daily life for every Israelite. This
was a most worthy object. The means taken to effect it were often
far enough from being worthy. They frequently served to nullify
the law by burdening it with a mass of details utterly foreign to its
fundamental principles. Beside the written law they placed the
unwritten one, made up of their own infinitesimal explanations and
applications. Little by little tradition took the place of Holy Scripture. It came to have not only an equal but a superior influence in
the conduct of daily life. The Talmud directly affirms that it is
more blameworthy to teach contrary to the instructions of the scribes
than to those of the law. By such a course the vital principle of
obedience was weakened at its centre. The letter was made more
important than the spirit, and the commandments of God rendered
of "no effect" by the tradition.

From the New Testament we get not a few significant hints of
what traditional Judaism was in its essential features. It required
the making "clean the outside of the cup and platter." The law
of tithes it so extended as to include mint, anise and cummin, while
the weightier matters were neglected. It increased the number of
fasts enjoined in the law from one in a year to two each week, and
adopted the unseemly custom of praying at the corners of the streets
"to be seen of men."[1] The Sabbath was made a day of painful
restrictions. Thirty-nine different forms of activity, illegal on the
Sabbath, are enumerated in the Talmud. In harmony with other
exaggerations the day itself was prolonged and made to begin before
the setting of Friday's sun. It is easy to see what must have been
the general effect of such a state of things. All spontaneity of religious service, along with sensitiveness of conscience, was effectually

---

[1] Matt. 15:3, 6; Mark 7:8, 9, 13.

crushed out, and religion was made to consist in a machine-like observance of outward rules alone.

8. THE PHARISEES.—The Pharisees formed the party of law, that is, the law as thus interpreted and applied by the scribes. The most distinguished scribes and a large majority of their whole number were always Pharisees. Just when this movement began it is not possible to say with certainty. It is seen in progress as early as the Maccabæan struggle. There existed at that time a small body, of whom scribes were at least the ruling spirits, who disputed on some occasions the authority of the Maccabæan heroes, and showed a marked distaste to their noble breadth of spirit. Once, in supposed loyalty to their principles, they went wholly over to the side of the enemy. They bore the name, probably of their own choosing, of the Assidæans or the Chassidim—that is, "the pious ones." Of these Chassidim the Pharisees were undoubtedly direct descendants. The latter title, however, has nothing to do with the former except that it has a somewhat similar meaning, "the separated ones," or, if given in derision by their enemies, as not unlikely, "the separatists." The title first occurs in the time of John Hyrcanus (B.C. 135–105), whose measures they violently opposed.

It is certain that they preferred to call themselves "Chaberim"—that is, "the companions." The brotherhood to which they belonged, in their estimation was the core of the true Israel in distinction from the mass of the people, who made no special effort to keep the oral law in its completeness. The contempt with which they looked down upon those who were not of their own order is well illustrated in a passage of the New Testament, where they remark to the officers who had been sent to arrest Jesus, "But this multitude which knoweth not the law are accursed."[1] It was on precisely the same ground that the Pharisees blamed our Lord for being a companion of publicans and sinners. In the Acts the Pharisees are spoken of as a sect.[2] It is not meant to be intimated by this that they were guilty of any departure from the orthodox faith of Judaism. No one better represented it. They were a sect only as making up a distinct body of purists, thousands in number, to whom the oral law was the highest duty.

9. Pharisaism cannot be said to have been a product of the Maccabæan struggle; but that struggle served greatly to emphasize a movement already in progress. It began with the first efforts to interpret in detail, and keep strictly, the ceremonial law. John Hyr-

1 John 7:49.   2 Acts 15:5; 26:5.

canus, the first successor of the Maccabæan brothers and son of the noted Simon, began his reign as a Pharisee; but before he closed it he went publicly over to the party of the Sadducees. The civil as well as ecclesiastical head of the Jewish people, politics interested him far more than religion. In the meantime the Maccabæan family to which he belonged, in the changes of the times, had fallen heir to the office of high priest to the exclusion of the regular Aaronic line. This was enough to enlist the sympathies of the Pharisaic party against it, and so, ultimately, against him. The better to counteract their opposition Hyrcanus became a Sadducee. Under his successors, Aristobulus I. and Alexander Jannæus (B.C. 105–78), the disagreement culminated in open revolution, in which many thousand Pharisees were put to death or went into voluntary banishment. On the death of Jannæus and the accession of his queen to the regency Pharisaic influence became again dominant, and remained so until the extinction of the Jewish state.

10. THE SADDUCEES.—The Sadducees, in distinction from the Pharisees, who were the party in best repute with the people, were the gentry, the aristocracy, of Israel. They put social position above conformity to the oral law, and, unlike their antagonists, instead of making a religion of their politics, they were much inclined to make their politics their religion. They reflect a far less distinct outline from the pages of Jewish history than do the Pharisees. They were to a far less extent a direct development of Jewish institutions. Given the work of the scribes in connection with the Mosaic law and the party of the Pharisees, sooner or later, was an almost inevitable result. The Sadducees, on the other hand, were more a party in opposition to the Pharisees than an independent growth.

11. The name Sadducee, it is likely, is derived from Zadok—that is, the Zadok who was high priest in the time of David. There are serious objections to deriving the word from the Hebrew *tsaddik*, meaning just, righteous. Moreover, it is clear that most of the priestly class were Sadducees. There were of course priests who were not Sadducees, just as there were scribes who were not Pharisees; but as the Pharisees best represented the scribes, so the Sadducæan party was best represented by the priesthood. This began to be the case, as it respected the Sadducees, from the time that the high priest John Hyrcanus joined them. It was obviously so in the times of the New Testament; and during the whole period of post-exilian Judaism to the beginning of the Christian era, the priests undoubtedly formed a sort of upper and privileged class. They

25

were the Jewish nobility, as far as any such distinction was tolerated or thought of among the Jews. Josephus begins his autobiography thus: "The family from which I am come is not an ignoble one; but I have descended from a line of priests from the beginning. Now as nobility among the several peoples is of divine origin, so with us it is the sure indication of the splendor of a family that it is of priestly origin."

12. But it was not on the ground that they were priests that the Pharisees were opposed to the Sadducees. Officially, especially as members together of the Sanhedrin, they stood in the closest relations with one another. We find them actually co-operating in their measures to check the spread of Christianity. Not a few priests in the time of Christ and later were adherents of the Pharisaic party. It was rather the dominant element in the priesthood, the men of highest position and greatest influence, that represented Sadducaism and became a theological, political and social counterpoise to the tendencies found in Pharisaism. It was the Pharisees, not the Sadducees, who were open to the charge of innovation. In theological belief the Sadducees may be said to have been the conservative party. They recognized the written word only as binding. They refused to sanction the additions which the scribes had made to it. It was formerly held that the Sadducees accepted only the Pentateuch as Scripture; but this was not the case. They looked upon the entire Old Testament as authoritative; but they were never strict constructionists. Their adherence to the Scriptures was more theoretical than practical; still in the several respects in which they differed theologically with their opponents they did so with no little consistency.

13. It was a doctrine of the Pharisees, for example, that every soul is immortal and receives in a future world recompense according to the deeds done in the body. The Sadducees, on the other hand, denied this, holding that the soul perishes with the body.[1] It would be too much to say with some that, in this respect, the Sadducees represented the position of the Old Testament. Our Saviour himself showed that they did not.[2] But inasmuch as the Pharisees had adopted the rule that any one who said that the doctrine of the resurrection was not to be derived from the law would have no part in the future world, the Sadducees went to the opposite extreme of denying that there was any authoritative teaching on the subject.

The same was true with respect to a belief in spirits and angels.

---

[1] Matt. 22:23; Acts 4:1, 2.   [2] Mark 12:24-27.

According to the New Testament the Sadducees denied the existence of either. Still further, the Sadducees denied, in opposition to the Pharisees, an overruling Providence. They taught that good and evil, fortune and misfortune, were matters wholly within human control. They made no allowance for circumstances. In questions concerning the relation of divine sovereignty and human free agency they attempted to escape all difficulty by eliminating the element of divine sovereignty. In all this it is not necessary to say that they did not represent the teaching of the Old Testament as over against a later tradition and philosophy. But it was that rather than the other; it was that in an exaggerated and so untrue form that they represented. It was not out of any special regard for what was old in distinction from Pharisaic novelties that they maintained such views. It was not because in their opinion it was in better keeping with the Scriptures. It was because it best served their partisan purposes; it was most in harmony with the worldly disposition and political aspirations which they cherished.

14. With all their extravagances it could not be denied that the Pharisees were eminently religious. The Sadducees, on the other hand, were eminently worldly. Forming a select *coterie*, which had little in common with the masses of the people, they were ready to submit gracefully to political connections with others than Jews and derive advantage from it. The Pharisee would submit if he must; but he denied the right of Cæsar to demand tribute. Pharisees in large numbers refused to take the oath of allegiance to Herod. It was a Pharisee, one Sadduc, who, with Judas the Gaulonite, founded the party of zealots whose aim was, by denying the right of taxation, to draw the Jews into revolt against the Roman power. All such conduct was distasteful to the Sadducees. They were content to take things as they found them. They rejected the idea of national isolation. It was for their personal interest, as men of wealth and high position, to be on friendly terms with the Greeks and Romans. Religious considerations, national hopes, scriptural teachings, did not greatly influence them.

Their own hereditary rights they were ever ready to defend. Many and dreadful were the conflicts which they waged in behalf of these during the last century before the Christian era. They especially insisted on the pre-eminence of the temple and its services as over against the growing influence of the synagogues, in which Pharisaism found its stronghold. The Pharisees depreciated the temple, and often with a very feeble logic as our Saviour himself showed.[1] It is easy to see how such a contest between people and aristocrats, the synagogues and the temple, would end. The Pharisees, from the time of their first great difference with Alexander Jannæus, slowly but surely gained one point after another: the management of the temple services; the mitigation of the penal code in the interests of the common people; the regulation of the festivals; a more general and rigorous observance of the ceremonial law as interpreted by tradition; and, finally, the almost exclusive control of the Sanhedrin where Sadducæan influence had been most felt. It was well for Christianity that the victory, as far as it is right to speak of victory in view of the later history of Judaism, remained with the Pharisees. Their religious zeal, even as misdirected, was a more valuable inheritance than the others' indifference; their hold on the Messianic hope and other precious Old Testament revelations, than the others' repudiation of them. Besides Saul of Tarsus, we are not to forget men like Gamaliel, and Nicodemus, and Joseph of Arimathæa, and many others to whom the Christian Church owes so large a debt of gratitude.

15. THE ESSENES.—Another religious division among the Jews at the time of our Lord was that of the Essenes. Essenism, although having its origin essentially in Judaism, differed so materially from it in many points that it makes upon one almost the impression of a foreign product. It had little concern with the things that most concerned the Pharisee and Sadducee. They were political as well as religious parties. The Essenes eschewed politics, and their attitude toward the national religion was such that they might be called rather an order than a party. In belief and practice they were far more nearly allied to the Pharisees than to the Sadducees; but from the former they were also widely separated. While zealous for some features of the law, for others they had no regard. They outdid the Pharisee in their devotion to Sabbath observance, outward purifications and the like; but it was under the influence of wholly different motives. They laid little stress on the national idea, and by the rejection of sacrifices even excluded themselves from the temple services.

16. The meaning of the name Essene, which appears in different forms in the Greek, is in dispute. It is most probable that originally it was Shemitic. The corresponding Hebrew term has not indeed been found; but a Syriac word meaning "pious," with great likelihood furnished the primitive title of the sect. According to

[1] Matt. 23. 16-22.

Josephus, the Essenes arose in the time of Jonathan the Maccabee. He makes specific mention of a distinguished member of the order as early as the time of Aristobulus, B.C. 105. This writer, while our principal source of information concerning the sect, is not the only one.[1] They are also independently spoken of by Philo and by Pliny. It is not known that the Essenes were to be found anywhere outside of Palestine. Within it they were gathered mostly in small communities in the larger towns and villages. According to Pliny one such community was also to be found in the wilderness of Engedi on the Dead Sea. At the beginning of our era their whole number was estimated at only about four thousand. They lived in houses by themselves, answering to the monasteries of later times, and were strictly organized.

17. At the head of the order stood a president, to whom unlimited obedience was given. A prolonged and severe probation was necessary in order to gain admission to the order. During the first year's novitiate an axe, an apron and a white garment were given to the candidate, as symbols of purification and other peculiar tenets of the brotherhood. Not until a probation of three years had expired was one fully admitted to membership. He then bound himself by a terrible oath to fidelity and, as it respected those without, to secresy. Only fully-grown men were received, although children were admitted to a course of preparatory training. For disobedience to the rules of the order the extreme penalty was expulsion. Besides the president, the governing body consisted of a council composed of at least a hundred members. One of the most characteristic of the tenets of the Essenes was the community of goods. The daily toil which was incumbent on all the able-bodied began with prayer. Returning from it, purification was required, both at noon and at night, before partaking of the common meal. Agriculture was the chief occupation, although no kind of manual labor was excluded excepting the manufacture of warlike weapons. Trade, on the other hand, as leading to covetousness, was prohibited.

18. The Essenes laid a particular emphasis on the freedom of the individual and on speaking the truth. They made much also of cleanliness of person, bathing not only, as we have said, before each meal, but also after every call of nature. On the Sabbath they did not respond to such calls. As a rule they rejected marriage. Their meals they regarded in the light of a religious exercise, much as did the Jews their sacrificial feasts. They were begun and ended

[1] Josephus, *Wars of the Jews*, 2, 8 : 2-13 ; *Antiq.* 13, 5 : 9 ; 15, 10 : 4, 5 ; 18, 1 : 2-6.

with prayer.   The opinion that they abstained from the use of animal food and of wine is not supported by the best authorities.   In philosophy and theology the Essenes occupied nearly the position of the orthodox Jews.   Their regard for the lawgiver Moses was unbounded. The use of his name blasphemously was punishable with death.   At their public services the Scriptures of the Old Testament were read and expounded.   According to Josephus, they showed special reverence to the sun.   He says, "And as for their piety towards God, it was very extraordinary; for before sun-rising they speak not a word about profane matters, but put up certain prayers, which they have received from their forefathers, as if they made a supplication for its rising." [1]

It seems likely that they looked upon the sun as somehow representing the effluence of the divine glory; and while not adoring it directly, they did pay it honors inconsistent with the precepts of the Mosaic code.   In addition to the Scriptures they had other writings which they held in almost equal authority.   The doctrine of the soul's immortality they held with great tenacity.   The body, in their estimation, was only its temporary abiding-place.   "For their doctrine is this: [2] that bodies are corruptible and that the matter they are made of is not permanent; but that souls are immortal, continue forever; and that they come out of the most subtile air, and are united to their bodies as to prisons, into which they are driven by a certain natural enticement; but that when they are set free from the bonds of the flesh, they then, as released from a long bondage, rejoice and mount upward."

19.   There is considerable difference of opinion among scholars on the question whether Essenism is a direct outgrowth of Judaism, more particularly Pharisaism, or the result of an effort to engraft some outside and alien element upon it.   The majority, perhaps, hold to the former view.   They regard the sect as for the most part simply an exaggeration of the Pharisaic tendency.   There is much to favor this theory, as the foregoing description shows.   On the other hand, the fact of the rejection of animal sacrifices by the Essenes and the peculiar honors they paid to the sun can hardly be harmonized with the fundamental principles of Judaism.   Their doctrine, too, concerning the relation of soul and body is in direct antagonism with Pharisaic teaching.   In these respects they approach nearer to that of Pythagoras than to that of their Jewish contemporaries.   It seems most probable, accordingly, that the origin

[1] Josephus, *Wars of the Jews*, 2, 8 : 5.   [2] Josephus, *Wars of the Jews*, 2, 8 : 5.

of Essenism must be sought in the peculiar associations and influences to which the Jewish people were exposed during the last two centuries before Christ, especially to the influence of Pharisaism modified by the teachings of Pythagoras.

20. THE THERAPEUTÆ.—The "Therapeutæ," formerly regarded as a sect allied to the Essenes, it is now held never had any real existence. The alleged work of Philo in which they are described is pronounced a forgery. Some person who set out to draw a picture of ideal asceticism assumed the name of Philo in order to give to his fictitious representations a wider currency.

21. PROSELYTES.—Proselytes to Judaism did not indeed form a sect; but they made up a large and distinct class of people whose peculiarities may be considered under this head. When we reflect on what Judaism was in the time of our Lord and what its relations were to the various nationalities with which it came in contact, especially to the Greeks and Romans, we find it somewhat difficult to understand how there could have been converts to it from other peoples. As a matter of fact there were at the beginning of our era thousands and possibly hundreds of thousands of such converts. It is to be remembered that at this time there were far more Jews living outside of Palestine than within it. Of the great numbers who from time to time, before and since the exile, had emigrated or been forcibly removed from the country, only a small proportion ever returned. Ten of the original twelve tribes were of this class, as well as no small part of the remaining two. Antiochus III. (B.C. 223–187) transferred at one time some thousands of Jewish families, previously settled in the regions of Mesopotamia and Babylon, into Asia Minor for the purpose of strengthening thereby his throne.

22. In a letter preserved by Philo, which Agrippa wrote to the emperor Caligula, concerning Jewish colonies outside of Palestine, the following graphic passage occurs: "Jerusalem is the capital not alone of Judæa, but, by means of colonies, of most other lands also. These colonies have been sent out, at fitting opportunities, into the neighboring countries of Egypt, Phoenicia, Syria, Coele-Syria, and the greater part of Asia as far as Bithynia and the most remote corners of Pontus. In the same manner, also, into Europe—Thessaly, Boeotia, Macedon, Ætolia, Attica, Argos, Corinth and the most and finest parts of the Peloponnesus. And not only is the mainland full of Israelitish communities, but also the most important islands—Euboea, Cyprus, Crete. And I say nothing of the countries beyond the Euphrates, for all of them, with unimportant exceptions, Bab-

ylon and the satrapies that include the fertile districts lying around it, have Jewish inhabitants."

These statements, extravagant as they might seem, are fully supported by information from other sources. So numerous were the Jews throughout the East near the beginning of the Christian era that they formed at Nahardea and Nisibis, on and near the Euphrates, an independent kingdom which even the Romans deemed it prudent to treat with respect. At Adiabene, the present Kurdistan, the royal family itself embraced the Jewish faith. In such numbers were they at Antioch and Alexandria that they enjoyed peculiar privileges and had their own ethnarch. If we may trust Josephus, ten thousand Jews fell at Damascus alone in conflicts with the Romans, and eight thousand in Rome supported a delegation sent from Palestine to ask certain favors from Augustus. . On the occasion of the first pentecost after the ascension of our Lord we read that there were sojourning at Jerusalem " Jews, devout men, from every nation under heaven. . . . Parthians and Medes and Elamites, and the dwellers in Mesopotamia, in Judæa and Cappadocia, in Pontus and Asia, in Phrygia and Pamphylia, in Egypt and the parts of Libya about Cyrene."[1]

23. Then it is to be remembered also that the Jews, wherever they were, remained, as a rule, true to their inherited faith and customs. Where other peoples were swallowed up by the surrounding heathenism, they presented almost as marked a contrast to the communities around them as Judæa did to Egypt or Babylon. They carried with them into every place where they went the Mosaic law in a written form. They established everywhere synagogues and *proseuchæ*—that is, resorts for prayer—which were not only a potent means of preserving their religious institutions intact, but became also important centres of social life, uniting the scattered people together and to their native land. From Jerusalem they were regularly informed of the periodic recurrence of the national festivals, and hundreds of thousands each year made their pilgrimage from various quarters of the world to the sacred precincts. With scrupulous exactness they made their annual contributions to the temple treasury, depositories being formed for the purpose in convenient places, from whence immense caravans conveyed, at stated seasons, the collected funds to their destination.

24. Here, now, there was a positive religious faith based on a written revelation and having a history which put to shame the

[1] Acts 2:5-11.

mythical outgrowths of Greece and Rome. It is not strange that it made a strong appeal to those who had been used to the empty forms of a materialistic worship. It is not strange that men like Cornelius of the "Italian band" found in it that which in some degree responded to the deeper longings of their souls. Then, besides the simplification of putting the one God, Jehovah, in place of the many gods of the heathen pantheons, Judaism required and expected of its disciples a strictly moral life. This was something which heathenism had never been able to achieve on any considerable scale. Such a life, as exemplified in its own communities, the Jews showed to be the highest wisdom as well as the highest duty. Its ways were ways of pleasantness and its paths peace. The successful industry of this people and their commercial prosperity were proverbial, and must always have made a profound impression on their pagan neighbors.

Sometimes, too, there may have been social reasons—especially the desire for intermarriage—which prompted persons to adopt the Jewish faith. Moreover, the Jews were themselves by no means uninterested in the matter of gaining adherents to their religion. Our Lord spoke of the Pharisee as one who was ready to compass sea and land in order to make one proselyte. It was no less true of the Jews of the dispersion than those of Palestine. This is shown by the character of the Jewish-Hellenistic literature, which had this for one of its principal objects. But whatever may have been the inducements offered, they were eagerly accepted by thousands if not hundreds of thousands. No disgrace or ostracism which they might incur from their own countrymen sufficed to keep them from the step. Josephus says that at Antioch the Jews "made proselytes of a great number of Greeks, perpetually, and thereby, after a sort, brought them to be a portion of their own body."[1] In the Acts it is recorded that on one occasion after Paul delivered an address in the synagogue at Antioch, "many of the Jews and of the devout proselytes followed Paul and Barnabas."[2] And he had the same experience in Thessalonica and in Athens.[3]

25. The relations of the proselytes to Judaism differed greatly according to circumstances. There were some who were such only in name. They still, in the main, adhered to their heathenish practices, while observing certain ordinances of Judaism. There were others who submitted to the rite of circumcision and took upon them therewith all the obligations of the Mosaic law. Between these two

[1] Josephus, *Wars of the Jews*, 7, 3 : 3. [2] Acts 13 : 43. [3] Acts 17 : 4, 17 ; cf. Acts 13 : 50.

extremes there seem to have been converts of almost every grade. Some contented themselves with simply giving up their gods and the worship of the same by means of images. Others, in addition, accepted a few of the principal injunctions of the ceremonial law, like that concerning clean and unclean food, and were more or less regular attendants on the services of the synagogue. But neither of these classes can have been regarded as proselytes in full, or proper members of the Jewish communities. They were "fearers of God," "worshippers of God," such as are frequently described in the Acts,[1] but not yet proselytes in the widest sense. This name was given alone to such as entered into the Israelitish communion by means of the distinguishing ordinance of circumcision, and, forsaking their heathenish practices, assumed without reserve all the obligations incumbent on the strictest Jew. It has been usual, accordingly, to speak of two classes of proselytes—"proselytes of the gate" and "proselytes of righteousness," the latter only being the full proselyte. It has been held that the seven so-called Noachian precepts simply were binding on the former, as, abstinence from blasphemy, idolatry, murder, disobedience toward the civil authorities, and the eating of flesh with its blood. It is doubtful, however, whether such a distinction can be maintained. The term "proselyte of the gate" first arose in the middle ages. The rules which are said to have been binding upon him appear to have been merely a matter of rabbinical theory and never actually in force. The "proselyte of righteousness," which was another name for a convert to Judaism, would seem to have been the only real proselyte; at least, the sole distinction found in the Talmud approaching the one named is between the heathen convert to Judaism and the heathen temporarily residing among the Jews. In the one case he is no longer an alien from the commonwealth of Israel; in the other, he still remains so.

26. Three things were needful for the reception of a Gentile into the Israelitish communion : circumcision (if a male), purification by water, and a sacrifice. After the destruction of the temple, the third condition was considered as no longer binding. In modern times it has been somewhat widely questioned whether proselytes were required to submit to the rite of purification by water. The affirmative is held, as it would appear, by the majority of the best authorities, and has the direct support of the Talmud and other early witnesses. Over against them too much emphasis should not be laid

---

[1] Acts 10 : 2, 22; 13 : 26, 43, 50.

on the silence of Philo and Josephus. Whether this purification by water is to be understood as answering to Christian baptism it is needless to discuss. If the native Jew in the time of our Saviour felt obliged, on the ground of certain passages of the Pentateuch,[1] to undergo as often as he did the ceremonies of purification, he would be likely to think them quite as needful for one who for the first time came out of the defilements of heathenism formally to embrace the Jewish faith.

[1] Lev. 11-15; Num. 19.

A Hebrew Scribe, with Roll and Frontlet.

INDEX OF SCRIPTURE TEXTS.

NUMBERS.

GENERAL INDEX.

www.ingramcontent.com/pod-product-compliance
Lightning Source LLC
Chambersburg PA
CBHW020234110726
47898CB00004B/1254